PLANTS AND TREES THAT GENERATE EMPLOYMENT

PLANTS AND TREES
THAT GENERATE EMPLOYMENT

Felix A. Ryan

Trees can live without people but
people cannot live without trees

GYAN

ISBN : 978-81-212-1250-2

Price : ₹ 990

First Published, 2016

Published by

Gyan Publishing House
5, Ansari Road
Daryaganj, New Delhi-110002
Phones: 9811692060
E-mail: books@gyanbooks.com

Printed at: G. Print Process, Delhi.

Cataloging in Publication Data—DK
Courtesy: D.K. Agencies (P) Ltd. <docinfo@dkagencies.com>

Ryan, Felix A., author.
Plants and trees : that generate employment / Felix A. Ryan.
pages cm
ISBN 9788121212502

1. Botany, Economic. 2. Trees—Economic aspects. I. Title.

DDC 581.6 23

Contents

Dedicated to my father

J. C. Ryan

Of the Indian Administrative
Service who had a
life-long commitment for
rural development, in whose
footsteps I have been treading
from the time I started
my career in 1955

Foreword

The Earth's trees, shrubs and soils hold about two trillion tones or carbon, roughly triple the amount stored in the atmosphere. When trees are felled and forests cleared and burnt, some of that carbon is oxidized and released in the air adding to the atmospheric pool of carbondioxide which is the single most important greenhouse gas. Because trees remove carbondioxide from the atmosphere through photosynthesis a two pronged stratege of stepping up reforestation and protecting remaining forests would reduce the build up of carbondioxide. Atleast 320 million acres of trees will be needed by the year 2000 to meet growing demands for fuel, fodder and industrial wood products and to stabilize soil and water resources. To-day the bulk of deforestation occurs in the tropics. Each year it is estimated that 28 million acres of tropical forests are destroyed though the combined action of land clearing for crop production, fuelwood gathering and cattle grazing.

Adequate supply of food, fuel and fodder consistent with employment generation and environmental protection is the major problem facing mankind to-day. Increasing population, expanding urbanization and rapid industrialization have posed severe constraints to extend area under production.

In India against the recommended forest cover of 33% of the land area, only about 13% of land area is under actual vegetative cover. Since the last decade, the rate of deforestation has been about 1.5 million hectares every year. Wood is the major source of cooking fuel in rural India, almost 85% of the total fuel needs in villages are met from trees including by burning dung and agricultural waste. By the turn of the century the annual demand for fuel wood alone will be around 200 million cubic metres, but the resource and supply position is dwindling rapidly. These statistics points to an impending ecological disaster if massive afforestation programme and tree planting programme is not implemented throughout the country. To meet this 200 million cubic metres of fuelwood and another 100 million cubic metres of industrial wood, the annual cut should be of the order of 20 to 30 million hectares of matured plantations per year.

In the context of ecological crisis looming large in the horizon of developing countries, the book written by Mr. Felix Ryan comes at a right time to focus attention and motivate people, particularly women to the much neglected sector of growing plants and trees for the benefit of mankind. This book has got a chapter on "CRISIS IN ECOLOGY" towards the end, which gives a glimpse of the current situation wityh a quotation of Mike Binge of the Agency for International Development, aptly summersing the issue "the real crisis today is not oil but wood".

Growing of trees and plants as an economic activity and for generation of employment is gaining importance with various committed programmes of the Government to promote this activity. This activity will not only provide gainful employment, but is also a very satisfying venture bringing in amelioration to people and environment.

Various plants and species of importance but remaining under utilized or commercially unexploited have been listed out in this book with their botanical names, description, the various uses to which the plant or its products can be put to at the household and village level. Their marks of identification, soil, climatic conditions, physical, chemical and medicinal properties are explained in clear and simple language avoiding technical jargons, other than botanical names. In fact the utilitarian aspect of the plants has been very vividly described with hand drawn sketches to make it acceptable as an appropriate technology.

The very many rural industries that can be promoted using these as raw materials, the millions of jobs they can generate in poor third world countries with negligible investment and by the application of appropriate rural technology, have been detailed.

Mr. Felix is an illustrious son of Mr. J. C. Ryan who has made a lasting contribution to the growth and development of co-operative movement in India and thereby etched a permanent place in the fields of cooperative planning, rural indebtedness and rural banking. Following in the same traditions, Mr. Felix Ryan has several books and inventions to his credit, particularly in the field of development of appropriate technology. I congratulate him for this laudable venture. Mr. Felix Ryan is qualified to do this work after various spells of jobs in the United Nations on employment generation attached to the UNIDO and the I. L. O as Adviser and Consultant. I hope this book will fulfill the long felt need in this field. In fact, this is the first book of its kind brought out In the series of adoption of appropriate technology in the field of growing plants and trees to generate employment to improve the economic condition of women and people living in rural areas.

S. JOHN JOSEPH
Principal Chief Conservator of Forests,
MADRAS – 600 006.

Preface

The Community Development Movement was officially launched in India in 1954 as an important organ of the government of free India, to educate, train and help rural masses in self-help enterprises for their own progress and the progress of the country. The movement was largely funded by the Ford Foundation of USA to extend information and services to the rural poor in the fields of agriculture, cottage and small industries, animal husbandry, poultry, piciculture, etc.

In July, 1955, I was commissioned by the Ministry of Industry, Government of India, to be in charge of training and extension services with headquarters in Bombay. Training and guidance and necessary help was given not only to the officers engaged in extension services but also to the rural poor who were to be uplifted.

For ten years, i.e., from the start to the official finish of the movement after which the movement was left to sail with its own wind I was engaged in this rural rehabilitation work. My field experience taught me that villages must be taught step by step ways and means of exploiting their native resources and promote and propagate new renewable raw materials and provide work and income for their families.

There were very few factories in India during the fifties and sixties to provide factory made raw materials such as plastic-granules, iron ingots, copper wire or chemicals to meet industrial needs. Factory made not-renewable raw materials were scarce and costly.

Land, labour, capital and organizations could be found but water, energy, transport and communication were not available suitable. There were no cell phones and even telephone connections and thousands of villages were not served with electricity and transport. People had no hospitals or doctors and had to be told about scientifically established herbal and rural medicines.

To work in such a scenario, I had to prepare officials deputed by the state governments to promote income generating projects for the rural poor. The only sensible and immediate possibility was to exploit readily available plants, trees, shrubs, weeds, reeds, cacti and halophytes (salt loving plants and trees which flourish in saline or sea water) to provide raw materials. (thereafter, live-stock, poultry, fish, etc. and their derivatives were included to the extent possible).

Many fibre and oil yielding plants and trees were introduced. There were excellent possibilities with these locally available raw materials but rural people were not exploiting or promoting them. Information from botanists and books were gathered by the team of officials and we kept notes and circulated papers to enlighten the extension workers and the rural communities.

This book is a result of our efforts which involved seeing, learning, discussing, experimenting, recording and communication, all put together. During those ten years we had sowed bags of seeds and many saplings planted, and several poor villages are now harvesting the benefits and the ideas were spreading from village to village.

Income generating plants and trees produce products that can be made out of them, and their medicinal uses are explained in this book.

For a cottage or rural industry to succeed in a remote village, the raw materials and technology must be local. Market should be local or nearly. Atleast two out of these three requisites should be local.

All parts of many drought plants and trees, such as castor, neem, tamarind, pongamia or bamboos of the grass family, have several uses. Leaves can be collected, dried and with tree gum (glue) or with starch from edible cereals such as corn or millet, can be made into briquettes to cook meals or steam distill well or tank water which is not potable.

Primarily, this book explains plants and trees that generate employment and livelihood and it does not focus on environment or climatic change which will automatically improve when a large number of plants and trees are planted. Trees can live without people but people can't live without trees.

Care for The Environment

INTRODUCTION

Oranges and pine-apples are abundant in Sierra Leone almost all through the year but their super markets have plenty of bottled orange and pine-apple juices imported from Spain or Honu-lu-lu. Markets in the Republic of Seychells have only imported goods. Many Third World Super Markets have German beer, Cyprus sherry, New Zealand lamb, Irish potatoes, Danish butter, South African grapes, Kenyan coffee and Indian Cashew. Yet, most of these can be produced and processed in many Third countries by rural communities to provide jobs for millions of people.

Third World Countries including the more progressive ones such as India or Phillippines which have been making several efforts to promote Small Industries for the past three or four decades have made very little progress to employ the poor in rural parts and as a result more and more unemployed villagers are moving towards urban cities giving rise to slums and squatter settlements. This trek can be arrested only by promoting vegetation and livestock based industries as it is common knowledge that for small and cottage industries to succeed, either raw materials or markets should be local. It will be excellent if even the technique can be native. But most villagers in the poor countries have no purchasing power for machine-made goods and therefore the market for manufactured goods is small or negligible.

To take metallic, plastic or any other machine-made raw materials from far away urban factories or centres to manufacture goods in rural areas and to send the finished products back to far away city markets is irrational and uneconomical. For village industries to be successful the only possibility is to exploit their cheap and dependable local raw materials like vegetation and liverstock and where suitable types of vegetation and livestock are not available they must be introduced into the area, grown, developed and exploited. In other words, rural areas that don't have raw materials must produce their own raw materials to promote and feed their industries and make urban centres depend on their supplies as they now make them depend for food-grains, cow's milk, edible oils, etc.

Industries based on local vegetation, livestock or fish as raw materials should be such as to command urban markets and not to demand patronage. Some countries which promote industries with village raw materials fail to meet this important objective and therefore, their products don't sell. Village pottery is organised, for instance, when urban people want stainless steel, aluminium or plastic utensils, or they make inferior quality products which do not attract limited urban markets. Greeting cards made out of palmyrah leaves or locally tanned leather goods are suitable examples of this folly.

When, village-made poor quality or unattractive products do not sell then the organisations that promote them underpay the workers resulting in exploitation. A report published by the Centre for Women's Development in 1987 has alleged that the Khadi artisans (Khadi is hand spun and hand woven cloth) "are being exploited to the hilt". In support of the conclusions of the study some figures about the income of the spinners in several states in India have been quoted to establish that a semi government organisation, like the Khadi and Village Industries Commission does not ensure the payment of even minimum wages to Khadi artisans. This organisation is moving in the right direction but over production, poor quality, restrictions on product mix, bureaucracy and red tapism are its sickness.

Almost the only solution to the problem of rural industrialisation is large-scale application of appropriate technology and breaking new grounds as emphasised by Gandhiji and Schumacher. It is in taking do-it-yourself machines and methods to rural people and not in taking them to machine-made machines and materials. As Gandhiji repeatedly put it' 'We need production by the masses and not mass production. Self-help and grass-roots development is what is wanted and not dependence on foreign aid and far away markets.,

Promotion of organic (leaf) fertilisers and insecticides is one such new ground which is gaining recognition and support. The leaves of ever so many wild growing shrubs, plants and trees and various types of nitrogen fixing bean plants have fertilising properties and others have insecticide (Neem for instance) or weedicide properties. A representative list including botanical name and marks of identification is given in the following pages. If these leaves are grown, ground, and put into village made fibre bags and sold as harmless organic fertilisers or insecticides, farmers and land owners, even governments and NGOs will purchase them for grain fields and orchards in preference to inorganic chemicals which are being discouraged these days by scientists and environmentalists as they are harmful to health and the soil. Organic fertilisers and insecticides are preferred also because they are cheaper and this industry will promote employment in dried-leaf grinding, mixing, packing and transportation in rural areas followed by store houses and credit unions.

In 40 hectare *gloria land*, a farm promoted and managed by the Aurobindo Ashram 17 west of Pondicherry (the former French Territory in India) not a pinch of chemical fertiliser, insecticide or weedicide is used.

In July, 1987 it was officially reported that every day 5,000 bananas and 250 kgs. of different vegetables were harvested in the farm. 394 adult coconut trees fetch the farm an annual income of Rs1.25 lakhs. The self-supporting farm stands as an exemplary organic model farm in India. Initially the yield with organic manures alone were not appreciable but promising. The soil was therefore supplemented with some doses of mineral fertilisers Slowly and steadily the soil built up humus and the chemical substitues were completely stopped, green manure crops rotated with biogas slurry, cereals and fish pond water have nourished the soil, improved productivity and the stability of crop yield. Two hundred indigenous cattle are kept in the farm in pink of health-without any vaçcination or laboratory made veterinary medicines and on an average each cow yields 4,500 litres of milk per lactation.

Organic fertiliser plants have recently been set up in the Philippines by the *Filipinas Foundation Inc.* (FFI) and it is claimed that this project will generate additional income benefits to small poultry farmers, *Ipil-Ipil (Leucaena leucocephola)* leaf gathers, and that rice and corn farmers can realise about US$ 20 savings per hectare through reduced fertiliser costs and also achieve 20 percent yield increase per hectare and an additional income of US$ 60 per hectare. Altogether 40 organic fertiliser factories are to be promoted by the FFI all in the rural areas of the country which will provide direct factory employment to about 400 people and indirect employment to about five times 400. It is claimed that the project will also stimulate foreign exchange savings by decreasing the need for imported chemical fertilisers.

There is need for a similar break-through in the field of pesticides Unfortunately, eventhough several pesticides which are banned or are on the restricted list in the industrialised countries many developing countries including the forerunner, India are being used on. These pesticides are Dieldrin, EDB, Sodium Cyamide, BHC, Aldrin,*Cholordane*, Heptachlor, 24-D, Cholrobenzilate, DDT and *Lindane*. All these harmful chemicals have to be replaced by harmless organic pesticides by rural industries and more research and field tests are required in this field.

Water hyacinth *(Eichornia Crassipes)* which is considered to be a global menace as it doubles itself every fifteenth day can be harnessed to provide a million rural jobs and many factories can be set up based on this aquatic weed. Experiments carried out by the Jorhat Research Institute of the Government of India with a grant from the United Nation Environment Programme (UNEP) has demonstrated and established that very fine quality paper can be made out of the stalk and leaves of the weed and the Agricultural University of Trivendrum, India, has used it to produce good quality fodder for cattle while according to a report in Research and Industry (Dec. 1983) excellent briquettes can be made out of the hyacinth as an alternative fuel for domestic stoves and industrial boilers.

Medicinal plants, fibre yielding trees and plants, pulp, dye and gum yielding trees and aromatic plants are all to be developed and exploited to promote rural industries and livelihood for millions of people and China is giving a lead to the world in this direction. Chinese farmers have achieved dramatic results by applying the rice-azolla fish systems in their fields. The new system minimises the use of insecticides and is ecologically sound, reducing environmental pollution to a great extent. "This system can be adapted in many irrigated fields of Asia", says Prof Liu Chung Chu, head of the newly formed National Azolla Research Centre. The system gives tremendars boost to the quantity of nice produced and also gives plenty of fish for the farmers and several fish based rural industries now seem on the anvil including fish meal, oil and bread-spread. The Chinese model of rural development is a fantastic story of success for that nation which feeds, houses, clothes, educates and provides health services for almost one fourth of the entire human population and does it from a landscape which cannot be regarded as excellent for livelihood activities. Cannot the poor Third Countries learn something from the Chinese model?

Chenna leaves (*Cassia Angustifolia*) popularly known in India as Senna or Sanai is a small shrub of Arabia and Somaliland and has been successfully cultivated in some tropical countries. In 1977-78, Rs 12 million worth of these leaves were exported from South Indian villages and the exports are nearly double now.

The country-side drought plant, *Catharanthus Roseus* (popularly called (*Vinca Rosea*) is being exported to Europe and the USA by India and many developing countries to extract the alcaloid which cures cancer and to manufacture the two drugs *Vincristine* and *Vinblastine*. This trend of exporting precious native raw materials as raw materials for foreign factories for the rich to get richer has to be stopped forthwith by the developing countries and they must start manufacturing in their own places and then export the finished commodities or drugs for a value added income.

Africa's backwardness is largely due to the fact that the African nations exported most of their raw materials as raw materials to feed factories in the West instead of using them to promote factories in their rural areas to employ their people.

Examples can be multiplied and the message to be emphasised is that rural sectors should endeavour to convert their local raw materials into finished products for urban markets and exports 'and this is the one and only sound way to promote small-scale and cottage Industries in rural parts and to check the flow of villagers into urban centres. All other approaches to rural industrialisation have miserably failed in the Third World at large, including China, India and the Phillippines.

It is heartening to note in the 1987 Administrative Report of AT International of USA that they are promoting, and encouraging palm oil extraction in Cameroon, protein enriched Cassava for pig feed in Thailand, Shea Butter Extraction in Mali, Potato Based Food Product in Peru, Dairy Development in Thailand, making and exporting grapple plant tea in Botswana, Hydro powered grain Mills in Zaire, Wool production in Guatemala and Wool Spinning in Nepal.

AT International has shown the right direction for national and international governments and NGO and Church agencies engaged in rural industrialisation and rehabilitation to take note and do like wise. Appropriate technology should be the order of the day and "Development" the new word for "peace".

INTEGRATED SMALL FARMING

The term 'Integrated farming' is used here in the sense of integrating several farm based activities in the same piece of land. Third World farm families which, on an average hold only about an acre have been following time worn methods of farming dividing their system broadly into wet weather crops and dry weather crops. Inappropriate and costly fertilisers and insecticides advertised and supplied by the government which very often reach them out of season take away much of farmer's income and the chemical fertilisers destroy natural land fertility. Thus, the small farm land is usually undernourished, or wrongly nourished and become unproductive without replacement of natural soil nutrients.

Uneducated farmers must be helped to learn new methods and appropriate technology and better farm management. Given below is a module which may be adopted by many small farmers in many Third countries: They should not change their traditional practices over night, but step by step they should:

1. Plant Sisal (cactus) all along the boundry of their land to prevent cattle straying in and use the fibre from them to make ropes and utility goods like bags and rugs.
2. Introduce 'Alley Cropping' with edible been plants, particularly protein rich Soya beans which fix nitrogen and enrich the soil (Handout 38) Soya plants may be allowed to go up the roof of the dwelling.
3. All along the boundry grow plants that give organic leaves to replace factory-made fertilisers and insecticides. Many such plants and trees have been identified by RYFO in Handout Nos. 112, 130, 151, 168 and 187.
4. Build a low-cost house by self-help in one corner of the plot and live there (several designs and materials are recommended in RYFO Handouts).
5. Dig a fish-pond in another corner and grow sturdy variety of edible fish such as Cutla or Thilapia and use the pond water which is to be circulated every day for the vegetable gardens.
6. Grow quick growing vegetables and spinach in the back-yard, consume a portion, sell a pottion and solar dry and preserve the remaining for the rainy day. Grow plenty of good variety papaya.
7. Make their own compost out of foliage, straw, cow-dung and dead fish in another corner of the plot and grow mushrooms on them.
8. Keep one or two buffaloes, consume more milk and milk products and sell the surplus; use a buffalo also for drawing a wooden cart for the family.
9. Grow in the boundry, trees with oil bearing nuts (handout 48) extract the oil by the village process for home needs and for the market. Trees may be planted in all vacant lands.
10. Keep fast-multiplying rabbits in he cage designed by RYFO for flesh, skin and manure and dehydrate the surplus. (Read the book, '*Spinning Rs6,000 per month from 6 rabbits*' written by this author and published by the Rotary club of Madras) (RYFO stands for Ryan Foundation).

The list can be endless and the 'HOW' of it all is explained in several handouts released by RYFO and 300 of them have been published by CARITAS (India) CBCI Centre, Ashok Place. New-Delhi-110001 (US $ 15 plus postage) When several farmers take to these mixed activities they can pool their small surplus for processing and reaching common markets. The BUKHAT project in the Laguna province of Philippines drawing world attention is an inspiration.

FERTILISE YOUR SOIL By LEGUMES

There are over 2000 plants, shrubs and trees in the Leguminosae family and most of them have the capacity to provide their own nitrogenous fertiliser, through bacteria that live in nodules on their roots. The bacteria chemically convert nitrogen gas, from the air into soluble compounds which the plants absorb. Most of the Leguminous are plants in tropical countries and they are highly drought resistent. Many of them convert nitrogen gas from the air into ammonia, a soluble form of nitrogen, which is readily used by plants. The nitrogen contribution maintains soil fertility. Therefore, in warm Third countries large scale promotion of *legumes* is the best and the quickest way to enrich the soil and augment production of food proteins. In fact, intensive cultivation of legumes has become a global movement now and national and international govts. have been spending billions of dollars on the movement, and books, reports and handouts are being released by the FAO, ILO, USAID, Tropical Institute of UK and many others.

Legumes in common use now in many Third countries include:-

(1) Soybean (*Glycine L*) (2) Pigeon Pea (*Cajanus DC*) (3) Hyacinth Bean *(nolichos L) (4) Common Beans or French Beans (Phaseolus lunatus I) (5)* Mug Beans (*Phaseolus Aureus Roxb*) (6) Cowoea (*Vigna Unguiculata L*) also called Cherry bean. (7) Chick Pea (*Cicer Arictinum L*) (8) Velvet Bean or Bengal Bean (*Mucuna Adans, Stizolobium L*) (9) Jack Bean or Horse Bean (Canavalia SP) (10) Bambarra Groundnuts (*Veandzeia Subterranea Thou*), peanuts, lentils, kidney beans, Alfa-alfa etc. Almost all edible beens are legumes.

All legumes bear pods and many of them give excellent flowers and flowering legume trees include the Flamboyant (*Delonix regia*), the *Golden Shower* (*Cassia Fistula*), the Bauhina species and the raintree (*Samanea Saman*)

Most popular, very fast growing and highly drought resistent legume trees which grow almost in any soil and climate (even in desert and sea sands in some areas) are: (1) *Acacia Tortilis.* (2) *Molden hauera floribunda.* (3) *Acacia Pendula.* (4) *Leucaena Leucocephala.* (5) *Pellophorum Species* (6) *Other Forage Acacias* (7) *Prosopis Species etc.*

All unwanted trees and plants that sap soil energy must be removed with roots and Legumes introduced on a large scale in rural areas. Alley croping should be made to replace use of chemical fertilisers by growing small variety bean plants in rows in the middle of paddy and other food grain cultivation. Compost heaps should be prepared with straw, legume leaves and cow dung in layers in cement tanks with holes on the side walls. Tanks should be 1metre high from the ground.

Many legumes also make excellent fodder for cattle. Legumes are living beings; God's gift to humanity and give us the 10 Fs, namely: food, fodder, fertiliser, fuel, flowers, fibres, fauna, fruits, furniture and fine chemicals. Legumes can survive without man but man cannot survive without Legumes. By promoting Legumes in rural areas we can give employment for the poor in their own villages and stop their trek into cities in search of jobs that do not exist.

POTENTIALITIES OF CASTOR

Botanical:- *RICINUS COMMUNIS LINN*
Family:- *Euphorbiaces.*
English:- *Castor oil plant.*
Hindi:- *Arandi.* Sanskrit-*Eranda.*
Tamil:- *Amanakkam.* Malayalam:-*Avanakka.*
Telugu:-*Erandamu or Amadam.*

There are three basic varieties; first with brown mottled seeds, second with purple bronze leaves and the third with large red seeds and woody stem. It is the third variety that is highly commercial as it yields an oil suitable for lubrication and illumination. The variety with mottled seeds is medicinal and the second variety is only ornamental. Description:- Tall perenial shrub with large leaves. Monoecious flowers without petals is red or yellow in colour. Globose oblong capsules have three seeds.

***Distribution*:-** Throughout India, Pakistan, Sri-Lanka, Bangladesh and most of the countries of Africa and Pacific islands with tropical climate. The plant grows uncared for in the islands of Republic of Seychelles and in waste lands depending only on rain water even in dry Somalia

The outer coat of the seed is poisionous but the oil from the kernal is medicinal used as a purgative and in skin ointments. The oil does not solidify at low temperature like many other oils and retains it's viscosity at high temperature. It does not dry up easily and has an iodine value of 80 to 90. It is therefore used as a lubricant and makes an important constituent of hydrolic fluids.

The oil is very suitable for making soaps, candles, cosmetics, fly papers, cutting oil, type-writer inks, and wood preservatives. Turkey red-oil used in dyeing and printing of fabrics is made out of Castor-oil. It is excellent as a dressing agent for tanned hides and skins and keep them soft and pliable. Hydrogenated oil is used in the preparation of splitting agents in industrial wax preparation and in *Calico printing.* Out of the seeds a blood coagulating toxin and the enzyme called lipase is extracted. The oil cake of Castor is a rich manure and restricted quantities of the cake can be given to cattle.

A good advise to villagers is to grow as much castor as possible of the commercial variety and send the seeds in bags to nearby oil mills. Alternatively, baby oil expellers may be installed for a group of about ten villages. The total cost of such baby oil expellers including the shelling, steaming and filtering attachments will be much less than Rs 50 thousand including instalation charges and the expeller can be operated either by electricity, diesel oil engines or bio-mass engines of the type supplied and subsidised now by the Energy Development Corporation of the Government. of Tamil Nadu. (the author installed a mini oil mill of the type explained above in 1988 in a village called Veerapalli in Cuddapah District. and the performance of it is very successful.)

USES FOR FIBRE

Handout 167 lists some good fibre yielding plants and trees. Handouts 176 and 180 explain Sisal fibre and different ways of extracting it. 96 shows a cot made of fibre while 118 and 156 explain more ways of extracting fibre. There are thousands of fibre yielding plants and trees and thousands of uses for fibre and fibre made products. Handout 232 explains AGAVE fibre.

Most fibre products are to be made after twisting the raw fibre into ropes and rope making is a typical village industry in the Third World Countries. In South India and Sri Lanka, one can see villagers using the palm of their hand and their bare thigh to join, roll and twist fibre into ropes. But this requires practice and skill and many Third world Country villagers have not learnt this method. Two simple wooden frames with metal gear wheels used in, India and recommended by VITA of USA and the machine popularised by the KVIC of the Government. of India are not easily available to villagers. They are to be fabricated in factories and cost more than what villagers can afford.

What is really difficult in rope making is the art of joining short staple fibre to make a long rope. The joining is the problem. In view of this difficulty RYFO recommands interweaving locks of strands of fibre like plaiting the hair of a school girl. This method will give a somewhat flat rope of three strands and everybody can make fibre ropes this way including uneducated teen age village children. Putting the fibre together and joining them is easy by this method.

Ropes made thus can be tied or woven into checks to be used in the place of window glass for security or as room dividers as shown in the picture above. Hammocks may be woven for babies and grown-ups as seen in the pictures above. Woven nets can be taken round plants and tree saplings to serve as plant guards. Used and discarded cement or fertiliser bags may be stitched to the fibre nets and used as roof for huts and as walls for tents. Net sacks may be made by unemployed youth to pack fruits, vegetables and leaves, which have fertilising properties or those that can be used as insecticides. Dressed rabbits in polythene bags and rabbit skins to be sent to tanning factories may also be packed in fibre sacks. Fibre net sacks woven in the villages may be sold as sacks in the market for packing and transporting various items in the place of jute bags and plastic bags which are expensive and take away rural jobs since there is so much potentiality in fibre more and more fibre plants and trees must be encouraged in villages to provide employment for the people. Commercial centres must be made to depend on supplies from the villages for their fibre woven sacks and nets and every region or state must produce its own requirements of fibre products.

TROPICAL SOFT WOOD

Some soft wood found in most tropical countries suited for making textile bobine, woodan toys carving light furniture etc are:

	Popular Trade name and English name	Botanical and family name
1.	Maha nim (trade)	Allanthus Excelsa Roxb (botanical)
	The tree of Heaven (English)	Slmaruba Ceae (family)
2.	Perumarom- T.	Ailanthus Triphyes Alston - B
	Arua-E	Simarubacea - F
3.	Jungi Akhrot - T	Aleurites Moluocena Wild - B
	Bengal welmit - E	Euphorbieceae - F
4.	Akola - T	Alanglum Salvifolium Wang - B
	Akola - E	Alangiaceae - F
5.	shaitan - T	Alstonia Scholaris R. ER - B
	Shaitan Wood - E	Apocynaceas - F
6.	Kadem - T	Anthocophalus Indicus A Rich - B
	Kadem - E	Rubiaceas - F
7.	Kattian - T	Celba Pentandra Geerta - B
	Kapok tren - E	Bombacacean - F
8.	Pengra - T	Erythrima Suberosa Roxb - B
	Madar - T	Leguminosae - F

(contd.)

9.	Geva. Geon - T	Exicoecaria Agallocha Inn - B
	Agaliochs - E	Eupborhiacean - F
10.	Umar - T	Ficus Glomerata Poxb - B
	Gular - E	Moraceas - F
11.	Rudraksha - T	Quaruma ulmifalia Lem - B
	Bastard Codar - E	Stereuliaceas -F
12.	Chelwa. Bola - T	Hibiecus Titiaceus Linn - B
	Yellow Mellow Tree - E	Malvaceae - F
13.	Kenju. Papri - T	Haloptolea Integriplia Planch - B
	Indian Kim - E	Ulmaceae - F
14.	Amle Amalaka - T	Emblica officinalis earth - B
	Emblic Myrobolan - E	Euphorblacese - F
15.	Beheda - T	Terminalia Bellerica Roxb - B
	Baleric Myrobalan - E	Combraiacase - F
16.	Kadam - T	Terminalts Procera Roxb - B
17.	Brich - T	Betula Linn. - B
18.	Bonaum - T	Phoebe neas - B
19.	Champ - T	Michelia Champaca Linn - B
20.	Chickrasay - T	Chukrasia tabulasia A Juss - B
21.	Chaplash - T	Artocarpus chaplasha Roxb - B
22.	Haldu - T	Adinacordifolia. Benth and Hook - B
23.	Kalam - T	Mitragyna panifolia (Roxb) - B
24.	Kanju - T	Holopteton. integrifolia planch - B
25.	Kuthan - T	Hyemodictyon Excelsum Wall - B
26.	Mango - T	Megnifera Indian Linn - B
27.	Pali - T	Pelaguim allipticum Eaill-B
28.	Silver Oak - T	Grevillea Robusta Stand - B
29.	Mapla - T	Aceral -B
30.	White Cedar - T	Dynoxylum Malabarium Bedd - B

CALLOPHYLLUM INOPHYLLUM

English - Alexandran Lourel. Hindi and Bengali - Sultana Champa

Botanically Known *Callaphyllum* I *Nophyllum* is a common tree in many tropical countries in the Republic of Seychelles the tree is called *Takamaka* and in south India as *PINAI*. In north of India people call it *Dilo*. Different African countries and the island countries of the Pacific have their own names. (*Callophyllum Parislorum* is slightly different within the same family). The wood which is considered good timber is used for furniture and for roof and wall panelling. There is a dense growth of this tree in most African countries,

Madagascar, Mauritius, India and Sri Lanka and it is also found in south America and the Caribbean countries. Being a sturdy tropical tree it can be introduced by seeds in countries having a warm dry climate with plenty of sunlight and moderate rain fall. The tree is of a large size and grows beyond 100 feet under normal conditions and spreads its heavy branches of deep green large leaves in all directions.It grows well on sea shore and grows generously in the Andaman islands

The perfectly round nuts of this tree are smaller than a lime (the fully developed nut has a diameter of about one inch). It is green on the tree and brownish and smaller when fallen and dried. The shell weighs about one third of the seed weight.

The kernel and shell together contain 40-70 per cent oil. The moisture content is about 25-35 per cent. The oil contains about 10 per cent resinous substances which give a strong olive green colour and bitter taste thereby making the fat non-edible. The oil is used in India for lighting lamps (especially in Hindu temples), for making soaps and in native medicines for skin disorder, including the treatment of leprosy.

The active principles are:-

(a) Calophyllolide.

(b) Inophyllolide.

(c) Calopyllic acid. Calophlloide is found to posses some active anti-inflamatory properties.

Fatty acid composition of neutral oil

Palmitic acid .... 17-19 per cent
Stearic acid .... 6-11 per cent
Oleic acid .... 48-52 per cent
Linoleic .... 21-24 per cent

The oil serves also as an alternative cooking energy, and it does not have a bad odour. In its crudest form, the oil can be poured into an old basin or flat empty tin and if a piece of rag, twisted and tied to stay like a rope, is soaked in it and used as a wick, it burns for hours together giving light and heat. In the interior villages of LDC's this can take light and warmth into the homes and cook meals for the poor. The leaves are *ideally used* for making leaf plant and cups, like the leaves of Terminatia Catappa (Indian Almond)

NEEM LEAF PROTECTS STORED GRAIN

The Ryan Foundation recommands the addition of a hand-full of green Neem leaves as an insecticide to every kilo of stored grain. It also recommends that fresh Neem leaves be soaked in water for about a month in large cemented open-air tanks (8' X 8' X 4') under hot sun and the greenish liquid used in rural toilets to keep off bad odour and infections to some extent.

Several experiments by different researchers have established that Neem leaves give effective protection against stored grain pests such as:

Moth (*Ephestinclavtella*)

Rice Veevil (*Calendra Oryzae*)

Red flour beetle (*Tribolium Castanevum*)

Angoumois grain moth (*Sitotroga Cercalella Oliver*) and

Lesser grain bover (*Rhizopertha dominica*)

Experiments have also established that Neem leaves (and other neem tree parts and products) can be used as repellent against insects, having chewing and biting mouth parts (taken from Utilisation of Neem and its By-Products - Report by C.M. KETKAR, published by the Non-edible Oils Division of the Khadi and Village Industries Commission of the Government of India, 226).

The extracts of Neem oil and Neem cake are found to inhibit the growth of types of bacteria such as Nitrsomonas and Nitrobacter (*ibid.*, p. 36).

Neem leaf was found to be an effective insecticide. "It was employed successfully to prevent infection of Cocoa leaves by *Ephestia Cautella* (*ibid.*, p. 152).

Leaves of Neem tree caused inhibition of development as well as morphological effects on Mexican bean beetle (*Epilanchua Varivestis Mulsant*), on the Diamond Moth (*Plutella maculipennis-L*) and the beet leaf bug (Piesma-*quandratum Fieb*) ibid., p. 134.

Seven tonnes of Neem leaves when applied to wheat crop, reduced the attack of termites by 8 to 0.7 per cent. Water extract of Neem leaves in ten gallons of water, gave effective protection against locus but 2.5 times the strength of the extract is essential for other insects.

Dried leaves and twigs of neem have been used in India from time immemorial for protection of woolen fabrics, books, leather goods, etc. (ibid., p. 149).

The active principle in Neem leaves extract appears to be derivative of Paraisin (ibid., p.156).

ALLEY CROPPING

Alley cropping is simply the planting of food crops in between rows of leguminous shrubs and trees, the leaves of which are slashed at regular intervels to supply nutrients to the soil. It is a low input soil management technology that can promote farming where farmers cannot afford expensive inputs and where increasing pressure on land does not favour the age-long shift cultivation. Alley cropping retains the basic features of bush fallow and can easily be adopted by resource poor farmers in tropical countries.

The shrubs and trees in alley farming provide green manure or mulch for companion food crops and thus plant nutrients are recycled from deeper soil layers.

An important advantage of alley cultivation over the traditional shift-cultivation, and bush fallow system is that the cropping and fallow phases can take place at the same time on the same land thereby allowing the farmer to cultivate for a longer time without returning the land for bush fallow for renourishment.

Some criteria for selecting shrubs and trees for alley cropping are: (1) heavy foliage, (2) roots that go deep, (3) easy eradication if necessary, (4) quick regeneration after pruning and (5) ability to provide useful by-products.

Leguminous plants and shrubs are preferred to non-legumes because of their ability to fix atmospheric nitrogen and the planting is usually done four metres apart in rows. Fast growing shrubs such as *Leucaena*, *Leucocephala* and *Gliricidia Sepium* require pruning once in two months.

Research has established that Alley cropping is a dependable alternative to the traditional systems as it retains the basic principles of traditional agriculture, while introducing very reliable improvements.

Based on the book on Alley Cropping published by the Institute of Tropical Agriculture *(IITA) Ibadan, Nigeria.*

Rural women do most of the agricultural work but modernization programmes are all addressed to men. The future of our farm communities and food supplies much depends on the help we give rural women in taking to inexpensive and appropriate technologies which alone can improve their farming and lifestyle.

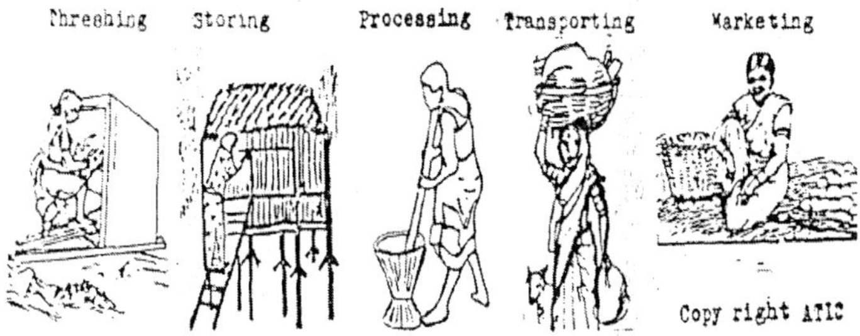

CAUSTIC SODA FROM BANANA BARK

Soap making has become a common cottage and village industry in many developing communities. The two important basic raw materials for making soaps are oil and caustic soda.

Several types of non-edible oils from locally available nuts are now being exploited, the chief among them being oil from Neem seeds.

Availability of Caustic Soda, however, remains a problem. Some DCs and almost all LDCs are not making but importing caustic soda. Frequently locally made soaps with imported caustic soda are more costly than ready-made imported soaps. The only way to reduce the cost of home-made soaps is to find suitable substitutes for imported caustic soda.

A good substitute can be obtained from the banana tree and extraction process is very simple. The outer barks of the tree are removed and crushed between two steel plates or thick wooden planks (on a small scale they may be hammered) By this process the liquid content in the barks can be removed and thereafter the barks may be dried in the open sun for about ten days. When completely dry, almost brittle, they are burnt in a cement floor and the white ash that is obtained is sieved and stored. This is caustic potash and a good substitute for caustic soda and can be used for making washing soaps. A simple method of preparing Caustic lye is explained below.

Among the wood or plant ash the banana burnt ash is found to be highly caustic. The soda thus made can be used only for making laundry soaps and not toilet soaps.

To make lye, make a hole at the bottom of an earthernware pot and mount the pot on a stand. Put some straw inside the pot to act as filter. Fill the pot with banana ash, scoop a hole in the middle and fill water into it. Add more water every day as the ash absorbs the water. The lye will drip through into the bucket placed below the pot. Continue this process for about three weeks. Then put a small raw potato into the lye in the bucket. If the potato floats the lye is ready for use, if not, give more time. Be very careful in handling this lye as it can burn your skin like caustic soda. In soap making use the lye in the same way caustic soda is used.

As good alternative to banana bark another common village plant *Adhatoda* may be used (Botanical *adhatoda Vasica Nees* family *Acanthaceae*).

PAPAINE FROM PAPAYA

A protein digesting enzyme is obtained from the latex (milk) extracted from unripe fruit of the papaya tree, which is botanically called *Carica Papaya.* The tree bears fruit when it is about a year old and the largest quantity of latex can be obtained during the first year. Second and third years give lesser amounts. By the fourth year the tree grows very tall and gives very little latex.

The latex is collected by making a shallow cut in the fruit. Within a few minutes after the tapping the fresh latex solidifies into a gel which is then processed. Sun drying is the country process while drying artificially under low temperature is the commercial method.

Chemical precipitation, solvent extraction, filtration and spray-drying are the operations which give different grades of commercial papine. The grades of papine are often standerdized by adding sucrose, lactose or starch as a dilutant.

Crude papine will have to be stored in a dark cool room in air-tight containers as it is easily oxidized when exposed to air or sun-light when crude papine is not fully dried it may be treated with a reducing agent such as sodium or potassium bisulphite or metabisulphite.

Uses: There are many uses for papine in the food industries, pharmaceuticals and cosmetics. Over 80 per cent of the papine produced in the world is used in chill-proofing compounds for the brewing industry and as a meat tenderiser. About two thirds of the papine used in the United States of America is used as meat tenderiser.

In the pharmaceuticals it is used as an aid to digestion particularly in cases of chronic dyspepsia and gastritis. It is also used in the treatment of infected wounds.

Caution: Papine produces lung diseases by acting as an inhalant allergen and it is a potent sensitiser for the production of respiratory diseases. As such it is likely to affect people prone to asthma and bronchial diseases.

Papine is also used in certain cleansing lotions, face creams and tooth paste.

In the food industry, it is usually used in bakery products and in the leather industry it is used in the preparation of baing compounds. (Bating is a process used prior to tanning, whereby skins are soaked in a fermenting solution to make them soft.) In the textile industry, it is used for degumming of silk and as a dry cleaning agent. In the fifties Sri Lanka was the largest producer of

Papine. In the seventies, it was Zaire followed by Tanzania, South Africa, Mozambique and India.

The world production of papine is about 300 tons a year and India's share is about 80 tons and India exports mostly crude papine. This is an industry which can be developed in many Third World Countries as Papaya does not grow in the cold countries. (Main source: Medicinal plants and their derivatives-UNCTAD-82)

DATURA STRAMONIUM RELIEVES ASTHMA

Basically there are two common varieties of *Datura Stramonium* the white variety and the black. More or less they have similar properties and the white is more common in most of the tropical countries. The plant requires sunlight and watering during mid-summer. Propagated by seeds the plant grows to a height of about five feet. At a distance of about 100 cms from each other the plants grow well. The leaves are ovate and triangular and the flowers large and white similar to Blue-bells. Flowering is during the second half of the year and the plant is called *Voomatham* in Tamil.

The dried leaves and flowers of *Datura Stramonium* contain a number of alkaloids mainly, hyoscyamine with small quantities of atropine and hyoscine (scopolamine) the black seed inside *Datura Stramonium*, (*Devils apple*) is poisonous.

The first harvest of leaves should be done just before flowering when the alkaloids content is at its highest. After the first harvest the leaves and flowers grow again and two or three harvests can be made.

"Preparations of the dried leaves and fruits of Datura Stramonium have similar action to those of the isolated alkaloids, they exhibit peripheral anti-cholingergic effects and may be used as antispasmodics in the treatment of asthma" (taken from the book *Medicinal Plants and their Derivatives*, published by the UNCTAD -1982.

The leaves and flowers of Datura Stramonium are to be sun dried and kept in air-tight containers. When an *asthma patient* has symptoms of going into an attack the dried mixture, which will look like smokers tobacco, may be burnt near the patient for the patient to inhale the smoke. If smoked well in time the smoke will prevent the on coming attack and relieve conjestion in the lungs. It is almost as effective as the asthma pump but after the attack catches on it can only reduce severity to some extent. In rural parts of India people commonly use Datura smoke to relieve or prevent asthma. *Datura Stramonium* is also called Thorn Apple in English, because its big round pods are full of long thorns. This flower does not open out like a trumpet while the other Variety. *Datura Suavealens*, opens out like a trumpet and it is nice to.look at. Both are medicinal, but *staramonium* is more effetive for asthama.

AGAVE-for excellent Fibre

Agave is highly drought resistant fibre plant. It is Short Stemmed and grows wild in drought prone areas. The: plant is said to bloom only once in it's life-time of 8 years and then dries and dies out. There are over 250 species of the genus but 3 varieties grow in many Third world Countries and they are *Agave Cantala*, *Agave Sisalana* and *Agave Americana.*

All the three species have coarse but strong fibre. The plants were introduced from America into several countries and in the USA they are used almost for all purposes for which coconut fibre. Jute or *Manila hemp* are used in the East, i.e., for making brushes, fishing nets, rugettes, ropes, Hammocks, etc.

As the fibre consists about 75 percent cellulose matter the waste that drops after extracting the fibre is excellent for making craft paper and boards. Hecogenin Acetate, a steroid extracted from the juice of the leaves is used in pharmaceuticals.

This drought plant is propagated by suckers and bulbs during rainy season. Bulbs are first sown closely, after three months transplanted spacing two feet between two plants and after about ten months the suckers are collected and replanted. The leaves can be cut only after three years.

The mature plants will have about 35 leaves every year and each leaf will be about a meter long. *Agava Sisalana* gives more and better quality fibre than the other two species.

From the third year onwards upto five years thereafter plants planted in about two acres can give more than Rs 1000, or about US$ 100 per year. The fibre can be extracted by the process shown in RYFO hand outs and the extraction should be done within two days from harvesting to get a good colour.

Ropes made out of this fibre are excellent to build low cost houses with RYFO shingles shown in Handout 192. for various other uses for fibre to promote jobs in rural areas and to make products for urban markets see handout 233.

USES OF PONGAMIA GLABRA

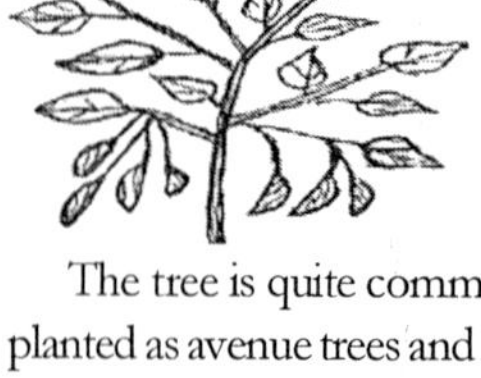

Pongamia Glabra is an evergreen and fast growing tropical tree. It belongs to the botanical family *Legtuninosae* and known in Tamil as *Punga* and as *Karan* in Hindi. In Karnataka, it is called *Honge* and in Andhra Pradesh as *Ganugachettu.* In Kerala, it is called *Unne.*

The tree is quite common in India and in many tropical countries. It is usually planted as avenue trees and in parks for shade. It is a hardy tree, drought resistant and can be propagated by seeds and cuttings during the rainy season. People use different parts of this tree for different purposes and some common uses are given below.

1. Fresh leaves are ground to a paste and applied for skin deseases.
2. Dried leaves kept in wardrobes and drawers keep away white ants and small insects.
3. Green twigs from the tree are used as tooth brush by villagers.
4. Honey-bees collect good honey from the flowers of this tree.
5. The leaves make excellent green manure, especially for flower gardens.
6. Oil is extracted from the nut of the tree which is used for preparing soaps and skin ointments. (many doctors in India advise their patients to use soaps that contain this oil to keep their skin healthy.)
7. The oil cake serves as a rich manure.
8. Trunks of well grown trees are used as timber.
9. Small branches are used as fuel wood.
10. Goats and rabbits are fed with these leaves.

RYFO recommands the propagation of this tree in rural settlements and refugee camps for creating self-employment opportunities for the poor people.

STARCH FROM CASAVA

Mature tubers are washed. On a small scale the skin peeled is by hand. Then the roots are chopped and crushed and the milk is drained out and seperated from the fiberous tissues. Clean water is added to the slurry when it is crushed to bring out all the stanch. The milky starch is collected and spread on broad flat trays or clean cement floors and left for about eight hours to set. In this process the starch settles to the bottom and the excess liquid partly drains away and partly evaporates.

The next day the surface layer of the starch will be of yellowish green colour containing impurities. It will give unpleasant smell. The top impure surface is scrapped off leaving the creamy white mass of starch below.

Water is added to the white mass and stirred vigorously and then left to settle. This washing and settling process is repeated several times until the Starch looks pure the starch oulto thus obtained is spread out well on the trays, or on the cement floor and allowed to dry. Finally, the hard dry lumps of starch are crushed into powder and sieved.

To prepare *Casava pearls* (also called tapioca pearls) the moist starch is rubbed through a sieve of about tweny holes to an inch and what comes out in damp form is put on perforated trays and vigourously shaken to shape them into pearls, (in factories excentric iberators are used) Then the pearls are roasted for about 15 mts. in hot pans seared with coco.nut oil. Finally, the pearls are dried in hot sun. The usual yield of tapioca pearls from fresh tubers to prepare Casava pearls is about twenty five percent.

INSTANT OKRA

Okra or Lady's finger, which is called in north India as *Bhindi* and in south India as *Vendai* is a common vegetable that is grown and eaten in most parts of the world. The small plant which grows to a height of 3 to 4 feet is easily propagated by seeds and harvested in about 3 months after sowing. It is a tasty and nutricious vegetable and can be preserved both in dry and wet form. Okra preserved in brine in air-tight bottles is commonly available in western countries and South Africa is a known exporter of preserved Okra.

To preserve, Okra it must first be blanched for about 5 minutes. Blanching is usually done by dipping in boiling water containing half a tea-spoon of baking soda or a tea-spoon full of salt. After draining the water, half tea-spoon of Sodium Metabisulphite may be spread on the blanched okra when it still contains a little water and mixed and shaken to spread well. The proportion of the mix is half tea-spoon of Sodium Metabisulphite for every ten kg of Okra. Thus prepared, the okra may be dried under open sun, preferably, inside a glass-top solar dryer. In about a week, the Okra will be completely dry and crisp and can be preserved for months together, in air-tight containers or polythene bags. About 12 kg of fresh tender Okra will give about one kg when dried and about three when reconstituted.

To reconstitute, the dried Okra may be soaked in water for about two hours and cooked in the same water used for soaking. Cooking is done with lid on and salt added to taste. If too much water is used the flavour will be lost.

Alternatively, the dried okra may be straight away fried in oil. It can also be added to gravy as dried rings. There is a belief in India that Okra is good for the brain and builds up a good memory.

There are different types of Okra. India, China, Africa, Sri Lanka, Philippines and many other countries have their own varieties. But the best table variety known so far is the Indian variety called *Pusha Savani*. This has now been successfully introduced by the ILO in the refugee camps in Jalalaqsi in Somalia and can be taken to other parts of the world without difficulty. Once grown, okra can be allowed to ripen and dry in the plant to provide more seeds. Recenty, the Indian Council of Agricultural Research released a Variety called *Pusha Chrisanti* which is claimed to be better than *Pusha Savani*.

Vegetable Growing Inside Automobile Tyres

Discarded car and lorry tyres are burried flat in the ground about one inch below surface level. The inside of the tyre is filled with sand free of small stones and pebbles. The sand used for filling may be mixed with poultry or cattle yard sweepings. Alternatively, different types of dried leaves may be mixed with the sand.

Delicate vegetable plants such as tomatoes, garden eggs (brinjals) Okra (lady's fingers), and spinich may be grown inside the tyre. Some cow dung and neem leaf may be added to the prepared soil mixture.

THE ADVANTAGE: When the plants are watered the manure-mixed sand inside the tyre absorbs and retains the water or moisture for two to three days and keeps the bed of the plant wet and therefore it will be enough to water the plants on alternative days during summer and once in three or four days in winter. Thus, there will be considerable saving in water and labour. The plant fertility will be greater and the plants will yield more and better vegetables in shorter time. Weed problem will be less inside the tyre and labour spent on weeding will also be less.

With the growing of vegetables in about ten tyres (four to five plants inside each tyre as shown in the diagram) a family can have vegetables all through the year. It should be noted that vegetables grow better when the plants are clustered together and support one another.

If two or three tyres are burried one on top of the onother their water holding capacity will be greater and the plants will also yield better results quikly. When layers are made with two or three tyres, watering may be done even once a week provided a good flow of water is ensured everytime watering is done.

The tyre system works well in flower gardens also, particularly in urban homes and roof-gardens. To grow plants to a height of three or four feet, it is necessary to have three tyres in layers. On roof gardens, the tyres need not be burried. The author has successfully demonstrated growing of vegetables in types on the sun shades over windows in the multi storied building in Bombay where the residents don't see soil for growing vegetables.

HYBRID SUNFLOWER

Rural communities in some developing countries are taking to sunflower cultivation for oil which has medical and commercial value. Common complaint about sunflower crops is that the seed setting is poor and many seeds are found not to be healthy but chaffy and half-filled. The plants frequently suffer from root and stem rot and develop alternaria leaf spots. These setbacks have been hindering large-scale cultivation of the crop for oil.

Recently the University of Agricultural Science, Bangalore, have successfully developed a hybrid variety for mass cultivation and the variety is free from most of the defects and problems mentioned above. This new hybrid variety is said to be highly tolerant to diseases, pests and drought conditions. They are uniform in growth and superior in their seed formation and reach the harvesting stage in about fifteen days ahead of the ruling variety.

The name of the new variety is *BS H-I* (Bangalore Sunflower hybrid). It yields about 35 percent more seeds than the ruling varieties. The university reports that BSH-I produced about 1.5 tons per hectare under rainfed conditions and about 2.8 tons under irrigated conditions and has become very popular with the cultivators in the State of Karnataka in South India. Scientists of the university claim that mass production of the seeds is almost as easy as producing hybrid *sorghum.*

This hybrid variety is excellent for intensive farming and inter croping with ground-nuts, wheat, *ragi* or *sorghum.* The BSH-I (Bangalore sunflower hybrid) may be obtained from the University of Agricultural science, Bangalore, Karnataka State, South India.

Sunflower oil is medically recommanded as a cooking medium for blood pressure and cholesterol patients. The residue left after the extraction of the oil can be mixed with cattle feed.

There is an ever rising demand in India and some other countries for Sunola oil and the supply is far short of demand. The plant grows well in most tropical countries and it is a field to be exploited. It can be grown between banana, sugar cane and Sorghum plantations.

GROWING MUSHROOMS ON PADDY STRAW

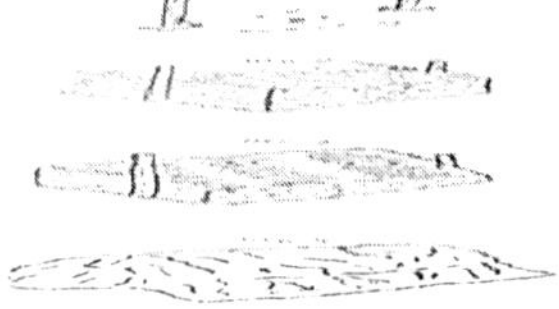

Select the spot on the ground where you would like to grow the mushrooms and strike two poles about two metres apart The poles may be nearly a metre high after they are stuck to the ground (diagram 1).

Before hand soak paddy straw for two or three days in a tub of water and make it Soft. Spread the straw between the two poles in an orderly manner as shown in diagram 2. When the spread is about eight or 10 cms high walk on it and compress the layer and simultaneously water the layer. The water may be mixed with common garden manure is nure without lumps or with cow dung. Cow dung preferable

Procure in advance mushroom culture (seeds) from the college of Agriculture or the government department of Agriculture, and have the seeds sprinkled on the layer of straw that you have made. Do the sowing about eight cms away from the edge of the straw bed. To prepare your own seeds (spawns) see RYFO booklet.

Make a second layer of soaked straw on top of the first and walk on it as you did on the first layer and at the same time water it, sprinkle the culture and water again.

Make several layers in the same fashion till the heaps come to the height of the two poles.

When you have made the last layer sprinkle the mushroom culture all over the surface including the edges and cover with one more layer of straw but lay this last layer perpendicular to the other layers as shown in diagram 3. *Pleurotus* and *volvariella* are the recommended variety of mushroom.

Finally, cover the entire heap with an opaque plastic sheet as shown in diagram 4 or cover them with woken coconut palm leaf.

Harvesting can commence after about 15 days and a heap built as explained Should yield about five Kgs of mushrooms in a month. If more harvest is desired the size of the bed and layers must be made bigger or many beds may be built in a row.

What is very important is that many mushrooms are poisonous... and one must be very careful in selecting them. It is always safe to procure the seeds or culture from a recognised institution or the agricultural department of the government. For detailed information see RYFO guide booklet growing mushrooms under your roof.

MORE ABOUT MUSHROOMS

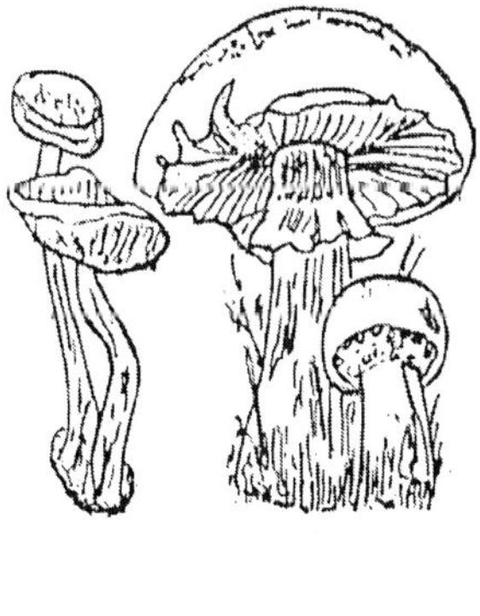

Among the few varieties of mushrooms that grow well on paddy straw the best is Oyster mushroom (*Peurotus Oatreatus*), It comes up well In temperatures ranging between 70 degrees and 100 degrees F. with about 75 per cent humidity. The Button mushrooms are the second best.

The straw bed explained in handout 67 must be watered and always kept moderately wet. The heap should be damp but should not drip water.

OYSTER MUSHROOMS

After the last harvest the straw heap must be removed and this decomposed and spawned straw which is rich in nitrogen compounds and protein must be given to cattle. They are easily digestible, and cattle like to eat them.

It is cultivated in about 30 Sq mts the annual returns, after meeting all expenses, will be well over Rs, 3000.

Composition of mushrooms.

Carbohydrates:- 4 to 5 per cent of fresh weight (mostly mannose).

Proteins:- 2 to 6 per cent of fresh weight (10 to 90 per cent digestible).

The caloric value of the above two items is very low.

Minerals:- Phosphorus, calcium magnesium, iron potassium, etc.

Vitamins:- Riboflavin (vit B2).

Thiamine:- (vit B2).

Folic acid;x Panothene.

Ascorbic acid (vit C).

Nicotinic acid, Biotin and ergosterine.

Note: In tropical climate, Oyster mushrooms don't stay fresh for long and their stem is more fibrous. So, the button mushrooms are in preference in tropical countries especially in Five Star hotels and Chinese Restos.

The best way to preserve and pack mushrooms is to break them into talis sun dry them crush them to granules and pack them is P.V.C Sacholi to be used as instant soup or gravy granules can be mixed with cutlets or

SISAL AND ACCACIA TO PROTECT PLANTS

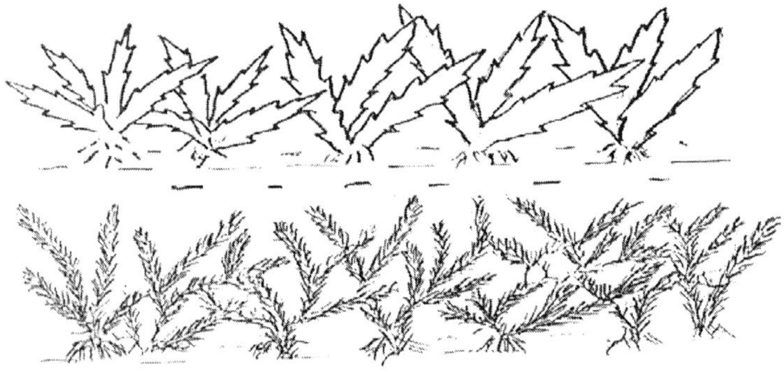

Vegetable gardens and social forestry are not developing as desired in the Third World for want of protection for the seedlings and saplings. Children and stray cattle destroy them and those who plant them cannot afford to erect walls or to fence them. When they make a fence with tree branches they are stolen for firewood.

For protecting plants from animals, children and trepassers sisal may be planted beforehand all along the boundry of the land or plot. As a second line of protection accacia may be planted. Both these are thorny plants and children and cattle keep away from them. This is a common way of protecting paddy and vegetable fields in south India.

Moreover, sisal is a commercial plant and its fibre has many uses while accacia bark gives dye for colouring. Commonly sisal fibre-is boiled with accacia barks to give the fibre a dark tan colour. Grown as a tree accacia gives good firewood and poor quality timber which can be used for certain purposes.

Both these plants belong to the cactus variety and don't need watering if planted during the rainy season and when they are available in commercial quantities they provide employment to many rural families. *Accacia Holo sericea* is another useful plant well suited for bunde cultivation (See page 139).Sisal is a major export earner for Tanzania.the pith, after the extraction of the before is used as a fertiliser.In India, this cactus with big sheets fund all along the raibiay track, is commonly called *Rail Kathalai.*

Sisal fibre Extraction and Uses

The botanical name of the commonly known sisal homp is *Agave Sislana Perr,* (family *Agavaceae*) This is a shrub with short and stout trunk bearing a rosette of thick and fleshy leaves. It is commonly seen in most of the countries having a tropical climate and has many uses.

The easiest way to extract the fibre from the fleshy loaves is to soak the leaves in water for about a week and beating the leaves with a wooden hammer. This process is called retting. During rainy season the rain water ponds in the village may be used to soak the leaves. To discourage mosquitoes and frogs breeding in the pond large quantities of neem leaves may also be soaked in the same pond along with the sisal. Neem leaf has properties of insecticides as explained in Handout 33. The rotting may be done beside the same pond, and fibre cleaned and washed in the same place.

The fibre may also be seperated from the flesh by using two spiked rollers to crush them as sugar cane is crushed for juice. The machine used for fibre extraction is very similar to the sugar cane crushing machine and can be assembled in a small mechanical workshop. The machine designed by the Khadi and Village Industries Commission for sisal fibre extraction works very well and rural communities can use them without difficulty.

The fibre extracted from the leaf (or sheath)is considered a good substitute for Manila fibre. It is used for manufacturing heavy twins, ropes, marine cordages and as a substitute for jute. It is also used for malting rugs, mats, sacks for packing onions, pineapple and other root crop products. Brushes, craft paper and paper boards are also made out of the fibre.

Pulque beer and Mexican brandy are made from the sap of the flowering stalk in the same way as from the sap of *Agave Americana.*

The Central Food Technology Research Institute of the Government of India in Mysore has the know-how to extract sugar out of sisal plant but the method has not been commercialised.

Most African countries grow sisal and some countries such as Tanzania have been exporting the fibre for the past several years. In India and China, sisal is grown all along paddy field boundaries to prevent cattle straying in. For information about protecting crops with sisal please see the Ryan foundation handout 76.

"SUN RISE SOLO" PAPAYA

There are many types of Papaya fruits, also known as Popos. Botanically Papaya is called *Carica Papaya.* The Tamil Nadu Agricultural University in South India has released four notable varieties and they are, CO1, CO2, CO3, and CO4. Excepting CO3, the others are dioecious, i.e., they have separate male and female trees. The CO3 variety is hermaphrodite, having both the sex organs in the same tree.

The variety called *Sun Rise Solo* introduced into India and many other countries from Hawaii is also hermaphrodite and this is an excellent variety. It is smaller than many other varieties but very suitable for home gardens and the table. The flesh is red in colour, the tree thrives well in well drained soil but do not stand water logging.

Nutritious Papaya has Vitamins A, B and C, protein, carbohydrates, calcium, phosphorus and iron and quite a few medicinal properties.

The tree yields fruit continuously from about the fifth month of planting and fertilisers may be applied in small doses from the third month onwards. If machine made fertilisers are available about 100 gms of urea, 300 gms of super phosphate, and 80 gms of muriate of potash may be applied. If not available, mere farm yard manure and cow dung may be applied at the rate of four kg per tree per month. If properly manured each tree will yield atleast 100 fruits per year for about two and a half years. The production will then fall steeply and fade away. RYFO recommands organic ferliliser.

A very useful product called Papine can be extracted from the papaya latex as explained in RYFO recommend organic fertilisers. handout No. 41. Besides tenderising meat papine is applicable in food industries, for chill proofing beer and. freezing food protein. Other applications are:

1. Textile industry - for degumming of silk.
2. Tanning Industry - shin dehairing and bathing of hides.
3. Brewing - beer stabilisation, barley and malt treatment.
4. Dairy industry - Cheese manufacturing.
5. Feeds industry - treatment of vegetable proteins.
6. Meat industry - fat extraction, concentrate.
7. Juice industry - fruit juices and wine mailing.
8. Pish industry - Hydrolysates -PPG, fish meals etc.
9. Dietetic industry - baby foods.
10. Baking industry - biscuits.

Papine is used also in pharmaceutical extracts, aromas and perfumery industries and in effluent treatment.

CEYLON SPINACH

The botanical name of the popularly known Ceylon Spinach is *Talinum Triaitgulare*. It is a small perennial plant that grows to a height of 30 cm. The stem is fleshy, the succulent and lustrous leaves contain plenty of vitamin A which is good for the eyes. Flowers are pink in small clusters and appear throughout the flower buds should be nipped to encourage growth of leaves.

Ceylon Spinach can be propagated by stem cuttings and if properly planted and watered the stems strike roots within ten days of planting. The natural spread of the plant is by seed dispersal and when seeds are allowed to form and spread, the spread of the plant is dense and quick. Seeds are also produced throughout the year. Fowls like to eat these leaves and as the fowls keep eating them new shoots and roots appear. Thus, Cylon Spinach can be nutriceous a and cost free chicken-feed in one's own garden or neighbourhood.

The plant is highly drought resistant and free of most deseases and pests that usually attack edible leaves. It grows luxuriously when irrigated and manured. It is enough to give the plant garden manure or fowl house or cattle yard sweepings. With such care the leaves can be harvested every week. The leaves can be eaten fresh like salad leaves.

The yield of leaves and stems is about 4.5 tonnes per hectare with casual care. The plant should be introduced and cultivated wherever refugees and poor communities live; wherever poultry is kept, around public taps and wells and in the backyard of homes where the bath water flows.

The Ceylons Spinach lends itself to several types of delicious preparations for the table. Tilapia fish and Ceylon Spinach make a fine comniation on the table. For information about Tilapia farming please see RYFO Handout No. 86.

NEEM TOOTH POWDER

Factory made tooth paste in collapsible tubes is costly for the rural poor. Factory made tooth powder which is now in the market is also quite costly for the poor. Both these are not available in the rural parts of many countries.

From time immemorial the rural poor in China., India and some other countries have been using twigs of certain trees to brush their teeth. Some of these twigs that are commonly used have certain natural medicinal properties and strengthen the gums but they hurt the gums and it is not convenient or comfortable to use a twig as a tooth brush. The twig that is most commonly used is taken from the Neem tree.

Neem leaf ash is an excellent alternative. The leaves are dried in the open sun until they are brittle, burnt, powdered and sieved. If a domestic kitchen sieve is not available, a closely knit wire mesh or just a bandage cloth may be used to sieve the ash obtained by burning the leaves. For taste and better effect some common salt may be added to the ash.

Neem (*Margosa*) contains a series of active ingredients of crystalline and amorphous bitter constituents. The main active principle is *NIMBIDIN* and it is a tonic for the gums. Several tooth paste manufacturers mix neem to their product.

The neem leaf powder may either be taken in the index finger and straight away applied to the teeth or the powder may be used in a tooth brush in the place of paste.

Experiments have established that neem kills several types of bacteria and has a healing effect on the human body. For further information about the chemical properties of neem please see Handout No 89.

ASPHALT VASAKA BUILDING SLABS

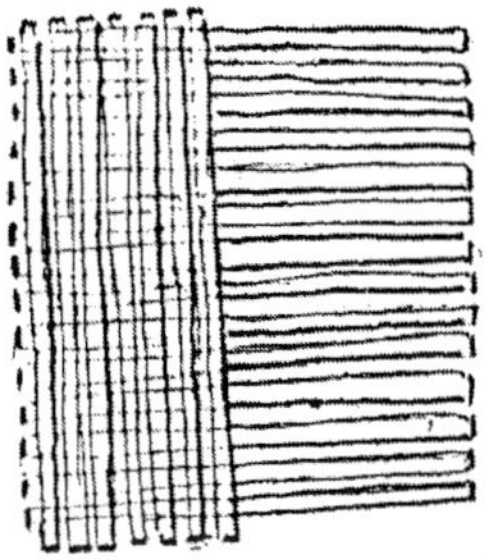

Adhatoda (botanical Adhatoda Yasica Nees family *Acanthaceae*) which is otherwise known as Adhatodai, Arusha or Vasaka, is a densely branched shrub, which grows wild to a height of four to six feet in many countries with tropical climate. The plant is not browsed by cattle and so it is commonly planted to reclaim waste land. The wood is used for burning country made bricks and for making charcoal. The ash which is very caustic is used for washing clothes by villagers. The stem and twigs are used for reinforcing mud walls in India. The leaves make excellent green manure and a durable yellow dye is extracted from the leaves. Leaves are also used as weedicide, fungicide and insecticide. Fruit dealers cover nearly ripe fruits in baskets with these leaves to hasten ripening.

It is easy to cut out the twigs and take the stem of this plant in straight lengths of three to four feet. A row of the sticks may be laid parallel to each other and tied to stay with a fibre rope or binding wire. Another row may be made on top of it perpendicular to the first layer as shown in the diagram. Thus a kind of mat made of sticks may be got. Bitumen or asphalt tar may be melted in a drum (an empty bitumen or oil drum may be used) and the mats dipped to give them a complete coating of bitumen. When dry, they may be dipped a second time to ensure better coating. (Acacia sticks may also be used.)

The *Adhatoda -Vasaka* slabs thus made are ideal for laying the floor and reinforcing mud walls in rural areas. They can also be used for panelling, as false celling and for protection against rain and. sun. Cages for chicken or rabbits and cattle sheds may also be built with them. Asphalt Vasaka building slabs are absolutely durable, convenient and economical. instead of mortar as phalt RYFO Mixture for mortars may used to drip the mats to till and close the crection for RYFO Mixture for mortars see Handout 270.

Tropical Trees that Yield Colours (Dye stuffs)

1. Botanical - *Acacia Catechu Wild.*

   Family - *Leguminosae.*

   English name - *Catechu Tree.*

   Indian names - *Khair, Katha, Khadia.*

   Identification - Medium size tree, branches dark brown, pinnate leaves 10-15 cms long, yellow flowers.

   Extraction - '*Cutch*' - a yellowish orange dye used in textile colouring.

2. Botanical - *Acacia Concinna Dc.*

   Family - *Leguminosae.*

   Indian names - Ritha, Shikekai.

   Identification - A prickly climber, branches have very many white spots and hooked prickles, leaves are 5-10 cms. long. Yellow flowers each containing 10-12 seeds.

   Extraction - the leaves yield a green dye with turmeric.

3. Botanical - Adenathera Pavonina Linn.

   Family - Leguminosae.

   English name - Bead Tree, Coral, Red Wood.

   Indian names - Kunchandona, Rakta Kambal, Val

   Identification - Large size tree with very long leaves, pale yellow flowers with a pleasant smell. Each flower holds about a dozen seeds.

   Extraction - the red dye extracted from the wood is used as a substitute for the dye extracted from Red sandle wood.

4. Botanical - Aegle Marmelos Correa.

   Family - Rutaceae

   English name - Bael Tree.

   Indian names - Bel, Bilva.

   Identification - Medium size tree which sheds its leaves annually (deciduous). Fruits are woody and smooth cover about 5 cms. in diameter with many seeds densely covered with fibrous hair embedded in a thick aromatic pulp.

   Extraction - The yellow dye extracted from the rind of the unripe fruit is used in calico printing.

5. Botanical - Albizzia Odoratisshima Benth.

   Family - Leguminosae.

   Indian names - Chikunda, Kala, Siris.

   Identification - Dark brown tall tree with plenty of leaflets; fragrant pale yellow flowers

   Extraction - The bark gives a brownish dye and it is used to colour yarn.

6. Botanical - Aleurites Moluccana Wild.

   Family - Euphorbiaceae.

   English names - Bengal Walnut, Candle Nut.

   Indian names - Japhol, Akhrot Jungli Akhrot.

   Identification - Large tree with long leaves and large white flowers and green fruits about four cms in dia. Fruits are fleshy with one or two seeds.

   Extraction - The roots yield a dye.

   Other trees that yield colours (dye stuffs)

7. Botanical - Alnus Nitida Endl.

   Family - Betuiaceae.

   English name - Himalayan Black Cedar.

   Indian names - Kunis, Sharol

   Identification - Big tree with blakish bark, average leaf size 12 cms. Leaves are thin and the wood light.

   Extraction - The bark yield a dye.

8. Botanical - Artocarpus Hetrophyillus Lamk.

   Family - Moraceae.

   English name Jack Fruit Tree

   Indian names - Kathal, Phanas

   Identification - Large tree with mottled bark, leathery leaves 10-12 cms long with shine on one side, flowers hang on short stalk from trunks and branches. Fruits are large and heavy.

   Extraction - Yellow colouring substance is obtained from the wood. By boiling the saw dust of the wood a reddish yellow colour is obtained. These colours are used in the textile industry.

9. Botanical - *Artocarpus Lakoocha Roxb.*

   Family - *Moraceae.*

   English names- *Lakoocha, Monkey Fruit.*

   Indian names - *Barhal, Dahua.*

   Identification - Deciduous, oval leaves 10-30 cms long, yellow fruits 5-8 cms in diameter, smooth and velvety.

   Extraction - Brownish dye from the roots.

10. Botanical - *Berberis Aristata DC.*

    Family - *Berberidaceae.*

    English - *Indian Barberry.*

    Indian names- *Daruharidra, Kashmal, Rasaut.*

    Identification - Reddish brown shrub, with tender branches also red in colour, leaves four-five cms long, flowers yellow and berry red.

    Extraction - Roots give a very valuable bright yellow dye and the stem gives a bright brown dye.

11. Botanical - *Bixa Orellana Linn.*

    Family - *Blxaceae*

    English name - *Annato.*

    Indian names - *Latkhan, Sendri.*

    Identification - Evergreen tree, leaves 10-20 cms long, flowers white or purple, fruits reddish brown, seeds enclosed by reddish pulp.

    Extraction - The red pulp gives an excellent red dye.

12. Botanical - *Frondosa Roxb.*

    Family - *Leguminosae.*

    English - *Butea Gum Tree, Flame of The Forest.*

    Indian names - *Dhak, Palasha.*

    Identification - Deciduous, trunk gnarled and crooked, large reddish orange flowers densely clustered, stalk dark brown and velvety

    Extraction - The flowers known as TESSU yield a brilliant yellow textile dye.

Leaves for serving meals

Clean water is scarce in many countries and people walk long distances to fetch water. Washing kitchen vessels and dining platen, therefore, is a problem and used vessels are nots washed properly leading to contamination of food and. people get sick. To get over this situation whore there is scarcity of water people must be encouraged to use leaves for taking meals as it is commonly done in India. In many parts of India, especially in the south, leaves are very commonly used even where there is no scarcity of. water, to save the labour of washing and wiping the used plates. In weddings and other functions which thousands of people attend invariably food is served on leaves of banana trees and Indian Almond trees. Almond leaves can be used even after they dry up.

The leaves are washed with very little water before use or simply wiped with a wet cloth and thrown away after use. (The size of Almond leaves in Africa is nearly double the size of Indian leaves and a single African leaves can take a full meal at a time).

Given below are botanical, English and Indian names of trees and plants that have very long and broad leaves many of which can be used as plates. All of them are tropical trees and can be commonly found in Africa and most other developing countries.

1. Botanical- *Agave Americana Linn.*

   Family- *Agavacuea.*

   Indian- *Bara Kanwar, Rakas-Palkah.*

   English- *Century Plants.*

2. Botanical- *Ailantiius Triphysa Alston.*

   Family- *Simarubaceae.*

   English - *The tree of distinction.*

   Indian - *Arua, Perumaram.*

3. Botanical - *Areca Catechu Linn.*

   Family - *Palmae.*

   English- *Aeca-Nut Palm, Betel-Nut Palh.*

   Indian - *Supari.*

4. Botanical- *Caesalpinia Sappan Linn.*

   Family- *Legutiinosae.*

   English- *Brazil Wood, Sappan Wood.*

   Indian - *Bakam, Patang.*

5. Botanical - *Canangium Odoratum Baill.*

   Family - *Annnaoeae.*

English - *Ylang-Ylang Tree.*

Local - *Cabanga, Yalang-Yalang.*

6. Botanical - *Curouha Zedoaria Rosc.*

Family - *Zigiberaceae.*

English- *Long Zedoary, Wild Turmeric.*

Indian - *Amb Halad, Kachura.*

There are many more to be identified. The Central Food Technology Research Institute (CFTRI) of the Govt. of India in Mysore, has invented a. small machine to mould cups and plates out of broad leaves.

PRESERVING SUGARCAN JUICE

Process-step by step

1. Extract the juice as quickly as possible after cutting the cane from the field to ensure fresh and high yield of juice.
2. Use the double roller cane crusher which is hand operated if you wish to go on a commercial scale.
3. On a domestic scale a home juicer may be used and in rural areas bits of sugar cane may be pound and crushed for juice.
4. Filter the juice with a muslin cloth.
5. Then, nearly boil the juice at about 80 or 90 degree. Centegrade.
6. As soon as the pot is removed from the fire, for every litre of juice add half a lime and half tea spoon of ginger juice and a pinch of salt for taste and better preservation.
7. When mixed properly leave the juice for 15 mts. to cool down at room temperature.
8. Add quarter tea spoon of the preservative, potassium meta bisulphite (KMS) for every litre of prepared juice.
9. Fill the juice in steralised bottles and close it airtight.
10. The juice thus preserved will roughly have the folloing;-

Sugar 21.5 per cent.

Ascorbic acid 1.5 mg. per 100 ml.
Phosphorus 6.8 mg per 100 ml.

Cost: In India, in 1986. the cost of 180 ml. of sugar cane juice (without the bottle) was about 25 paise or about one rupee for four bottles.

If properly made the juice will last six months or longer and will not deteriorate in quality or taste while in store.

Sugar cane juice is an excellent tonic for the liver. Those who consume excess of alcohol and those who suffer from jaundice are advised to take pleanty of sugar cane juice.

DROUGHT TOLERANT TAMARIND

Tamarind, a commercial crop of India, has not been identified as a money earner in many tropical countries even though it grows and flourishes well in several countries in Africa and the Far East. The soft fruit pulp taken from the pods is used liberally in Indian cooking and there is no home in South India without everyday use of tamarind pulp. The tender pods are used as vegetables and for making pickles and livestock are fed with the leaves which have high animal food nutrients. The seeds arc roasted and given to animals.

Tamarind tree makes good timber in the commercial market; can be used as good firewood and for making high quality charcoal. The white of the seed, crushed and boiled yields a paste which is a good weather proofing material used especially against sea water and salt breeze erosion. The paste can also be used as table gun, or used in factories.

The tree grows well with little care. Seeds when kept in water germinate in about a week and the. germinating seeds are raised in elevated seed bed's. After about a year they may be removed from the bed and transplanted in the fields. Planting is done with gaps of ten metres and the tree is seldom affected by pests and diseases. After the third year practically no care is required and it grows like trees in a forest.

Trees bear fruit from the sixth year but economic returns are got only from the 15th year. Yield is good in alternative years and the yielding stage lasts for over 80 years. A fully grown tree can on an average bear nearly 200 kgs of ripe pods which in India can sell for more than Rs 1,000 (US $100). Ten trees are enough to give a comfortable living wage for a farm family of five.

A heap of pods will have 55 per cent pulp and 34 percent seeds. The rest is fibre and. shell. One of fruits will have about 1800 seeds. The tree can grow to a height of 30 metres.

In India several village industries are based on the Tamarind tree. Collecting the pods (men), removing the pulp from the pods (women), separating and cleaning the pods (girls), crushing the fiberous pod, shells and grinding them with the leaves to make cattle feed (women and children) Weighing and packing the pulp, transporting, glue making, etc., is done jointly by the village community. These industries provide part time employment for many. Enterprising farmers grow the Tamarind tree all along the boundary of their fields for additional money.

MORE ABOUT NEEM

The information contained in this handout are excerpts from the article of Elizabeth Hoddy which appeared in the D + C of Germany, No 1 of 1986.

"Scientists in both Britain and West Germany have demonstrated the Azadirachtin (which is extracted from the neem leaves) prevents insects from shedding their skin and impairs their development, frequently causing abnormalities. The active substance clearly interferes with the insects hormone balance."

"One thousandth of a gram of *Azadirachtin*, which was isolated by British scientists towards the end of the 1970s, is sufficient to curb the appetite and significantly reduce the growth rate of cricket larvae."

"A neem extract applied to adult insects appears to act as a birth control agent. The insects egg laying capacity is greatly reduced and a few eggs that are laid are more susceptible to fungal infection. Pests such as locusts and mites often produce 95 per cent fever off springs."

"Dr. B.G. Joshi at the Central Tobacco Research Institute in Rajahmundry, Andhre Pradesh, India, believes that his team, was the first to demonstrate that a suspension of neem seed kernel effectively repels the moth of the tobacco caterpillar (*Spodoptora Litura*), a major pest of the tobacco plant. The results wore spectacular. There wore far fewer moths, fewer eggs and fewer caterpillars, which can destroy thousands of seedlings within the space of a few days."

"Neem cake, which comprises between 70 per cent and 90 per cent of the crushed seed, is now widely used in many parts of India as a fertiliser to grow tomatoes, cabbages, cauliflowers, potatoes and grapes. IRRI has found that it can boost crop yields by upto 1.3 tonnes per hectare. Weekly treatments of urea blended with neem cake have increased rice yields by upto 40 per cent and sorghum by more than 25 per cent in field experiments."

"In some parts of the Indian state of Andhra Pradesh farmers regularly feed neem cake to their cattle." It's got a bitter taste but once the animals get used to it they take it very well", said one marginal farmer.

"But the research that has attracted the most attention is being conducted by Dr S.S. Riar of the Defence Institute of Physiology and Applied Sciences in New Delhi. He and his colleagues have demonstrated that undiluted neem oil is 100 percent effective as a *vaginal contraceptive* in trials using rats, rhesus monkeys and humans. Subsequent experiments indicate that neem oil could also be used as a. postcoital contraceptive, preventing implantation of the egg.

Cutting trees to live in Sudan. Reproduced with courtesy to the Commission of the European communities from their dossier Enemy for the people.

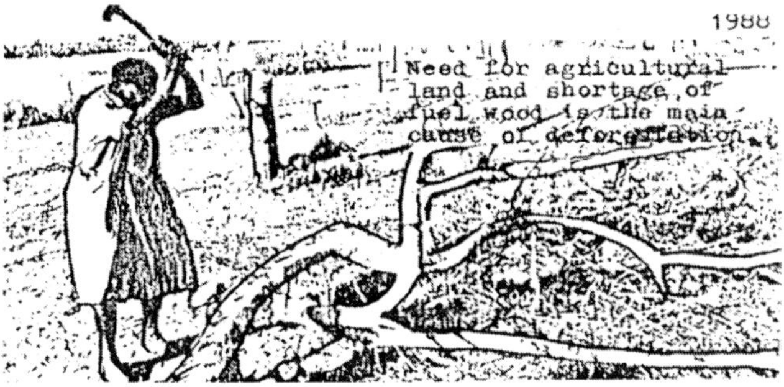

Issued as a poster by The Ryan Foundation.

If you cut trees ruthlessly and don't replant them this is how your land will erode and you will lose land which is the basic and most important factor of production for your livelihood and progress (Issued as a poster by Ryan Foundation, India).

Trees that give Gums and Mucilages

Brief description of some trees are given to help identification. Many of these trees are commonly found in several Third World countries and are already commercially exploited for various uses. The gum or mucilages will be in most cases suitable to bind ground bio-mass into briquettes. Experimentation and field tests are necessary to establish the cheapest and the best suited gums for different areas.

1. Botanical - *Abeclnoschus Moschatus Medic.*

   English name - *Music Mallow.*

   Indian Name - *Mushk dana.*

Description - Herbaceous, leaves coarsely toothed, large Yellow flowers with crimson centre, seeds musky and scented and musk seed oil is extracted out of it. Available throughout India, Pakistan and Bangladesh. The roots contain a good mucilage and it is used for sizing paper in China.

2. Botanical - *Acacia Arabica Wild.*

   English name - *The Babul tree.*

   Indian names - *Kikar, Babul.*

   Description - About 12 mts high, trunk and bark rough, bright yellow flowers, seeds deep blaking brown,-available throughout the Indian Sub-continent. Mucilage from the bark.

3. Botanical - *Acacia Catechu Wild.*

   English name - *Catechu tree.*

   Indian - *Khadira, Katha, Khair.*

   Description - Medium sized tree, bark greyish brown and rough, glabrous leaves about 12-15 long, flowers yellow, pods brown in colour and beaked at the apex. Lac insects thrive on the tree. The gum that exudes from the tree is one of the best substitute for the true Gum Arabic.

4. Botanical - *Acacia Senegal Wild.*

   Indian - *Kumta, Kher.*

   Description - Spiny, flexuous branches, small spines, leaves pinnate and about three Cms long, leaflets numerous and glaucous green, yellowish flowers five-eight cms long, Pods have five or six seeds. This tree yields the true Gun Arabic of commerce.

5. Botanical - *Adenathera Pavonina Linn.*

   Indian - *Feed tree, Coral pea.*

   English - *Bead tree, Red Wood, Coral Pea.*

   Description - A large deciduous tree, leaves 30-60 cms leaflets many and flowers scented and pale yellow. Pods about 20 cms long and about a dozen seeds in each pod. The gun that exudes from the bark is known as Madatia.

6. Botanical - *Aeglc Mormelos Correa.*

   English - *Baal, Sol, Indian-Bilva, Bel.*

Description - Deciduous, strong spines, small flowers, Gum from the bark makes excellent adhesive.

MORE TREES YIELDING GUM

1. Botanical: *Albizzia Procera Benth.*

   Family: *Leguminosae.* English name: *White Siris.* Indian name: *Safed Siris.*

   Description: Large deciduous tree, yellowish white, smooth, marked with horizontal lines, leaf axis 30-45 Gms, flowers sessile whitish, corolla pubescent, stamens greenish yellow. Pod strap shaped 10-20 Cms long, orange brown.

   The gum that comes from the bark is used in the manufacture of Nepal Paper.

2. Botanical: *Anacardium Occidentale Linn.*

   Family: *Anacardioceae. English- Cashew apple, Cashew Nut.*

   Indian: *Hijli badam, Kaju; Munthri.*

   Description: Evergreen tree, leaves 10-20 Cms long; petals yellowish with pink stripes. Nut kidney shaped. Flower stalk orange or yellow.

The gum from the stem is insect repellent and therefore it is used for binding books.

3. Botanical; *Anogeissus Latifolia Wall.*

   Family: *Combrateceae.* English:*Axle wood tree.*

   Indian: *Dhaura, Dhawa.*

   Description: Large tree, stem tall and straight, bark mottled-Flowers in small, dense, globose heads on short axillary stalks. Small fruits, several crowded in a globular head, yellowish brown. Seed solitary.

The gum from the trunk is extensively used in calico printing, for sizing paper and in confectionery.

4. Botanical: *Galophyllum Inophyllum Linn.*

   Family: *Guttiferae.*English name: *Alexanderean Laurel.*

   Indian - *Dilo, Pinai* (used for burning lamps in Hindu temples).

   Description: Evergreen tree, leaves opposite and shining on both sides. Flowers stalked, white, fragrant. Flower buds clothed in minute rusty hair. The aromatic gum from the bark is known as *Tacamahca* and it is used as a perfume.

5. Botanical: Canarium Strictum Roxb.

   Family: *Burseraceae.* English name: *Black Dammar Tree.*

   Indian: *Dhup, kala dammar.*

   Description- tall bushy tree, leaves alternate, pinnate, upto 60 cms long, leaflets ovate-oblong, hairy beneath and flowers are usually in clusters, Drupe four–five Cms long, one seeded.

6. Botanical: *Cochlospermum Religiosum Alston* (or C. Religiosum Alston). Family: *Cochlospermaceae.*English name:*Buttercup tree, yellow silk cotton tree.* Indian: *Galgal, Kumbi, Katira.*

   Description: Deciduous tree, thick bark, leaves near the end of branches, alternate golden yellow flowers upto 18 Cm dia, unequal silky petals (usually five petals in a flower) Pods dark brown with numerous seeds covered with silky wool.

The Gum from trunk is *Katira* or Hog gum of commerce. It is used in calico printing, finishing paper, in the manufacturing of cosmetics, for thickening ice-creams and in book binding.

PLANT INSECTICIDES

1. Botanical: *Adhatoda Vasica Nees.*

   Family: *Acanthaceae.*

   Indian: *Arusha, Adhatodai, Vasaka.*

   Description: Densely branched gregarious shrub with pubescent branches, leaves opposite, pointed at both ends, elliptic, 13-20 Cms long. Flowers white with red spots and Three-Nine Cms long. Single flowered (not in clusters). Distribution: throughout India, Pakistan, Bangladesh, Sri Lanka and many tropical countries.

The leaves are not only used as green manure in rice fields but also as weedicide, fungicide and insecticide. As a weedicide, they are used for eradicating aquatic weeds in rice fields and as an insecticide they have the same use as tobacco leaves. As a fungicide they control the growth of moulds in fruits.

2. Botanical: *Trigonella Foenumgraacum Linn.*

   Family: *Leguminosae.*

   English: *Fenugreek.* Indian: *Methi.*

   Distribution: Throughout India, Pakistan, Bangladesh and most other tropical countries.

Description: An erect, strongly scented herbaceous herb. Pinnate leaves, flowers lemon yellow, pods five-seven Cms long, thin and long beaked. 10-12 seeds in each pod.

Uses: The herb contains the alkaloid *trigonelline* and an essential oil which is an insect repellent. The herb is used for protecting stored grains from insects.

3. Botanical: *Vitex Negundo Linn.*

   Family: *Verbenaceae.*

   English: *Indian Privet.*

   Indian: *Nirgundi, Indrani.*

   Description: Small tree, branchlets densely white tomentose. Blu purple flowers in short cymes, forming erect, tapering panicles.

   Distribution: throughout India, Pakistan, Bangladesh, Sri Lanka and many other tropical countries.

   Uses: the branches and leaves are insect repellent and are therefore used for preserving stored grains against insects.

4. Botanical: *Azadirachta Indica Adr Jugs.*

   Family: *Meliaceae.*

   Indian: *Limba, Neem.*

   English: *Neem.*

   Description: Large tree with rough bark, flowers white. Drupe yellow when ripe, ovoid-oblong, one seeded. Distribution: Throughout the tropics and Africa has plenty of neem.

   Uses: very effective insecticide. effective deterrent to locusts. Oil cake is a useful fertilizer; it is a good substitute for pyridine and other agents used in the manufacture of alocohol denaturonts. For more about Neem please see RYFO Handouts No, 33 and 107.

BEANANA FIBRE EXTRACTION

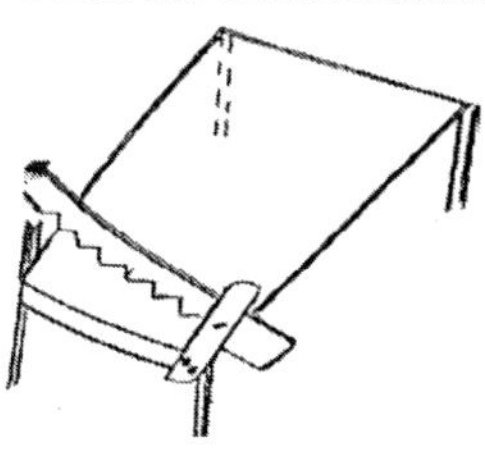

Banana is a life supporting tree and yet it is not all banana growing countries that put the tree to full use. Often only the fruits are eaten and the other parts thrown away. The poor must learn to promote and exploit bananas fully for their survival.

Some common uses of different parts of the tree are:

1. Fruits are eaten fresh and in several converted forms.

2. Raw bananas and banana flowers are commonly cooked for meals in South India and chips are made for outdoor eats.

3. The long white core of the trunk, (*thandu*, in Tamil) is cooked for meals in different forms.

4. Leaves are used in the place of plates to serve food for big gatherings, usually during weddings.

5. Chemically, vegetable protein, caustic soda, etc. are extracted from the leaf and the bark (see Handout 45).

6. Several native medicines are prepared from the tree. The trunk (*thandu*) is eaten to disolve store in stone 'lader.

7. Fibre is extracted and used in several industries.

Fibre is a profitable by-product and the Philippines leads the world in making high quality banana fibre products including furnishing fabrics and costly dress material which is an export earner for the country.

On a village scale, common people can extract coarse fibre using a simple device are. On to an old table a metal saw, like the carpenter's handsaw, is fixed. three saws in three different sizes are required to be used one by one. For the first operation, teeth distance one Cm; for the second, 1/2 and for the third 1/4 Cm.

After the thick outer layer (bark) of the tree is spread on the floor and hammered flat the bark may be fed under the saw (fibre extracter) and pulled by a woman or child. Another woman or child may place her foot in the loop hanging from the blade and press it down to give adequate hold and pressure when the fibre is pulled through. This process is repeated with the three saws in three different operations to get clean and flesh free fibre. Then, like wet clothes, the fibre is dried on poles in bunches.

In its crude form the fibre can be used for making ropes and some household articles such as bags, baskets or table mats. They may be dyed for different colours (for vegetable dyes see RYFO Handout 91 and 92).

This method of extracting banana fibre can be commonly seen in Sri Lanka.

SOUTH INDIAN WAY OF THATCHING

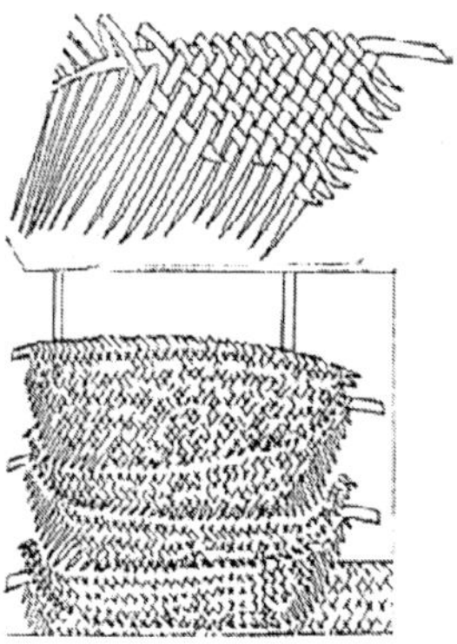

This is how palm Leaf is woven.

Roof laying is the most difficult part in house construction. Suitable materials have to be found and the laying must be leak proof. Palm leaves of coconut trees are good for making roofs and yet they are used only in some countries in the world where coconut trees grow (for a complete list of countries where coconut trees grow please see handout No. 121). A good thatched roof can be made out of palm leaves provided they are woven well as done in South India.

And this is how the woven mats are them arranged and tied to rafters to make a roof.

The method of weaving palm is shown clearly in the diagram. Note that all the palms on one side of the stem of the leaf is folded and pressed to fall on the palms on the other side of. the stem to make weaving possible. Palms on the left side of the stem are then interwoven with the palms on the right side as shown. The weaving must be close and tight and gaps must be avoided as far as possible.

When fresh leaves are dried in shade for about three days they bend better for weaving and if they dry too much weaving becomes a little difficult.

The woven mats are arranged one on top of the other on pre-built roof frames or rafters. Bamboo, causarina, or eucalyptus (called gum tree in Australia) may be used to build the frame work.

Where plastic sheets are available they may be spread out on top of the frame work and the mats arranged on top of the plastic sheets. Two layers of mats may also be laid one running perpendicular to the other layer. For tying the mats to the roof-frame coconut fibre ropes may be used.

Coconut growing countries which have not learnt to weave coconut palm for thatching would do well to learn this method of weaving.

Palm mats can also be used for building cattle sheds, partition walls and pandals (halls) for community meetings and wedding receptions as commonly done in South India.

SOAP WITH VILLAGE MATERIALS

Only three basic components are required for making washing soaps and they are: 1. caustic soda, 2. oil and 3. soft water.

Eventhough soap making process is so simple many villagers do not make their own soaps because of three reasons and they are: 1. caustic soda is not available in their market and when available it is too costly. 2. Edible oil is costly and non-edible oil is not always available in the village market and this is also costly when available. 3. The water from village wells is usually hard water and hard water does not make good soap.

These difficulties may be got over by - 1. making their own caustic soda out of banana barks as explained in Handout No. 45 (page 18).

2. Crushing their own non-edible oils out of oil-bearing nuts available in their area. For non-edible oil bearing nuts see Handout No. 4-8. 3)

Using rain water which is soft water to prepare the lye as explained in Handout No. 45.

Soap can be made in domestic equipment and the quantity of materials required are:

Three bottles of any non-edible vegetable oil (one lit. capacity).

one Kg of Caustic soda lye (rain water to be used in the preperation of the lye.

First the oil is warmed to about 40 degrees C and then the caustic soda lye added to the warm oil and mixed well with a wooden laddile. As the mixture cools soap will form and before it solidifies it may be poured into a wooden tray or into wooden moulds. After three days when completely dry, the soap in the tray may be cut to pieces.

Caution:

1. Do not touch the lye as it will burn the fingers.
2. To mix use only an earthen ware bowl (mud pot) or wooden container.
3. If caustic soda lye is prepared by RYFO Method addition of water in the process of soap making is not necessary since the lye contains water.
4. If the soap is found to be too soft for the feel about five per cent of chalk by volume may be added as a filler. (not always done), Neem leat powder sieved to 300 to 400 mesh may also be added as filler.

WATER PURIFICATION IN SMALL WELLS

Chlorine and bleaching powder and other chemical agents are not easily available in villages and they are expensive. Moreover, use of these machine made chemicals should be avoided as far as possible. Rural communities should find their own appropriate methods to purify drinking water to the extent possible. This can be done without difficulty in small community wells from which upto 1000, litres. of water is drawn every day. Some of the traditional and scientifically proven native methods are:-

1. By throwing a small log (or parts of) the Nelli tree into the well. (very commonly and. traditionally done in India) Botanical name of this tree is *Phyllanthus Enbelika*. Sanskrit name is Dhatriphala. This tree is very commonly available in tropical countries and can be grown easily. The fruits are edible and medicinal.
2. By throwing ground seeds of Drumstic (after removing the outer skin of the seed) into the well. Botanical name of Drumstick tree is *Moringa Oleifera Adans*. This very common tree has properties of water purification as reported by Somia John of Care German Agency (cited in the book Science and (technology for Women, Dept. of Science and Technology, Govt. of India).
3. By throwing Tulsi leaves into the well. Botanical name of Tulsi is *Ocimum Basilium Linn*. It has insecticidal properties and repells mosquitoes and flies as reported in Science for villages, India No.77, Feb. 1984. Tulsi is a very common plant and can be propagated easily.
4. By throwing neem leaves into the well. For chemical and insecticidal properties of Neem see Handout No.33.
5. By throwing dried and burnt banana peal ash. This ash contains antifungal and antibacterial substances (Source: *Useful Plants of India & Pakistan by* J.F. Dastur, Page 22; Published by Taraporevalas, Bombay).
6. By throwing leaves of Adhatodai (botanical -*Adhatoda Vasica Nees)*. These leaves have properties of weedicide, fungicide and insecticide. As an insecticide they have the same use as the tobacco leaves (Source: Useful Plants of India and Pakistan by Dastur.)
7. By dropping burnt lime stones or roasted river or sea shells into the well. This is also commonly done in India from time immemorial.
8. By throwing Papaya (Popos). This is done in some parts of Africa. Papaya smell is said to repell mosquitoes and prevent mosquito larvae in the water. (In Sierra Leone people boil Papaya leaves and bathe in the water to prevent mosquito bite and malaria.)

At least four out of these eight items may be pound to granules in dry form and filled in equal parts by volume into a perforated five Kg plastic container and reduced into the well with a fibre rope and the contents replienished every month (three small holes at the bottom and three at the top will do).

The 8 items can be pound or ground and the mixture made readily available in 5 Kg packets and may be distributed free by aid agencies.

Wood Suitable for Small House Construction (for Piles and Beams)

AFRICAN REGION

Botanical name	Region where available	Common Local names
1.Danta-Nesogor-donia papaverifera	East Africa from Sierra Leone to Cameroon & Gabon	l. Otutu (Nigeria) 2. Owoé (Cameroon) 3. Kondo finde (Zaire) 4. Abumana, Ajumaba, Epro (Ghana) 5. Kotibe (Ivory Coast) 6. Arborbora (Gabon) 7. Naouya (Angola)
2. Opepe-Nauclea diderrichii	From Sireea Leone to Congo on the eastern side, upto Uganda.	1. Akondoc (Cameroon) 2. Jusia (Ghana) 3. Masa (Angola, Zaire) 4. Badi (Ivory Coast) 5. Aloma (Gabon) 6. Kilingi (Uganda)
3. Afzelia Afzelia bipindenis (also, A.pachyloba, A.Africana, A.Quazensis)	West Africa, Middle Africa, East Africa	1. Angola – Bolengu 2. Ghana - Alinga 3. Higeria -Doussie 4. Senegal- Lingue 5. Comeroon -Doussie 6. Tanzania-Chanfuta 7. Mozumbique-neli
4. Opepe-Nauclea diderrichiie	From Sierra Leone to Congo to Uganda.	1. Ivory Coast-Badi 2.Cameroon-nasa 3. Ghana-Jusia 4.Uganda-Kitangi 5. Gabon- Aloma.

ASIAN REGION

Botanical name	Region where available	Common Local names
5. Kempas Koompassia	Sumatra, Malaysia, Indonesia, Borneo.	1. Sumatra (sabah) 2. Malaysia (Impus) 3. Indonesia (Sarawak) 4. Borneo (Mengaris)
6. Kapur-Dryobalanops aromatica.	Sumatra Borneo	1. Kapoer (Sumatra) 2. Keladan (Borneo)

D. Lanceolata	Malaysia	3. Kalaysia (Kapur)
D. Becarrii		
7. Keruing-dipterocarpus Spp.	Indo-Maiaysian region. (Gurjun)	1. Malaysia and Indonesia (Keruing) 2. India and Burma 3. Philippines (Apitong) 4. Thailand (Yang) 5. Burma (Engor In)

MOSQUITO SMOKE

Strong smell of any smoke keeps mosquitoes away. Hut dwellers cook inside their huts mainly to keep mosquitoes away. In some slum areas the residents burn dried leaves and garbage to keep away mosquitoes. This is far better than using artificial (chemical) insecticides. Some people get asthma when they inhale chemical insecticides and chemicals must be avoided as far as possible.

(I am Mr Mosquito suck your blood and bring you deadly diseases. Beware of me especially when you sleep.)

Several leaves comminly available in tropical countries have insecticide properties and the smoke of these leaves, when dried and burnt, chase away mosquitoes. Some of these leaves are:-

1. Botanical - *Adhatoda Vasica Nees.* Family: *Acanthaceae.*

   Indian names:- Arusha, Adhatodai, vasaka.

2. Botanical - *Trigonella Foenum-Graeium*, Family: *Leguminosae.*

   English: *Fenugreek.* Hindi: *Methi.* Tamil: *Vendhiam*

3. Botanical - *Vitex Negundo Linn.* Family: *Verbenaceae.*

   English: *Indian Privet.* Indian: *Nirgundi, Indrani.*

4. Botanical - *Azodirachta Indica Adr Juss*

   Family: *Meliaceae.* Indian: *Limba, Neem. English: Neem.*

5. Botanical - *Moringa Oleifeha Adans.* English: *Drum-stick tree.* Tamil:-*Murungai.*
6. Botanical:-*Ocimum Basilium Linn.* Indian name: *Tulasi.*
7. Botanical: *Carica Papaya.* English: *Papaya or popos.*
8. Botanical:-*Zanthoxylum Alatum* (local name in Nepal where plenty of it is available -*Bokhe Timur or Aule Timur*). The small seeds are more effective and the leaves are less effective.
9. Botanical:-*Cymbopugon Winterianus.* Bnglish-*Citronelia.*
10. Botanical:- *Cathabanthus Roseus.* English: *Vinca Rosea or Peri-Winkle.* Family: *Apocynaceae.* Hindi: *Sadabhar* .Tamil-*Nithya. Kalyani. Malayalam-Vanapoo.*

Non of these leaves are poisonous; in fact most of them are eaten and some of them are highly medicinal. However, as far as possible people should avoid inhaling any smoke. Atleast four of the leaves listed above should be collected, dried and kept in a closed container and a handful burnt in a tray every night before going to bed. If necessary, a handful may be burnt once again at mid-night.Smoke from a mixture of these leaves is very effective in driving away mosquitoes. For chemical properties of some of these leaves see handouts 33, 112 and 120.

SOME USEFUL SHRUBS (FOUND MOSTLY IN THE NORTHERN HEMISPHERE)

Shrubs are small trees with many branches capable of growing in the most derelict terrain. Several of them, especially the legumes fix nitrogen that enrich the soil. They are highly drought resistant, and provide food for people and fodder for livestock. Many of them provide ingredients for medicines, pulp for paper and industrial products such as resins, gums, oils and fibres. Shrubs also provide plenty of fuel wood.

Names and uses of some shrubs:

1. *Pigeon Pea* - Excellent fuel, wild growth.
2. *Dhaincha* - also known as SESBANIA - fuel wood, two harvests a year. Seeds contain a water soluble gum used for sizing textiles and paper. The shrub is excellent for alley croping, as it is a natural fertilizer for food crops, especially on saline soils. It is also a good cattle fodder. The stem of Dhaincha gives fibre to make gunnysacks and fishing nets.

3. *Calliandera*, very quick growing fuel wood.
4. *Leucaena Leucocephala*, is a native of South America, spreads fast to a height of two metres. Cattle like the leaves and the shrub spreads without replanting. The
5. Leaves of Leucaena which are similar to ALFALFA in digestibility and nutitional value are particularly suitable as fodder for cows, buffaloes and goats.
6. Jojoba (*Simmondsia Ghinensis*), native of North America. Contains high quality vegetable oil used in cold-rolling steel, leather finishing, and as a lubricant in very delicate machines. It is also used in the textile industry.

About 20,000 hectares of Jojoba are being cultivated in the arid southwestern regions of USA and plantations are coming up in Australia-Argentina, Costa Rica, Mexico, Israel and India.

7. GUAYULE (*Parthenium Argentatum*), native of North America. Contains a rubber, which when purified equals the rubber from a rubber tree. It grows even in poor desert areas. The entire plant contains rubber and to obtain the rubber the entire plant is taken The yield is upto twelve percent from improved varieties.
8. *Ricinus Communis Linn* (Castor oil plant), a very common tropical plant known for its non-drying oil. which has several domestic and industrial applications. The oil cake is a valuable manure and the leaves of the shrub when buried in the soil enriches the soil.

MULTIPURPOSE MANGIUM

The Mangiura, which is a leguminous tree, growing dense in the humid Australian tropics, has been taken to several countries all over the world including Malaysia and India. It belongs to the acacia family and botanically it is known as *Acacia Mangium*. The tree grows very fast and gives good quality brown timber, firewood, charcoal, pulp for paper and chips for particle boards. Because of its dense and attractive loaves people like to have it as avenue trees and they are also planted to prevent soil erosion. The tree grows straight to an average height of 30 metres and has small white flowers. The diametre of the trunk of a medium size tree will be about 90 cms.

The tree grows healthily in different soils, temperature, altitude. and moisture and is highly drought resistant. Its growth potentiality is very similar to Subabul and Eucalyptus.

Like most legumes, Mangium forms a mutually beneficial symbiosis with soil bacteria of the genus Rhizobium. It has large and prolific nodules and does not require nitrogenous fertilizer because the Rhizobium bacteria provides enough nitrogenous compounds to sustain its growth.

Mongium can be propagated by seeds and cuttings and the tree gives plenty of seeds. If dried well and kept in air-tight containers the seeds have life for several years.

As a preperation before sowing/boiling water must be poured on the seeds and after 30 seconds the hot water must be drained and replaced by cold water and allowed to soak over night. (ten parts boiling water for one part of seeds). The seeds germinate in about a week and the seedlings grow 25 cms in about three months and then they arc ready for transplantation. Planting is done during rainy season in about 3m X 3m spacing.

According to the Forest Products Laboratory, Madison, USA; the timber qualities of this tree are similar to those of black walnut, one of the finest cabinet wood of North America. Australia has found this wood excellent for making paper. The leaves of Mangium are relished by cattle.

Use Leaves as Insecticides

Use of chemical fertilizers, insecticides and weedicides are to be discouraged for better health of the people. There are several leaves with properties of insecticides. Those are to be used and the results they produce under different conditions will have to established. Some of them are:-

1. Botanical: *Acorus Calamus Linn.*

   Family: *Araceae.*

   English name: *The sweet Flag.*

   Distribution: Throughout India, Pakistan, Bangladesh and many tropical countries.

   Description: Erect herb, aromatic, leaves four-eight cm long, Yellow-green dense flowers. Angular berry with about 3 seeds. Uses: The leaves of the root stock are commonly used in India as an efficacious insecticide for the control of household pests and insects attacking field crops, stored grains and woolen clothes.

2. Botanical: *Derris Elliptica Behth.*

   Family: *Leguwinosae.*

   Indian names: *Etam Chali, Bakal Bip, Mokoi Sopu.*

   Description: Tree with wide branches. Big leaves -about 30 cm long. Leaves are green and glossy on the one side and brownish on the other. Flower stalk densely clothed with brown pubescnce. Corolla whitish, pink or red. Winged pod with about three seeds.

Distribution: Colder parts of north India- grows in tropics 2000 feet above sea level.

Uses: The roots are of great insecticidal value, and are used in the control of many insect pests in horticultural crops, agricultural farms, as also in cattle, poultry, cats and dogs.

3. Botanical: *Moringa Oleifera Lam.*

   English name: *Horse Radish., Ben Tree.*

   Indian Names: *Sainjna, Mungna, Shevgi.*

   Description: Medium sized tree about 10 M high, corky bark, very long leaves, white fragrant flowers in large panicles. Long pendulous and winged pods with ribs.

   Distribution: Throughout India, Pakistan & many warm countries Uses: The twigs and leaves are lopped for fodder. The leaves are rich in CAROTENE and ascorbic acid. The leaf juice has strong antibacterial properties.

4. Botanical: *Pongamia Pimata Pierre.*

   Family: *Leguminosae*. English: Indian *Beach*. Local-*Karanj*. *Description*: Small tree. Bright green leaves, about 12 cm long, purple and white flowers, woody pod having one or two seeds.

   Distribution: Many tropical countries (plenty in India) Uses: Leaves are used for manuring rice fields and the seed oil is an insecticide.

5. Botanical: *Vttex Negundo Linn.* Family: *Verbenaceae.*

   English: *Indian Privet.* Indian-*Nirgundi. Indrani.*

   Description: Small tree, dense branchlets, blue and purple flowers.

   Distribution: Throughout India, Pakistan and many tropics.

PLANT TREES FOR PROSPERITY

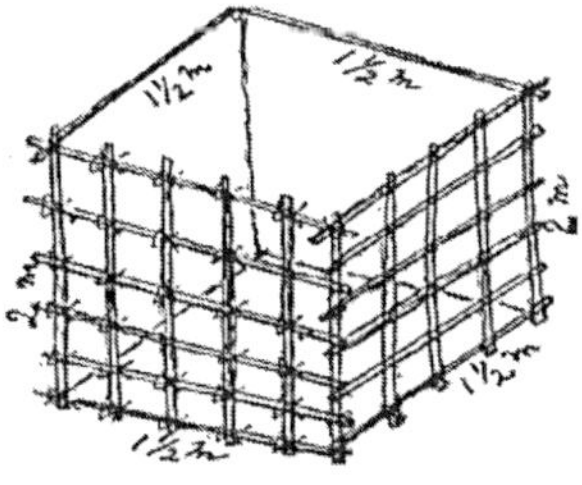

Trees are living beings. They give us oxygen, prevent air polution, regulate the climate and help in the accumulation of rain water, prevent soil erosion, landslides and floods. They give shelter to birds and animals and give us the 10 Fs. Namely, food, fodder, fertiliser, fuel, flowers, fibres, fruits, fauna, furniture, and fine-chemicals.

A good person should always be interested in planting trees for general human welfare. Gautama Buddha has said that to be a good Buddist, One should plant trees in one's life-time.

It is not difficult to get some seeds, seedlings and saplings and plant them and many people would happily do so. The difficulty is in protecting them and caring for them. Watering three or four trees is not a problem but the problem is to save them from animals, children playing about and from firewood collectors.

Usually villagers put acacia or other thorny branches around a plant but this is haphazardly done and does not stay long. The fence to protect must be built strong and sturdy to stand almost for two years and only then the plant can grow into a healthy tree.

Diagram shows the type of fense that should be used and it is made out of tree and. plant branches and does not require money to make. They may be tied together with any fibre available locally. After building the fence wall, acacia and other thorny bnanches may be placed or tied on all sides of the fence so that animals and children will not go near. This is the best way of protecting small plants in villages.

Every village home or hut should plant atleast four saplings and care for them till they grow into a tree. This will lead the family and the village community to prosperity.

RYFO Handouts 135 and 136 give some recommended trees that are sturdy and drought resistant and require little watering and care and can grow into big and useful trees in tropical soil and climate.

BLESSINGS FROM TREES

There is a common and very sensible belief among the Chinese peasants that a person is blessed by the trees he or she plants. If the benefits are not directly for the planter they are for his family or community. Therefore, everybody must plant a seedling or sapling wherever there is open land if a tree can grow there. Trees may be planted in one's own lands, in common public lands or in unclaimed or uncared for lands. After all a tree that is planted is for the benefit of somebody and carries development and goodwill with it. When everybody plants trees there is bound to be prosperity.

RYFO Handout 132 explains the best way of protecting trees and Handout 134 lists several trees suitable for villages in the tropical countries (Your local forest department can guide in the selection) see pages 55, 56 and 57.

Since trees are a blessing every family should plant around their dwelling as many trees as the number of members in the family and each tree may be named after one member. As soon as a baby is born along with the naming ceremony there may be a tree planting and tree naming ceremony. The parents of the baby may care for the tree as they care for the baby and develop the interest of the baby for the tree as it grows up along with the tree. By this way trees around hamlets will all belong to people and time and tradition will establish a ownership right for them.

Even the village administration should not cut a tree without the permission of its owner (who may be called a patron) and without compensating the owner with another tree near by. People in rural areas should be helped and encouraged to establish such relationship and ownership with trees.

There may be a tree committe in every village to select, plant, supervise, and regulate the cutting of trees. The forest department should regularly reach seedlings and saplings to these committes free of cost and should not interfere or even regulate the administration of the committes.

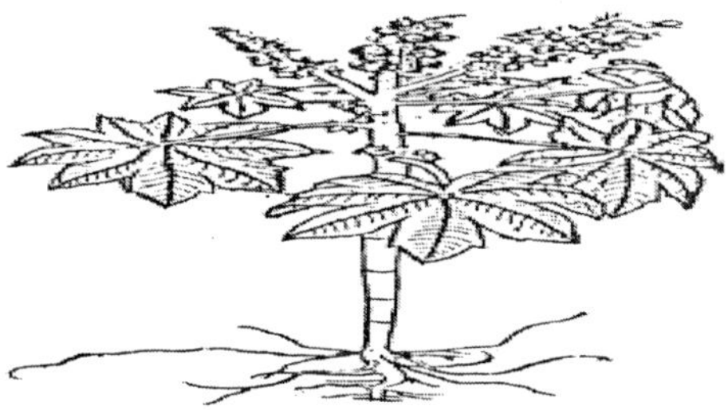

Issued as a wall poster by The Ryan Foundation.

Forests around the world, particularly in tropical countries, are rapidly being depleted Every year, many thousands of hectares are lost to population growth, clearance for farming, land speculation, commercial ranching and industrial development.

Most trees are being lost in Latin America, Southeast Asia and West Africa, as the following figures for randomly selected countries show.

Countries	*Closed forest area. 1980 in thousand hectares*	*Annual rate of deforetation 1981-1985(%)*	*Area lost annually in thousand hectares*
Brazil	396,030	0.4	1,480
Colombia	47,351	1.7	820
Indonesia	123,235	0.5	600
Mexico	47,840	1.2	595
Ecuador	14,679	2.3	340
Nigeria	7,583	4.0	300
Ivory Coast	4,907	5.9	290
Peru	70,520	0.4	270
Malaysia	21,256	1.2	255
Thailand	10,375	2.4	252
Zaire	105,975	0.2	182
India	72,521	0.2	147

***Recommanded Tropical Trees* — List One**

Trees recommeded below for villages and public places are common all over India and in very many countries with tropical climate. They are drought resistant and require little water and have a variety of uses.

1. Botanical: *Acacia Catechu Wild.*

   Family: *Leguminosae.* English name: *Catechu Tree.*

   Indian Names: *Khadira, Katha, Khair.*

   Description: Medium size, rough bark, yellow flowers, pods stalked and strap shaped, five-eight cm long.

   Uses: very hard and durable wood, resists white ants, used for making agricultural implements, boats, furniture and fire wood. A yellowish orange dye is extracted from the wood and the gum taken from the tree is as good as Gum Arabic

2. Botanical: *Adansonia Digitata Linn.*

   Family: *Bombacaceae.*

   Indian Names: *Gorakh Chichi, Gorakh Amli.*

   English - *Monkey bread tree, Baob tree.*

   Description: Short tree with broad trunk rapidly tapering upward. Solitary white flowers, cup shaped with 5 petals, fruits pendulous.

Uses: soft wood commonly used for making craft paper. Bark gives fibre. The ash of the woody shell, the seeds and the bark are used as manure. The acid pulp of the fruit repells mosquitoes and other biting insects.

3. Botanical: *Adenathera. Pavonina Linn.*

   Family: *Leguminosae.*

   Indian: *Rakta- Kambal, Kun Chand.*

   English: *Coral Pea, Bread Tree, Red Wood.*

   Description: A large deciduous tree, leaves 30-60 cm long, pale yellow scented flowers, pod 15-25 cm long.

   Uses: Seeds are used as beeds for rosaries and for necklaces. The gum that exudes from the tree known in India as Madotia has several common uses.

4. Botanical: *Aleurites Moluccana. Wild.*

   Family: *Euphorbiaccoa.*

   Indian names: *Candle nut, Bengal nut.*

   Description: A large tree, white flowers, roots yield a dye, fruits are 2-5 cm long in diameter, fleshy and green in colour, 1-2 seeded.

   Uses: Bark used in tanning and the *roots* for dying cloth, oil is extracted from the edible nut known as Kekuna and it is superior to linseed oil. It is used in the manufacturing of paints and varnishes. The oil cake is excellent as cattle feed and fertilizer.

5. Botanical: *Azadirachta Indica Adr Jess.* Family: *Mehaccae.* Indian- *Neem.* Neem See Handout Nos - 33, 89 and 107.

6. Botanical: *Bridelia Retusca Spreng.*

   Family: *Euphorbiaceae.*

   Indian: *Khaja, Ekdania.*

   Description: Medium size, leaves alternate, greenish yellow flowers, fruit globose.

   Uses: Wood hard and durable is used for agricultural implements and for furniture, leaves make good cattle fodder.

RECOMMENDED TROPICAL TRESS - LIST TWO

7. Botanical: *Butea Frondos Roxb.*

   Family: *Leguminosae.*

English - *Flame of the forest, Butea Gum Tree.*

Description: Large deciduous tree with large velvet flowers, petals deep orange red, pods 15-20 cm long.

Uses: The beautiful flowers yield a brilliant yellow dye; seeds have insecticidal properties. From the trunk the gum called BUTEA is taken.

8. Botanical: *Casuarina Equisetifolia Linn.*

   Family: *Cusuarinaceae.*

   Indian: *Wilayati Saru, Jangli Saru.*

   English: *Casuarina, Beef wood tree.*

   Description: Large evergreen tree with pendulous branchlets

   Uses: Planted on coasts to reclaim sandy dunes. The straight stem or trunk is used as beams and posts and as fuelwood. A brown dye is extracted from the bark.

9. Botanical: *Emblica Officinalis Gaerth.*

   Family: *Euphorbiaceae.*

   English- *Emblic Myrobalan.*

   Indian: *Amla, Amalaka.*

   Description: Small deciduous tree, greenish yellow flowers densely clustered, fruits globose and fleshy about 2 cm in diameter; 6 seeded.

   Uses: wood is used for making agricultural implements and furniture. Charcoal is also made. The twig bark is excellent tanning material. Twigs and wood chips are used to clarify muddy water. Fruit is edible and has plenty of Vitamin C. It is commonly used for making writing ink and hair dyes.

10. Botanical: *Lagerstroemia Speciosa Pers.*

    Family: *Lythraceae.* Indian: *Taman, Jarul.*

    English: *Pride of India.*

    Description: Medium sized deciduous tree, purple flowers in large terminal panicles:

    Uses: Excellent timber, hard and durable wood is used for bridge construction, boats, agricultural implements, etc.

11. Botanical: *Lawsonia Inermis Linn.*

 Family: *Lythraceae.*

 Indian: *Mehndi, Henna.*

 English: *Henna.*

 Description: The leaves yield a very popular cosmetic dye which is used by rural women to colour the palm of their hand, feet and other parts of the body. An aromatic oil is distilled from the flowers.

12. Botanical: *Morus Alba Linn.*

 Family: *Moraceae:*

 Indian- *Tut.*

 English: *White Mulbury.*

 Description: Shrub sized tree, greenish flowers which are inconspicuous, fruits are a collection of numerous drupes upto five cm long white, pupple or black in colour. Sweet taste.

 Uses: Wood is used for making sports goods, bark yields fibre and can be used for making paper. The leaves are eaten by silk worms.

Recommended Tropical Trees - List Three

13. Botanical: *Pongamia Pinnata Pierre.*

 Family: *Leguminosae.*

 Indian: *Karanj.*

 English: *Indian Beach.*

 Description: Small deciduous tree, leaves odd-pinnate 13-35 cm long and bright green, purple and white are common colours. Pod woody, oval-oblong. one-two seeded.

 Uses: The Seed oil is used as an illuminant, as an insecticide and in the manufacture of soap. The seeds are used as fish poison and the leaves as manure in rice fields.

14. Botanical: *Randia Brandish Gamble.*

 Family: *Rubiaceae.* Indian: *Maniphal, Ghela.*

 Description: Small deciduous tree. Leaves usually clustered on the suppressed branches are smooth, shiny and oval shaped. The white flowers turn yellow as they fade. The fragrant flowers are two-three together. Fruits are globose and seeds numerous.

Uses: Hard wood is used for making agricultural implements. Seeds contain essential oil. Crushed fruits are used as insecticides to protect stored grains.

15. Botanical: *Sapindus Trifoliatus Linn.*

    Family: *Sapindaceae.*

    Indian: *Ritha, Areeta.*

    English: *Soap Nut Tree.*

    Description: Large deciduous tree, bark scaly, leaves alternate 13-30 cm long. White flowers, monoecious, fleshy fruits.

    Uses: Hard and strong wood is used for building carts and agricultural impliments. Fruits contain saponin and therefore used commonly as a detergent and as a substitute for soap. The root-bark also contains saponin. Fruits and the powder of the bark are used also for washing clothes.

16. Botanical: *Zizyphus Jujuba Lam.*

    Family: *Rhemnaceae.*

    Indian: *Ber.*

    English; *Jujub Tree.*

    Description: Medium size. Bark irregularly cracked, branches drooping. Dark green loaves vary in shape. Flowers greenish yellow. Berry differet in size, shape and colour.

    Uses: Hard wood takes good polish. Used for furniture, building construction, agricultural implements, sports goods, etc. The bark contains five-nine per cent tannin and is used as a tanning material. Edible fruits are used for making beverages.

17. Botanical: *Prosopis Juliflora.*

    Indian: *Gandobavla* (meaning the mad one).

    English: *Dry zone wonder tree.*

    Description: Extremely drought tolerent. Grows well in saline soil. Leaves are a good fodder for livestock. The wood is excellent as fuelwood. Needs no care, no water after it takes root.

18. Botanical: *Causarina Junghuniana.*

    Family: *Gasuarinaceae.*

    English:*Thailand variety of Causarina*

Description: Highly drought tolerent. Does not set seeds and it is female sterile. Propagates by air layering or rooting of springs (small branchlets) Tolerates saline soil.

Uses: Crude furniture, firewood, building materials. Leaves are excellent as manure.

FLOWERING TREES FOR THE TROPICS

Some flowering trees which are common in India and many other countries which have a tropical climate are listed below. They are very suited for planting on either side of the roads in towns and villages. Most of the trees are sturdy and some are drought resistant. In general, the trees listed below require only initial care and watering. Host of them are uncared for forest trees, which look after themselves.

	Botanical Name	*Colour of Flower*
1.	GREVILLEA ROBUSTA	YELLOW
2.	COLVILLEA RACEMOSA	ORANGE-RED
3.	JACARANDA MINOSAEFOLIA	BLUE
4.	GUL-MOHUR	SCARLET ORANGE
5.	ERYTHRIINA INDICA or SCARLET ERYTHRINA	SCARLET-RED
6.	AMALTAS	YELLOW
7.	BAUHNEA-PURPUREA	PURPLE
8.	GLARICIDIA MACULATA	
9.	CASSEA NODOSA	PINK
10.	BAHNEA–VARIEGATA	WHITE
11.	PETTOPHORUM FERRUGINEUM	GOLDEN YELLOW
12.	LAGERSTROEMIA FLOS–REGINAE. ...	
13.	SPATHODIA NILOTICA	ORANGE-CRIMSON
14.	CASSIA FISTULA	
15.	POINCIANA REGIA or DELONIX REGIA	
16.	CASSIA NODOSA	PINK

The following are ornamental trees but do not flower. These are also very suitable as avenue trees:

1. *Melia Aradirachta*
2. *Sterculia Alata*
3. *Anthocephalus Cadamba*
4. *Putranjive Roxburghil*
5. *Tamarindus Indica*

6. *Averrhoa Caramboal*
7. *Pithecolobium Sahan*
8. *Callistemon Lanceolatus*
9. *Pulyulthia Longifolia*
10. *Sugenia Operculata*
11. *Moulsari (Mimusops Elengi).*
12. *Ficus Retusa*
13. *Melia Azadiracta*
14. *Pakur.*

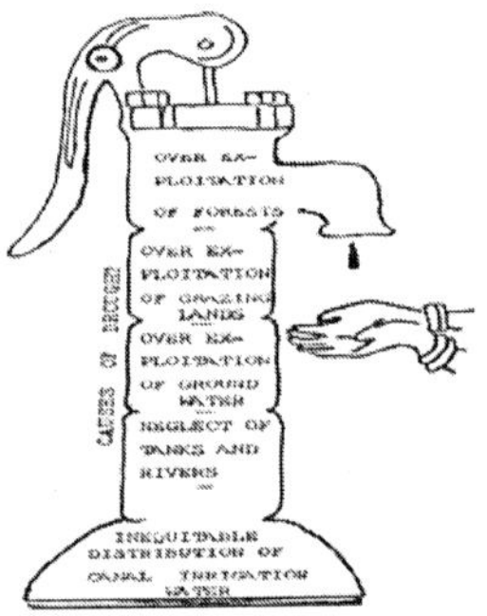

Wall Poster Issued by The Ryan Foundation.

EMBLICA (*Indian Gooseberry*)

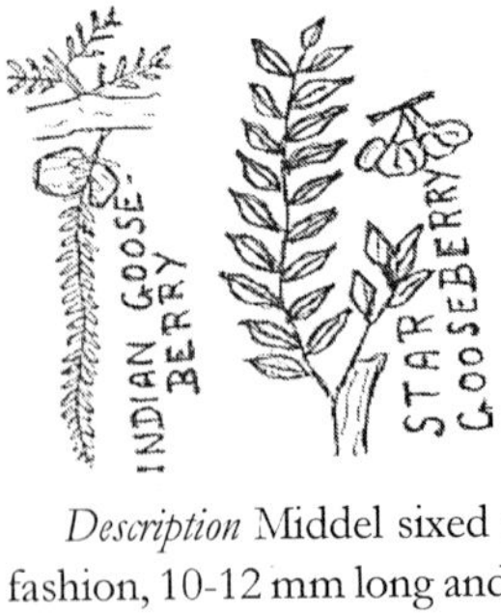

Botanical: *Emblica Officinalis Gaerth.*
Family: *Euphorbiaceae.*
Hindi: *Aonlo Aamla.*
Bengali: *Araloki.*
Malayalan: *Amlakam.*
Tamil: *Nellikai.*

Description Middel sixed decidious tree. Leaves very closely set in pinnate fashion, 10-12 mm long and two-three mm broad. Flowers pale green in small dense clusters below the leaves. Fruits one-two cm in diametre, fleshy, round.

Uses: Both fresh and dried fruits are highly medicinal. They are excellent as a liver tonic and for jaundice and scurvy. Raw fruits cool the human system and work as a mild laxitive. The fruit is a very rich source of vitamin C. The vitamin G of this fruit is more quickly assimilated in the human system than the synthetic vitamin C. Dried fruits are given for dysentery and diarrhoea. Seeds, powdered and made into a decoction if taken regularly is said to build the lungs against asthma.

The Aamla fruit is used commonly for making pickles and preserves. The fruits are used for making writing inks and hair dyes and shampoos. Leaves and fruits are excellent cattle fodder.

The wood is hard and mottled and is used for making agricultural implements, cheap buildings and furniture. The wood is also good for charcoal.

The fruit, bark and leaves contain a large amount of tannin and the twig bark is particularly valuable as a tanning material. In Indian villages branches of this tree thrown into the well to purify water and make it less salty. Children like to eat emblica with some salt.

Triphala Chooran, the well known Indian general medicine, and tonic which is given for several ailments contains equal parts of powdered Aamla, chebulic and Belleric Myrobalam.

Grow your own *fodder* - I

1. Botanical: *Cyperus Rotundus Linn.*

   Family: *Cyperaceae.*

   Indian names: *Mustaka, Motha.*

   English: *Nut Grass.*

   Description: Perennial grass with woody tubers. Rhizome (rootless stem, commonly horizontal or oblique in position, either lying on the ground or subterranean, which usually produces roots below ground and send up shoots from the upper surface. The rhizome is upto 20 cm long.)

   Distribution: Throughout India, Pakistan, Bangladesh, Sri Lanka, Malaysia, Indonesia and many tropical countries.

   Uses: The spongy rhizome yields an essential oil which is used in pharmaceuticals and perfumery. It is also used as an insect repellent.

   The leaves and stems are excellent fodder for cattle. The rhizomes are given to fatten pigs.

2. Botanical: *Ficus Glomerata Roxb.*

   Family: *Moraceae.*

Indian names: *Umar*, *Gular*.

Description: A large spreading tree with dark green leaves. Figs in clusters and red when ripe. Distribution: many countries with tropical climate.

Uses: The soft wood which lasts long under water is used for making toys and packing boxes. The leaves are excellent as cattle feed.

3. Botanical: *Helicteres Isora Linn.*

   Family: *Sterculiaceae.*

   Indian names: *Marorphali, Bhendu, mrigashinga, Jon kaphal.*

   English: *East Indian Screw Tree.*

   Description: Small deciduous tree, solitary red flowers while young; they turn blue when old. Greenish brown fruits 2-5 Cm long.

   Distribution: Many countries with tropical climate.

   Uses: Inner bark gives fibre. The leaves and other tender parts of the tree make excellent cattle feed. They are palatable for animals and rich in essential nutrients, especially, Vitamin A.

4. Botanical: *Hymenodictyon Excelsum Wall.*

   Family: *Rubiaceae.*

   Indian names: *Bhramarchhallika, Bhaulan.*

   Description: Deciduous tree. Leaves 10- 25 Cm long. Greenish white flowers all over the branches.

   Distribution: Common in several tropical countries, upto a height of 1500 Mts.

   Uses: Leaves arc excellent cattle fodder.

5. Botanical: *Kydia Calycina Roxb.* Family- *Malvaceae.*

   Indian names: *Pula*, *Polao.*

   Description: Small deciduous tree. Leaves alternate. Flowers are light purple in colour or greenish white

   Distribution: throughout India, Pakistan, Bangladesh and many tropical countries.

   Uses: The bark yields a fibre. Leaves are valued as fodder.

PULP GIVING GRASS

(The grass varieties listed below may be grown along with waste paper to make panel boards explained in ATIC Handout 75).

1. Botanical- *Eulaliopsis Binata C.E. Hubbard.*

   Family- *Gramineae.* English name- *Sabai grass.*

   Indian- *Bhabar, Baib, Sabai.*

   Description-Perenial tufted grass about 120 cm long. erect, slender and wooly at the base, leaves sharply pointed.

   Distribution- Throughout India, Pakistan, Bangladesh, Sri-Lanka. Thailand and many countries with similar climate.

   Uses- The grass yields an excellent pulp for making paper. Mats are woven out of the grass.

2. Botanical- *Imperata Cylindrica Beauv.* Family-*Gramineae.*

   English-*Thatch grass.*

   Indian- *Siru, Dabh*

   Description- perennial, tufted, creeping, scaly, climbs upto 3 Mts. Leaves densely bearded with white hair.

   Distribution - same as 1.

   Uses- Stem yields fibre for making ropes, brushes, bags, baskets and mats. The blades of the grass are used for getting paper pulp. The plant is planted to reclaim dry and desert areas.

3. Botanical- *Saccharum Spontaneum Linn.*

   Family- *Gramineae.* English (also) *Thatch grass.*

   Indian- *Kans.*

   Description-Perennial, thick stem, about 5 cm high, solid above and hollow below, slender, silky hair below the flower heads.

   Destribution- same as 1 and 2

   Uses- Soil binder. Leaves used for thatching and for making mats. The reed gives excellent paper pulp and buffaloes love to eat the grass.

4. Botanical- *Themeda Arundinacea Ridley.* Family-*Gramineae.*

   English- *Ulla Grass.* Indian- *Ghas, Ulla, Kapur.*

   Description- Perennial, tall and tufted, stem 20-40 cms. yellow in colour, long leaves rough on both sides.

   Destribution- Tropical countries with extremes of climate like North-India.

Uses- Pulp of grass makes high quality paper. Stem is used for making cordage.

5. Botanical- *Vetiveria Zizanioides Nash.*

   Family- *Gramineae.*

   English- *Ehue-khus grass.*

   Indian- *Vetiver, Khus-khus.*

   Description- Densely tufted and perennial. Stem branches underground. Above ground stem is 2-3 Cms, smooth and glabrous. Roots aromatic, leaf blades 40-80 cms long and erect and firm. Flowers in conical pinnicles 30 cm long.

   Distribution- same as 1,and 3.

   Uses- Great commercial value. Aromatic oil extracted from roots to make scents and soaps. Fibrous roots are used to make *tatties* (window blinds), mats, fans etc Grass is excellent for making paper but other uses are more remunerative.

Some *Aromatic plants*

1. Botanical: *Aqularia Agallocha. Roxb.*

   Family: *Thymelaceae.*

   English: *Eagle Wood, Aloe Wood.*

   Indian: *Agaru, Agar.*

   Distribution-Bengal, Assam and hilly places with similar climate.

   Description; Evergreen tree with very small white flowers in silky umbels. Velvety fruits 4-6 Cm long.

   Uses: It is true Agar of Eagle Wood which is commercially used and the wood is highly scented. When the wood is loaded within Olco-resinous matter it gets infected with fungus and when the infected wood is distilled it yields *agar attar*, an essential oil which is very valuable as a perfume.

2. Botanical; Cananglum odoratum Baill.

   Family. *Annonacae.*

   English: *Ylang-Ylang tree.*

   Description: Large evergreen tree with large leaves, long stalked flowers, fragrant and yellow in colour. Fruit globose and have about a dozen segments and about a dozen seeds.

Distribution: Throughout India, Pakistan, Bangladesh and many other tropical countries.

Uses. The flowers on first distillation gives the well-known perfume Ylang-Ylang. Second distillation gives the inferior oil called Macassar or Cananga. Ylang Ylong is an important ingredient of high class scents, face powder, hair oil, soaps, etc.

3. Botanical: *Cedrus Deodara Loud.*

   Family- *Pinaceae.*

   English: *Himalayan Coder, Deodar.*

   Indian- *Deodaru.*

   Distribution- Cold hilly slopes and valleys usually at a height of 3,000 ft above sea level.

   Uses: Wood is oily and aromatic and not attacked by insects. It is a costly timber in India. Destructive distillation of the wood gives deodar tar oil which is used as a substitute for *Cedar Wood Oil.*

4. Botanical:- *Cinnanmomum Camphor.*

   Family: *Lauraceae.*

   Indian- *Rohu, Nepal Camphor*

   Distribution: *Cold hilly ranges of tropical countries.*

   Uses: Wood is aromatic, insect repellent.

5. Botanical- *Curcuma Zedoaria Rose.*

   Family- *Zingiberaceae.*

   English- *Wild Turmeric, Long Zedoary.*

   Indian-*Kachura.*

   Distribution- Most deciduous tropical forests of tropical countries.

   Description- Large root-stock with many tubers. Whitish or palish yellow inside, long stalked leaves about 50 cm long. Pale yellow flowers.

   Uses- The rhizome which is aromatic is used mostly in cosmetics and in the preparation of medicinal oils. The rhizome is rich in starch in commerce the Shoti starch. The starch is a substitute for barley and arrowroot and it is a very nutritious food given to infants and invalids.

PLANT AND TREE POTASH

In areas where vegetables are grown, if warm and dry winds blow, inadequacy of potash in the soil will adversely affect their growth. Rabbit manure, cow dung, or chicken house sweepings, mixed with wood ash or dried-leaf ash of the trees plant listed below will make excellent potash, so much better than machine made potash. Loaf fertilizers should have potash, phosphate, nitrogen and some chemicals such as sulphur and zinc in small quantities. Many of the plant and tree fertilizers listed below contain one or the other of these chemicals.

1. Botanical: *Achyranthes Aspera Linn.*

   Family: *Latjira, Apamaga.*

   English: *Prickly Chaff flower.*

   Description: Erect, ash coloured shrub with many branches; velvety leaves and bisexual flowers in spikes of the length of about 40 cm while in fruit.

   Distribution: Throughout India, Pakistan. Bangladesh, Sri Lanka and many African countries.

   Uses: Leaves are used for washing clothes, for making Caustic Soda as explained in Handout No 45 and as a fertlizer.

2. Botanical: *Adhatoda Vasica Nees.*

   Family: *Acanthaceae.*

   Indian: *Arusha. Adhatodai, Vasaka.*

   Description: Densely branched shrub, leaves opposite and pointed at both ends, about 15 Cm long. Has white flowers with red spots and are 4 seeded.

   Distribution; same as 1 above.

   Uses: Leaves are excellent green manure in rice fields. Ash is used for washing clothes and to make Caustic soda. The leaves are also used as funglide and weedicide.

3. Botanical: *Carica Papaya Linn.* Family: *Caricaceae.*

   Indian: *Papita, papaya.*

   English: *Papaw.*

Description: Errect soft wood tree with cluster of leaves at the very top. Leaf stalk long and hallow. Small pale yellow flowers. Large edible fruit with many seeds. See Nos 41 and 85.

Uses: Leaves contain vitamin C and E, a glycoside, carposide and an alkaloid, Carpain. It can be used as a detergent and as a green manure.

4. Botanical: *Musa X Paradisicalinn Linn.* Family: *Musaceal.*

   Indian: *Kela, Valhai.*

   English: *Plaintain, Banana.*

   Description: Broad long leaves, large flowers with bunches of fruits each bunch having 50 to 100 fruits.

   Distribution: Common in many tropical countries, abundant in South India.

   Uses: Fruits are edible. When unripe they are used as a vegetable. The ash of the banana peal is rich in potash, There is potash in the leaves also and the leaves and the peal of the fruit can be chopped and used as manure.

SOME SIMPLE WAYS OF EXTRACTING FIBRE

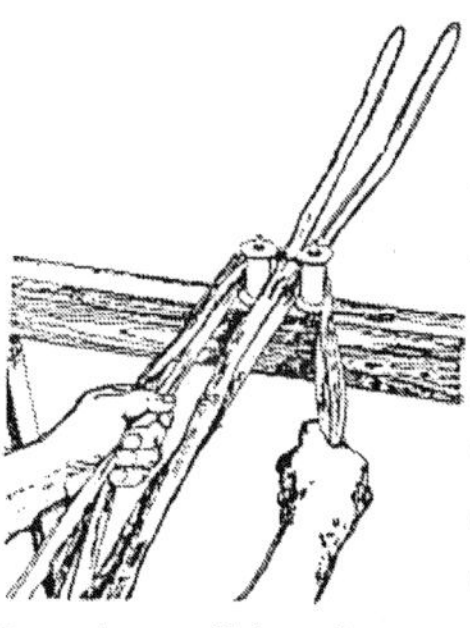

1. Leaf fibres such as sisal or abaca (Manilla Hemp) can be extracted by hand retting. The long flat leaves or fleshy blades are cut and made into bundles and soaked in water, preferably in moving water for about two months. Thereafter, the leaves are beaten with wooden hammers and the flesh is removed from the fibre. As the flesh gets loosened the fibre must be rinsed and boated again and then dried in shade. Sun drying will darken the colour of the fibre.
2. A small hand-operated machine may also be used for extracting leaf fibre. This simple machine is made of two spiked iron rollers and set close to each other - with about one inch gap between the rollers in a mild steel frame. The leaf is fed between the two rollers and pulled out on the other side; and between the rollers. By this process the flesh drops out on the feeding side of the rollers. These rollers may also be power operated.
3. Bark fibres such as Kenaf, Urena Labata or jute can be extracted in a simple hand operated bark fibre ribboner shown in the picture developed

by the Tropical Products Institute. The. top edge of the bark is loosened and drawn back until it can be gripped firmly. By pulling the bark around the spools the stalk can be stripped completely and the long fibre can be separated.

4. Soft fibre like banana fibre can be extracted between two knives or between a table top or a guillotin blade. Also sisal, abaca or lobata, after the hard flesh is removed by initial retting, can be pulled through this device to completely get rid of the flesh that may be sticking in lumps here and there.

5. There are power operated machines and chemical process to Seperate fibres from the fleshy portion but these are not suited for rural communities. Simple hand and power operated machines are commonly used to extract coconut fibre in India, Sri Lanka, Philippines, Thailand and other countries

SOAY FOR PROTEIN DIET

Soaybean belongs to the family of legumes and has a high food value. It is a very valuable source of protein, minerals, vitamins and other food ingredients. An analysis of Soya bean shows that it contains:

Protein	-	43.2 per cent
Fat	-	19.5 per cent
Mineral matter	-	4.6 per cent.
Carbohydrate	-	20.9 per cent
Fibre	-	3.7 per cent
Calcium	-	0. 24 per cent
Phosphorus	-	0.69 per cent and
Iron	-	11.5 mg. per cent.

Vitamin content of Soyabean is as under

Vitamin A	-	710 I.U
Thiamine	-	0.73 mg per cent.
Riboflavin	-	O.76 mg. per cent.
Niacin	-	2.4 Mg. per cent.
Biotin	-	60 mmg per cent
Pantothenic acid	-	1.68 mg per cent

Pyridoxine	-	0.64 mg per cent.
Vitamin E	-	6.11 mg per cent per 100 gms.

The energy value Soaybean is very high - about 4-32 per cent per 100 gms. Soyabean is rich in alkaline-bearing salts and hence it is regarded as a corrective diet. It contains little or no starch but large amounts of Carbohydrate. Therefore, it is considered a very suitable food for diabetic patients.

Soyabean gives plenty of Lecithin which is a natural emulsifier. Lecithin which is rich in substances for the proper functioning of all living cells. in the body also helps disperse deposits of cholesterol and fatty materials in certain vital organs of the body. Soyabeans has so much Lecithin that most of the lecithin produced commercially is extracted from Soyabean.

Soyabean is said to be a natural food medicine to cure skin diseases and eczema. When eczema sufferers eat plenty of soyabean they say. intensive itching diminishes within a few minutes after eating it and some say, that eczema even disappears if Soyabean is eaten regularly for about three months. Perhaps the lecithin present in soyabean is the active ingredient that cures eczema.

Fibre yielding plants trees

1. Botanical: *Abroma Augusta Linn.*

   Family: *Sterculiaceae.*

   English: *Perennial Indian hemp.*

   Indian: *Ulathambel.*

   Description: Shrub with whitish and darkish purple flowers. Numerous seeds covered with silky hair.

   Distribution: Throughout the hotter parts of India, Sri Lanka, Pakistan, Bangladesh and many African countries.

   Uses: The bark yields fibre which is very soft and durable and considered superior to hemp and jute. It is so soft that sometimes it is inter-woven with silk.

2. Botanical: *Acacia Prnnata Willd.* Family: *Leguminosae.*

   Indian: *Shambi or Aila.*

   Description: Prickly climber. Leaves 10-15 cm long. White and yellowish flowers. Pods 10-20 cm long. brown or yellow.

   Distribution: Peninsular India and several tropical countries with similar climate.

Uses: The stem yields a long and strong fibre. The charred fibre is used for cleaning mirrors.

3. Botanical: *Agave American Linn.* Family: *Agavaceae.*

   English: *Century plant.* Indian: *Rakas-paltah or Bara Kawar.*

   Description: A stout plant bearing a rosette of leaves on a short trunk, leaves about 160 cm long.

   Distribution: Throughout India, Pakistan, Bangladesh, Sri Lanka and many tropical countries.

   Uses: The leaves and roots yield high quality fibre.

4. Botanical: *Annas Comosus Merril.* Family: *Bromiliaceae.*

   English: *Pineapple.* Indian: *Ananas. Tamil: Annasi.*

   Description: Several countries, warm and about 2,000 feet above sea level.

   Uses: Leaves give soft and white fibre. It is strong and does not weaken in water. Thread used by cobblers to stich leather. After extracting the fibre paper is made out of the waste material left.

5. Botanical: *Cocos Nucifeba Linn.* Family: Palme. English: *Porcupine Wood* or *Coconut palm.* Indian: *Nariyal.*

   Description: Very tall palm - 20 to 40 feet high. Leaves also very long. The fruit coconut is eaten raw or cooked. Fibre from the husk is the coir of commerce.

   Uses: Cordage, upholstry, hard board, etc. (for a list of 84 countries where coconut grows see Handout 121.

6. Botanical: *Cordia Dichotoma Forstf.*

   Family: *Lasora, Bahuvaraka.* English: *Sebestan.*

   Description: Low spreading tree with crooked stem. Small flowers white and fragrant in large open panicles. Distribution: Throughout India and many tropical countries.

   Uses: Strong wood. Bark yields coarse fibre used for making cordage. Pulp is used as glue. Lac insects grow on this tree.

Use Leaves as Fertilizers

1. In Africa, Marechea Seeds (Grcpolania Ocholenca), when applied in layers in grain filled sacks, repel harmful insects. Leaves of the Marechea plant

is also used as green manure, as weed supressor and fodder for cattle and feed for fish - report in GATE of Germany, NO 4/85.

2. Botanical: *Pongamia Globra* - leaves make excellent green manure especially for flower and vegetable gardens See Handout-53 (Page 22).

3. Botanical: Lencauena Leucooephala, a highly drought resistant tropical tree found in many countries also make excellent fertilisers. The tree is called Epil-Epil in Africa.

4. Botanical: Adhatoda Vasica Nees is a shrub commonly found in the fields in the tropics also makes excellent organic fertliser. The green leaves are usually buried in the soil.

5. Botanical: *Pongatuia Pinnuta Pierre.*

   Family: *Leguininosae.*

   Indian name: *Karanj.*

   English: *Indian Beach.*

   Description: Small deciduous tree. Leaves about 15-30 cm. long. Purple white flowers, woody pods oval-oblong with a short beak. One or two seeds.

   Distribution: Throughout India, Pakistan, Bangladesh, Sri Lanka and many tropical countries.

   Uses: The leaves are excellent for manuring rice fields. The seed-oil is an insecticide.

6. Botanical: Emblica Myrobalanc. Family: *Euphorbiaceae* Indian names: *Amla, Amlica.* Tajmil- *Nellikai.*

   Description: middle size tree with plenty of small leaves. Pale green flowers in clusters. Fruit-1.5 to 2.5 cm in diameter, roundish with 6 divisions (lobes).

   Distribution: Many countries with tropical and sub-tropical climate. Leaves are used to fertilise vegetable gardens.

7. Botanical: *Mallotus Philippinsis.*

   Family: *Euphorbiaceae.* Indian: *Sendurl, Kamela, Rohini.*

   Tamil: *Kopila podi* Telugu: Kunkuma.

   Description: middle size tree, ever green, very small yellow flowers Roundish fruit, 8-12 cms in diameter.

8. Botanical: Leugaena, Leucocephola, Gliricidia Sbpium, etc. The leaves are used for manuring paddy fields and vegetable gardens. See Handout—38.

9. Botanical: *Madhuga.* Family: *Sapotaceae.* Bengali: *Mahua.* Malayalam: *Poonam.* Tamil: Elluppai.

   Description: Large deciduous tree, leaves 12-25 cm long, dull white flowers are small and fleshy and fall at dawn.Fruit-2.5 -5 cm long.

   Distribution: tall tree common in submontane regions. In Many tropical countries it is commonly found in the forests. Leaves are used as manure but Mahua cake, after the oil is extracted is more effective as a fertiliser.

USEFUL PLANTS OF KHOLLI HILLS

The following are some of the medicinal and other useful plants identified and collected at the Kholli Hills by a team of 40 members of the ABVA Mandal, Ahemedabad, Gujarat in 1987.

Botanical Name	*Tamil*	*Sanakrit*
Erythrine Indica	Kalyana murukku	Pariphatra
Veronai anthelmlnlicum	Kattu jeeragam	Aranys jeeraks
Chenopdiurn embroaldos	Paruppukaaral	Soganda vastuku
Piper nigrum	Mlagu	Maricha
Poristropha bicatyculats	Nangal	Kakashanka
Montha arvenis	Puthins ·	Pothlka
Tamarindua Indica	Puli	Chincha
Elotteraris cardamum	Elam	Els
Alpinis galanga	Pararathal	Deelpanther vachs
Clauaena dantata	Kattu karuvepila	–
Jatropha curcas	Kattuamanakku	Karnsetanda
Bryophyllum calicum	hankalli	Parnar peelam
Mollugo pantaphyila	Thura	Peroada
Sida cordifolia	Karunthotti	Bala
Bryonopsis lacinioss	lyvisalikovai	Slvalings
Cyclas peltats	Sirpatha vath	Raspaths
Mallotus philippinees	Kornils	Kampillako
Timisoara condifolls	Soenthail	Guduchl
Trida procumbens	Veslukayapochilal	Pitha bringaral
Prantma tomantoss	Pidanku nari	Agnlmankh
Plper sttenuatum	Kattu milagu ·	Jangli Maricha
Classis occidantalis	Ponthagaral	Kasamrds
Classis lomentoss	Pal thagaral	Kasamrda
Classistora	Ooal thagaaral	Chakamsda

(contd.)

(Table Continued.)

Solanum verbaac Holiun	Kattu sundal	Bahathi
Cardioapannum halicacabom	Mudakkartan	Kamaapta
Litses wightill	Vakkanal	Medasses
Gynoaporis montana	Nanduna	Vutkakata
Anamirts cocculua	Kakaikoili	Kakanaalsks
Sclrtdapaus ollcioalla	Analthlppill	Calalpill
Rubia cordifolia	Chevallikadi	Vidanka
Embelia ribes	Valvidankam	Valvidanka
Symplocos spicats	Velli lothiram	Swads lodhrs
Argyrais apecious	Samudrapalal	Vridhadaru
Cinnamomun zeylanicum	ttavangapattal	Twak
Cinnamomum tamals	Havanaapattal	Tamalapatrs
Smilax zalanics	karuvilanjikudam	Chospchini
Randia duomolorum	Marukkarai	Madhans
Asparagus racomosus	Tharurvittankuha	Sathavari
Tarminalls bellerics	Thantri	Bibithuki
Oldenlandia corymboss	Parpadagam	Parpads
Elolvalusalsnoidcs	Visnukiranthi	Visnukiranthi
Clarodandrum serratum	Siruthakku	Bhargi
Caottalls aslatica	Vallaral	Mandoogabhrami

Leucaenaleu COCEPHALA

This is a drought resistant tropical tree with several uses. It grows well in different soils and varying temperature upto an altitude of 1,000 meters under various weather conditions. The tree gives not only excellent fuel wood and timber for furniture but also fodder by its leaves, honey from its flower and dye (colours) from it's bark. In some parts of Africa the tree is known as Epil-Epil. This fast growing tree reaches a height of five mts within a year and 20 mts in about three to four years.

The pods contain hard Beeds and African women make neck-laces, hand-bags and fancy items out of them. Big bunches of white flowers on the tree look beautiful.

Leucanena which belongs to South America has been introduced into Indonesia, Philippines, Australia, India and several other countries.

A very important feature of this tree is that it fixes nitrogen from the air through fungi adhering to it's roots and this enriches the soil in which it grows and benefits plants and trees planted around it.

The leaves of the tree fall throughout the year and farmers use them as mulch (green manure) to increase soil fertility and also as fodder for animals and feed for chicken. But only one fourth of the total quantity of feed given to livestock should be Leucaena leaves. If more is given livestock suffer ill health.

RYFO recommends the promotion of this multipurpose tree on a large scale in rural areas to develop rural economy.

GROWING MANGOSTEEN

Mangosteen, botanically known as Garcinia Mangostana, belongs to the family of Guttieerae. Deep reddish and about the size of a tennis ball, it has a very fine flavour and grows well in the tropics ideally at an elevation of 400 to 1,000 metres and an annual precipitation of about 150 cm.

The slow growing tree which takes about ten years to give the first crop, is grown at spacings of 8 to 10 metres on either side and 150 trees can be grown in a hectare (Seeds treated with gibberelic acid quickens germination and growth of the plant). Yields continue for more than 100 years, and each tree will produce about 500 fruits in both seasons, January to March and July to October. In a year one single tree is capable of yielding even upto 3,000 fruits if properly cared for.

It is necessary to manure the trees and manuring is best done in June-July and the recoinmanded manure is a mixture of 75 Kg. of cattle manure, one kg of nitrogen, three Kgs. of Potash and 0.8 Kg. of phosphorous.

Watering the trees during the bearing season will improve the size and quality of the fruit. The fruits which grow well in many elevated parts of south India are delicious, nutritious and very much in demand in the market. It is eaten raw or made into jam with a mixture of other fruits. The edible part is the pearl-white pulp with a fine flavour.

The hard outer covering of the fruit is believed to have several medical properties. In areas where they are grown the dried and powdered shell is taken as a cure for stomach ailments.

The fruit is cultivated on a commercial scale in Sri Lanka, Malaysia, Indonesia, Philippines and India.

Gambog is the only disease of the crop and spraying with copper fungicides can prevent the infection.

The tree can be cultivated excellently well by rural communities living in humid sub-tropics and as it does not grow into a big tree it can be grown by families in their front or backyard.

EMPLOYMENT POSSIBILITIES WITH JAMBOL

Botanical: *Syzygium Cumtni (L) Skeels Syn Eugenia Jambolana Lam.*

Family: *Myrtaceae.* Indian names are given below:

Sanakrit: *Jambul.*	Hindi-*Jamun.*
Tamil: *Nagai (Nagam phalam).*	Malayalam-*Yavel.*
Bengali: *Jam, or Bada Jam.*	Gujarati -*Jambu.*

Description: Very big tree, shiny and long leaves opposite to each other, small flowers in large clusters pale white in colour. Fruits are purple and the small ones are about one cm. long while the big ones can be upto 4 cms long. Ripe fruits are juicy and tasty with a single seed like the seed of a date fruit (a little bigger in size). Natural growth is in forests, especially, along water channels. However, the tree grows well and bears plenty of fruits if planted in the plains provided the climate is tropical.

Uses:

(1) All parts of the tree excepting the leaves are medicinal and the very astringent bark is used to cure bronchitis, sore throat, dysentry and asthma. These may be procured and supplied to manufacturers of herbal medicines.

(2) The fruits and seeds are very effective in keeping diabetes under control and cases of complete cure have been reported. The active ingredient responsible for this has been established by research laboratories. Employment can be given to people in collecting the fruits to be eaten raw by patients, to convert the fruit into jams, pickles and wine. The fruits can also be solar dried and sold all through the year.

(3) More than the fruits the seeds are effective in controlling diabetes. These may be collected dried, pound, put into gelatine capsules, packed in lots and sent to drug stores.

In the forests monkeys eat the fruit (birds also eat them) and drop the seeds which can be collected in large quantities. Large quantities may also be purchased in rural markets during season.

(4) It is reported that when the active ingredient is separated from the seed and prepared injections are given to patients it has a very quick and better effect.

Note: The other fruit known to be effective on diabetes patients is the Indian Kino (Bija Sal) Botanical name of it is: *Pterocaphus Marsupium Roxb.*

Family:- Papilionaceae.

Sanskrit name: *Mahakutaj*. Hindi:- *Bijasalor Piasal.*

Malayalam: *Kino*. Gujarathi: *Bibla*. Kannada: *Honne*. Marathi: *Honi*.

Indian *Kino* is a large tree with beautiful yellow flowers in big bunches and with a fine smell.

METHI in Hindi and several Indian languages known as *Vendiai* in Tamil which is commonly used in Indian cooking is also known to suppress blood sugar and experiments have proved this Botanical: *Trigonella Foenum* (Eng: Fenugreek).

All three of these, the active ingredients of which have been established, if mixed in equal quantities and packed in capsule form can be a good tonic and medicine for people suffering from diabetes.

THE AIDER TREE

Among the forest trees that produce humus (organic manure) for the soil the Alder tree, botanically known as Ainas Nepalensis is an excellent example. The tree grows well in hill slopes above a height of 1,000 feet. Besides it's roots that produce nodules (clusters of bacteria) it's leaves and twigs fix nitrogen in the soil. The tree is popular on the hill slopes of Nagaland where the farmers cultivate and care for it and use it to fertilize soil and grow maize, millet, barley, wheat, potatoes as well as secondary crops such as pumpkins. cucumbers, melons, casava, taro or chillies.

Branches of Alder, are excellent fuel-wood and they burn well even when they are not fully dry and women find it easy to split them. When the tree grows about three metres. high the middle trunk is cut horizontally about two mts. above ground level and all the branches are cut and removed. This operation is called pollarding of the tree usually done between December and January. About 5 to 10 years thereafter the tree shoots branches. The second and subsequent pollaring is done after intervels of five years. Under such spacing the tree gets new branches even if it is pollarded over a hundred times. The leaves may be pruned and the small branches cut every year. During the second and subsequent pollaring about half-a-dozen vertical branches are left to grow further.

If the tree is left unpollarded it grows wild, and tall and straight with one main trunk like an Eucaliptus or Causarina tree. Soon after pollaring the fuel-wood is separated from the twigs and leaves and allowed to dry. When dry, the twigs and leaves are burnt and mixed with the soil at the time of sowing food grains.

Male and female flowers bloom in the same tree between September and October and the male flowers are much larger than the female and the tree is propagated by wind pollination. If the saplings are transplanted after a year they grow into healthy trees and percent the soil from erosion. The Alder seeds are found inside small dark-brown eases or shells called catkins and the seed life is only four months.

The foliage of the tree dries and becomes rich mulch, enriches the soil and helps other plants to grow well in the soil. The roots of the tree spread sideways and don't go deep into the soil and nodules are formed in it's roots as in legumunous trees eventhough an Alder is not a legume. Food grains are sown between February and April.

To cultivate Alder 6 to 9 months seedlings should be procured in May and planted at intervels of 5 metres. and for two years from the date of sowing cattle should not be allowed in the area as cattle will brouse the tender shoots and hamper the growth of the tree.

(Condensed from a publicity booklet released by the Govt. of Nagaland in April 1985).

INDIAN ALMOND TREE

(Otherwise called Bengal Almond)

Botanical: *Terminalia Catappa.* Native of India and Malayasia but now found in almost all countries with tropical climate. The islands of Seychelles and the semi-deserts of Somalia have plenty of it.

Uses and Employment.

(1) The leaves are broad and big and commonlv used for serving meals. The African variety has much bigger leaves than the Indian and Malaysian variety.

(2) The fully ripe fruits are Turkish -red in colour and taste like plums and children relish the fruits.

(3) Jams and pickles are made out of the fruits and this is a village industry for urban markets.

(4) Good quality wine is also made out of the fully ripe fruits by the usual process of making grape wine and wine making can give employment for some urban communities.

(5) The kernel inside the nut is very tasty and children break the nut and eat the kernel,

(6) When the kernal is collected in lots, fried in ghee, dalda or any edible oil, peppered and salted, it gains in commercial value. It can be packed like cashew kernels and sold as evening eats. Village women can process the kernels for sale in city markets and even for exports. (Frenchmen used to export them from Pondicherry to Paris).

(7) A valuable oil, like the Almond oil, is extracted from the dried fruit and the kernel by simple steam distillation village process and this oil has medicinal and commercial value and can also be used as a cooking media.

(8) Butter paste or Almond butter can be made out of the Ķernel similar to peanut butter and it tastes like peanut butter.

(9) Leaves can be used as fodder and animals like them.

(10) Plates and tumblers are made out of the leaves by a simple hand-operated machine invented by the Central Food Technology Research Institute of the Government of India, Mysore, and many families are engaged in this industry now in India.

(11) The soft wood of the tree is excellent for making wooden toys and montesorry toys.

(12) All parts of the tree can be chopped and used as manure.

(13) When the fully ripe fruits are boiled they give a beetrootish liquid which is used, to dye fibre-made articles like bags and rugs.

(14) The twigs and leaf when dried burn well in 'Stovel Pumps' (Stoval pump, invention of Dr Ryan is a stove to use dried leaves as cooking fuel.

AILAANTHUS FOR SALINE SOIL

Botanical: *Allanthus exceisia.*
Family: *Srmarubaceae.*
Hindi: Ardu.
Tamil: *Peru Maram* or *Pimaram.*

Native of South India, this highly drought resistant large tree grows well in hot and dry climates, in saline or calcareous (containing calcium carbonate) soil, in the sea shore and river beds. The tree is now popular all over India and can be easily introduced into other tropical countries. The average height of the tree in three about 25 years is 20 mts with a girth of over one metre. It grows excellently well in farm yards and tank bunds and does not take away the soil nutrient of other plants. Its soft wood is commonly used for match sticks and the leaves are used as fodder. The tree can be lapped once in two years and over 1000 kgs of green leaves can be gathered from each tree and sold in village markets as fodder. Cattle eat the dried leaves also and the protein content of the leaf." is about 19 per cent. Honey bees are active where these trees are in plenty and silk worms can be grown on these trees. The worms eat the leaves as they eat the leaves of mulberry plants. So, where mulberry does not thrive these trees may be introduced or both the trees may be cultivated side by side. The leaves have about two per cent calcium.

The tree is propagated through seeds. Raised in nurseries, the seedlings are transplanted in about eight months, at intervals of 10 mts, and given plenty of farm yard manure. Chemical fertilisers are not necessary. Stump planting is done in some areas but nursery saplings are the best.

Tribals claim that the bark of the tree is medicinal but nothing so far has been scientifically tested and established. The leaves mixed with paddy straw and cow dung make good humus. Eventhough Ailanthus does not spread out to give shade it is considered good avenue trees. Seeds of ripe fruits are collected during May-June dried and sowed immediately. They should not be stored. Germination takes places within two weeks.

The trunk of the tree is long and straight like that of a casuarina or eucaliptus and therefore it is used in low cost building industries and in thatched houses. Only low quality furniture can be made out of it but the wood is ideally suited for making wooden toys and packing cases. Soft wood packing cases are a scarce item in several industrial centres and therefore this tree, if promoted in the villages all around industrial cities, can provide employment for hundreds of village carpenters in making packing cases. Planks made of this wood can be cut to uniform size, say, two feet by one foot, and used in the place of roofing tiles (shingles) in low-cost houses.

INDIAN ACALYPHA

Acalypha Indica

Botanical: *Acalyha Indica L.*
Family: *Euphorbiaceae.*
Indian names: Hindi: *Kuppi, Khokali.*
Sanskrit: *Harittaman jari.*
Tamil: *Kuppamani.*
Halayalam: *Kuppamani.*
Telugu: *Kuppamani.*
Gujarathi: *Vanchi Kanto.*
Bengali: *Muktabarsi.*
Trade name: *Acalypha.*

Description: Perenial herb about 70 cms. high. Tooth edged ovate leaves are about six cm. long. The stalk of the leaves are longer than the leaves. Fruits are small and flowers are in erect spikes.

Distribution: Found throughout India. Pakistan, Srilanka, Bangladesh and in many African countries. It is highly a drought resistant herb and grows like a weed in barren lands.

Uses: The drug Acalypha is extracted from the entire plant collected when it is about to flower. Acalyphay is useful in pneumonia, bronchitis and asthma. Laxatives are also made from the leaves and thee roots. Fresh leaves are ground and applied on wounds.

Properties of Acalypha are very similar to those of Ipecac of the Rubiaceae family and Tyiophora Indica of the family Asclepiadacae. The roots of all these plants have an excellent export market and pure herbs (roots) can be packed in one Kg. plastic pouches are exported either directly to pharmaceutical buyers abroad or through registered merchant exporters who are already in the trade. These herbs are not at present treated as items of commerce eventhough they are being exported by different exporters to different countries from different countries.

Herbs collection centres have to be set up in different regions of the Third World as only then the villagers will have an incentive to collect and supply the herbs and the price per kilo,. for different herbs must be fixed by the NGOs organising the collecting centres. It is advisable for each centre to specialise only in five to 10 herbs to prevent mixing up of herbs and accounts. Such collection centres will promote several indirect employment such as making of plastic pouches, fibre bags and sacks, testing and grading laboratories transportation, etc.

The collection of *Vinca Rosea* which cures certain types of cancer, *chenna* leaves used as laxative and some other herbal plants arc already well organised, controlled and managed and tons of these are being exported from India every year. There are thousands of other useful plants from which curative and life-saving alkaloids are extracted are waiting to be exploited. Villagers should exploit all their local resources instead of applying to the govrnment for metals and chemicals which are in short supply, waiting indefenitely and cursing authorities for corruption and mal practices.

GO SLOW WITH EUCALYPTUS

The exotic native tree of Australia, Eucalyptus a very fast growing species has become very controversial after it's introduction in new habitats and reclaimed areas. Environmentalists are much against the tree and say it dries up wells, fast depletes soil nutrients and fails to meet fuel, fodder and fertilizer needs of farmers but only produces toxins.

The Food and Agricultural Organisation (FAO) of the United Nations came out with a review of the various findings of different field agencies from different countries in a publication under the title, 'The Ecological Effect of Eucalyptus.' The report points out that there is evidence from the tropics that Eucalyptus plantations consume soil water and dry up wells. The report also says that if the trees are planted in barren lands, they draw down water tables. The FAO document further adds the Eucalyptus totally change the eco-system which exists prior to their introduction.

However, the Eucalyptus cannot be completely given up. The ever-green Eucalyptus related to the Myrtle family is found in many parts of the world and it is the largest source of pulp for rayon and paper industries. Botanists have identified about 500 species of the tree. Many of them yield essential oil and gum. In fact, the tree is popularly known in its native country, Australia, as the *Gum tree.*

The oil and gum are used in preparing medicines. The long and straight trunk of the tree, which is not attacked by white ants, are required for building low-cost houses for the poor, for fencing and for erecting cow-sheds and goat-pens. The twigs are also needed to be used as domestic fuel-wood.

Therefore, patches of secluded areas of rocky and rugged grounds must be earmarked to grow about 1,000 trees in each village. The tree may be grown on either sides of roads and in between large-size ever-green trees already existing on road boundaries. Even here, the species that don't suck the soil too dry should be introduced. Along with other employment generating and useful trees such as the bamboo, Causarina, Subabool, tamarind, Neem, etc. Eucalyptus is also very much needed for rural people to progress. These trees are ideal for initiating self-help employment projects based on appropriate technology and local resources. The FAO and forest departments and Tree Lovers Clubs (which are gaining popularity now all over the world) should now promote and popularise the harmless species of the tree out of the 500 identified so far. They should also popularise the highly drought resistant and quick growing Thailand variety of Casuarina *(CausArina Junghuniana)* which is propagated by air layering or rooting of springs.

Issued as a poster by The Ryan Foundation

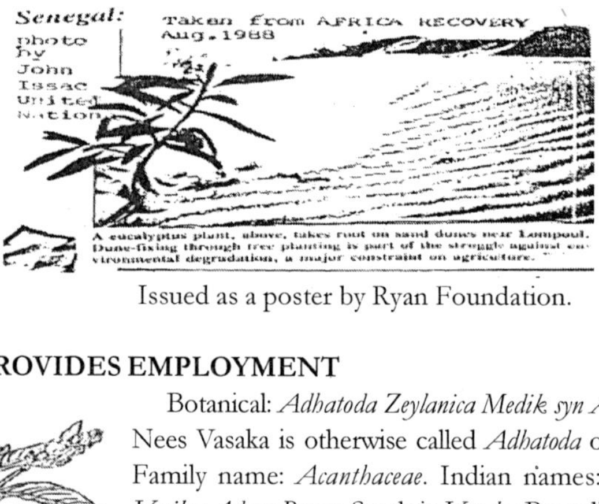

Issued as a poster by Ryan Foundation.

VASAKA. PROVIDES EMPLOYMENT

Botanical: *Adhatoda Zeylanica Medik syn A.* Vasica Nees Vasaka is otherwise called *Adhatoda* or *Adusa.* Family name: *Acanthaceae.* Indian names:- Hindi: *Vasika, Adusa, Bansa.* Sanskrit: *Vasaka,* Bengali: *Vasaka.* Kannada: *Adusoge,* Gujarati: *Ardusi* or *Aldusco.*

Malayalam: *Atalotakam.* Marathi: *Adulsa* Telugu: *Adasaramu.* Tamil: *Arathorai* or *Adadorai.* In and around Delhi the plant is popularly known as *Piya-bansa.*

The international trade name is *Vasaka.*

Vasaka is about two to three cm tall evergreen shrub with large leaves. It grows uncared for all over India, Burma, Sri Lanka, Pakistan, Bangladesh, and several African countries and other countries with tropical climate. Nepal has plenty of it.

Stalks of the spikes are shorter than the leaves and dense flowers grow in the short spikes. Capsules have four seeds. Petals of the flowers are white with purple shades and fruits are round.

Uses:

(1) The leaves contain an essential oil, and people can be employed in steam distilling the oil as shown in handout 7.

(2) The oil may also be sold for burning lights (handout 99), for cooking (handout 48) and for lubrication of wheels and pumps.

(3) The leaves contain an alkaloid called *Vasicine* which acts as an expectorant. As the alkaloid is to be chemically extracted fresh leaves can be sent to chemical factories. Collecting and packing the leaves will give employment for women and children.

(4) The leaves are excellent manure both in green form and dry. They can be dried, pound or ground by one of the methods shown in earlier handouts along with other leaves having fertiliser and insecticide properties and sold (Handout 112 and 130).

(5) The leaves yield a yellow dye which may be extracted and sold to handloom weavers or those engaged in fibre industries.

(6) Parts of this plant is not attacked by insects or fungi and therefore, can be used in the frame work of Shingles (H-192).

(7) As the plants are not eaten by cattle it can be grown to reclaim soil and as field and plant guards.

(8) The leaves can be collected and sold to wholesale fruit markets to ripen fruits and to preserve them (commonly done in India).

(9) Villagers boil the leaf of this plant, take the essence of it and give about ten to twenty drops to those suffering from chest cold. Larger doses is said to irritate the stomach.

(10) Sticks can be used for making building slabs (handout 90) and this work can employ several teenage boys and girls.

(11) All parts of this neglected plant can be used in Ryan's cooking pump.

SOLANUM

(Solanum Incanum)

Botanical: *Solamum Incanum*
Family: *Solanaceae*
Hindi: *Ringni or Kateri*
Tamil: *kandankattari*
Bengali: *Kannada,Telugu,Halamulaka.*
Trade name: *kantakari.*

Description: Creaping herb, with several branches full of thorns. Minute star shaped hair cover the tender branches. The leaves are about ten cm long and flowers in bunches are purple and about two cm. long. Round pale yellow fruits with green veins are more than a centimeter in diameter. The plant has a wild growth throughout India, Pakistan, Sri Lanka and Bangladesh and grows uncared for. Cattle don't brouse them because they are very thorny.

The Indian Pharmaceutical Codex and the Pharmacopoeia of United States of America, refer to the roots but not to the fruits eventhough the fruits are used in the treatment of several diseases.

Medicinal: The dried roots of the plant have the active ingredient used in asthma, bronchitis, colds and hay fever. Some tribals drop the juice of the fruits into the ears to relieve ear ache. The tender leaves and fruits are eaten as vegetables in rural homes believing that to be a good lung tonic. However, this has not been scientifically established. Some ayurvedic (green medicine) doctors claim that a soup made of the roots, leaves and fruits of Solarium is as good as Water Burry's compound for the lungs.

To the same family belongs Solarium Melongena Linn known in the West as Garden eggs or *Egg plant* and in the south of the World as Brinjals. In Tamil it is known as Katharikai, a very common vegetable especially in south Indian homes. This plant also has some medicinal properties and its unripe fruits are cardiotonic. It is said to enrich the blood and improve appetite.

For Asthma: This plant is particularly known as a fortification against asthma. A spoonfull of concentrate decoction of the fresh roots is given with honey to patients as a tonic against asthma. Roots are dried and burnt for the patient to inhale the smoke before the oncoming of an asthma attack. (it has no effect absolutely after the attack catches on.) The roots may be powdered and mixed with other leaves, roots or flowers like datura that relieve bronchial conjestion to prevent asthma. All parts of the plant, dried and burnt helps easy breathing but the roots are most effective. Therefore, the roots are in demand by licensed factories manufacturing herbal cures. Collection, packing and cleaning the roots can provide employment for many women and children.

SEETHAPAL OIL

Custard Apple.
Seethaphal (Indian name).
Annona Squamosa (Botanical).

Custard apple grows in many tropical countries and the white pulpy fruit is usually eaten raw. The fruit contains large number of black seeds which contain oil. The oil is commonly used in the preperation of paints and varnishes, soaps and medicines. Following are the characteristies of the oil:-

Sp Gr. at 15°C	0.92116
N. 60°d	1.4558
Sapohification value:	181 to 183.5
Iodine number	85.6 to 88, 2
R/M. Value	0.6
Poplenske Value	0.2
Unsaponification matter	0.2 per cent.

The acid contained in the oil are found to be in the following percentage:

Oleic	18.1
Linoleic	55.1
Palmitic	14.7
Stearic	10.7
Cerotic	00.9

Common uses for the acids mentioned above are:

(a) *Linoleic acid:* medicines, food-stuffs, chicken feed, special driers for protective coatings, soaps, emulsifying agents, bio-chemical research etc.

(b) *Oleic acid:* in the preparation of ointments, polishing compounds, cosmetics, lubricants etc.

(c) *Palmitic acid:* starting point in the making of various metalic palmitates, lubrication oils, soaps, water proofing materials, etc.

(d) *Stearic acid*: soaps, candles, lubricants, pharmaceuticals, cosmetics, rubber compounding, polishes, etc.

Seetaphal seed oil is ideally suited for making soaps, paints and varnishes and the oil can be extracted on a cottage scale and used in the village soap industry.

To preserve the pulp of Seethapal a process is available with the Central Food Technology Research Institute of the Government. of India, at Mysore, India. Mixed fruit jam can be made out of this pulp along with other fruit pulps. Annona Squamosa can be cultivated in most of the tropical countries without difficulty. The trees need little water and animals do not eat its bitter leaves.

HOME TREATMENT FOR POTABILITY

ATIC handout, 40 explains with diagrams how drinking water can be filtered to an extent in three pots arranged as shown in the diagram there. Handout 120 gives details of about eight commonly available plants and trees the leaves of which can be thrown into small wells to purify and disinfect the water to a certain extent.

Intensive research in Germany has revealed that seeds of raw drum sticks (*Moringa Oleifera*) clarify water of low and medium turbidities with a 98.99 per cent reduction in faecal coliforms. When the seeds are broken to bits and stirred vigouriously in a pot of drinking water the dangerous microbes don't die but settle down in the bottom of the pot in about an hour. After an hour 3/4 of the water in the pot may be gently (without shaking) cloth filtered into another clean pot and the 1/4 sediment remaining in the first pot may be thrown out.

Indian time worn experience based on several experiments is that neem seeds dried and broken and gooseberry seeds dried and broken have the same effect and these seeds may also be used in the process explained above. If all these three seeds are easily available they may all be mixed and used.

Where these seeds are not available some of the common leaves listed in Handout 120 may be put into pots one and two shown in Handout 40. They should be washed well, dipped in boiling water if possible and then used. Old leaves must be removed everyday and replaced by fresh leaves. To make the removing easy the leaves may be bundled in thin cloth and thrown in as a bundle. Seeds and leaves may all be mixed if available for better effect.

The water must be boiled before being filled into the top most pot. If fuelwood is scarce and costly the water may be solar heated as shown in Handouts No 2 or No 166.

Villagers will do well to grow all the trees mentioned in their neighbourhood. All of them have several uses other than what is mentioned here. Some are medicinal and produce oil bearing nuts and others can be used as fodder and fertilizers too. Drum stick tree for instance, is medicinal and honey yielding and the leaves are eaten by people and animals; they are rich source of vitamin A and prevent eye ailments.

(Handouts referred here may be found in the two volumes Better Life Technologies for the poor by the same author)

SCHOOL CUM COMMUNITY HALL

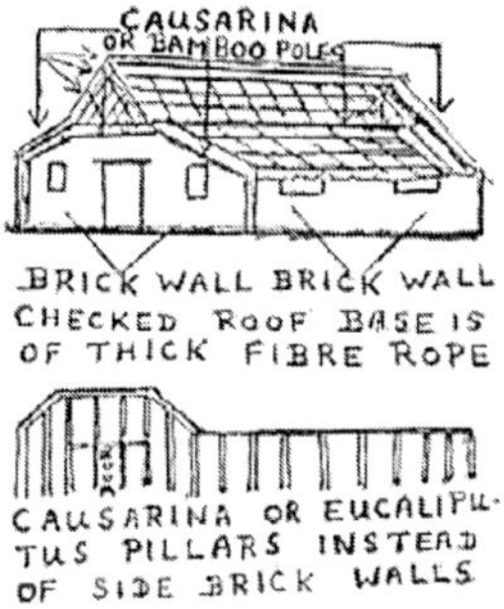

Every village or refugee settlement needs a school cum community hall. Diagram shows a simple and inexpensive school cum community hall which can be built by villagers by their own effort and with locally available raw materials. If some bricks and cement are available the side walls alone may be built of bricks and cement and the roof may be laid with palm or palmyrah leaves. If coconut leaves are available they may be woven and then laid in layers to make the roof.

The roof is designed to be built with the trunk of Causarina or eucaliptus or with straight tree branches. If tree trunks and wood are scarce or costly in the village, fibre ropes of one inch thickness may be tied in a check pattern in the place of wood and the leaves may be laid on them. Bisal or any other fibre that is available in the village may be used.

If bricks and cement are costly and scarce, in the place of side walls in pillars may be laid. Pillar construction will reduce labour and the total cost and will provide more ventilation.

The floor may be rammed with mud and rubbles and raised atleast one foot above ground level.

It is possible to give a school cum community hall of this type to every village; weddings, common functions and festivals may be conducted in these halls and carpentry, tailoring and adult education classes may also be conducted. They can be also used as a common cow-shed but if used as a cow shed it should be used only as a cowshed.

If used as a common hall, poor people who don't have proper ventilation in their house may sleep in this hall. If the village community grows Causarina and eucaliputus and fibre trees and plants the hall can be nut up almost at no cost with free community labour. Self-help is the best help and this must be drilled into the ears of our villagers.

RYFO SHINGLES

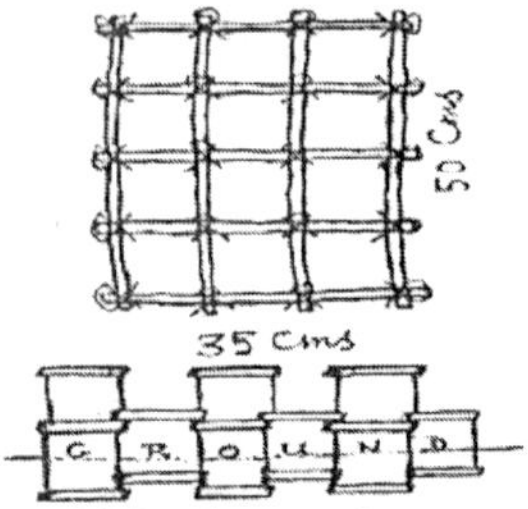

RYFO shingles are made out of used and thrown away cement fertilizer/chemical bags which are made of HDPE or *HDPP bags* (plastic group) Some bags are water proof and for making shingles water-proof bags are required. Bags which are not water-proof should be coated with bitumen (black tar which is spread on road top) (see handout 90).

Sticks, three or four cms. thick of Causarina, eucaliputs. accacia. bamboo, neem, mongamia, vasaka etc may be cut into two uniform lengths - 50 cm and 35 cm and tied with fibre strings into check frames as shown in the diagram. Each frame is inserted into one bag and the bag is heat sealed. Before sealing about quarter kilo of neem leaves or any leaves with insecticidal properties (see handout 112 and 130) may be put into the bag.

On the roof frame-work, also made either out of Causarina, eucaliputs or accacia branches or out of binding wire or used electric wires as shown in handout 173, the bag-and-frame shingles may be arranged like tiles as shown in handout 114.

The same frame tiles may be used also to build walls of huts. They may be buried in horizontal position 40 cms. deep in a row as shown in diagram. A similar parallel wall may be made with a gap of 20 cms between the two walls. In between the parallel walls clay soil may be filled. If clay soil is not readily found spits may be dug for clay as explained in handout No 184. If clay soil is not available in the area, ordinary earth may be mixed with thick starch and other materials and filled (see handout 109).

If necessay the walls may be given a final coat of bitumen after the huts are ready.

RYFO shingles cannot be used as floors but car tyres cut into slabs may be used to make the floor (see handout 1140. Floors made of car tyre slabs are excellent and durable. They can be swabed like mosaic floors and kept clean. Molten bitumen (*tar*) may be used to stick them and the crevices may be filled also with bitumen. If bitumen is not available ordinary clay may be used.

PEANUT BUTTER AND BANANA CAKE
(conversion for preservation)

Peanut Butter: Shell peanuts, roast and cool. While cooling remove thin inner skin. Grind nuts in two stages. During the second stage add two percent salt and five percent vegetable oil by volume. Alternatively, butter or margarine may be added (three table spoons of oil or butter for every cup of peanut). One per cent sugar by volume may also be added into the grinder. The peanut butter is now ready and may be packed in air-tight containers.

All processing may be done conveniently in a domestic electric blender or a small hand-operated mill.

Banana Cakes; six table spoons of milk for every medium size banana. Mash the fruits well, add the milk and also add half cup of sweet potato flour and make a stiff dough. Form into a slab on greesed foil or banana leaf. Bake in slow fire for about 30 mts.

For information on preservation by conversion regarding other items of food, based on appropriate technology, see Handouts 16, 17, 18, 20 to 25 and 55.

THE INDIAN JUJUBE

Botanical: *Zizyphus Mauritiana.*
English: *Indian Jujube* or *Bor.*
Distribution: Throughout India, Pakistan, Bangladesh, Srilanka and many counties with tropical climate.

Description: A prickly tree, that yields edible fruit. The tree does not grow high and has zig-zag branchlets. The leaves are small, elliptical, It is green above and velvety white or brown underneath. The flowers are tiny, greenish and have a thick disc filling their centre. The fruit which is very variable in size, shape and taste is fleshy with a large seed enclosed in a shell.

Uses: The fruit is used mainly for making a sherbet (soft drink) and can also be eatend raw. Jujube gives good timber, excellent fuelwood and it's prickly branches are good for fencing. The leaves are good as fodder and both cows and goats relish the leaves. Many parts of the plant are medicinal. The Tussore and Iri silk-worms are fed with the leaves and the lac insects are reared on the tree. The wood is hard and durable and takes a fine polish. It is commonly used for making agricultural implements, building construction and for making *Persian wheels.*

Fruits of the tree that grow wild in jungles are rather small in size compared to those of trees cultivated but the jungle variety makes better sherbet and soft drinks. Cultivated fruits are bigger in size and also tastier to be eaten raw. The plant grows well in dry and sandy lands and provides fodder for camels in African semi-deserts and the leaves are used as manure in some African countries. Picking the leaves, putting them in bags and transporting them provides employment for the poor.

After removing the bony stone in the centre which contains the seed the fruit can be dehydrated and preserved as such or in honey. The preserved fruits fetch a good price in foreign markets. Pickles and chutney are made from the fruits and also used in cakes and puddings.

Where soil and climatic conditions are not suitable to grow mulberry plants to rear silk-worms Jujube trees may be introduced and cultivated. In some areas both the trees con grow side by side. Mulberry fruits are also edible and make excellent jam.

SUBABUL - DRY-LAND BOON

Botanical: *Leucaena Leucooephala.*

Highly drought resistant, grows under different soil and climatic conditions and needs watering only until the roots spread. It grows very well in black soil with moderate rain fall. A well known leguminous plant (small tree) which fixes atmospheric nitrogen through its roots and builds up fertility of soil. The leaves are used as green fodder and organic manure.

When inter-cropped with food grains like jowar, paddy or maize the food grains are enriched and grow well as the tree does not take away but fixes soil nutrients. The tree prevents soil rrosion and checks flow of rain water.

The succulent green leaves of Subabul contains about 25 percent protein. Seeds soaked in water also have large amount of protein and are mixed with cattle feed but the leaves contain an alkaloid called minosine which is harmful to cattle if eaten in excess. So, the mix of leaves with other feed must be limited to 30 per cent of the whole to cattle 50 per cent to goats. 10 per cent to pigs and rabbits and five per cent only to poultry.

Livestock eat dry leaves also and usually dried leaves are soaked in water and given. But the mimosine content is quite low in dried leaves and therefore, as far as possible fresh green leaves are given to cattle.

Subabul yields about 200 tons of fuel per acre under normal conditions and rich regrowth takes place after every harvesting. The wood gives a high calory of heat and makes excellent charcoal.

If the trees are left to grow for about ten years they give straight tall poles like casuarina or eucaliputs with broad girth and timber can then be used in low-cost housing and for making furniture.

In some African countries the natives use the dry seeds to make "Coffee" and they call the drink "Subee" The tender leaves are also cooked in various forms for its protein contents.

Before sowing, the seeds have to be treated for about 5 mts in very hot water (not boiling) and then soaked in cold water for about 24 hours to soften the tough waxy coat on them. If some soil and root nodules of mature trees are ground and mixed with the seeds they germinate quickly.

If two or three seeds are mixed with equal parts of soil, sand, and compost and filled into small polythene bags with holes and watered every day the saplings appear and grow and they can be transplanted in about three months and planting should be done during the cold or rainy season.

Every farm community should own atleast ten Subabul tree either in their own lands or in waste lands or in no man's property and they should be allowed to enjoy the benefit from these trees. NGOs working in rural parts should bring about this as a movement.

SUNFLOWER IS PROFITABLE

Sunflower plant is highly income generating in rural parts. It is compulsory in India for all vegetable ghee (oil) manufacturers (like dalda) to blend 7.5 percent by Volume of sun flower oil. This Government. order is in view of the fact that sunflower oil reduces cholesterol and heart ailments. The seeds contain more than 30 per cent unsaturated fatty acids (contains lino-letic acid 68 per cent).

Sunflower is a tall drought resistant plant commonly grown in most tropical countries. The big bright yellow flowers look beautiful in the morning sun and the cultivation of the plant is easy. As the main stem is thin and slender it needs support and therefore it is frequently planted along with sugar cane, bananas and grain plants which grow as tall as these. The initial sowing need not be intense as the plant self-propagates itself by the help of wind, birds and breeze.

Compared to ground nuts, Sunflower cultivation is more than four times cheaper and the plant is rarely attacked by pests unlike groundnuts which suffer from nematodes and leaf folder.

Several Hybrid varieties of Sunflowers have been developed in India, the best so far being BSH-I and MSH-I which yield seeds within 100 days after sowing. They are both short, sturdy and drought resistent. Of late a much better variety is being imported into India from Russia for higher yield of oil.

Seeds are sown at intervals of 40 cm so that the tall plants can support each other as they grow up and the sowing is usually done with the onset of monsoon. If watered liberally, weekly watering is enough and organic fertilisers and farm yard manure give good results and therefore chemicals may be totally avoided.

Breeze and bee pollination takes place in a natural way yet, keeping bee hives amidst the cultivation is recommanded for quicker pollination. Honey from Sunflower is considered to be of superior quality and good for heart patients and honey gives additional income to the farmers. Well cared for, a hectare under Sunflower should give about 2,000 kgs of seeds and several oil mills readily buy the seeds. In fact, the seeds and the oil are in short supply everywhere the price keeps rising. Seeds may also be hand-crushed as explained in Handout 209 or expelled in mini-oil mills as shown in handout 210. Crushed seed residues may be mixed with cattle feed or used as farm yard manure. In India several State Ownwed Corporations collect, crush and sell the oil under the brand name *Sunola* but it is better to leave the industry to private initiative and rural communities. NGOs working in rural areas should propagate the best varieties of seeds to give better income for the people.

COCCINIA GRANDIS
(may be called *mini cucumber*)

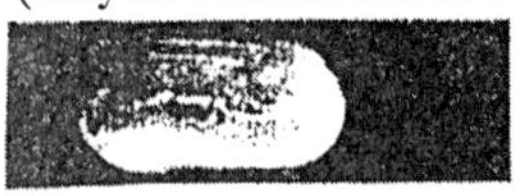

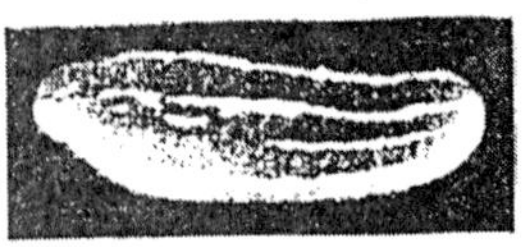

Family: *Cucurbitaceae.*
Hindi: *Kundru.*
Kanada: *Thonde Kai.*
Tamil: *Kovakkai.* Marathi.*Thendle.*
Malayalam: Kavakkai.
Konkani: *Thendle.*

Coccinaia a creaping Vegetable and native of Asia. It is tasty and grows well in different climatic conditions but not nutrtiously rich eventhough it contains a good amount of Vitamin A and C. A favourite vegetables in south Indian homes, it is cooked in various forms and made into pickles and salads. The fairly drought resistant creeper requires warm climate and little water. Usually, the creeper is allowed to spread on fencings and on the roof of thatched huts in villages. Village homes grow the creeper in their backyard on a commercial scale.

Green pods become bright red when ripe and there are three types in Coccinia, namely, the long and slender variety, long and thick variety and the stout and short variety, which is the most common of all.

The fully grown creepers develop nodes and three or four nodes are cut and planted to propagate the plant. They are usually buried in pits of 50cm X 50cm X 50cm with portions of the cutting sticking out of the ground. In each pit two or three cuttings with nodes may be planted.

The pods appear in about 3 months and give plenty of fruits thereafter for two to three years. The creeper grows in different type of soils and usually planted during winter in India. If good organic mulch, cow dung and limited quantities of wood or leaf ash is applied to the soil the yield is better. Water is required only once a week. If adequately manured with mulch, bean leaves and cow-dung it is enough to water the plant once in 10 or 12 days.

A fruit fly makes holes in the ripe red fruits penetrates and makes the fruit non-edible as it produces a gummy substance in the fruits. If flies are noticed the fruits may be sprayed with neem. leaf extract (essence) mixed with jaggery water.

RYFO recommends the growing of Coccinia along with bean plants on fences and thatched roofs by small farm holders.

VINCA ROSEA

Botanical: *Catharanthus Roseus.*

Family: *Apocynaeeae.* Englisn name:*Periwinkle.*

Hindi: *Sadabahar.* Bengali:*Nayantara.*

Tamil: *Nithya Kalyani* or *Sudu Kaatu Malli.*

Malayalam: *Nithya Kalyani* or *Ushamalari* or *Vanapoo.*

Telugu: *Billaganneru or Tirukumalli.*

Kannada: *Turukumallige.* Marathi.*Sada phuli.*

Oria: *Ainskati* and Punjabi: *Rattanjot.*

Highly drought resistant perennial plant with rose or white flowers each having five petals bright and nice to look at. Stem and leaves are green and seeds black and very small. Grows uncared for in waste lands under different climatic and soil conditions in tropical countries upto an altitude of three to four thousand feet above sea level and the plant is not browsed by cattle or attacked by pests.

Seeds are sown or roots are transplanted usually when the rains set in and the soil is wet. If cultivated, watered and managed well the plant blooms better and gives better quality roots but water logging should be avoided.

Main Uses: An alkaloid is extracted from the roots to cure curable cancer. From the leaves also the alkaloid is extracted but the recovery is very low. The well known drugs *Vincristine* and *Vinblastine* are made from this plant and in Indian villages a decoction of the roots is given to diabetes patients and many Indian villagers say that there is no better medicine for diabetes than Vinca Rosea. However, scientifically this has not been established so far.

Since the roots are medicinal, no chemical fertilizers but only organic manure and cow-dung should be used in cultivation. Seeds may be mixed with river sand and neem oil-cake or dried cow dung (all in equal parts by volume) and sowed. About three Kg of such seed mixture can cover about one acre of land. After about three months the saplings will have to be transplanted with intervels of 30 cms between two plants.

Before pulling out the plants the roots should be soaked in water to get all the roots out and the pulling out easy and they may be pulled out in about 6 months after the sowing of the seeds. While the roots will have to be dried in hot sun the leaves will have to be dried under shade.

In 1988, the roots fetched Rs15 per Kg in India and well dried leaves Rs five per Kg. Export price varied from country to country and there is a rising demand for the roots from USA and Europe, especially, from Germany. A few million dollars worth of roots are exported from India and Africa every year and the entire growing, collection and supply is done by poor villagers living in remote areas.

NEW STRAINS OF MULBERRY

Mulberry is propagated by cuttings from healthy mother plants which are nearly a year old. The diameter of the cuttings should be about a centimeter and the length about 20 cms. They should be planted in prepared pits of 30 cubic centimetre and the distance between two pits must be about a centimeter. Four cuttings may be planted in the middle of each pit in a square fashion with a gap of about 15 cms between them. Plenty of farm yard manure must be used in the pits and some neem leaves may be mixed with the manure.

The first harvesting of leaves is done on the sixth month and the second, three months thereafter. There can be a third harvest three months after the second. During a year over 6,000 kgs of leaves can be picked and transported in wet gunny bags or baskets.

After three harvests the plants should be pruned before the onset of rains. The stem must be cut with a sharp knife about 20 cms above ground to get a healthy yield during the second year. At this stage weeding, ploughing, manuring and watering must be done. Plenty of from yard manure must he applied after preparing the bed.

During the second year,picking of leaves must be done on the tenth week of pruning. Subsequently seven or eight pickings may be done at intervals of eight weeks.

The Central Sericultural Research and Training Institute *(CSRTI)* at Mysore, India, have developed three high yielding strains of Mulberry and they have labled them S13, S14 and S34. It is reported that these varieties yield nearly 20 tonnes of leaves per ha. in one year. These varieties are now popular in South India and will have to be taken to other tropical countries both for silk worms and for paper making. Mulberry gives employment and a living wage for women and children. For 451 the method of paper making out of Mulberry, see Handouts 450 of 451.

SEA-WATER PLANTS

Botanical: *Zostera Marina.* Family: *Potamogetonaceae.* English name: *eelgrass.* Native of Northern hemisphere, this flowering plant grows fully submerged in sea water. Ripe grains break-loose and float and drift to the shore and can be harvested. The plant holds potential to be grown as a food crop in tropical estuaries. People of the West coast of Mexico are known to separate the fruit from the grain, dry and powder the grain and prepare porridge and other food items. Chemical analysis reveal that the starch and protein content of the grain is rich.

The leaves of eelgrass look very much like pine apple leaves but much longer and broader and have no thorns on either sides. Therefore the leaves are used as fodder and for thatching huts. There are certain other varieties of this plant which have very broad and long leaves and give bigger fruits and more grain. This is a plant on which much research has to be done before propagation for human benefit.

SALTBUSBES:

Botanical: name of one variety is a Atriplex Nummularia and that of the other is a *Atriplex halimus.* Family *Ghenopdiaceae.*

This is also a very highly salt resistant plant and grows in sea water, though not submerged in sea-water. It is an ever-green saline soil plant that grows all over the world under different climatic conditions. They usually flourish on shores that are washed by sea water and the leaves, which are not thorny, are relished by sheep. This plant has been introduced on a large scale in Israel, Tunisia and North Africa from South America. Of the two varieties Atriplex halimus is especially highly salt tolerant and grows well in sea-water. The plants grow to a height of more than one meter in about two years when they are harvested.

(Information culled out from the book *'Under Exploited Tropical Plants with Promising Economic Value'* published by the National Academy of Sciences, USA).

MELONS BRING MONEY

Melons include a family of fruits including muskmelon, watermelon, snapmelon. Long melon, round-melon. All melons have plenty of vitamin A minerals and carbohydrates. They belong to the Cucurbitaceae family and are either creepers or vines. These fruits are mostly grown in summer but roundmelon and snap-melon are also grown in rainy season. All melons require a warm and dry climate, sandy-loam soil and good sun-shine. Duration of crop is between 80 and 100 days depending on the variety.

Seeds are sown directly and not transplanted and sowing is done as the rains or cold weather sets in. Before sowing the soil is tilled and made friable and plenty of farm yard manure is given. Weeds must be completely removed till the plants start vining and weeding may be done once a fortnight.

Only longmelons and roundmelons are harvested when they are tender and raw (immature) All other varieties are harvested only when they are ripe and turn yellow. Watermelon is quick in maturing and takes only about 40 days.

Recommanded varieties for tropical countries

1. *Asahi Yamata*: native of Japan now introduced into several countries. Large fruits weigh about Seven kgs or more and the outer colour is light green while the inner flesh is deep red or pinkish red. The fruit is very adaptive to different soils. In Tamil Nadu, the fruit is called *Darboose*.

2. *New Hampshire Midget*: Native of USA. Small size and weighs only about two Kg and the shape is oval. Outside colour is light green and inside flesh is red. Takes 30 days to mature from the date of pollination and it is ideal for home gardens.

3. *Sugar baby*: Also native of USA. Round medium size fruits weigh about five Kgs. This variety also takes a full month to ripen and the colour of flesh is red.

4. *Arkat Jeet*:- Native of India. Ripens in 90 days. Outer colour is yellowish orange and medium size fruits weigh about 600 gms. Tastes very sweet and contains high percentage of Vitamin C.

5. There are others which belong to hybrid variety such as Arka Jyoti and Push Bedana, both Indian. Being hybrid it is difficult to get their parent seeds for propagatlon.

Most varieties of the melon family cross polynate by wind, bees and birds excepting watermelon and roundmelon. Therefore, different varieties of melons should not be grown together as they would cross polynate and the varieties will be contaminated and lose their specific appearance and taste.

Melon seeds may be dried in the sun and when well dried sown directly in prepared and manured beds for best results.

MANGROVES AND THEIR USES

Mangroves are trees belonging to a particular species which adopt themselves remarkably to conditions created by tidal backwaters. Their roots spread in all directions to get a firm hold in the loose ground that is washed every day by the saline sea water waves. Mangroves need hot and humid climate and sloping shores and Mangrove forests are many and dense in East and West Africa and Madagascar. There is a dense growth between Senegal and Gabon and in these areas 15 to 20 tonnes of excellent bio-mass is formed by their litter in one hectare per year. Mangrove trees are of soft wood and the branches break easily.

Employment Potentialities

1. Fishing, fish-meal, fish oil, fish fertillser, fish-paste, etc.
2. Acquaculture, including shrimp and oyster cultivation and growing mushrooms.
3. Forestry for fuel wood, charcoal, furniture, honey and bee's wax.
4. Salt in pans by boiling the sea water using dried mangrove wood for fuel. Cattle lick-salt may also be made.
5. Rice growing in the neighbourhood if there is a river or good rain fall in the area. On the fringes of Mangrove forests the soil is rich and nitrogenous.

6. Mining of iron ore and bauxite as done in Cote d'lvoire in Africa.
7. Sinking petroleum wells in the area as done in Nigeria and Cameroon.
8. Making bricks out of the clayey sediment soil. If the soil is good clay unburnt bricks may be made in Cinva rams. If not clayey they will have to be burnt using dried mangrove wood and twigs along with dried leaves.
9. Low-cost houses out of the timber and twigs (RYFO Shingles).
10. Making road-side plant gaards out of mangrove tree branches.
11. Making compost out of the litter from the forests.
12. The leaves of some species may be given to cattle as fodder.
13. The foliage of Mangrove is fine for making briquettes and for burning in '*Stovel*' pumps.
14. Medicinal properties of mangroves have not so far been investigated.

KHUSKHUS OR *VETIVER*

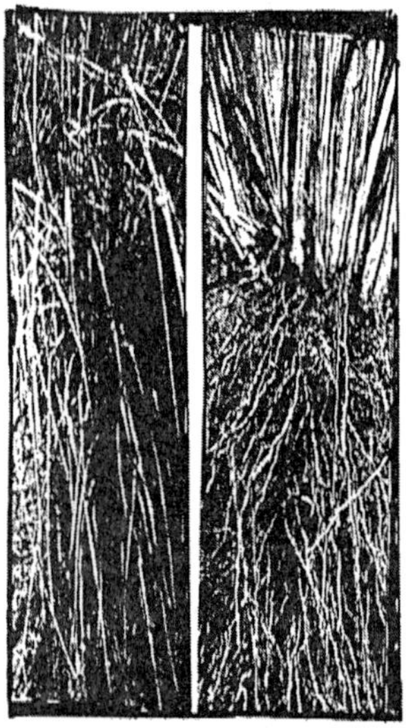

Botanical: *Vetlveria Zizanioides.* South Indian languages: Vetiver.

Grass with thick broad blades growing to a height of more than a meter. Grass blades are spongy without thorns. Dense matty roots spread deep and wide and gives a fine smell when removed from the ground and crushed. It is highly a drought resistant grass uncared for and shoot out luxuriously during rainy season and stay unnoticed during summer. Villagers weave the roots and make window blinds and when water is splashed on the blinds they retain the water for a long time and blow cool and fragrant breeze into the rooms. An essential oil is extracted from the roots which is used in cents, soaps, cleaning liquids and some medicinal ointments.

As the grass grows dense with tufted clumps it holds the soil and helps the soil to absorb rain water. In recent years it is being recommended by the FAO and the World Bank for conserving soil from erosion. Propagated by root strips the grass grows well in different soils and very well in marshy lands. Usually nurseries are raised in river banks and tank bunds. Bunches of roots are planted in raised beds prepared with farm-yard manure and the weeds removed every fortnight. If weeds are not removed regularly seperating Vetiver roots from the weed roots will be a problem.

Vetiver is not attacked by pests and diseases and rodents which don't like it's smell keep away from it. The grass is not browsed by cattle, goats or sheep. Surprisingly, the dried grass does not catch fire easily.

The best time to plant the grass is before the onset of rains. Planting of the tillers (bunches of the roots) in beds must be done repeatedly for two or three years and then the roots hold on for self propagation. After 18 months the grass gives high quality roots which contain under normal conditions, one percent oil which is usually steam distilled by the village process or in the simple distiller shown in Handout No 7.

For removing, the top grass is cut 15 cms from ground level and then with a digging fork the roots are uprooted from a depth of about 20 cms along with the clumps. It is important to collect the roots with the clumps. The left-out roots and clumps will shoot again. Roots and clumps which are thick, hard, dry and yellow contain a higher percentage of oil. From a hectare about five tonnes of clean washed roots can be taken when the grass is about 18 months old. If watered and given organic manure the yield of roots and oil will be better.

PROFITS FROM MULBERRY

If mulberry gardens are watered regularly, manured and taken care of, one acre will give the owner leaves five times a year and he or his village community can rear 2,000 laying silk worm eggs. Approximately, this will give 450 kgs. of cocoons in one year. In the Government. of India cocoon market a kg, fetches Rs 30 in India or say, US $ 3 (1908 price). This gives a gross income of about Rs. 12,000 (about US$ 1,000) per acre. The cost of eggs, leaf and labour will be about Rs 4,000 After giving allowance for disease and damage we may recover Rs 7,000 net profit per year.

Sericulture is very labour intensive and it is an ideal village industry, especially, as side income for women and children. One acre of mulberry can generate employment for five women for 300 days in a year upto the stage of weaving. The weaving industry can empoyy many more. Before the weaving stage only Rs 600 is required to employe one woman which is so low and attractive. Moreover the risk of failure in the industry is almost nil unless the mulberry plants are attacked by pests.

Raw silk from India has a tremendous export market eventhough China, Japan and Korea are already exporting large quantities of raw silk to different countries. All these three countries produce silk in their own countries with appropriate technology, Japan, the largest producer of raw silk in the world is also the largest importer of raw silk.

India exports about 40 crores (400 millions) Rupees worth of silk and silk good every year, (1988 figures) and most of it is in the form of handloom fabrics. To increase the export India must replace its native variety of silk called *Mulivltines* by the international variety called *Bivoltine.* All Third world countries which try to introduce silk in their country should straight away import the *Bivoltine* variety from China or Japan and make a beginning. Parts of tropical countries which have a little lower temperature have excellent potentialities for silk even though the industry has been quite successful also in the warmer parts as demonstrated and proved in the state of Tamil Nadu in South India. But the fact remain that in an elevated place or a cool place and in slopes or hillocks mulberry plants thrive well and the productivity in the industry is more.

Indian silk sarees, scarfs, ties and cushion cases are now popular all over the world and the market is steadily rising.

Several biproducts can be made out of the cocoon shells and they fetch fancy price both in India and abroad. The empty cocoon shell is a good raw material for making handicrafts and novelties. Jams made out of mulberry fruits are common and nutritious.

TREE TRUNK THEATRE

Entertainment is an essential part of education and community life, especially in remote villages cut away from transport and communication. Audio education is cheap and possible by Transister and radio but visual entertainment is what villagers. especially children, like to enjoy. Local schools, church or social groups can train children and arrange for skits, dialogues. dance, and skill demonstration but to do this a small open-air theatre or stage is required in a convenient location where all the community can meet.

The Picture shows a Tree Trunk Theatre which gives a clear idea about the way it must be built. In a prominent and convenient location, two or three trees standing in a row side by side may be selected and a stage built there using the trunks as the rear wall. The gap between the trees may be partly blocked with poles and fibre ropes and or plastic sacks leaving only a door-like opening for the actors to enter in and out from the rear.

The stage is built by dumping stones and rubbles available in the village and covered with clayey soil and then with common earth mixed with fibre and twigs and rammed at every stage as it rises. Casuarina, bamboo or palmyrah tree trunks may be planted as pillars to mark the four corners of the stage. Thinner pillars may be planted in a row inbetween the 4 pillars to make a boundry line fence for the stage.

With such a fencing filling the middle portion with rubble and rubbish, stones and sand will be easy. If the poles parallel to the ground are closely arranged and lined with jute sacks or used cement or fertilizer bags, the walls of the stage will be strong and during heavy rains the sand inside will not be washed out. Dimentions of the stage be 6M X 5M and one Mt. high. If the boundry walls are strong and the "fillers" used to raise the stage is rammed well it will make a fine stage where the community can gather not only for entertainment but also for programmes and prayers.

As an alternative, to building a fenced wall eight heaps of rubbles, pebbles, sand and stone may be made in two parallel rows, of four heaps in each row, and after they are well set the middle portions may be filled and hardened to make a table like a stage.

TREE MONUMENTS

Many people all over the world, especially Christians and Muslims, build monuments in brick and mortor or marble and granite to honour and remember their near and dear ones, who are dead and gone. Tree, Lovers Clubs have innovated something in the place on tomb and that is, planting a beautiful flowering tree in memory of the dead in a "Memory Park"

If you pay a fixed sum to the Park you can plant one sapling of your choice and the management will water and look after it. The name, dates of birth and death of the deseased will be displayed on the plant guard and transferred to the tree when it grows up. If you like you may fix the symbol of your religion on the tree and this will help all religious sentiments to co-exist inside the park.

Every year on the death anniversary of your loved one you will get a colour photo of the tree which will be sent also to whomever you want it to be sent witha a suitable prayer.

You are free to visit the tree anytime and pray to God for the dead and also sit and relax and distribute sweets to children and food or clothes to the poor

Some clubs plant trees also to mark happy events in parks called "HAPPY PARKS" – events such as births, marriage, promotion, anniversary etc. In both cases the idea is not only to grow trees, improve ecology, make you think of the dead ones and pray to God but also to disuade people from wasteful and vulgar spending on big ceremonies and large gatherings.

The Smrita Vatika Society has a 15 acre plot in Delhi city for this purpose. for a remittance of Rs 1,150 (about US $ 100) you plant and they look after the tree for good until the tree has a natural death. Usually people select trees which their grand-children can see. The grandchildren, if they like, may plant other trees in It's place to perpetuate the memory.

Everybody likes to have happy parks to plant trees to mark happy events. Let there be a call by the Tree Project Wing of the United Nations (or the General Assembly) to the International Community to promote Happy Parks and one day in the year may be declared as the Happy Parks day for all those who own trees in these parks to gather and rejoice birthdays and anniversaries. And this will be one sure way of getting people together for a better ecology.

SAKTHI SOYA'S SEED SERVICE

Sakthi Soyas Limited is a Joint Sector undertaking with TIDCO (Tamil Nadu Industrial Development Corporation). Their registered office address is 180 Race Course Road, P.B. No.3841, Coimbatore - 641 018, Tamil Nadu, India.

Sakthi Soyas render all help for taking up soya bean cultivation in the State of Tamil Nadu. They supply the required quality seeds at Rs 5.27 per kg (as on October. 19). The seeds supplied are cleaned, graded, treated the required fungicide and bacterial culture and packed in five kg cloth bags and the cost of treatment and packing is included in the price quoted (Rs 5.17 per kg in Coimbatore).

Soya bean can be cultivated as a lean crop or intercropped with coconut, rubber, tapioca, sugarcane, cotton etc. About 12 kgs are required for sole sowing and about seven kgs for intercrop sowing.

Sakthi Soyas give an undertaking that the entire produce grown by the farmers will be purchased by them at Rs 3.75 per kg (October 1988 price) on the spot of growing and the actual cost or freight charges from the field to Pollachi (Coimbatore District) will be borne by them full cultivation details will be sent by them on request.

All those NGOs or private agencies who want to introduce Soya cultivation in their area for promoting income generating activities may roughly calculate the seed requirements and send a bank draft taken in the name of Sakthi Soyas Ltd payable at Coimbatore.

For large scale or collective operations undertaken by registered or recognised private agencies, bank assistance may be obtained. If a written proposal is submitted with details of income and expenditure and repayment, banks will be happy to finance projects, especially when they know that the recommending agency takes the responsibility of supervising the cultivation, collection and recovery and repayment.

Soya is excellent for soil, oil, health and income and has several uses. For more about protein rich and nitrogen fixing Soya, see Handout 158.

MORE ABOUT SOYABEAN

Protein-rich soyabean which helps enrich the soil with nitrogen loaded root nodules is an excellent cash crop for tropical countries and the variety called CO-1 developed in Coimbatore thrives well in countries with South Indian climate. The legume which yields in 90 days is very adaptable and can be grown as a sole crop or intercropped with bananas, sugarcane, grapes, paddy, cerals, etc. Marginal farm holders and families living near uncared for government lands can grow Soya and Soya can be grown also on field bunds for additional income. CO-1 is highly resistant to drought, pests and diseases, has better and more oil and protein and gives better Soya flour. This improved variety also flowers profusely and matures uniformly.

If only Soya is planted about 40 kg. of seeds are required to cover two acres while for intercropping about 20 kg and for field bund planting about seven kgs per acre are required. Bund crop will yield about 100 kgs of seeds per acre.

To eliminate seed-borne pathogens, the seeds may be dipped in water mixed with ground neem leaf (ground like chutney) and dried in hot sun for a day. The seeds are usually planted to a depth of 2.5 cm, 40 cm apart, in a row and 20 cms apart between rows. Every 15th day the seeds or saplings must be watered with neem water solution. Under good climatic conditions and care an acre should yield about one tonne of beans. A week after harvest the second sowing can start and crops can be grown throughout the year excepting in the months of October and November. It will be good to plant some other crop during October, November, and December, to retain soil fertility.

Fully matured plants will shed all leaves and at that stage they should be cut at ground level leaving the nitrogen fixing modules undisturbed. The pods and stalks are dried well and threshed by beating with sticks or in an Appropriate Technology thresher.

The leaves make excellent mulch for sugar-cane crops and in a single row intercroping of sugar cane at least 300 kgs of Soyabean can be harvested per acre and over 500 kgs in double row planting. It is reported that when sugar cane and Soya are intercropped the cane yield goes up by about ten percent.

THE COMMON PEA

Botanical: Pisum. Sativuml. Family. Papilionaceae.

Native of Europe now grows well in several countries including tropical countries. Several local strains have developed in every country and exotic varieties are also seen. It is a cold/mild weather plant with a vining habit and grows wild on the hills and in the plains during winter. In the tropics, It is adoptive to different cold clitmates and soil composition. The common pea is rich in vitamin A and C, carbohydrates and protein.

The pea can be grown in flat or raised beds and can either be broadcast or sown behind the plough to a depth of about three cm, and about 60 to 80 kgs of seeds are required per hectare depending on the size of the seed. The wrinkled seeds may be soaked overnight in water before sowing for better germination.

The early varieties produce less - about 30 Q/ha while the medium variety produces about 60 Q/ha and the late varieties produce about 100 Q/ha. The common pea cannot be kept for more than a week in room temperature and therefore it is advisable to sun dry or otherwise dehydrate it soon after picking.

There are four improved varieties of the *common pea*, namely, Arkel, Early Badger, Bonneville. and Meteor. The Arkel, taken to other countries from Europe, is sweet with good pod quality and can be harvested throughout the third month of sowing.

The Early Badger, introduced from the United States of America is a small variety with wrinkled seeds (the plant is small in height). The pods are quite big and tasty. The Meteor, which was spread from England is a round seeded early variety and the Bonneville, a tall prolific bearer is also a native of America. The pods of this are about seven cm long and can be picked throughout the fourth month from the month of sowing. This wrinkle-seeded variety grows well in most parts of India where the soil and climate are favourable. It is advisable to go in for the Bonneville pea cultivation to give food and employment for the poor.

Several tasty dishes can be prepared out of dehydrated peas and there was a time when a multinational had flooded the Indian market with dehydrated peas under the brand name 'HEMA'. Dehydrated ones can easily be reconstituted by boiling and they can be given also to chicken and cattle. Even pigs relish them and the pea leaf is a good fertilizer for pea plants.

BAMBOO SHINGLES

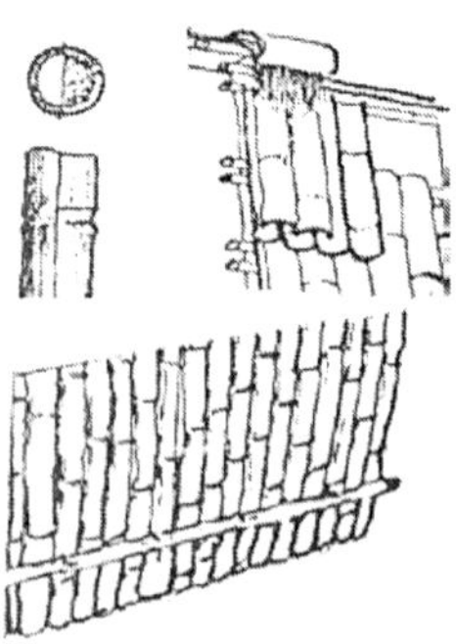

Bamboo of the grass family is the fastest growing grass in the world reaching a height of 20 to 25 meters and an average diameter of 15 cms above the roots. They can be cut to convenient sizes to build low cost houses and excellent roof, can be built(laid) with them. First the bamboo is cut to pieces notch-to-notch and the cylindrical pieces split lengthwise into two halves to be arranged like Roman tiles (or Indian country tiles) as shown in the diagram. at the eaves (the overhanging lower edge of the roof) a batten with a bigger diameter may be fixed to serve as a gutter.

The four pillars and the roof frame-work may all be built with bamboo but it is better to build the four corner pillars with rammed and sun-dried bricks and to use Casurina or eucaliputs trunks to make the frame of the roof. However, six to 10 cm bamboo sticks and smaller poles may be added to the casurina and eucaliputs to make the frame.

The bamboo tiles need not be nailed for laying excepting here and there to prevent them from sliding and only two cm long nails may be used as longer ones may crack the bamboo. For grip, the best is to use mortar mixture and after laying the side curves and crevices may be filled with mortar.

Before the tiles are arranged on the frame-work plastic sheets. agrifilm or used cement or fertliser sacks may be spread on the frame. The plastic lining will not only make the laying easy but will also prevent leaks during rains.

Bamboo tiles may also be used to build side walls of houses as shown in the diagram. When used for side walls the inward curved portion of the tiles will have to be filled with mortar after fixing or planting in the ground. If necessary two rows of walls may be raised parallel to each other with a 15 cm gap in between and the gap filled with mortar. The portion of the bamboo which goes into the ground may be coated with tar (bitumen) if available or with a semi-liquid paint made out of ground neem leaf, chillie and tarmeric. Alternatively, they may be painted with waste engine-oil or castor oil to keep away white ants.

If desired, the bamboo walls may be plastered with mortar on either side (inside and outside) Excellent low-cost houses can be built with bamboo walls and fibre roofs explained in handout 271.

FIBRE/STRAW ROOF

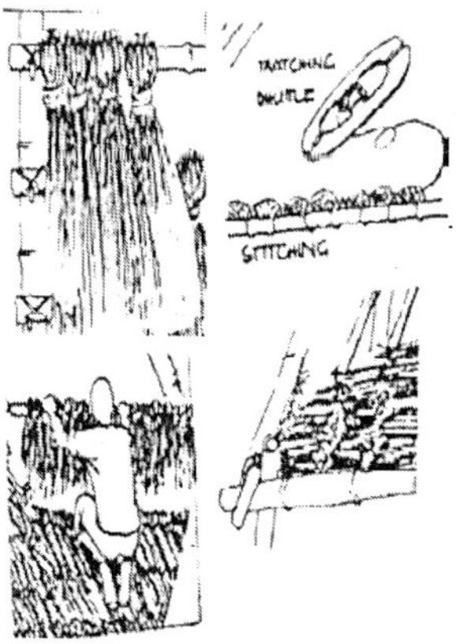

Paddy straw, "Korai" grass and all types of fibre are the cheapest and most easily available materials for low-cost rural housing and they are traditionally used in several countries. Some fibre yielding plants and trees are listed in Handout 167 and some simple ways of extracting fibre are explained in handout 156, Paddy straw or fibre (or both together) may be combed with one's own fingers and got into uniform bunches and tied on to the roof frame-work as shown in the diagram. It is not necessary to make the entire roof frame—work with bamboo or Casurina poles.

Well twisted 6 cm fibre ropes can be tied to make checks on four strong pillars and a square pole frame (only the four sides) and the fibre bunches laid on the network.

If a big plastic sheet or agrifilm is available it may be spreadout first on the top square frame and then the network tied on top of it. Alternatively, used and thrown away cement or fertiliser bags may be stiched together and used. The plastic lining will prevent rain water penetrating the roof.

Two cm thick fibre ropes may be used to tie the bunches to the framework and the ropes can be easily twisted in villages with available fibre. The spun ropes may be rolled in wooden shuttles as shown in the diagram to make work easy.

When the entire roof is laid and tied to stay extra ropes may be taken over the roof and tied frame to frame in a cris-cross fashion to prevent breeze lifting.

Straw and fibre ropes do not last long as they are eaten by moths. To prevent this and to preserve them for five to six years they may be soaked in in big oil drums or a cemented garden tub in a semi-liquid solution of neem-leaf, chillie and turmeric or in any other paste-solution of leaves listed in handout 112. and 130 having insecticide properties.

If a hard roof is wanted a semi-liquid mortar solution may be sprinkled on top of the fibre roof and allowed to set and harden.

INSTANT LIME JUICE & FACE CREAM

Common kitchen lime grows well in most tropical countries and in several areas there is an over production making cultivation uneconomical. The solution is to find better and more uses for the fruit. Teaching people to make instant lime juice is an excellent way of promoting lime and stabilising the price.

Take a full size empty bottle (750 ml), wash with boiling water or with rain water and dry it in sun. Get the bottles ready first.

Wash 15 large size lime dry, cut and squeeze the juice. Your hand must be perfectly dry. Squeezing in a wooden or aluminium squeeze is advisable. Filter the juice in a clean, dry strainer and transfer the Juice into a bottle (15 limes juice in each bottle). Then fill the bottle with white sugar upto the neck and fix the lid and put the bottle in the sun. You may add a pinch of salt for taste before closing. Expose the bottle to sun light for three weeks or leave it in the open terrace. The white sugar will obsorb the juice and turn brownish and in about two weeks the entire sugar will turn into a thick brown syrup. Your job is over and now the lime is ready for instant use. You have only to mix two table spoons of it to a glass of water and serve. The drink is not only delicious but also nutritious and contains plenty of vitamin C.

If you wish, you may squeeze 30 fruits, add some modern sweetener (used by diabetic patients) and produce a more concentrated syrup in which case one spoon full will be adequate to mix a glass. But it is better to avoid anything syn. thetic. Down with synthetics.

The instant juice can be kept for about a year and does not need repression but it is advisable to expose the bottle to bright sun once a week. Lime, sugar, salt and sunlight all act as preservatives and no additional preservatives are required. Instant lime juice can be supplied to canteens, hotels, ships, railways, airways, and wayside shops in bulk quantities at half the cost of synthetic stuff now in the market and the profits on the industry will be atleast 50 per cent on the total investment after meeting all expenses. Profits will be more if more juice is made during lime season and kept in store for off season sale (the author recently commissioned a semi-commercial unit for a poor community living on the hill slopes in Andhra and the industry is fast picking up and the price of lime cultivated by be community is stabilising).

Don't throw away the skin as useless. Dry it chop and powder it, add equal quantity of tinned milk-powder, green gram powder (Mung bean) and ten neem leaf powder, make paste with water and apply on your face to keep it cool, fresh, fair, wrinkle-free and lovely. Most of the face cosmetics contain lime skin.

Give the seeds to chicken which like them or roast, grind and add them to neem-leaf tooth powder explained in Handout 89.

If you mix half glass of instant lime juice to half glass of preserved sugar-cane juice explained in Handout 102 you will get an excellent soft punch, plsohinstant. There is money in lime. Cash it. Medical science reports that line skin taken in any form fights cancer.

KATDAMANI FERTILISER

Kettamani (Botanical: *Iipomea Cornea*) is an ever green perinial shrub which grows wild and uncared for in many Third Countries in barren lands. It looks like a crotten with broad and bright green leaves and not attacked by white ants or browsed by cattle. Therefore farmers plant them to mark their field boundry and prevent cattle straying in. The leaves which supply micro-nutrients and preserve soil fartility are used, from time immemorial, as organic manure, in green or dry form but green form gives better results.

Thick branches of the shrub cut and planted also where daring rainy season watered for a month if dry saason take roots and grow fast (the author has planted them in his garden to experiment on their growth and survival and propagated the shrub in several countries).

The leaves make best manure if plucked once in 6 or 7 weeks when still tender and directly burnled in crop lands or put into compost pits or tanks and used when required.

Calotropis suganha (*Krukkam* in Tamil and *Muddar* in Hindi) and *Adhatoda Vasica Nees* (*Adhatoda* or *Yasaka* in South Indian languages) are other two similar shrubs with more or less similar properties that grow wild in villages with dry climatic conditions. See Handout 230 for more about *Vasaka.*

A mixture of the leaves of these three shrubs and neem leaves all in equal parts have proved to be not only excellent fertiliser but also an effective insecticide. If it the mixture is conposed with an addition of some cow-dung in an above-ground-level compose tub as explained in handout 229 to make the soil rich and productive.

For generating employment ATIC international advisee unemployed villagers to dry the leaves and grind them into granules by the village methods, pack in used cement or fertiliser bags or village made fibre bags and sell them to local farmers to replace harmful chemical fertilisers and also sell in open markets.

Other organic fertilisers listed in handout 168 may also be mixed. The mixing and packing is a remunerative job oriented village industry for a family living on wage.

The stem and sticks of all the shrubs mentioned above are ideally suited for building low-cost houses and they are explained in the Ryan Foundation booklet, Shelter From Village Materials. These stems and sticks are strong available free and are not attacked by white-ants.

There are many farms in several countries today using only organic manure and having high yields. Gloria Land in Pondicherry in South India is a striking example and we need more and more farmers to take to organic manures in preference to factory made chemical fertilisers. Down with chemical fertilisers for economy, better soil and better health of the people.

EDIBLE OIL FROM KOKAM

Botanical: *Garcinia Indian.* Marathi: *Brindonia.*

Kannada: *Murugals.* Hindi: *Kokas.*

English: *Kangosteen oil tree* (this is different from the Mangosteen fruit tree botanically called *Garcinia Mangostana*).

The Kokam tree, which contains plenty of seeds has not been exploited in several countries and very few prople know this tree which is common in peninsular India. The pulp of the fruit is medicinal and has industrial uses. The trunk resembles the girth of a Papaya (*popos*) tree but with some branches.

ie. it is tall, errect and slender and grows to a height of about ten meters. The branches droop like those of a Christmas tree and the dark green leaves are oblong and six to nine cm long. Flowers are polygamous with four petals and the fruits which are about 3.5 cm in diameter are globose and each fruit contains about six seeds, and has a sweetish taste, pungent, somewhat like vinegar. The recovery of oil from the seeds is about 25 per cent and the oil is called not as Kokam oil but as Kukam butter and it is used in the preparation of skin ointments. In some countries and in some parts of India, people use it as a cooking media. The outer rind is used for preparing beverages and the juice of the fruit is used in dyeing. The mongosteen oil is rich in a combination of stearic and oleic acids. The butter of Kokas is used as confectionary butter and in the manufacture of candles, cosmetics and soaps.

The tree is hardy and drought, resistent and grows in different types of soils but takes a long time to grow and about ten years to yield fruits, seeds and oil. This perhaps is the reason for not commercialising it in many countries.

Botanists recommend to sow the seeds, and grow some saplings first and when the saplings are about two years old graft them to well grown end yielding trees, in about eight month time the grafted trees integrate with each other and the baby trees get full nourishment and support from the mother tree. After a year the small tree can be separated from the big tree and planted in a flower pot or plastic bag and nurtuted for about three months and then transplanted in the field.

Kokam is a tree to be promoted in wastelands and tank bunds and villagers have to be educated about the tree and the useful edible oil it gives. The tree holds tremandous employment potentialities with negligible investment and NGOs in third countries must turn their attention to this tree. Further research has to be done on various other possible uses of the tree. the fruits, the roots, the leaves, the oil the bark etc.

BITTER GOURD OR BITTER CUCUMBER

Botanical *Momordica Charantia.*

Sanskrit *Kaaravella.* Hindi *Kerala.*

Malayalam *Paval.* Tamil Pava Kai.

Description: A climbing creeper with yellow flowers, native of many tropical countries. Though bitter, it is a popular vegetable. Fruits are about 25 cms long and about Six cms broad. They are green when raw and bright yellow when ripe. Turns orange red when allowed to over ripe. The outer skin is more bitter than the inner flesh. Leaves, fruits, seeds, roots are all medicinal. Grows wild in China, Malaysia, Philippines, Caribbean, Sri Lanka and India. In all these countries people take bitter gourd in various forms to control sugar (diabetes).

Medicinal: Fruits which are stomachic pain help relieve gout, rheumatism, spleen and liver trouble. Easily digestible, it also relieves constipation. The vegetable, seeds in particular, contain hypoglycaemic or insuline - like active ingredient called "plant insulin" and tests on patients have established that it lowers sugar level in blood and wine without side effects. Diabetic patients are advised to dry the seeds, powder it and take it regularly. It is claimed that bitter gourd, does not substitute the work of the pancreas glands but strengthens the gland to function better. The most important nutrient needed by diabetic patients is manganese which is required to produce natural insulin. Manganese is found in Citrus fruits and green edible spinach). Bitter gourd is rich in Vitamins A, B, B2, C and iron and help relieve hypertension and build up general body resistance. In India it is now being completely dehydrated and powdered.

A spoonful of juice from the leaves or powder mixed with a glass of butter milk relieves piles; boils and scabies. The juice can also be mixed with lime juice, tomato, carrot or any fruit juice for that matter. The juice of the roots of bitter gourd mixed with the juice of the roots of Holy Sasil (Thulasi) in equal proportion and taken with honey helps resperatory disorder and liver trouble due to alcoholism.

Bitter gourd is so bitter, that it is difficult to eat it. In powder form it is difficult to swallow. An easy way of taking the powder it to put it into geletine capsules and swallow the capsule. But capsules are machine-made and expensive for the rural poor. Ryan foundation which promotes these native medicines for Villagers without depending on imports and taxable raw materials recommends that the powder be converted into pellets as explained in Handout 501. In Pellet form it is easy to swallow and can be taken regularly along with meals.

Ref:

(1) Diet cure for common ailments.

(2) Health the Natural way.

(3) Foods that Heal - all authored by H.K. Bakhru and published by Orient Paper Back and Jaico Publishing House.

GUINEA GRASS

Botanical: *Panicum maximum*.

Family: *gramineae*.Hindi.*Ginighas*.

This is a drought resistant grass, which grows to a height of nearly Three mts. with dense and perennial growth forming short and stout root stocks in well drained soils. It needs barely 40 to 60 inches railfall. When animals graze the surface grass it grows again and it's dense and deep fibrous roots help to consolidate the soil. During very dry summers, the grass fades and whithers but picks up life when the climate changes with a few drops of rain. Seeds shatter by wind and take root but if collected, dried stored for about four months and then sowed the results are excellent. It is advisable to sow dry seeds once a year as the rains set in and about 10 kgs of seed are required for one hectare.

The grass combines with lucerns, and perennial legumes such as centrosema pubescenis, Desmanthus Virgatus and Desmodium species and grows well under coconut trees and saline soil. The grass is grown all over India especially in South India.

Some scientists claim that the guinea grass is better than the *Napier grass* because Napier grass contains Oxalic acid which the guinea grass does not have. The Guinea grass is rich in protein and dry matter easy to digest. It can be propagated both by seeds and root cuttings. Since the collecting of seeds is difficult, usually root cuttings are transplanted and once in three or four years from other fields, and planted with a spacing of 30 cms between two transplantation and 60 cms between rows. If seeds are used they may be transplanted in about a month from the date of sowing.

Two to three days after planting, the transplanted grass must be watered once and thereafter once a week for four weeks. Farm yard manure, cow dung and kitchen, waste may be applied during the first month and after each harvest, Sewerage waste may be led into the field if possible. Now and again weeding must be done and the grass may be first harvested two months from the date of planting and thereafter every month. Harvesting intervals depend on the soil, the rain and flourish of the grass. Cattle eat the grass even when they are dry and dried grass can be mixed with other materials to prepare cattle feed. Guinea grass is good fodder and cattle prefer this grass to many others.

TREES FOR SOCIAL FORESTRY

In India the following trees are usually promoted in Social Forestry Programmes. However many of them are suited for many countries with tropical elimate. In fact most of them are found in many warm countries.

1.	Acacia Catechu	Katha, dye and gum
2.	Acacia Nilotica	Agricultural implements, leaves for fodder, gum and fuel-wood.

3.	Aegle marmelos	Medicinal fruits, gum from seeds and stem.
4.	Albizzia lebbak	Poles and shafts, beams and building materials, gum and tan from bark.
5.	Alstonia Scholaris	Tea boxes, match wood.
6.	Artocarpus Integrifolia	Furniture, building materials and edible fruits.
7.	Bombax Cuba	Packing cases, plywood and gum
8.	Butea Frondosa	Gum, oil seeds, tan bark, yellow dye from flowers
9.	Bauhinia Purpurea	Low quality furniture, gum, fibre, tan bark, leaves as fodder.
10.	Bauhinia Variegate	Gum, furniture, fodder, oil-seeds.
11.	Bambusa Arundinacea	Building materials, baskets and pulp
12.	Cassia fistula	Poles, fruits, medicinal seeds, tan bark.
13.	Cassia Siamea	Building materials and agricultural implements
14.	Casuarina Equisetifolia	Pulp, fuel-wood and low-cost housing.
15.	Dalbergia Sissoo	Furniture, building, toys & tools, oil from wood for skin ailments.
16.	Diaspyros melanoxylon	Handle for tools, Tendu leaves
17.	Dendrocalamus Strictus	Furniture, baskets, pulp. Agricultural implements.
18.	Syzygium Cumini	Boat making, tan, bark edible fruits, building materials, low-cost furniture.
19.	Eucalyptus Citriodora	Essential oil from leaves, poles, pulp, insecticides.
20.	Grewia Captiva	Fuel St Fodder
21.	Leucoena Leucocephala	Poles, pulp, fuel, fodder and bio-gas.
22.	Lagerstrodmia parviflora	Building, boats, shafts, village carts.

AZOLLA-THE NATURAL FERTILISER

Azolla is a tiny aquatic fern which floats in water. When introduced to grow and float in paddy fields it acts as a natural fertiliser for paddy plants. It actually promotes (plays host) to Ambabena Azollae, which is an alga greenish-blue in colour. This alaga converts the nitrogen in the atmosphere in a form which are used by plants. When the floating Azolla dies, it decays, decomposes, and gets digested in the soil and frees nitrogen for the paddy plants to thrive.

Azolla can be cultured and propagated in water and used also to fertilise vegetable gardens, fruit trees and other types of vegetation.

Further, Azolla can be given as feed to fowls, ducks, pigs and fishes and also be eaten by human beings in different types of culinary preparations. It tastes good when used in omlettes and burgers.

Azolla can be used also in home-made bio-gas digesters along with other bio-mass. It produces sufficient methane gas to meet domestic needs of a small household including lighting, cooking, and working of incubators.

The sludge from the digester is also used as fertiliser. It is claimed that rice crops fertilised only by azolla can produce 1.5 tons more per hectare than chemical fertilisers.

All what has been stated above has been demonstrated and proved by Memerto Fantilanan of the Philippines who was twice named as the Philippine Farmer of the year. Hundreds of other farmers in the Philippines are now resorting to azolla for fertilising crops and producing gas for domestic use. For more information, contact the International Rice Research Institute (IRRI) Communication and Publication Department, P.O. Box 933 Manila, Philippines, Photo credit to IRRI.

TEAK (TECTONA GRANDIS)

Family: *Verieraceal.* Hindi: Sagwan.

Teak is essentially a tropical tree and needs plenty of sunshine. The wood is strong and excellent for fine furniture, musical instruments, and as building material. Waste wood is converted into particle boards and chip boards. The broad leaves can be used for serving meals. They yield a good dye which is commonly used for dyeing wool and silk.

Teak raising in waste land is not difficult and they tolerate saline soil. Seeds are collected from good mother trees and for about 10 days soaked in diluted cow dung slurry. Seed beds are made about eight metres long and one metre wide and about 30 cms high. They are planted (buried) on the bed with cans of 30 cms. In about eight months seedlings grow to a height of 20 cms with stem thickness of about two cms. At this stage their height is cut to about 15 cms and the saplings allowed to remain on the bed for a week. Thereafter they are transplanted in trenches 60 cm wide and 60 cm deep. The spacing between trees is about 3 mts x 3 mts. There will be roughly about 1,000 replanting to a hectare. In the interspace, neem, banana, soya or sunflower may be grown. Neem and banana have shown excellent results. Subabool, Ailanthus, Panaye, Tapioca etc., may be grown in between the trenches. If watered, teak can grow upto a height of three metres in a year. To encourage straight growth and wide girth the young shoots sprouting beside the main ones should be removed. In about 10 years when the birth attains a size of 20 cms diameter and a height of about two metres from the ground alternate trees may be cut and each tree fetches now a big sum. The remaining trees are cut after 28 years when they have a girth of about 50 to 60 cms.

Strictly speaking a teak tree should, be out only after 50 years to get quality wood and big girth. In Burma, trees used to be cut after 50 years but now they are cut after 30 years. They say in Burma fathers must plant teak for children to benefit.

PALM TREES FOR SUGAR A LIVELIHOOD

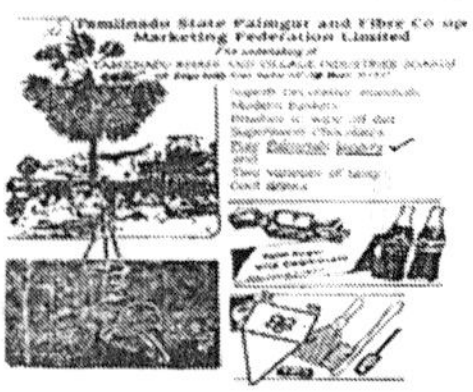

There are trillions of palm trees in India and several trillions in the other 82 palm growing countries of the world (Handout 121).Palmyrah and coconuts grow very well on sea shores washed by sea water. In the palm family, there are three well known species which yield plenty of sugar —

1. Palmyra: Botanical, *Borassus Flabellifer Linn:* In Hindi, Bengali and Marathi, it is called *Tal* or *Tar.*
2. Wild date palm: Botanical.*Phoenix Sylvestris Roab.*
3. Coconut: Coco Nucifere Linn.

Several products are made out of palm as can be seen in the picture. The floral bunches of the three varieties mentioned above possess plenty of sap which is sweet and tasty and drips readily when the boat-like branches are is slit with a knife at the and of it. A mud pot tied under the dripping slit and the juice collected overnight becomes intoxicating toddy by the action of yeast floating in the air. But when a handfull of mineral lime (chunam) is applied inside the pot the sap does not ferment but remains as a sweet juice called

Neera which is a healthy and delicious drink. Sugar or jaggery is obtained by boiling the unfermented Juice (neera) into a syrupy semi liquid and then allowed to cool and harden.

Jaggery, brownish in colour, is formed into lumps or caste into moulds and sold. It melts in warm weather and to have it bleached and crystallised it costs much more than cane sugar.

If only the Governments of countries which have palm promote and encourage the use of liquid brown sugar of palm packed in sachets as they now market intoxicating drinks, milk, fruit juices and ghee they will be lowering the price of cane sugar and creating millions of jobs for the people. Instead, Governments are now promoting capital intensive and centralised cane factories and cane cultivation because there is money for politicians, beaureorats and middlemen in centralised factories for making sugar and fertilizers, for cane cultivation and in their packing, transportation, distribution and licensing, creating scarcities in rural areas and developing black markets. It is a tragedy that many palm growing countries import white sugar, topple in balance of payment and turn to the IMF or the ESC for loans and remain inbonds as LDCs eternally. USA is trying to market protein rich synthetic *Thaumatin* which is 1000 times sweeter than sugar to wipe out cane cultivation. (Whither Development?)

ORANGE OIL FOR GALLSTONES

There is enough scientific evidence now that orange peel oil dissolves gallstone (*Hindu,*6th Feb, 3rd April,1991). The easiest way of extracting oil from orange peels is by steam distillation in a simple steal bowl designed by the Ryan Foundation and published as one of the 100 best Appropriate Technology ideas of 1990 by the Innovations for Development Association (IDEA) Sweden.

Fresh peels yield one to two percent oil only and therefore domestic scale extraction with small collection of peels can yield only an ounce or two of the oil. However, factories that prepare ready-mix orange juices and squashes can use the skin and extract large quantities of oil which has a rising demand as the oil is not only medicinal but also aromatic. Pectin can also be extracted where oranges are used in factory scale and presently Brazil is the largest producer of orange oil in the world. The oil can also be used as a refrigerant.

D-Limonene is the active principle of orange oil constituting 90 percent. The remaining ten percent is made up of trace components. According to Chemical and food technology reports from various sources the D-Limonene in orange oil seems to play the most important role in disintegrating the gallstone by fragmentation which begins within an hour after the patient takes orange oil. Ryan Foundation medical experts recommand the taking of orange oil to get rid of gallstone and to avoid surgery. Some scientist think that besides the D-limone some of the trace components may also play the therapeutic role in curing gallstone.

Ryan Foundation steam distillation equipment is small, simple and cheap. However, on a domestic scale to treat one family member the peels may just be put in a stainless steel bowl with water and boiled in a pressure cooker and the oil will form the surface layer on the water in the container. Ten drops of the oil may be taken in a spoon full of milk or with some honey.

There is an aurvedic tablet called *CISTONE* now available in the market which is reported to dissolve gallstone in one month without any side effects.

Some More Aromatic Plants

1. Botanical: *Hedychium Coronarium Koening.*

   Family: *Zingiberaceal.*

   English: *Garland flower. Ginger lily.*

   Indian: *Champa, Dulaba.*

   Distribution: Most tropical countries upto an altitude of 2,200 m.

   Description: Perennial, rhizomatous plant with stout root stock, fleshy and horizontal. Fragrant white flowers in dense spikes about 10 cm long. Calyx green, Corolla tube eight cm long many seeds.

   Uses: Stems are used for paper making. Rhizomes contain starch similar to arrowroot. The white flowers field a pleasant smelling perfume.

2. Botanical: *Mammea Longifolia Planch and Triana.*

   Family: *Gultifere.*

   Indian Names: *Surgi, Nag Kesar, Surgiri.*

   Distribution: Rainy slopy areas with high altitude in tropical countries

   Description: Evergreen tree with scaly bark. Leaves opposite and about 15 cms long. Flowers Polygamous, small, white or pinkish, in clulsters. Fragnant. Fruits 2.5 cms long one to four seeds in each.

3. Botanical: *Trigonella Foenum - Graecum Linn.*

   Family: *Leguminosae.* English.*Fenugreek.*

Indian: Methi.

Distribution: Throughout India, Pakistan, Bangladesh, Sri Lanka & many countries with tropical climate.

Description: Erect, strongly scented herbaceous annual with pinnate leaves. Lemon yellow flowers. About 5 to 7 pods each 5 cms long having about a dozen seeds.

uses: The herb contains the alkaloid Trigonelline and an essential oil Which is an insect repallent much used to protect grains in store. The seeds are used in perfumery.

4. Botanical: *Viola Cdorata Linn.* Family: *Violaceae.* English: *Vilet.* Indian: *Banaf Shah*

   Distribution: Cold Hillslopes 2000-3000 feet.

   Description: Low trailing plant about 12 cm high. Underground stem thick and scaly leaves broad & smooth. Flowers fragrant. Corolla deep violet inside with bluish white base dark blue outside.

   Uses: Flowers yield an excellent and strong perfume. The essential oil extracted from the leaves is used in perfumery and cosmetics. See Handout 152 for more Aromatic Plants.

Mosquito Sticks (non chemical)

Mosquito menace and the sickness they bring need no explanation. Attempts are made globally to eradicate or reduce mosquitoes but they get immune to chemicals and multiply. Electronic killers and coil burners are costly and do not reach the poor. Chemicals in the coils trigger asthma and other respiratory diseases. Some people are allergic to the smell and get skin rashes.

Ryan Foundation Mosquito sticks are the best solution so far to drive away mosquitoes as field tests establish. Rural preparation is explained below:

1. Soak newspaper or waste paper in water for atleast a week, grind in a traditional stone grinder and make pulp (papier mache).
2. Separately grind for every kilo of paper-paste one spoonful of Fenugreek. (Methi in Hindi and Vendiam in Tamil). Along with this grind also one medium size onion or garlic, ginger or some orange peals. This is to prevent contamination and unpleasant smell.
3. Powder well dried cow dung separately.
4. Grind fresh neem leaves into paste.

5. Mix neem leaves one part, paper pulp one part, and cow dung one part.
6. Some saw dust or charcoal dust, paddy straw bits or coconut fibre bits may also be mixed if available easily.
7. Cut out three or four cm plastic tubes used for electric wiring 20 cm long. Metal, glass, bamboo, or papaya stalk may be used instead of plastic. But three cm diameter aluminium tube is the best.
8. Oil the inside of tube, fill the ground mixture and dry under sun for two days. On the 3rd day remove sticks out of tube and dry them further for a day or two.
9. Where neem is not available use papaya leaf, or vasaka (which prevents chest cold) or murunga, or Thulasi (Basil) (very mild antibiotic) or any other leaf listed in (RYFO Handout No.123) Available leaves may be mixed in equal proportion but neem is the best. Every night one stick is fixed in a candle stand and lighted to burn like a mosquito coil which is now commonly used. Neem has about 20 active ingredients that mosquitoes cannot get immune to all of them, as reported by Elizabeth Hoddy in D+C 5/91 of the Government of Germany.
10. Sell each stick for Paise 20 or ten sticks for Rs two (US 0.8) to the consumer. The margin of profit looks low but there is 100 percent profit and the fast turnover will bring you a fortune. Sticks can be exported to countries where the said leaves are not available. Rural poor can make the urban rich depend on them for these sticks. Keep the quality high and the cost low to reach the poor. See RYFO Booklet Do-It-Yourself Mosquito Sticks.

NOTE: Formula rights and quality certificate (RYFO emblem) may be obtained from Ryan Foundation international. Registered Public Charity, 8 West Mada Street, Srinagar Colony, Madras - 600 015, India (RYFO Emblem rights reserved).

RYFO Organic "Ferticide"

The new word "Ferticide" coined by Ryan Foundation means fertiliser and insecticide combined RYFO *Ferticide*" is composed of nine leaves of common trees and shrubs of the tropics. Dried, granuled and mixed in the following proportion, it may be mixed with the soil and sprinkled on the plants.

1. Botanical : *Azadirachta Indica* — 30 parts

   English: *Neem or Margosa*
2. *Eucalyptus* (any species) — 20 parts

3.	*Subabool* and/or leaves of any bean plant	10 parts
4.	*Humus* or paddy straw or any pith after extracting fibre	10 parts
5.	Botanical: *Calotropis Jigantia* English: *Humble Plant, Tamil:Errukkam*	5 parts
6.	Botanical: *Adhatoda Vasica Nees* Family: *Acarthacea* Indian: *Arusha, Adhatodai, Vasaka*	5 parts
7.	Botanical: *Datura Stramonium* (and/or castor) English: *Angel's Trumpet/Devil's apple* Tamil: *Voomatham*	5 parts
8.	Botanical: *Catharanthus Roseus* English: *Vinca Rosea or Periwinkle* Tamil - *Nithiyakalini or Sudukattu Malli*	5 parts
9.	*Papaya or Ailanthus*	5 parts
10.	*Wood Ash,Charcoal dust* and/or farm yard manure	5 parts
	Total	**100 parts**

Field tests confirm that some of these leaves control army worm, diamond back moth, thrips, spidermites, mango-leaf-hopper and nematodes. Some of them control several other pests as reported in different issues of Sustainable Agricultural Newsletter, CUSO, Asia(In August 1989 issue). Field tests of the mixture of leaves done through some farmers by the Ryan Foundation showed excellent results.

Income: Women and children may collect, dry, pound and pack the leaves in used gunny sacks (jute bags) or HDPP legs (Cement/Fertiliser plastic bags)

If a 20 kg bag reaches the consumer (farmer) for Rs 10 or US $ 0.75 it will leave a net profit of Rs five per bag. A regular turnover can give a family Rs 1,000 per month and for a hundred families in the same village.

Only the bags mixed and packed under the supervision of Ryan Foundation Field Cooperators should carry the Emblem of the Foundation. Beware of adulteration.

RYFO Foliage Briquettes

Sweep or collect the dried leaves in and around your house and neighbourhood gather and store them in jute or *HDPP* (cement or fertiliser bags). It will be good to add plenty of Eucalyptus and neem leaves and those of shrubs, weeds and Cacti, Dry them well in open sun and break them into granules. This can be done either in a circular mineral lime-crusher with a rolling wheel made of stone (Handout 103) or in an oil crushing-unit-like device (Handout 165), in sea saw grinders (Handout 217) or just hand pound in a traditional village hand pounders.

Separately, prepare a bucket of gum. This may be tree gum collected from various trees, tamarind seeds, casava, or yam crushed and boiled. (Gum oozing from trees need not be boiled but straight away soaked in water and diluted). In coastal areas where non-edible fish and fish waste is available they may be converted into good quality gum as explained in Handout 501).

Make a pit 1m x 1m x 1m in the rear or frontage of your cottage, brick line and plaster it. Don't use cement but use mortar mixture recommended by Ryan Foundation (Handout 270). If this pit is properly walled and plastered the foliage may be dried and pound in it.

When broken to bits add the prepared liquid glue and mix well using a convenient pole.

Take a *Cirnva* ram (Handout 231) oil the cavity with unwanted oil, load the mixture into it and compress it just as clay blocks are compressed in it. You will get briquettes in the form and size of building blocks. Dry and break these block into 5 or 6 parts and these burn very well. In the absence of a Cinva ram wooden hand moulds may be used (Handout 109).

When cooking is done using these briquettes the Eualy smoke keeps mosquitoes away, especially when neem, Eucalyotus and other leaves listed in Handout 123 are used.

More Papain from Papaya

Co-5 Papaya is exclusively suited for papain production.

The various uses and increasing demand for Papain is well known. See *Papain* from Papaya, Page 19. After repeated research the Tamil Nadu Agricultural University has come out with a new variety which yields an unusually large quality of Papain. The University isolated from CP 15, an American Variety and released it in India as Co.5.

Cp.15 is of medium height, a dioecious variety. The tree flowers at a height of 90 to 100 cms with deep purple, fruit stalk and stamens. The size of the fruit is larger than the variety called Co2 which is popular in India at present for papain extraction. While Co 2 gives three to four gms of dry papain for fruit the Co.5 variety gives nearly three times. The University claims this as the worlds highest record in papain production.

Hence, this new variety (Co. 5) is excellently suited for the production of Papain.

After the papain is extracted, the Papaya can be used as a vegetable or can be dehydrated and preserved. The University claims the latex that can be used as a raw material or starting material for several industries due to it's high proteolytic acticity (11.6 units) and protein (72.2 per cent).

This improved variety, Co.5 grows in all soils and seasons in almost all tropical countries but cannot grows tolerate extremes of climate The tree needs poor rainfall and good drainage and therefore grows well in sandy hillocks and mole hills upto a height of about 100 M.

It is reported that in about two years the tree yields about 70 fruits every year each weighing over 2 kg. The average yield is 500 tons of fruits from one ha thus over 1,500 kg of dry papain per ha.

The profits on the industry is claimed to be nearly four times the money invested and the industry is recommended for drought areas, for marginal farmers and hill slopes.

Tutti-fruitti can also be made from the raw or ripe papaya after extracting the latex.

SALINE AGRICULTURE: SALT—TOLERANT PLANTS FOR DEVELOPING COUNTRIES

(Taken from Biomass users Network July-August 1990)

1. Scientists exploring seashores, estauries, and saline seeps have found thousands of halophytes with potential use as food, fuel, fodder, fiber, and other products. Many have already been in traditional use, and there are also a number of plants that, although not halophytes, have sufficient salt tolerence for use in some saline environments.

2. The seeds of *Zostera marina,* a sea grass, were used as food by the Seri Indians of the Southernwestern United States: in recent tests, these seeds were ground to flour and used to make bread. Seeds of Distichlis palmeri, *Palmer's saltgrass,* were harvested from tidal flats at the head of the Gulf of California by

Cocopa Indians. The seed, about the same size as wheat, has also been used for making bread.

3. Amount the grasses, kallar grass (Leptochloa fusca) tolerates waterlogging and recovers well from cutting and grazing. Its economic value as fodder for buffalo and goats has already been demonstrated in Pakistan and is now being examined in other countries. Members of the Spartina genus (cordgrasses) have also been used as fodder. These tough, long-leaved grasses are found in todal marshes in North America, Europe, and Africa. The salt-tolerant grass Sporobolus virginicus has also been used as cattle forliage.

4. Among trees, Acacia species are widely used in arid and saline environments as supplementary sources of fodder. Acacia pods provide food for livestock in large areas of the semi-arid zone of Africa. Acacia cyclops and A. bivenosa tolerate salt spray and salinity. They are grown on coastal dunes as small trees or bushy shrubs. Pods and leaves of both are consumed by goats.

5. *Leucaena leucocephala* is a tree legume widely cultivated in tropical and subtropical countries. Leaves, pods, and seeds are grazed by cattle, sheep, and goats. In Pakistan, it has been grown on coastal sandy soil through irrigation with saline water. When seawater comprised 20 per cent of the irrigation water, yields were reduced by 50 percent, however.

Botanical: *Solanum Nigrum*
English: *Black Night-shade.*Tamil-*Mana Thakkali.*
Bengali: *Gurkamani*, or *Kakmachi.*Punjabi:*Pilak.*
Cannada: *Kachigida.*

Description: Drought resistant tropical garden plant which grows in clusters to a height of about a meter. Green pods in bunches bigger than a black pepper and smaller than a green pea. When pods ripen they take the colour of deep pink grapes and have the taste of sweet and sour mixed. Children like to eat the fruit.

Growth: Commonly found in many tropical countries. Can be propagated through roots during rainy season. When the roots take to the soil they spread on their own. Some weeding and occasional watering helps good growth.

Medicinal: Solanum Nigrum is an important ingredient in Indian Medicines. All parts of the plants are used -roots, stem green pods, ripe fruits and leaves. They are ground and the juice is given for dysentery and to promote urination.

The juice is also applied on mouth ulcer and skin diseases. The fruits have more of the active ingredient than other parts of the plant. The fruit is also a laxative and an appetiser.

The raw pods, dried and powdered are administered to suppress asthma and loosen phlegm in the lungs. Asthma patients say that with increase in urination asthma conjestion gets reduced but one has to investigate the scientific base for this claim.

Commercial: The whole plant, without uprooting all the roots, may be washed and soaked in mineral lime (Chunam) plus common salt-water for about an hour and then dried in the sun for several days. RYFCT dehydration tray. . . may be used. When completely dry it may be stored in air tight containers and a spoon full of it may be added to soups and gravey and "Rasam".

The dehydrated plant matter may be packeted in double layer polythene sackets, labled and marketed, in half and one kg packets.

Many South Indian homes cook Nigrum leaves as a spinich but not regularly because it is neither available in the market in large quantities nor regularly. It is an ideal plant to be grown inside tyres (page 38) and in roof gardens. They can also be grown by city flat dwellers on top of sun shades over windows inside tyres.

Derris Root to kill predaceous fish

When you begin fish culture in a new pond it is not necessary to put derris root poison (rotenone) in it to get rid of unwanted fish. But in old ponds before every stocking of fishlings a derris spray cleaning is necessary. The roots are hammered flat, squeezed into a bucket of water until the water turns milky and then sprinkled in the water in the pond when the pond has less than 10 cms of water. Then about half kg of the root is enough to poison a pond of 100 m x 100 m. Spread the poison during day when the water temperature is high to make it more effective. Leave the poison for a day or two and then let in fresh water and introduce the fish 6 days thereafter. During these 6 days the poison effect in the water will go.

Botanical: *Derris Elliptica Benth.* Family: *Leguminosoa.*

Indian names *Etam Chali*, *Bakal bip*, *mokoi sopu.*

Description: A large creeper. Leaves about 30 cm long Flower, stalks densely clothed with brown pubescence. Corolla, pink, red or white. Winged pods have one to three seeds. Distribution-hilly slopes. Can be cultivated in cold climates.

The roots contain several toxic compounds but rotenone is the most important and less important toxins are tephrosin, deguelin and toxicarol.

Thin end of the roots have more of the toxic compounds than the thick ends. Derris is a strong insect killer and a well known fish poison. The roots are not available freely and everywhere and therefore when available the essence may be extracted kept in glass bottles.

When Derris is not available some of the common plant insecticides listed in RYFO Handout 112 may be used. Calotropis gigantia (humble plant), Datura (Voomatham) or Vinca Resea may be used.

The bark and seeds of Oliander flower plant "Arali Poo" (Bot-Nerium Indicum Mill) commonly found in gardens may be ground and a spoonful of the paste may be mixed in a bucket of water and used but this is very highly poisiomous and can kill birds, animals and human beings. Extreme care is necessary when this is used and the water in the pond must be completely flushed and sprinkled with a thick solution of quick lime before the fishlings are introduced. Quick lime is "Chunam" used for white washing walls made out of roasted sea-shells (what is made out of natural lime stone is called slaked lime).

RFYO organic insecticide mixture when mixed well and sprinkled in the pond has produced excellent results. One may use the poison that is easily available. Pond poisoning may be done before every stocking to be totally free of unwanted fish in the pond.

SESBANIA ROSTRATA

This is an aquatic legume recently discovered in Africa and it absorbs nitrogen from the atmospheric air and releases it into the soil. Thus, the weed is an excellent substitute for chemical fertilisers according to the International Rice Research Institute of the United Nations. Sesbania differs from many other nitrogen fixing plants in that it has nitrogen fixing nodules not only on its roots but also on its stems and has nearly ten times more nodules than most legumes. Microbiologists say that combined with azolla, Sesbania can replace nearly 50 kg of nitrogen fertilisers per acre. Within 2 months the plants grow well over a meter high.

In rice fields, soon after harvest, Sesbania can be broadcast or drilled. About 12 kgs of seeds will cover about one acre and as the seeds sprout some watering is required for about 10 days. Sesbania should be harvested in about 50 days and if left longer they become tough and harvesting becomes difficult and ploughing the field also becomes difficult. The leaves produce a large volume of biomass especially if grown in summer months. Many farmers in the Philippines have taken to Sesbania plantation guided by the IRRI and they are happy with the results. The University of the Philippines in Los Banos is promoting the use of Sesbania, Ryan Foundation International recommends the use of *azolla* and *Sesbania* in paddy and maize fields and to reduce the use of chemical fertilisers.

Head Bold Ideal Legumes for Rabbits

Siratro and Stylos anthus are good fodder legumes for feeding rabbits and they are drought tolerant and grow in all types of soil throughout the year. The seeds are usually broadcast during rains so that they germinate quickly and take root. They grow well even if the rainfall is as low as 600 mm per annum. Being legumes they fix atmospheric nitrogen in the soil and make the soil fertile and productive.

About 20 kgs of seed are cast in an hectare of land in prepared shallow beds. The spacing between rows of the beds is about 45 cm.

When these legumes grow no weeding is required but will have to be watered once in 20 days and oftener during mid summer. The first harvest is three months after sowing and subsequent harvesting can be done after intervals of one and a half months.

Usually, farmers sow some 10 to 12 kgs of seeds after every harvest to keep the growth continuous. Even in dry and neglected land the yield is about 20 tons per ha in a year. Strictly speaking reseeding is not necessary as the legumes are self seeding and self-propagating. A good practice is to recast seeds once in three or four years to maintain the density of the growth.

As rabbit feed, both these legumes are excellent and rabbits like them. An adult rabbit must be given about 400 gms of green fodder everyday. Several green leaves to be given to rabbits are explained in the booklet "Spinning Rs 6,000 per month from Six Rabbits" published by the Ryan Foundation. Siratro and Saycosanthus are additional legumes (rabbit feeds) which may be added to the list —

Desert tree called Carob Tree

Botanical: *Ceratonia Siliqua.*

Hindi: *Kharnub.* Also called *Locust tree* in English.

Family: *Caesalpiniaceal.*

Description: Large evergreen tree, deep roots, grows well in dry and rocky soil fruits (pods) are rich in proteins and sugars and excellent food for cattle. Native of Syria now taken to many countries and grown in Punjab, India. Seeds are light brown surrounded by sweet pulp. Pods contain over seven percent surcrose and sugar can be extracted from pods, and molasses as by-product. Flowers are without petals. Seeds which contain over 14 per cent protein can be used as cattle feed and the seeds contain Vitamins A, D and E. Seeds can be dried, ground to flower and mixed to wheat flower in the ratio 1:4 for making bread. Bread which contains Carob flour are tastier and healthier with Vitamins and in America this bread is made and called *St. John's Bread* and claimed to be good for diabetics. A gum known as *TRAGASOL* or Carob gum is made from the endosperm of the seed. Botanists estimate that 450 Kgs of pods will give 45 Kgs of seeds out of which 15 kgs of gum can be extracted. The gum is used in paper industry, textile industry, in printing, tanning, for flavouring, and in medicines (pods are used in preparation of cough syrups). The wood of the tree, heavy and hardy, is used for furniture making and a textile dye called agarrobin is extracted from the wood. This highly drought resistant desert tree which can be propagated by seeds may be introduced in saline soil, rocky mole-hills and hillocks. The life of the tree is said to be over 50 years and when over a hundred full grown trees are available several industries and income generation activities may be started based on the tree and its by-products. The tree gives shade and can be promoted also as avenue trees on highways.

Reference: (1) *Dictionary of Economic Plants in India*, ICAR Government of India, (2) *Useful Plants of India and Pakistan* by Dastur, Publisher, Taraporevala, Bombay, (3) *Journal of Economic And Taxonomic Botany*, October 1982 Scientific Publishers, Maan Bhawan, Ratanada Road, Jodhpur - 342001, India.

RYFO Balm for Boils

Everybody gets boils in some part of the body especially during summer. Village children who play in the sand and bathe in dirty ponds get boils more frequently and some of them are big and painful. RYFO balm is specially composed for treating boils but they can also be used to heal open sores or cuts. The ingredients are all herbal already in popular use in many villages in India and in some Third world Countries. But villagers do not make a combination of the ingredients mixed in proper proportion. After chemical analysis and study of active ingredients Ryan Foundation prescribes the composition given below which can be prepared by the villagers with the materials easily available to them.

1. Vinca Rosea roots ground to paste 4 parts (for details see handout 242.
2. Castor oil (medicinal) 4 parts. (for details see handout 128).
3. Turmeric powder one part.
4. Neem leaf paste 2 parts (for details see handout (33).
5. Chiotropis gigantia latex - one spoon (for details see page).
6. Papaya latex - one spoon (for details see handout 32).
7. Moringa seed paste one spoon.
8. One spoon of honey or white sugar.

Mix well, make cream and bottle and apply with a finger. Spread well and rub for atleast five mts. There will be neither burning nor itching sensation. In about 4 to 5 days the boil will either ripen and break open letting the pus out or subside and heal.

The ointment does not burn or itch open sores and cuts but should be applied to open wounds only if prepared under hygenic conditions.

RYFO balm may be packed in small used ice cream cups which have lids or in used paper board fruit juice satchets (Tetra Pack) with paper labels on top the balm can enter the market. 50 grams may be sold for Rs five and the Home Industry can bring an attractive side income for a family.

JULIFLORA BRIQUETTES
(Mesquite)

There are absolutely dry and drought prone villages in some Third world Countries where, people believe, income generating activities cannot be promoted. This is a wrong notion as humanity cannot survive there if nothing can be done and people live there only because there are ways of living.

Briquette making is one thing that can certainly be done. The thorny bush which grows into a tree now commonly seen in many Third countries called Prosopis Juliflora (P- Chilinsis) and popularly known in English as the Mad Tree because it grows on rocky mountains, on river beds, on saline sea shore, in areas where there is plenty of rain and places where there is no rain and in any type of soil or climate. Uncared for is a boon to dry and drought ridden areas and should be introduced and propagated in dry areas. In peninsular India this shrub tree is called '*Vaeli Kaathaan*' meaning fence-protector as it is thorny and human beings and animals keep away from it, RYAN Foundation has been promoting Juliflora briquettes and providing employment and a living for the poor in many Third world countries and this is how briquettes are made.

After removing the leaves and thorns, fairly straight twigs are cut to the length and thickness of a standard size led-pencil. Three such twigs are first tied together with any fibre available in the village. (there is no Third World barren village including semi-deserts which do not have or cannot grow atleast a dozen fibre giving plants and trees). Then, five of these twig bundles are put together and tied into a bigger bundle consisting of 15 twigs. Each bundle is a briquette and burns for a long time almost like charcoal. If not in bundle form, they bum out quickly. If unwanted leaves and foliage are ground to paste in a traditional village oil crusher (*Ghani* in Hindi and *Shekku* in Tamil), then, the ground leaves made into a semi liquid by adding water and the briquettes dipped into it, they burn for a much longer time. The idea is to block crevices and make the briquettes solid blocks. (cattle eat the pods of this tree but not the leaves).

There are several other desert plants and shrubs which give high thermal energy and can also be used and among them are Acacia, Acacia Spp, Pitecellabium dulce, Zizyphus Spp, Sesbania Spp, Dichrostachys glomeruta, Chlorophospermum mopane, Cryptostgia grandiflora, Datura (Voomatham in Tamil), Ipomoea fistula, Vasaka (Adathoda in Tamil) and the croten like plant called in Tamil *Katamani*. Semi-liquid clay fill crevices better and burnt clay (surki) is excellent for brick-making. See handout 184.

Villagers may use these bundle briquettes for their domestic cooking and also send them to nearby urban markets. For cooking one simple routine meal for a family of four ten briquettes may be required. If the price per bundle is fixed as low as five np (in India) a household will have to spend only 50 np on fuel per meal which is about one fourth the price of cooking gas, electricity, coal or kerosine. A family of four can make 500 bundles in one day in their spare time, i.,e. Rs 25 per day. If Rs 5 is set apart to meet transportation to nearby urban markets there will be a net profit of Rs 20 per day or Rs 600 per month which is a good family living wage. Transporting may be done by several families jointly by animal drawn carts. Care must be taken to replant what is cut. Other commercial uses for the shrubs are explained in other handouts of RYFO.

Yield and Extraction of Commonly Known Oil (Only those which are to be Dried and Crushed or Boiled and Crushed)

	English	*Botanical*	*Percentage of oil by weight*	*Processing*	*Uses*
1.	Castor	Ricinus Communes	48 percent	Seed crushed, then Kernel mashed & boiled in water, floating oil skimmed off	Sopps, lubricants, paints, medicines, etc.
2.	Cotton seed	Gossypium family - several varieties	16-24 p.c.	Cooked & Crushed	Soaps, Vanaspathi
3.	Groundnut	Arachis hypogaea	46-54 p.c.	Dried & Crushed	Edible
4.	Linseed	Linum usitatissimum	42 p.c.	Dried & Crushed	Edible
5.	Musk Melon	Cucumis melo linn	33 p.c.	Dehulled crushed & cooked	Nice to munch giver to poultry & birds
6.	Mustard	Brassica Juncea	35-48 p.c.	Dried & Crushed	Used as a spice
7.	Neem	Azadirachta Indica (Linn)	4 5 pc in Kernels	Dried & Crushed	Soaps & native medicines
8.	Orange seed	Citrus Meticulate	37 percent	Cooked & Crushed	Soaps
9.	Pongam	Pongamia Glabra	35 percent in Kernels	Dried & Crushed	Soaos & native medicines
10.	Rubber seed	Hevea brasiliensis	25 percent	Kernel is first decorticated, then the seed is cooked & crushed	Paints and soaps
11.	Sesame	Sesamum indicun	45 to 52 p.c,	Dried & Crushed	Edible
12.	Alexandria Laurel	Collophyllum Inophyllum	40-70 p.c. Kernel & shell together	Dried & Crushed	Soaps, skin, ointments
13.	Soybean	Glycine max	18-21 percent	Whole or Dehulled cooked & Crushed	Refined oil is edible
14.	Sunflower Seed	Helianthus	33 to 4 6 p.c,	Dehulled seed is cooked & Crushed	Edible
15.	Tea seed	The a sasanqua	18-34 p.c.	Decorticated, cooked & Crushed	Raw oil-soaps refined edible
16.	Watermelon ceed	CitruLus Vulgaris Schard	27 percent	Whole or dehulled cooked & crushed	Cil edible even in raw form.
17.	Indian Almond	Termanelia Catappa	–	Kernel is dried and crushed	Edible
18.	Custard Apple seed	Annonna Squamosa	–	Dried & Crushed	Soaps, medicinal

BOON FROM BAMBOO

1. Bamboo is the fastest and tallest growing grass in the world and has hundreds of uses. Pickies are made out of the shoots, baskets and thatches out of the leaves, pulp, furniture, ladders, buillding materials from the poles etc See RF Handouts 76, 96, 100, 316, 323, 350, 397, 400 etc.
2. Raise seedlings in polythene bags or elevatecd Sand beds and transplant them in mid summer. Obtain saplings from hilley regions, Kerala coast, Nepal, or Kashmir. Many countries in the African continent and Australia and South America have a dense and luxurious growth of bamboo. Every village, even every home, should get some saplings from nearby and propagate them.
3. Plant them in one cubic metre pits with 30 mt gap in between pits. Fill the pits with farm yard manure or sewerage silt. Bamboo thrives on poor and saline soil and very well in coastal villages. Water them only for a month or two.
4. In 3 years bamboos grow more than 4 mts high and each bush will yield about 40 shoots. The thin thorny sticks (shoots) may be cut from the 3rd year and used for fencing or fuel (or sent to paper mills). They should be cut only during summer and sold by weight.
5. Regular harvesting may start from the 7th year when they attain five to six cms in dia and from each cluster or bush five or six poles may be removed now and again to encourage growth and maturity and also for a regular income.
6. In South India a good bamboo pole of the type used for making ladders is sold now for Rs 20 each, and one hectate of the bush can yield Rs 25,000 every year after expenses.
7. 10th year onwards the growth is steady, healthy and mature and the yield will continue for half a century. It is a life time gross.
8. The best part of bamboo business is that whenever the poor need money, they can cut a pole, two or three, and sell them for their daily breed.
9. Pests don't attack bamboos, they resist strong winds, animals don't eat them. They need very little care.
10. In-between bamboo bushes grow Alanthus (202) Mopane (387) Papaya (377), Sunflower (249), Urena Labota (266), Acacia Halosericea (355).

Citrus Oils

Many developing countries which have good sunshine and rainfall have tremendous potentialities to grow and improve their Citrus cultivation and citrus grows almost in all soils. Citrus group of fruits such as limes, lemons, oranges (tight jackets and loose jackets) have very many commercial uses in food and industry besides the conventional uses. There is plenty of pectin, citric acid and essential oils in lime and lemon seeds and there are different species in limes and lemon family.

According to the Oil Technology Research Institute (OTRI) in Anantapur, Andhra, India, the common kitchen lime contains 38 to 40 per cent fatty oil and 16 to 18 per cent protein. The inner Kernal alone if separated gives 52 to 55 percent fatty oil and 27 to 29 per cent protein by weight.

The Institute report that the common sweet orange contains 16 to 18 per cent protein and 36 to 38 per cent fatty oil. The Kernel alone of the sweet orange fruit gives 18 to 20 per cent protein and 50 to 52 per cent fatty oil.

In sum, seeds of most citrus fruits contain plenty of essential oils and protein. The oil is bitter, but on refining becomes tasteless, odourless and almost colourless.

The citrus seed collection from squash factories, 5 star and smaller hotels, clubs, canteens and restaurants and homes can become in important industry in the non-formal sector. The price for a kilo of mixed seeds may be fixed at Rs 10 in India and Centres be promoted to collect crush and steam-distill the oil. This is not an elaborate process and the oil can be distilled like the lemon grass. or Citronella oil even on a domestic scale. A small semi-commercial distiller for decentralised domestic production is now made in Madras by Raja Pinteiro and Co, Thambu Chetty Street, Madras - 600 001, India.

The oil makes excellent soaps and can be hydrogenated to make tallow grade fats for industrial use. The oil cake is excellent fertilizer and insecticide seeds must be sown within 15 days of removal from the fruits.

BOTANICAL INSECTICIDES

Much research has been done on pesticide properties of neem both in India and abroad and the effectiveness of neem as a pesticide has been well established and neem, in various forms, is in use now in farms or fields(RF Handouts 33 and 107). But neem alone cannot meet the demands of organic farming and other botanical insecticides also will have to be applied. Pesticide properties of several other common leaves have also been researched and established but not adequately popularised to educate villagers. Some are explained below:

1. *Annona Squamosa*: English–Sugar apple, Hindi-*Sitaphal*, explained in RF handout 39 (According to the *Dictionary of Economic Plants*, ICAR, Powdered seeds and leaves possess insecticidal properties).
2. *Vitax Negundo*: Vavili in Telugu and *nochi* in Tamil.
3. *Tephrosia Villosa*: Called *Vempali* in Tamil.
4. Pongamia Pinnate: English-*Pongam*, Hindi-*Karanja*. Common on Banks of streams and rivers and near sea-shore. Fruits are edible. See RF Handout 53.
5. *Tephrosea Purpurea*: English-*Purple Tephrosia*, Hindi-*Sarphonka*. In Tamil they call this also *Vempali* (powdered leaf, like Detura, releaves asthma and a die can be extracted from it).
6. *Cleistanthus Collinus*: Hindi-*Gari*. This is excellent as an insecticide and also for making paper (*Dictionary of Economic Plants*,ICAR).
7. *Mundulea Suberosa*: English-*Lilac*. Tamil-*Konda Vempali*.
8. *Munoulea Sercea* of the same family also has insecticidal properties. They are toxic to caterpillars, cockroaches and house flies. Stem and bark are insecticidal.
9. *Apocynacoae* (*Oleander* in English). Dried powder mixed with equal part of wood ash and sprinkled at the level of roots of plants. Keep away insects (leaves of Oleander is ground and applied for skin eruption. Flowers and stem bark possess cardiotonic properties according to the *Dictionary of Economic Plants*, ICAR). Oleander seeds are highly poisonous and can kill animals and human beings.

Gram Coffee for Vitality

Refreshing coffee and tea certainly do not contribute to better health and people often get addicted to these beverages. Health beverages (compositions) now available in the market are costly and often contain chemicals. Ryan Foundation recommends coffee or extract made out of the following grams.

1. Cotton Seed: *Gossypium Indioum*. Hindi: Binaula. Tamil: Paruthi. Very good in general disability, cough and asthma. (*Book of Home Remedies* by Hakeem Saheb, Orient, Paperback, Delhi-110 006).
2. Bengal Gram: *Cicer Aretinum*. Hindi: *Chenna*. Tamil: *Sundal Kadalai* Good general tonic–Hakeem Saheb.

3. *Black gram*: *Phaseolus Rox burghii*. Hindi: *Mash* or *urad*. Tamil: *Vulundu*. Increases vigour in men and increases breast milk in women
4. *Fenugreek*: *Trigonella Foenum Gareceum*. Hindi: Methi. Tamil: *Vendhiam* Releaves rheumatism, lumbage and constipation
5. Cummin Seed: Hindi- *Zira*; Tamil- *Jeerangam*. Well known for its carminative effect, relieves nausea and vomitting among pregnant mothers, increases breast milk - Hakeem Sahab.

Roast and powder each separately and mix in equal parts. Use the powder just like coffee powder to make coffee and add sugar

Since the mixture contains Fenugreek and Cummin Seed the flavour is fine and the drink is quite tasty.

The powder can also be added to curry or chutney for taste flavour and vitality. Ready mix packets may be marketed and the business can earn quite a living wage for a family. Sachet and lable packing will keep the cost down and make handling and transportation easy.

Reference *Complete book of Home Remedies* by Hakeem Abdul Hameed Saheb,Orient,Paper Backs, Kashmere Gate,Delhi-110006,Revised publication 1988.

Some Improved Strains of Oilseeds

1. *Soyabean*: PK471 and PK472 suited for countries having South Indian climate average yield 2,600 kg per hectare.
2. *Groundnut*: CGC4018 known as Girrar yields about 2,000 kg per hectare C364 yields about 2,700 kg per hectare. These possess high resistance to foliar diseases and pests. Grow well both in Kharif and rabi seasons. The Indian Technology Mission. on Oil Seeds (TMO) claims that these varieties yield atleast 25 per cent more per hectare than the traditional varieties.
3. *Safflower*: Sweta or JSF seed yields on an average 1,900 kg per hectare. Strains called HUS 305 and NRS 209 are also high yielding and drought resistant.
4. *Castort*: SHB18 strain yields about kg per hectare with average rain fall and it is resistent to several diseases. It is superior to *Gauchi* which is quite popular in India.
5. *Mustard* or *Rapeseed*: YSB 197C (yellow sarson types has an average yield of 1,000 kg per hectare and the RH819 (Indian strain has a yield of 1,400 kg per hectare).The yield of these are 20 per cent more per hectare than those being grown now.

6. *Linseed*: Popular name Kiran (RLC6) popular now in peninsular India. Yield is 50 per cent more than local varieties.

7. *Sunflower*: MSFHI7 seed can be cultivated anywhere in India. Has an average yield of 1,600 kg per hectare easily gives 20 per cent more oil than the existing strains.

For more information and seeds supply position contact: The Director, Technology Missions on Oilseeds, Dept. of Agricultural Research & Education, Ministry of Agriculture, Krishi Bhavan, New Delhi - 110 00 1.

Fruit Tree Species for Agroforestry and the Corresponding Propagation Method

	Species	*Common PhilippineName*	*Propagation Method*
1.	*Anacardium occidentale**	Cashew	Send, grafting
2.	*Annona muricata**	Soursop	Send, grafting
3.	*Artocarpus altilis*	Breadfruit	Send cutting
4.	*Artocarpus heterophyllus**	Jackfruit	Seed, grafting
5.	*Artocarpus odoratissima*	Marang	Seed
6.	*Awerrhoa bilimbi**	Kamias	Seed
7.	*Aweirhoa carambola*	Starfruit	Seed,grafting
8.	*Canatium Oratum*	Pili	Seed, budding
9.	*Chnsophyllum caihito**	Starapple	Seed,grafting
10.	*Citrus grandis**	Pummelo	Seed, budding
11.	*Citrus madurensis**	Caamansi Calamondin	Seed, budding
12.	*Citrus reticulata*	Mandarin orange	Seed budding
13.	*Durio zibethinus*	Durian	Seed, budding grafting
14.	*Lansium domesticum*	Langsat. Lanzones	Seed, grafting
15.	*Malpighia glabra**	Aceroia Barbados cherry	Seed, marcotting
16.	*Mangifera indica**	Mango	Seed grafting
17.	*Maniikara zapota**	Sapodilla, chico	Seed, grafting
18.	*Musak paradisiaca**	Banana, plantain	Sucker
19.	*Nephelium laopaceum*	Ranbutan	Seed, budding, grafting
20	*Persea americana**	Avocado	Seed, budding grafting
21.	*Psidium guajava**	Guava	Seed, grafting
22.	*Sandcricum kostjape**	Santol	Seed, budding, grafting
23.	*Syzygium cumini**	Dhat	Seed, grafting
24.	*Tamatindus indica**	Tamarrd	Seed grafting

*Cited by Hensleigh and way (1988).

Reptotuced by the Ryen Foundation with courtasy to the authors and the journal.

The Sustainable Agriculture Newsletter, September 1990.

Acacia Senegal

This is the famous tree which produces the golden sap popularly called *Gum Arabic* in English and *Kumta* in Hindi and it is common in the *Sahal* region of Africa and some other tropical countries. It is now grown in Punjab, Haryana and Rajasthan in India. Different trees of the Sahal region have their own ways of resisting the vagaries of weather. For instance, Acacia tortilis delays blooming until the rainy season ends because the onset of the cool season fluctuates. The baobab tree conserves water within its trunk. Many trees of this drought region develop long and deep roots which can go far and deep to find water. But of all the trees of this region the Acacia Senegal has perhaps the most interesting drought defence machanism to avoid dehydration. When insects, animals or wind damage its trunk, it secretes a viscous liquid which is the Gum Arabic. This gum is of a very high quality and man is yet to discover a substitute for this gum in nature. It is used for glue, wine, soft drinks, in paintings, ceramics, starich, cosmetics medicines, paper, paints, matches, etc. Goats, cows and camels eat the leaves.

The tree needs only 250-270 mm rainfall and can withstand ten to eleven months of drought and an average temperature of 45°C. Each tree produces 5 to 10 kgs of gum every year.

85 percent of gum arabic is produced in Sudan. The Sudanese farmer grows millet for five years and then switches over to the gum tree. As the gum tree is highly leguminous and fixes atmospheric nitrogen into the soil it revitalises the land after 15 years. So, the farmers of Sudan live by producing millet and gum alternatively.

Other Acacia species which yield fairly good quality gum are A Catechu (from bark); A farnesiana (from stem). A ferruginea found in Gujarat, Vidharba and peninsular India; A Jacquemontii (Hindi-Kinkar) is found in Punjab, Rajasthan and Gujarat and yields an edible gum; A nilotica (Hindi-Babul) grown in Central and South India and gum is obtained from the bark. All these acacia species have different uses besides the gum they produce.

Next to Acacia Senegal, Acacia Catechu is known to give the highest quality gum from its bark. This is a small tree which grows well in the drier regions of India, Africa and many tropical countries and can be cultivated without difficulty as a commercial crop.

Anti-erosion Setaria

The deep rooted grass called Setaria is much better suited than Vetiver to fix soil and embankments. Vetiver which was once widely used in Rawanda, Burundi and Zaire upto the sixties have been completely given up now in preference to Setaria. This plant fixes anti-erosion embankments and is also useful as a foliage plant, since animals like it and it has good nutritive properties.

There are atleast six popular species in Setaria they can all be propogated in almost all warm countries:

1. Setaria Gluca: Bot - *Panicum glaucum.*English: Cat. Tail millet. Hindi - *Bandra.* An annual grass occurring throughout India and used as fodder. Grains are edible.
2. Setaria pallide: fusca. English: *Kavatta Grass.* Found in Tamil Nadu, Gujarat and Maharashtra. Grains are edible.
3. Setaria Italica: Botanical: *Panicum I talicum.* English -*Thalian Millet.* Hindi - *Kangni.* Cultivated in Andhra, Tamil Nadu, Maharashtra, Gujarat and Karnataka. Grains are edible and are also used as fodder.
4. Setaria Sphacalata. English: Kazuagula Grass. Introduced from Brazli and grown only as fodder Not edible.
5. Setaria palmifolia. English - Palm grass. Hindi -Bahapatia. Grown only as fodder.
6. Setaria Verticillata: English: Bristly foxtail. Hindi: *Laptuna.* Cultivated in peninsular India and used as fodder. Not edible.

Out of these six the first and the last viz. Cat tail millet and Bristly foxtail are excellent for holding the soil. All Setaria species grow luxuriously and are highly drought resistant. They are to be cultivated during the rainy season. S. Gleuca should be preferred because it is edible.

Leaf that Controls birth

Botanically the leaf is called Vicoa-Indica and in North India as Banjauri Dr P.L. Sharma, Dean and Head of the Department of Pharmacology of the Post Graduate Institute of Medical Research and Education, New Delhi of the Govt. of India, who has been researching on this leaf for the past several years declares that the leaf can not only stall. pregnancies but create permanent sterility in women without disturbing the normal menstruation or producing side effects. The plant has no toxic effect and has been declared absolutely safe for human consumption.

It is reported that Banjauri has been used by the Adivasis (tribals) of the area called Sokhodeora in the Nawadah district of Bihar for creating temporary or permanent sterility in women and to prolong the interval between births.

The entire plant-the roots, the stem, the leaves and flowers are all dried and powdered, mixed with some water sugar or honey and a pinch of black pepper and administered in three doses during three successive menstrual cycles. Only 15 gms of the powder is given in every dose. Dr Sharma has announced that this has proved quite successful in controlling pragnancy for atleast six months. When taken immediately after child birth for three months it causes almost permanent sterility.

Several experiments on fast multiplying rats have been absolutely successful and new experiments and observations are being done on women in the Institute. Over a hundred women who have taken this powder from the institute are absolutely normal, physically and mentally and no side effects have been reported so far.

The Department of Pharmacology of the Post Graduate Institute of Medical Research and Education, is optimistic about this discovery, Dr Sharma, the Dean, believes that this discovery will reduce the population in India and the cultivation of the plant will give rural employment to tribals and Adivasis. Perhaps the powder may be capsuled or tablated and exported to other countries. Some say that even if eaten as spinach the leaves reduce fertility. However, no authentic information has been released so far about this.

BIO–INSECTICIDES

1. To kill or keep away rice bugs, cutworms, army worms, caseworms, whorl maggots and leaf rollers use dried and ground leaves and roots of Red Pepper (Capsicum Frustesceus); Tinnsphora linii and Derris Sp Gliricidia. Green or dried leaves may be spread in the fields at the rate of about three kg per 100 sq. mts. while preparing for transplantation. Leaves may also be buried one or two inches below ground and their insecticidal effect lasts for about ten days.
2. Boil leaves of Derris Sp and obtain a thick essence. Mix one litre of concentrate to 4 buckets of water and spray on plants. Each spraying keeps insects away for about 10 days.
3. Dried roots of "tubli" (seems to be Philippine language) mixed with tobacco leaves and neem leaves if buried in the soil keep away insects for about a month.
4. One table spoon of crushed soap (soap chips) mixed with one kg of red pepper or chillie is boiled in a bucket of water and sprayed on plants once in 10 days.
5. Any crude (non-edible) oil mixed with ash of dried neem leaves is used to treat seeds in store to preserve them.
6. Tinospora leaves and red pepper ground together and thrown in the fields are found to keep away rats and rodents.
7. A concentrate of red pepper, turmeric and onion, if sprayed on rice fields keeps away pests.

8. According to many reports farmers in the Far East, in the Philippines in particular, have been following these practices. An important study of scientists sponsored in 1989 by the Asian Development Bank, FAO, IRRI, and he PCARRD (Philippines Council for Agriculture, Forestry and Natural Resources Research and Development) which studied 13 provinces in the Philippines observed many of these practices and called for R and D on the subject as reported by the monthly of PCARRD during the 1st quarter of 1990.

Medicinal - Hog Weed

Botanical- *Borhawia diffusa.* Family- *Nyctaginaceae.* Variety with red flowers - local name in South India Rakta Punarnava Variety with white flowers is called Svetha Punarnaga

Availability; Growers wild in many tropical Countries, particularly in the Indian sub-continent. Highly drought tolerant and grows on hills, plains, valleys, roadside and forests. It is a low spreading perennial creaper and grows well also in saline soil and on sea shore.

Propagation by root spreading is done in summer months and farmyard manure is applied in large quantities. Initial watering is necessary. The creaper can be harvested five to six times a year and the cut plants grow again and strike fresh roots, A little weeding and watering increases and quickens the growth.

Villagers cook the tender leaves which has plenty of Calcium and iron. Medicinal uses are many and the active element is an alkaloid called Punarnavine. The root is used as a laxative, diphoretic, stomachic, anthelmintic and in the native treatment of kidney and heart disorders. Roots are also used to treat dropsy, gonorrhoea, anaemia, oedema, cough, pleurisy and intestinal colic and asthma. The roots are ground to a paste and applied on boils and to cure skin ailments.

Decoction of the leaf is given for liver trouble and jaundice in the form of "tea" or mixed with honey. Drops of the juice of the leaves mixed in a spoon of water is given to babies as laxative and also put into eyes to cure chronic opthalmia.

The foregoing information was taken basically from an investigated report by Salikutty Joseph and Meagle Joseph of the Department of Olericulture, Kerala Agri University, Vellanikkara 680 654, India, which was published in the Hindu dated 18th April, 1990. It is also based on direct investigation made by the Ryan Foundation in 10 villages in peninsúlar India and on discussion with the tribals of the Yellagiri hills.

Saline Agriculture

The following information has been culled out from the 143 pages book entitled *Saline Agriculture: Salt-Tolerant plants for Developing Countries* published by the National Academy of Sciences-1990.

Salt tolerant plants (halophytes) usually have poor agronomic qualities (e.g., there may be wide variations in germination and maturation times). They may be cultivated in land and water that are unsuitable for salt sensitive plants.

1. Leucaena Leucocephala is growing in coastal sandy soil in Pakistan irrigated by saline water. Trees even survived when 20 per cent seawater was used although yield came down by 50 per cent.
2. Jojoba grows near the Dead Sea in Israel with brackish water irrigation.
3. Quinoa germinates in a mixture of 1/3 sea water and 2/3 fresh water, that it did not continue to grow for a long time. In the salt flats of Southern Bolivia, Quinoa is grown.
4. Azadirachta indica (Neem) grows successfully in Pakistan on sandy soil using irrigation water with about 10,000 ppm salt(pure sea water is 35,000 ppm). A neem plantation has been established near Mecca in Saudi Arabia to provide shade for Muslim pilgrims. Water with about 2,500 ppm date palms grow very well in brackish water.
6. Asparagus is remarkably tolerant of salt. In Tunisia, where irrigation water contains 6,500 ppm salt, asparagus yields are about the same as in areas irrigated with fresh water.
7. Barley is the most salt-tolerant cereal grain. At the University of Arizona good results have been demonstrated. California experiment produced 458 kg of barley from one ha of land when cultivated entirely by sea water.

The book or further information may be obtained from the Board of Science and Technology for International Development, Publications and Information Services, Office of the International Affairs. National Research Council, 2101 Constitution Avenue, Washington D.C.-20418, USA.

MOPANE

Colophospermum Mopane is the botanical name of an exotic tree taken to many countries from Zimbabwe. It is a fast growing, drought tolerant. multipurpose tree and improves soil fertility, From a. distance the tree looks like an Acacia. It is planted, as a wind breaker, shade provider and soil binder, especially where the soil) is Sandy. The tree grows 10 to 15 mts high and the wood makes good fire-wood.

The flat thin kidney-shaped pods which are about one Cm long contain single seeds which are highly resinous. Seeds get propagated by nature and germinate in any most soil but not in cold wet weather.

In Africa low quality furniture and building materials are made out of the trunk of the tree which is not attacked by white ants. Carpenters powder the resinous seeds, mix the powder with country brewed liquor and use the semi-liquid to give colour and polish to furniture. They also dry and powder the bark of the tree for the same purpose.

The leaves make good fodder. More than half the leaves of the tree may be lopped at a time and frequent does not stunt its growth. Botanists have researched and published that Mopane leaves have a remarkable quality of retaining nutritional value for Soil and fodder long after they fall and dry on the ground.

The tree can be planted as avenue trees in village roads. Heavy winds do not uproot it even during rainy season when the soil is loose. The roots evolve Carbondioxide which helps lower soil alkalinity. Indeed Mopane is ideal to fight poverty, provide fuel wood fodder and furniture. It should be introduced and propagated in waste lands in poor and warm countries.

Acacia Holosericea

This tree which is leguminous and drought resistant with a high calorfic value grows in different types of soils and climatic conditions. It is small in size, ornamental, fast-growing and belongs to Australia but thrives in all countries where it has been introduced and propagated. The nitrogen loaded nodules of the tree enrich the soil and therefore it is ideal for wasteland reclamation.

The trunk has a girth of about 30 cm and branches starting from a height of 50 to 60 cm from the ground level. Only till the roots catch the soil the saplings are to be watered and thereafter nature and annual rainfall takes care of it. If planted as rains set in no watering is needed. The climate most suited ranges from 30 to 40 degrees c. but the tree can survive dry spells for eight to nine months in a year with scanty rainfall of about 125 mm annually.

The wood of the tree gives high quality charcoal and the tree has natural self-regene-rating property. Branches grow upward and the leaves are 12 to 24 cn long and five to eight cms broad (almost like mango leaves) and cattle don't brouse them. As the leaves have insecticidal properties white ants don't attack the wood. The tree has proved excellent as an avenue tree inside institutions like schools, colleges, hospitals and on either side of small roads.

The *Auroville township* in Pondicherry South India, introduced the tree in it's campus a decade ago and the tree has been propagated from there to several parts of south India by the Social Forestry department which has realised the potentialities of the tree.

The branches of the tree are good for making roof for low-cost huts after making them into shingles. See explanation of RYFO shingles in handout 192. The twigs are excellent for making briquettes as explained in RYFO Handout 319.

From a distance the tree looks similar to an Oliander tree without flowers and the leaves are broader than the Oliander. All Third World countries should propogate this tree to save fuel wood crisis, to enrich the soil and reclaim waste lands.

Wonder trees called Mesquit

Some information has already been given about Mesquits in handout 319 on Juliflora Briquettes (Page 124). Mesquits belong to the genus Prosopis and they are well known arid zone trees of a medium size. There are over 40 species in the family of Mesquit and the one most popular and flourishing in India and many warm countries is the species called Prosopis Juliflora. Two other common varieties are Prosopic Cineraria (synonym P. Spicigera) and Prosopis Africanus. All these species grow well in arid tracts having a rainfall of less than 600 mm per year. They spread wild and provide fuel wood for the rural poor.

If the seeds of Mesquit strains are soaked in hot water before sowing they germinate quickly. The seeds which are eaten by goats, horses and donkeys and carried in their droppings also germinate. Thus, nature has its own way of propagating this useful tree. The seeds that germinate from animal droppings reach girth of about 40 cm and a height of about 4 m in about 3 years.

Since the leaves contain an amino-acid derivative called prosarina, animals don't eat them but only the pods which are available even during mid summer.

In about three years, Mesquits yield about 40 tonnes of biomass per ha. (The current market price per tonne in India at site is Rs.300 and gives the owner atleast Rs 15,000 per ha per year) The sticks are used in the building industry.

Mesquit wood makes good charcoal. Since the ash content is very low the Charcoal is much in demand for the production of acetylene.

Recently the Tamil Nadu Agricultural University in South India introduced a new species of the Mesquit family from Hawaii called Prosopis Pallida with straight and multiple stems almost like a bamboo tree. The advantage with this species is that its leaves can be dried overnight and given to goats. This species also yields plenty of honey and much of the honey produced in Hawaii is collected from this tree.

Promote Pomegranate

Family: Punicaceae. Hindi. Anar. Tamil. Madhalam:

Pomegranate, native of Iran, is excellently suited for arid and semi-arid lands. It requires relatively low humidity and cool climate (15°C to 20°C) and grows well in tropical countries upto an elevation of 2,000 meters. The tree requires very little water and can be best irrigated by the drip irrigated system where there is water scarcity. It also grows well in saline soil and sea coasts and even when watered by sea water as experiments have proved. See Handout 403.

Pomegranate is suited for dry land horticulture along with custard apple (Seethapalham), Guava (Koiya), ber (Seemai Ilandam Palham), fig (Athi Palham), Sapota (Chiku).

The improved variety of Pomegranate called "Ganesh" which is very popular in Maharashtra State of India is seedless (has very soft seeds which can be easily chewed and swallowed).

There are other good varieties such as Bassein (seedless), Kabul (small soft seeds) and Jyothi evolved by the University of Agricultural Science, Bangalore. All these varieties are big, sweet and have soft seeds which can be chewed and swallowed.

Medicinal: The raw fruits help proper functioning of the stomach and the fruit is often called "stomach tonic". The thin yellow skin between the fruit seeds and the thick outer coat binds the bowels and may be eaten raw, ground to paste and taken with curds, boiled in water and taken as a decoction. The essence of the yellow skin is usually mixed with honey and given to babies and little children to set right stomach •irregularities (not if constipated). The yellow peals are commonly used in ayurveda to cure diarrhoea and dysentery. The dry seeds and yellow skin may be dried and powdered and kept ready in homes in airtight bottles to control loose motion and stomach ache.

The yellow skins are also boiled and used as a fast yellow dye to colour fibre and cotton. It is also mixed with other Vegetable colours like that of Mendhi (Marudhani), onions and beetroot to get different shades.

Bark and fruit shells are crushed and used to tan leather. They are specially very good for initial processing of rabbit skins. The rind which is valuable tan is used for tanning rabbit skin and morocco leather. The root bark contains 22 percent tannin and it is used for making jet black writing ink and the rind is used for making hair dyes. The leaves and outer coat of the fruit make good fodder and they deworm animals.

The fruits can be dehydrated and preserved (better with honey). Delicious wine, jams and pickles are made out of them.

The flowers known as balustine or balustium yield honey and they contain quality tan. Thus the pomegranate has several uses to sustain life in Villages and should be cultivated in coastal areas in particular.

Duckweed (Lemnaceae)

An acquatic weed which grows anywhere under any climatic conditions excepting in deserts and where the temperature nears freezing point. Has extraordinary property of cleansing waste and creating protein. When dried, its protein content is over 40 per cent which is similar to Soya. Since 1985 Duck-weed is being used in some parts of USA to purify municipal waste water. The weed grows prolifically and doubles its wet weight within 3 days. it grows ten times more than Soya in a given area and all it takes to multiply is water rich in nitrogen, potassium and phosphorus nutrients found in water polluted by animal and human waste or agricultural residue. The weed is an excellent fish feed and faten fish very fast. It is also good animal and chicken feed.

Under controlled condition one hectare yields one tonne of weeds in Bangladesh. The weed can be cultivated in small household ponds into which domestic (Kitchen and toilet) waste water is let in. Where domestic waste is available the effluent of 100 people is sufficient to fertilise an area of quarter hectare which is a manageable size for one family.

A family must channel its polluted water into the pond and divide the pond into compartments by floating bamboos or long light poles to prevent the crop from being swept by wind against the bank of the pond. Duckweed is a tiny green weightless round leaf frond with rudimentary roots, grow best when evenly dispersed. When it spreads out well and grows harvesting is easy and quick. With a butterfly net the whole pond can be harvested is 3 to 4 hours. Some healthy leaves (Plants) must be left uniformly for further growth and propogation. The ideal water temperature for the weed is 20 degrees centigrade.

Common Carp-grass carp, Chinese and silver carp thrive well in these ponds. Eating duckweed exclusively the carps grow upto four kgs in weight. Annual production of 10 tonnes of carps per hectare can be raised without change of water or airation. Scientists say that the fish eats the weed without consuming the oxygen in the water. as the weed itself contains oxygen. Moreover fish raised in duckweed ponds purify water and make it fit for human consumption in course of time. In multiplying, the plant consumes excess nutrients and releases oxygen which purifies water.

There appears a possibility of growing duckweed and fish in ponds mixing municipal sewerage with sea water. This however has to be researched and established.

MULTIMEDICINAL AMRITA

Botanical- *Tinospora Cardifolla.*Trade name: Tinospora. English name: *Moonseed plant.* Sanskrit- *Amritavalli*; Bengali- *Cuian cha.* Telugu- *Guduchi.* Tamil- *Thippa Thega*; Malayalym- *Amrytu.*

Description. Drought resistant creeper which grows in many tropical countries and found in abundance in India, Burma Sri-Lanka, Pakistan, Bangladesh, Nepal and most African countries. Heart shaped leaves resemble betel leaves and the red fruits are of the size of a pea. When the thin outer skin of the stem is pealed, a greyish green dotted stem is seen.

Medicinal Amrita is a highly valued creaper in Ayurvedic system of medicine and it is used to cure several diseases. When the stem is crushed and boiled in a small quantity of water and condensed to almost a semi-liquid state and taken with an equal quantity of honey, it acts as an antibiotic against several common ailments. For diabetic patients the condensed juice is given without mixing honey and in about ten days the sugar level in the body is found to fall. Quarter teaspoon of the semi liquid in the morning and quarter after dinner before bed is the usual dosage.

Handy Powder, After removing the skin from the stem the stem is chopped, ground and made into a paste and the paste soaked in water (4 parts of water by volume to the quantity of paste) and kept overnight to settle. On the following day when the water is drained off a white starchy paste is left back which is spread on a plate and dried in shade (not under direct sun) The dried paste is powdered and kept in an air-tight bottle. The powder so prepared is called Guduchi Satva or Amrita Satva.

About quarter teaspoon of the powder is "mixed with ghee, milk, sugar, honey or glucose and taken to relieve fever, general weakness, insomnia, hyperacidity, guidiness, restlessness etc. It is an excellent blood purifier. Ayurvedic doctors claim that Amrita satva strengthens the metabolism of the human body. Some also claim that it slows down the process of aging but this claim has not been scientifically proved. A decoction of the roots of this plant is taken to relieve diarrhoea and dysentery. It is claimed that Amrita Satva does not give any side effects even if taken in excess or too often.

Ready made powder of *Amrita Satva* is available in some native medicine shops in several parts of India and Nepal.

For reference:-

1. *Home Remedies* by Hakeem Saheb, Orient, Paper Back, Delhi.

2. *Science Express* dated 5-12-89.
3. *Medicinal Plants* by S.K. Jain, National Book Trust of India,
4. *Medicinal Plants of Nepal*, Ministry of Forests, Nepal.

Ecualy leaves make good briquettes

In many Third world Countries the favourite tree in the Social Forestry Scheme is the controversial Eucaiyptus. However, Eucaly has to be given a limited place for certain advantages that it has. See Handout 226.

Fallen Eucaly leaves do not retain any moisture but remain dry even if the rainfall is intense. There is no mulching and because of the acidic nature, cattle do not graze on the lands with Eucaly foliage and consequently, there is no animal dung droppings in these areas and the top soil is lifeless. The roots of Eucaly Spread far and dry up wells and ponds. The wood is neither used as fuel nor fodder.

But the dried fallen leaves of Eucaly is excellent for making briquettes by various methods that are innovated by the Ryan Foundation. They are only to be ground to granules by any one of the village methods of grinding or pounding and mixed with a little gum oozing from the very Eucaly tree and when compress in a hand press or a Cinva Ram fine briquettes are got. The smoke from these Eucaly briquettes do not burn the eyes, they are good for the lungs and free respiration and more than that the Eucaly smoke is a good mosquito repelient.

Ground Eucaly leaves may be mixed with ground neem leaves for making mosquito sticks.

Many NGOs and Environmentalist are trying to bring about an anti-eualy movement as in Karnataka and Chenglepet District of Tamil Nadu, but it is wrong to do so. Eucaly, like water hyacinth, has good uses which must be exploited.

Paper from Mulberry

Mulberry is a drought resistant plant which grows well in tropical climate in different soil condition though it grows better in elevated places and when water (the author has a tree flourishing in his garden in Madras). People only think of rearing silk worms with, Mulberry but excellent paper is made for writing, mosquito coils, candles, joss sticks, umbrellas, lamp shades, writing paper,etc. The pulp is durable and paper strong and insect resistant. This industry is popular in Northern Thailand. The Ban Ta Leh village in Lamrang province is the largest paper making village where about 140 people in 182 house-holds produce mulberry paper as a profession as on 1st July 1990. (*Network News*, July 1990, Bangkok). Mulberry is called SA in the Thai language. Japan, China and Korea are also making SA paper especially for artists to paint on them and for printing certificates and documents and making artificial flowers and kites. SA paper is now used in hospitals as tissue paper and as sanitary bags the to is absorbing capacity and durability.

The small tree to be out must have a dametre of 1-3 inches. Cut trunks are literally roasted for easy peeling. For peeling device see Handout 156. The burnt bark is used as soil fertiliser/insecticide and the ramaining peeled bark is taken to the boiling process where the bark is softened with ash. Ash of the same tree or any wood ash may be used to make a basic solution. After rinsing in the soluti on the bark is bashed with a wooden hammer and turned into pulp. About two kg of bark must bebashed for about? hours. The pulp thus obtainech may now be used, the way pulp is used for making hand-made paper, ie., it is spread into bamboo frame screens fittecd with mosquito nets, made of wire or plastic. This spreading process is done under water (the screen portion of the tray is immersed in a tub of water). Screens are then removed and allowed to dry under the sun and the dried material is paper and can be easily remoned from the tray (please do not replace the ash with sodium hydroxide to soften the bark).

A family of five can produce 50 sheets of paper a day and one kg of pulp will give 12 sheets of paper of 40 gms weight each of the size 55x77 cm or 65x125 cm. The producer's price of each sheet can be Rs four and that gives a family Rs 200 per day.

Traditional Paper Making: Northern Thailand

Figure 1: Umbrellas made from hand-made paper in the town of Bo Sung. Chiengman Provinent

Figure 2: A full grown Sa tree.

Figure 3: Bark being bolted acousta.

Figure 4: The pulp being spread evenly onto a bamboo frame screen in the working area of a household in Ban Ta Loh, Lampang Province.

Figure 5: Pulp being dried on bamboo frame screen.
(Contributed by Supatra Indrbhakdi, Network News Assistant Editor).

With Courtesy to the author and the Journal reproduced by Ryan Foundation International, India.

SAVE THE MANGROVES

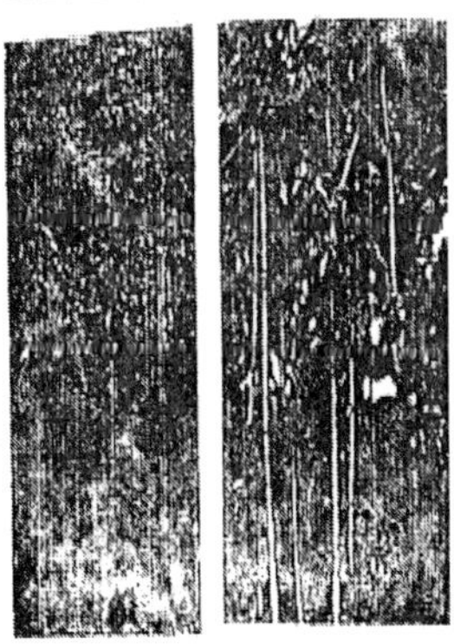

A typical Mangrove bush

Mangroves* otherwise called Mangels is a salt tolerant forest ecosystem usually found between high and low tide levels of the sea forming a labryinthine interface between sea and and rivers. Mangrove trees consolidate the shoreline and nurtures fishes, prawns, crabs, oysters etc. They provide several income generating activities for people besides wood. cane, bamboo, food, fruits, fodder, salt, fibre, oil dye, wax, medicines tannin* tree gum, organic fertilisers, etc. Rhizophora, a common species of mangrove which nurtures seedlings on the parent plant.

According to the Ministry of Environment and Forests, Govt. of India, the total area of mangrove forests left in India in 1990 is about 6,740 Sq.Km and the rest have been destroyed or reclaimed but based on LANDSAT Satellite imageries of 1980-82,the National Remote Sensing Agency. Hyderabad, there are only 2,650 Sq. Kms of mangroves in India now.

Very poor tribal communities inhabit the mangroves under trying conditions and it is criminal to deny them of their traditional rights over the mangrove resources in return for their hard toil. There is large scale destruction of Mangroves going on in India today. In Goa, for instance, there were only about 2,000 hectares left in 1909 along the Mondovi-Zuari estuarine complex.

However, it is gratifying to note that 14 sites have been selected by the Govternment of India for setting up biosphere resources out of which 5 are in Mangrove estuaries. They are Gulf of Mannar, Little Rana of Kutch* North Island of Andamans Sunderbans of West Bengal and the Great Nicobar.

Mangroves are a challenge for environmentalists and they will have to fight the Governments and poachers and preserve mangroves and the wealth, food and employment they provide besides helping the formation of the fast depleting one layer. Man must benefit by Mangroves. The idea of digging sea water canals parallel to rivers with about five Kms gap in between the rivers and the canals and promoting Mangroves in the middle should be implemented wherever possible. when the rivers go completely dry the sea water may be turned into the river to keep it flowing and the ground wet for mangroves and marshy land plants and trees. Plants and trees that grow well in saline soil and sea water have been identified by the Ryan Foundation. the USAID and several international research agencies. (see handout 343 also and Ryan Foundation booklet Survival by Sea Water).

USES OF MORINGA OLEIFERA (otherwise called Horse Radish)

Botanical: *Moring Oleifera*, English-*Drumstick*, Hindi-*Munga or Shajna*, Tamil-*Murungai*, Malayalam-*Murinna* or *Moringo,* Sanskrit-*Shobhanjana* or *Shigru*, Gujarati-*Midhosairavago* or Saraga, Telugu-*Munaga* or *Mulaga*, Orissa-*Sajina*, Marathi-*Achajhada*, Punjabi-*Soanjna.*

Uses: The seeds contain 35 percent medicinal oil which is rubbed to relieve goiter pain and rheumatism. Seeds act as antibiotic against the chemical called benzyl Isothiocyanate (V.M. Gogate,*Dravyaguna Vidnyan*,1982, Continental Prakashan, Pune). Leaves are rich in Vitamin A and C. Decoction of leaves is given for hypertension bronchitis, diarrhoea and ear infection by tribals. The leaves, ground with turmeric are applied on boils and closed wounds (acts like iodex). Eastrogen is prepared from the leaves (*Hindu* 18.10.89).

When people are over intoxicated by alcohol wet bark of the tree is held near their nose to reduce the effect of alcohol. Some claim that the juice of the bark is a good antidote for alcohol.

The bark is pound and used as an antidote for cat, rat and dog bites in rural Africa. In India the leaves are ground with turmeric and salt and applied externally.

Decoction of the flowers is given for digestive disorder and worms and as a general health tonic.

Indian Chemists have successfully isolated from the stem of the tree hydroxyl mellein, a fertility regulatory agent (proper use of African Natural Coagulants for rural water supplies: research in Sudan 1986-GTZ, Germany and Samia Jahn, in Traditional Water purification in Developing Countries 1981. G.T.Z.).

The flowers also contain the wax called quercelin and the ash of the wood is rich in calcium and potassium. Flowers yield plenty of honey.

Crushed seeds clarify drinking water, sugarcane-juice and honey. The drumstick tree is highly drought resistent and the soft wood can be used for paper making. The tree is propogated by sowing seeds in pits of one cubic feet three metres apart (1,125 trees per hectare) and five seeds per pit. Soil and farm yard manure may be mixed half and half to fill the pits.

Leaves and twigs are given as fodder and unlike many other leaves eaten by animals they do not contain tannic acid which lowers the digestibility of proteins.

The tender pods are cooked and eaten as a vegetable and also pickled. Fried seeds taste good and the roots are dried, ground and used as condiments. Seeds germinate in about 10 days and when the saplings are 15 cm high thinning should be done, leaving one plant in each pit. When the plant is about one metre high, the buds may be nipped to encourage side growth.

If there is surplus production, drumsticks can be cut into small pieces, boiled in water for 5 minutes and sun dried and preserved for months together.

FLAME OF THE FOREST (or *BUTEA GUM TREE)*

Botanical- *Butea Frondosa*. Family *Leguminosea* Hindi- *Dhaka or Palasha*. Tamil- *Kattumurukku*, *PALRSU*, Bengali- *Palas*. Sanskrit-*Palasha*. Telugu- *Passamu*. (*Butea Superba Roxb* (Hindi- *Palsa Lata*) is a different species of the same family).

DESCRIPTION: Many people wrongly call the Flambyont tree, "Flame of the Forest" but the two belong to different species, even though both have large bright red or deep orange flowers which look alike from a distant. Both bloom in mid summer and have plenty of flowers densely clustered and both are highly drought resistant and thrive in different climates and soils. The stalk of the Butea flower is dark brown and the Calyx jet black and velvetty. The immediate striking difference between the two trees is that the Flame of the Forest has very big leaves while the Flambyont has very small leaves. FOF has twisted branches and is found in jungles. It is medium in size and desiduous. Trunk has thick brownish bark on which lac insects thrive. Wood is not durable unless kept in water. Each leaf of the tree contains three leaflets and whithers in winter. Pods are flat with a single seed called Monosperma. Mature pods have white silvery hair and dried ones are carried by wind for natural propagation, saplings transplanted along with the root nodules thrive better than what is grown by sowing seeds.

Distribution: Dry forests and waste lands are found throughout India and countries with warm climate and minimum rain fall. They are more dense in forests not far away from sea and many tropical countries have the tree.

Uses: Wood is excellent for fuel and roots yield strong fibre. Both wood and fibre are used in building low-cost houses. The dark brown seed gives a non-edible fatty oil (18 to 20 per cent) which is good for making soaps. Flowers boiled in water yield a dye which is not fast colour. The gum called Bengal Kino or Betea Kino is used in native medicines and in tanning industry and thin gum is taken from the stem of the tree. Value of the tree is really in the Lac that thrives on it as lac which has very many uses are in demand all over the world. French polish, seeling wax and several other fast moving consumer and industrial items are made out of *Lac*. The flowers yield good honey. Thus, the Flame of the Forest generates employment by yielding Lac, honey, oil, fibre, fuel-wood medicines, leaves for making plates and several products in which these are used as raw materials. From the inner bark a strong fibre is extracted for making cordage and paper. The root fibre is so rough that tribals weave and make slippers out of it. Seeds are insecticidal and cattle eat the leaves.

Medicinal: Seeds are used in the treatment of Roundworms, tapeworms, and ringworms. A durable blue dye is made out of the gum which contains tannin and gallic acid used in the treatment of diarrhoea. Research done on this oil by the Oil Technology Research Institute, Ananthapur reveals that the oil of seeds stops balding and strengthens hair roots. Five full grown trees in a village can give a living wage for one family all through the year.

RYFO SLIMMING PORRIDGE

This is a natural fibre food without fat, excellent for diabetic, cholesterol and obesity patients. It fills the stomach, gives energy, keeps you healthy and active and does not make you feel hungry. Ideally suited for those who want to slim and lose weight, it is instant breakfast-food for the family, handy for working women and inexpensive.

Ragi powder — One cup — Kelveregu — Tamil
Horse gram — one cup — Hindi-Kulthi (Kollu in Tamil)
Green gram — one cup (Mung or sabut) — Pacha payer in Tamil
Cow pea - one cup (Lobia) — Karamani — Tamil
(You may omit one or two ingredients if they are not easily available, but Soya Bean or Cow Pea is a must.)
Red gram — one cup — Pigeon pea; Arhar-Hindi
Thuvarai-Tamil
Green Pea (Mutter) — one cup
Soya bean — One cup (Hindi-Bhar)

Dry the grains well, powder and keep air-tight. Do not aid any colour or flavour. For breakfast, boil required quantity, add Milk and sugar and take as porridge. If you stick to this breakfast your weight is likely to reduce by one kg every month and this result has been seen in several cases. There are women, who take this as a regular diet even for lunch and dinner with some boiled vegetables, salads, fruits or pickles as side-dish. RYFO slimming porridge is found to be more effective than the internationally used weight reducing tablet called Andorax. If natural smell of the cereals is not liked add to the poridge quarter tea spoon of coffee or cocoa powder, Vanila or rose essence or home made essence of cummin seeds.

BUSINESS RYFO porridge powder may be packed in half kg plastic packets and put in the consumer market/for daily use of common people and the poor. Atleast half kg must be consumed in one month to see results. The ingredients (composition) may be printed on the label to inspire consumer confidence. Bulk supplies may be made to hospitals and nursing homes. They may even be exported to African refugee settlements. Ten neem leaves, dried and powdered may be added to every half kilo packet as a preservative. Even though neem preserves well it is advisable to consume the powder before the expiry date printed on the label. If kept longer have the powder sieved in a kitchen sieve once a fortnight to prevent formation of worms and lumps.

Energy value of Soyabean is very high and it is rich in alkaline salts and hence regarded as a corrective diet. It contains negligible percentage of starch (20.9 per cent). Therefore, it is very suitable for diabetic patients. Soyabean gives plenty of Lecithin which is rich in substances for the proper functioning of all living cells in the body and helps disperse deposits of Cholesterol and fatty materials from certain vital organs of the body. It is also a natural food medicine to cure or prevent skin diseases and eczema.

If making for the markets don't spend on containers. Pack in transparent colourless polythene sachet and put the packed sachet into another sachet and seal. Labels may be put between the two layers.

Money in Citronella Java

Botanical- Cymbopoon Sp is a perenial grass which yields an essential oil with fine flavour and several uses. The grass grows about a metre high and can be hard-rested 12 times in 4 years, can be raised by seeds and about one Kg. of seeds cover one acre. Usually they are raised in a nursery and then transplanted in ridges and furrows with a spacing of 60 cms by 90 cms before transplanting/ farm yard manure must be applied liberally. The grass should be cut in about 6 months and before it flowers. If allowed to flower the oil recovery will fall. About one tonne of grass will yield about ten kg of oil under normal conditions.

The oil can be steem distilled useing a simple still shown in RF Handout 13 and the residue can be given to cattle. A kilo of Lemon grass oil sold for Rs. 80 in India (1989 price).

Citronella fields should be watered, manured and weeded regularly. The second and subsequent harvests may be once in three months. Ants are the common pests and to keep them away neem-leaf powder may be used. For soil fertility all kinds of organic manure and crushed neem cake may be used and it will cost about Rs 5,000 a year to cultivate one acre.

Now a new variety of Citronella has been introduced by the Central Institute of Aromatic Plants (CIMAP) in Lucknow called CIMAP/BIO-13 the oil yield of which is double that of the existing variety from a given quantity.

Citronellas oil/is effective mosquito repellent and used in ODOMOSE and other similar preparations. Army men rub the oil on their body while living in jungles to keep away mosquitoes and elephants (It is surprising that mosquitoes and elephants cannot stank the smell of citronella). Citronella oil is widely used to manufacture of good quality soaps (the author of this note commissioned one unit for the poor in Sierra Leone financed by the ILO of the United Nations) and also in the manufacture of perfumes and medicines and confectionary. To thicken the oil it may be mixed with any of the oils mentioned in RF Handout 310 that may be extracted in the village. Thicker the oil, better the soap.

The grass grows very well in hills, plateaus and even in plains if looked after well and the grass can be seen to be growing wild in many tropical countries, especially. in Africa and the Indian Ocean islands. The oil can be extracted in cottage kitchens and for wholesale markets, there are nearly one thousand cottage units in Kerala and established buyers purchase the oil from them and export them to Europe and USA.

To reduce the price of soap, caustic lye extracted from banan barks as explained in Handout 45 may be used. If one uses citronella soap and takes a bath before going to bed mosquitos will keep away from him or her.

If a family in India produces about 30 Kgs of citronella oil per month (about 1 Kgs per day) it can make a net profit of Rs 5000 per month after meeting all expenses.

CATTL S FEED FORMULA

FEED Formula Recommended by the Animal Husbandry Department of Kerala

FORMULA-ONE	*Component*	*Percentage*
1.	Tapioca	43
2.	Groundnut cake	28
3.	Rice Bran	25
4.	Urea	1
5.	Mineral mixture	1.5
6	Salt	1.5
	Total	100.0

FORMULA-TWO	*Component*	*Percentage*
1.	Tapioca chips	22
2.	Gapioca leaf meal	30
3.	Groundnut cake	15
4.	Gingilly cake	10
5.	Black gram bran	10
6.	Wheat bran	10
7.	Mineral mixture	1.5
8.	Salt	1.5
	Total	100.0

Note: four formulae are given in Handout 272 and two in Handout 273.

Depending on the price and availability of the components on the village the appropriate formula may be followed small variations in the percentage of the components mixed will not matter.

Cattle must be given clean water to drink every day. Feed and water served the previous day must be removed and the feeding area must be kept absolutely clean and tidy.

CATTLE FEED FORMULA

Recommended by the National Dairy Research, Institute, Karnal

FORMULA-ONE	*Component*	*Percentage*
1.	Tapioca flour	25
2.	Coconut oil cake	25
3.	Groundnut oil. cake	20
4.	Gram churt	30
	Total	100

FORMULA-TWO	*Component*	*Percentage*
1.	Tapioca flour	25
2.	Horse gram	25
3.	Groundnut oil. cake	25
4.	Wheat, bran	25
	Total	100

FORMULA-THREE	*Component*	*Percentage*
1.	Tapioca	30
2.	Distillary Waste (dried)	35
3.	Fish, or meat meal	15
4.	Molasses	10
5.	Gran	10
	Total	100

FORMULA-FOUR	*Component*	*Percentage*
1.	Tapioca flour	20
2.	Groundnut oil cake	20
3.	Gram churi	20
4.	Wheat bran	20
5.	Groundnut oil cake	20
	Total	100

Feed formula is are recommended by the Animal. Husbandry Department of Kerala.

GOOSEBERRY PRESERVE

Gooseberry is basically of two types, the small type grown in domestic gardens and the large type grown mostly in villages and forests in many tropical countries including Africa, South Pacific and Indian Ocean Islands. Very rich in vitamin C gooseberry contains several other vitamins and it is frequently used in Indian medicines. They can be processed and preserved during season for consumer markets and exported to several countries which do not have them. The large type is better suited for preservation and commercialization,

Process: Collect or purchase a kilo, wash in salt water, dry well, cut each into two equal halves and remove the single seed. Take a porceline jar of 3 Kg capacity, clean, dry and put a 1 cm high layer of sugar into it. Spread (don't heap) one layer of the cut gooseberry and spread a layer of sugar on top of it. Make as many layers as you get, cover the opening of the jar, not with the lid but with a piece of mosquito net (no other cloth) and expose to open sun for ten days. On the eleventh day remove the net and filter the liquid. This drink is a delicacy and stays for months together tastes like sweet wine and does not ferment. It is also a tonic and an apetiser and can be served to visitors in small wine glasses. In these days of anti- alcoholism gooseberry syrup is a good substitute for sweet wine.

After filtering all the juice, spread the juiceless fruit bits in a dry plate and again expose to sun. Close the plate with a fly cover made of wire and net or use a ready made plastic fly cover. After two days of drying squeeze a full lime (for every Kilo of fruit) and spread two spoons of honey and dry again. Shift and turn the fruit bits the next day and dry for two more days and now the gooseberry is ready as a preserve to be bottled and packed in plastic food pouches or aluminium foil. They are excellent to taste almost like dried Apricots and can be cut into smaller bits and used as Tutti Frutti. The label can read dehydrated gooseberry in honey.

Don't add any chemical preservative. If you like, add 20 drops of ginger essence. To reduce cost on sugar you may mix sugar and jaggery in the ratio 3: 1. Please note that sunlight. Sugar, jaggery, lime (citric) honey are all excellent natural preservatives.

While packing put the bottle or hold the plastic pouch upto the neck in very hot water, fill in that position (while the container is still in water), close and seal it. This will make shelf life longer.

Cost of one Kg of gooseberry Rs two; cost of all other inputs Re one. Total cost of production of one kg of syrup and one Kg of fruit Rs three. Price to distributors of one Kg of syrup and fruit Rs eight. Net profit on one kg Rs five Price to exporters Rs 10. On a commercial scale especially in rural parts where gooseberry is plenty and cheap, a family can make a good monthly net profit of Rs 3,000.

There are several uses for the removed seeds which is explained in another handout. Gooseberry pickles are common in India. After extracting the juice, without adding anything the residue can be chopped and dried crisp, powdered and added to gravy or soup to add to taste and enrich food value. Holes are drilled in the seedis and used as beads for making garlands and for flower arrangement.

TUTTI-FRUTTI

Tutti-frutti is now a household word and children and grown-ups ask for bread, bun and biscuits with tutti-frutti. Hostel cooks, restaurants and railway caterers use more and more of it these days especially in warm countries where fruit and vegetable jackets are easily sun-dried. Plums and cherries are not usually grown and are therefore scarce and costly in warm countries and tutti frutti is an excellent substitute. Different types can easily be made by a woman in her kitchen out of fruit and vegetable shavings which are usually thrown away.

Materials used in Third world Countries for preparing Tutti-frutti are fleshy jackets (shavings) of raw Papaya (without the outer skin), pumpkin, chow-chow, carrots, beeat-roots, orange (loose jacket) peals, the big great water melon called in India Tarboose (not the soft yellow variety), etc. The most commonly used is the raw papaya (Popose) which is full of vitamins and medicinal properties like papine for soothing sore stomach.

Process*:* Wash and cut fleshy coat into half cm by half cm bits. Steam in pressure cooker or any vessel in a dry container placed inside the cooker or vessel with water around the dry container with the bits. Duration of steaming depends on hardness or softness of the materials steamed. Usually under full steam it is kept for five mts.

Remove with dry spoon and spread bits on dry porcelain or aluminium plate and sun dry for two days. (In countries where there is no sun a baking oven or a room heater may be used). On the third day, squeeze a full free lime for every kg of bits. Separately roast white sugar, char it brown and sprinkle a spoon full of charred sugar on, roughly, one kg of bits. To reduce cost you may mix with the sugar an equal quantity of powdered jaggery. A spoon full of honey may also be spread on the bits. Protect the bits from flies, insects and dust with a net dish closer while exposed to sun for ten to twelve days. Please note that steam, sun-light, lime, sugar, jaggery, honey are all natural preservatives and therefore no cynthetic preservative need be used.

Remove from plate with dry spoon, and pack bits in polythene bags. Packets may be in quarter, half and. one kg in weight. After removing the milk from the plastic pouches the pouches may be washed, dried and used for packing tutti-frutti. The packets may contain bits of one fruit or vegetable or a mixed lot. Seal each packet, staple lable, briefly explain content, process and mark consumer price. suggestesd wording for the label. Tutti-Frutti - raw papaya sun dried with lime, sugar & honey and packed under hygenic conditions by Educated women members of the WHEN FOUNDATION which promotes Women's Home Enterprises. No chemicals, artificial colours, smell. or preservatives. Rich in Vitamins.

CASSAVA BREAD

Making bread (and income) from *cassava*

YOUTHWORKS offers an FAO recipe for bread made with cassava flour as an income-generating activity for rural youth.

This bread is easily and inexpensively made from ingredients which are available locally across the tropics of the developing world, is good-tasting and, because of the addition of egg-white or soya flour, contains more protein than simple cassava products. Once baked, the bread will keep for 7-10 days, much longer than wheat breads.

Ingredients

250g cassava flour	15g sugar
5g salt	10g cooking oil

2 egg whites or 40g soya flour

2 teaspoons dry yeast

(1) Mix 30g cassava flour and 250ml water and heat to boiling while stirring constantly. Cook for 3-4 minutes, until the mixture becomes translucent. Remove from heat.

(2) Stir in remaining cassava flour (220g), salt, sugar, oil and egg white or soya flour. Allow batter to cool.

(3) Mix 2 teaspoons dry yeast in 40ml water, wait for 5 minutes and add to batter.

(4) Mix batter for 5 minutes. Pour batter into baking tins (fill 1/3 full) and let rise in warm, humid place for 15-25 minutes (cover with damp cloth).

(5) Bake at 210°C for 45 minutes.

(6) Allow bread to cool for one whole day before slicing.

Notes:

(1) You may want to experiment by using more or less cassava flour until you get the texture you prefer.

(2) This bread can also be made with millet or sorghum flour instead of cassava in that case, the egg white or soya flour are not needed.

Reproduced by RYEO (International) from *YOUTHWORKS* (journal of the Food and Agricultural Organisation of the United Nations dated April 1988.

BUNS FROM CASSAVA

Buns are made very much like bread, but with much finer and soft flour of high absorptive capacity; more water, upto ten percent sugar (even more for a sweet roll); say, about five per cent of milk and a similar quantity of fat. Usually, also twice as much yeast is used as in making bread. All this gives the bun a sweetish, chewy quality and a more plastic crust. Once the dough has been mixed, it is divided, rounded, proofed, formed and baked in individual pans much as is done for bread.

Buns from Cassava - reproduced from the book *Everyday Indian Processed Foods* by K.T. Achaya, Published by the National Book Trust of India.

Versatile Side-Tables

Any inexpensive wood such as tamarind, neem or Jack tree wood may be used to make these small many purpose tables. The advantage of the design is that the tables of uniform size can be stacked in spiral form to save space.

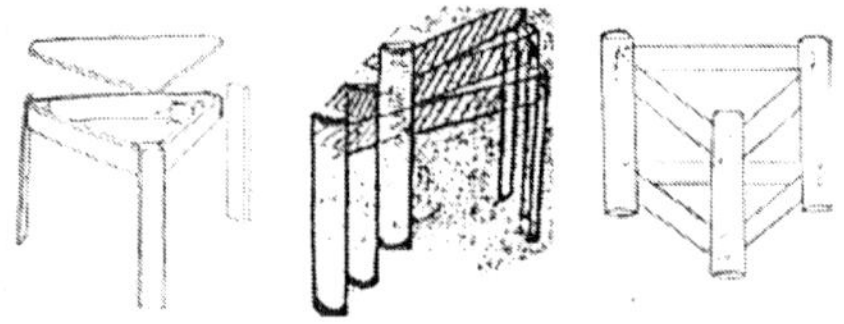

Construction: Cut 6 pieces of the size 40cm X 2cm X 2cm. Use three to make the legs and the remaining three to make a triangular top as shown in the diagram. Make also three equal size triangular blocks of the size two Cms on all sides. Fit these blocks into the inner triangle of the table top and screw then. Gum may be used before screwing. These three blocks will hold the triangle and the three legs firmly in position. You may fix the top either wooden plank, plywood or glass but the best will be to weave the triangle with a fibre rope or tape as weaving will give further strength to the table and the table can also be used as a stool to sit on and shifted to the garden conveniently.

If one likes, a triangular cushion filled with straw bits, waste cotton, jute, tailors waste or dried flowers may be used on top of it.

The table can also be made out of bamboo but if so made there has to be a triangular bottom frame like the triangular top frame in which case they cannot be stacked. If made out of bamboo care must be taken not to split the bamboo while cutting, making holes or nailing. Screws are not necessary if made out of bamboo. However, if some joints are found not strong enough screws may be used or the joints may be tied with wire or tape for added strength.

Diagram 1 explains constructional details. Dia 2 shows how the tables may be stacked and Dia 3 shows how the table will look if made out of bamboo.

For diagram and assembling instructions for making sitting room chairs out of bamboo.

RYFO Wood Paint Cum Preservative (for Villages)

Price of ordinary paint and brush is very high and the poor who cannot afford food cannot afford paint as well. Rural carpenters who make simple stools, chairs and tablet out of country wood sell them without paint or varnish. They are easily attached by white ants and wood insects. RYFO wood paint cum preservative not only preserves but also gives a good colour. It is prepared with organic matter available in villages. The ingredients are given below. Every ingredient must be ground well (like butter and mixed in the given proportion. The paint may be applied either with a brush or with a piece of cloth (rag) made into a bundle as big as a lime. The grinding is best done in a village oil crusher (Cow driven chekku) or put in an electrically or hand operatic pulveriser. For various other methods of grinding see RYFO Handout Nos. 285, 2, 145, 165, 212, to bring the paste to required consistency add country brewed alcohol or kerosine. Water may be added only of Kerosin or alcohol is not available.

Composition

1.	Eucalyptus leaf paste	one cup.
2.	Neem leaf paste	two cups.
3.	Tamarind seed glue	2 cups.
4.	Turmeric	One table spoonfull heap.
5.	Red Chillis	One tablespoonfull heap.
6.	Wood ash	One cup (Sieved well).

7. Paste of Beetroot or Methi (Marudani) or Acacia tree bark, any one or all three mixed) — One cup
8. Mineral Lime (Chunam) — One cup
9. Kerosine oil if available or country brewed alcohol — One cup
10. Any waste oil (non-edible) — One cup

Mix thoroughly and paint. Repainting may be done once a year.

BAMBOO FURNITURE

Picture is self explanatory. Excellent furniture can be made out of good quality bamboo of uniform diametre, several varieties of bamboos are available in different regions of the world and the varieties available in one's own country or region may be used. Almost all varieties are suitable for making furniture.

The tools required are the usual hand-operated carpenter's tools, and no power need be used. For cutting and sawing the Ryan Foundation Device for cutting poles and planks may be used (handout 25).

Two similar chairs like the one shown in the diagram and one double piece (sofa) will make a settee and a small central table and a smaller peg stand (whisky glass stand) may also be made to required size.

In the picture the bottom and the back rest are made of strips of bamboo but it is better to weave these out of cotton tapes, fibre ropes or HDPP (plastic) woven tapes'. It will be easier, nicer, quicker, and stronger to make the seat and back rest out of tapes or ropes.

The furniture must be made when the bamboos are green, so that when they dry and became yellow, the holes become smaller and the joints grip tight. Strictly speaking no gum or wire nails or screws are required to make bamboo furniture. However, when the grip in certain joints are not tight enough country glue (tree gum), animal tatow. (Vajaram), gum Arabic or Fevicol and some nails and screws may be used.

The seat back cushion for the chairs may be made out of HDPP woven sack cloth (the material commonly used for packing cements and fertilisers). This cloth is much cheaper than jute, and it is sold by weight. However, where this man-made fibre cloth is not available, jute cloth may be used and in India jute is now offered at a concessional price under the Internal and External Market Assistance scheme for diversified jute product by the Jute Manufacturers Development Council of the Government. of India, Ministry of industry. 3 Park Plaza, 71 Park Street, Calcutta-700016' The cushions may be stuffed with jute waste, tailor's waste, fibre waste and neem leaves, all mixed in equal proportion. Cottor or foam flling will it make it costly.

Bamboo which is the largest and quickest growing grass in the world is highly drought resitant and can be grown by villagers in tropical countries. If the bamboo furniture industry is promoted there will be more growing of bamboos and less cutting of trees for timber A chair like the one shown in the dia, will give a profit of nearly one hundred percent,

DEMAND FOR DRIED FRUITS

The Demand in USA, Europe and Japan for dried fruits of other Countries is basically for people's own consumption and for re-export in further processed or converted forms to other Countries by merchant exporters or "luxury edibles" manufacturers.

On an average about 40 per cent of processed and preserved fruits imported by these countries are re-exported in the same form or added to biscuits, chocolates. jams, fruit salads and several other products into which the imported fruits are used as ingredients or components.

To give an idea regarding one country, the Netherlands, in 1986 the Country imported processed fruits worth of 185 million weighing 19.100 tons costing on an average £ 2.30 per kg. The total imports in 1987 was for £ 175 millions weighing 20.800 tons and costing on an average £ 2.15 per kg.

In general, the import market of advanced countries for processed fruits, is steadily increasing in value, approximately by four per cent every year. In Netherlands the import of dried fruits increased by five per cent between 1983 and 1986.

The Western and Japanese buyers want processed, preserved and dried fruits to be packed in their natural juices. Fruits in syrup is quite popular and light syrup is preferred (18 to 20 per cent syrup) This is due to growing consciousness of health and eating habits of people in these advanced countries.

An increasing number of consumers are prepared to try new, unknown products. The number of Asians, Mediterraneans, Caribbeans and Africans (settlers in these countries) like tropical fruits and many locals like fruits not grown in their own country.

Dried fruits are often used in what are called luxury (food) products, so the consumption of them is a status symbol. The health food movement in these countries shows a growing interest in dried fruits. These is also a noticeable increase in the demonstration of status symbols in these Countries.

The importers ask for:

1. Uniform size
2. Attractive colour typical of the fruit devoid of chemicals
3. Good eating properties, i.e., good bite/texture and not fibrous or sticky
4. Well dried-fruits not sticking together
5. Good packaging quality
6. Food colours and preservatives within tolerance level or not at all.

Developing new applications/uses for processed, preserved and dried fruits is one of the possible ways of capturing or increasing export market share to these Countries by the developing countries and creating new rural job opportunities. Fruit growers, dealers, home science specialists and women's groups and NGOs in general should come up with new ideas.

It should be noted that several small innovations such as dried mango, and dried papaya or plantain have not been very successful because they did not conform to the 6 requisites of the foreign buyers. Care must be taken to meet the requirements of the importers and final consumers.

OIL DISTILLER WITH VILLAGE MATERIALS

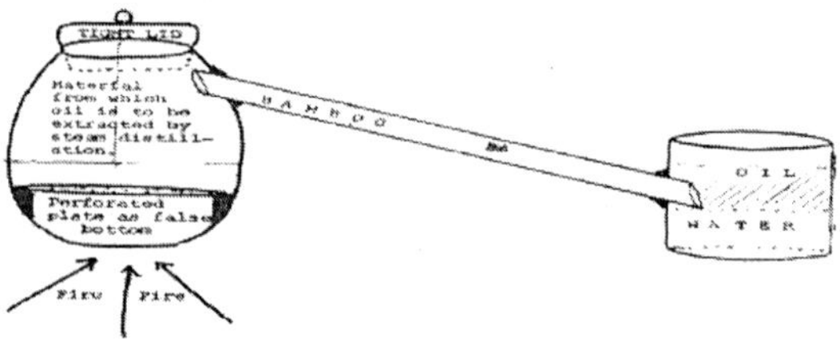

Construction: The height of pot must be atleast one metre and breath half metre. The lid must be tight and leak proof. A wire belt may be tied round the pot; and the lid connected and tied to it with a binding wire as shown. The earthen pot must be as strong as possible/made of good clay, surki (burnt clay powder), mineral calcium (Chunnam), some Jaggery and plaster of Paris (natural gypsum stones burnt and powdered. If cement is easily available a little may be added. The bamboo must be two metres long and smooth inside. The two joints must be tight and plastered as shoen.

How to Use: Mount the pot on three stones and put fire underneath.

Fill water upto the perforated false bottom. The steam will carry the oil and flow out to the water bath and condensation will take place inside the bamboo. To hasten condensation the bamboo may be wrapped with wet cloth. The pot may be lodged inside a tank or small chamber built of bricks on the ground of the size 11/2 m X 11/2 m to prevent accidents in case the pot breaks due to excess pressure inside. But this should not happen, as the excess steam will' escape through the bamboo. If metal wire is not available to be used as a belt around the pot a strong fibre rope may be used.

All types of nuts, barks, seeds, leaves or roots that have to be steam distilled/for oil may be put into the pot. The oil in the steam will condense and float on the water in the bath/as shown and can be siphoned off. In every village about a dozen families may distill the oil and make it available for all those families who supply the raw materials. This distiller will provide rural employment save tandrees from being cut and keep the surroundings clean.

BAMBOO PIPES

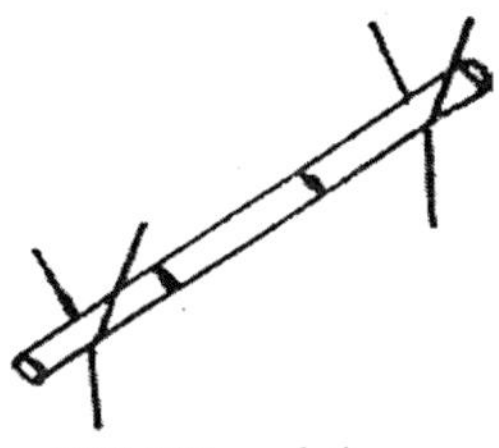

Bamboo; of the grass family, grows fast and high under hazardous conditions of soil and climate. It is a highly drought resistant forest shrub-tree/offering several livelihood possibilities and yet neglected. Bamboos make excellent sewerage pipes in remote rural areas where they can be grown and processed.

RYAN Foundation recommends standardisation on bamboo pipes to lengths of 3 mts and 8 cms. internal diametre. Mature bamboo may be cut at either ends uniformly with a saw and projections outside may be chopped with a chissel and hammer and then the inner cavity cleaned and broadened. To do this, a long iron rod 1,1/2 mts long sharpened at one end like a chissel may be used. The bamboo may be placed on two 'Y' stands as shown in dia. and chiselled from either end. Only in this position one can see through easily and knock out internal projections and smoothen ruggedness. Whether used above ground or under all bamboos have to be treated. The best rural technology for treating is to boil Castor oil with neem, vasaka, datura leaves (3 parts) and turmeric, chilli. powder and wood ash (one part) and paint the bamboos with the solution inside and outside. On a commercial scale the solution may be prepared in a long concrete pit-tub and the bamboos put into it and soaked for about a week. This treatment prevents bamboos from cracking or being attacked by white ants. If bituen (*tar*) is available it may be melted and painted outside (not inside) Inside must be as smooth as possible. If tar is not available, used cement or fertilizer bags (plastic or fibre) or locally woven crude fibre cloth may be wrapped around the bamboos and tied.

30 cms long and 10 cms in inner diametre pipes may be similarly prepared and used as sleeves to join the pipes where required. Mortar mixture explained in RF Handout 294 may be used as the binder to plaster the joints.

These bamboo pipes may also be used to take water to fields and for domestic supply to drinking water.

In Tanzania region of Arusha, Rukwa, Morogoro and Dar-es-Salam several bamboo processing and installing units have been established financed by the Dutch Government (US $140,000), NORAM (US$ 196,000); SIDA (US $ 280,000); and the EEC. The processing method is different in Tanzania from what is recommanded by the RYAN Foundation. For RF processing only local materials available in the village need be used and nothing need be imported.

Raw materials being free or the industry can provide full employment for atleast a dozen families of the village in the cultivation, processing, laying, repairs, replacement and maintenance and it is an ideal industry for rural women. For Castor see Handout

SUN DRYING POTATO SLICES

Large size and odd shaped potatos can be pealed, cut into thin slices and sun dried for preservation on corrugated metal roofing sheets or inside boxes with a glass lid or thin transparent polythene covering.

Before exposing to sun the pealed potatos may be washed several times in fresh water to remove as much starch as possible and then blanched (dipped in boiling water for about five minutes.) A teaspoon full of table salt may be added to the water kept for blanching. If the sun is bright complete dehydration will take place in about three days (morning nine to evening four) If the sun is mild, drying may take five to six days. If corrugated metal roofing sheets or glass sheets are not available slices may be laid on plain cloth or on a news paper.

To preserve for several months pealed potatos are treated in the preservative Sodium Metabisulphite which is cheap and readily available in city shops but to preserve for one or two months this treatment is not required and it is advisable to avoid the chemical.

Dried potatos may be packed in new one kg polythene bags for the market or in used milk sachets for domestic use. What goes to the market must have a brand name and price tag.

The pelled skin may be mixed in moist form to cattle feed, or dried, ground and mixed to chicken feed. They may also be boiled with little water to get a paste and if a good pate is required wheat flour (maida) may be added to it one third by volume.

Similarly, onions may be dried as flakes; ginger, the common pea and several other vegetables may also be dried (dehydrated) and preserved or sold. Most of the dehydrated vegetables may be reconstituted by boiling in water. Some vegetables and edible leaves (spinache) can be dried, ground and preserved in powder form for the market or for exporting to countries where they are not available. Mixing and blending of different powders may also be done to obtain different taste and flavour and nutrition value. Blending of carrot powder and drumstick leaf powder is excellent as an eye tonic as both carrot and drumstick leaves have a high percentage of vitamin A. Field mint, (pudhina in Tamil) and curry leaves (Karuva pillai in Tamil) are other two leaves which are almost every day used in Indian cooking and these also may be dried and preserved either as dried leaves or in powder form.

Sun dried preservation of fruits, vegetables and edible leaves for culinary and medicinal purposes is opening out new avenues of livelihood and these industries can be an entire monopoly of rural people. Very low investment, high decentralization and pooling for wholesale markets is all possible in the industry. The only thing to be ensured is cleanliness and free from adulteration.

Following these chain of industries is the commercialisation of medicinal plants. Some of these plants are available only in some poor countries and these countries can capture a world market. Separate handouts are available on processing and packing different medicinal herbs and leaves with the Ryan Foundation. Sky is the limit.

ORGANIC INSECTICIDE

Plants and trees are attacked by various pests and scientist recommand chemical pesticides. Many pesticides found to be hazardous to health and banned in advanced countries are sold in India and many Third world countries by Governments and multinationals but they will soon be defeated in the chemical warefare. They are products of the twentieth century and farmers of the bygones centuries did not have or use them. This 'awakening' is spreading and people are trying to find sane alternatives.

The best alternative is the organic pesticide invented and manufactured by God Almighty for the survival of humanity. This can be in powder, liquid or granule form and they kill several pests and prevent many plant diseases, basically organic insecticides consist of neem leaf, wood ash and a small quantity of turmeric. For kitchen and home-garden use these may be ground like paste, then mixed with water and made into semi-liquid and brushed with a soft paint-brush on the stems and leaves of plants and small trees.

Several village leaves and jungle shrubs with insecticide propeties are listed in Ryan Foundation Handout Nos 112 and 130. Any of these available leaves may be added to the mixture as one or the other ingredient kills or drives away one pest or the other and the research in this field is just starting and we have miles to go for one to say which leaf for what pest.

For large plantations orchids and crop fields the insecticide may be dried, ground and mixed on a village community scale and the mixture can be in the composition 20 parts leaves (mostly neem) 5 parts wood—ash and one part turmeric and they may be in liquid, powder or granule form but the granule form is the easiest to prepare, store and transport. Third world farmers, who do not have electrical or mechanical sprayers or stirup pumps prefer to use it as powder spray or mix the granules in the water flowing into the fields.

The type of leaves used in the mixture depends on their availability in a given region or country. In peninsuler India leaves such as neem, vasaka, datura, papaya, rubs, bull, 'Yerukkam' etc are being used. Other types of leaves are also used in *GLORIA LAND* in Pondicheery, a flourishing farm where only organic fertilizers and insecticides are used.

RYAN Foundation favours the preperation of organic insecticides in granule form (broken to small particles) by village communities and sold to farms, institutions and governmente to generate income for millions of families in the Third world. If packed well without adulteration, they can very well be exported to the advanced west. Already neem leaves are exported to Germany from India to make insecticides there.

Granules may be packed in HDPP (plastic) bags like cement or chemical fertilizers, The producer can earn one hundred percent profit. per. The initial investment will be on bags and used (bags can be reused. By quick turn over both the working capital and profits can be built up. Non-Government organizations working in rural areas may quickly get villagers organised for this livelihood.

DROUGHT RESISTANT MESTA

There axe two varieties of this excellent fibre. Hibiscus Cannabinus and Hibiscus Sabdarifa. After much investigation Ryan Foundation field experts recommand the propagation of *Sabdariffa* in very dry areas having below average rain fall as this variety is highly drought resistant even though it takes longer time to get ready for harvest. Short duration Cannabin us which is better in quality and fetches a better price may however be introduced in areas which have average rain fall.

Mista does not require chemical fertilizers but plenty of organic and farm house manure and the harvest time for sabdariffa is May-June. If left for about six months beyond harvest time the plant yields plenty of seeds for resowing. The seeds must be drilled into the soil and about 14 kg can be sowed in one hectare. As the plants grow, repeated weeding is necessary and the first weeding should be done in about a month from sowing. Spraying of organic liquid fertilizer and organic liquid insecticide, helps healthy growth. Water logging should be prevented to avoid formation of fungus.

The fibre yield of Sabdariffa is about 15 quintals per hectare, and the fibre is of long staple and not very tough. It is easy to it, clean and weave into coarse cloth. The stem should be cut close to ground to get long fibre.

Harvesting is done five to six months from sowing depending on soil and climatic conditions. The best time to harvest is when the flowering stage is mid-way. Cut stems are bundled and left in the field to shed their leaves and the leaves make good manure. When dry the stems are soaked in water in a pond and retted in the same way as jute is retted.

The fibre is in the skin or peal of the stem or bark and the pealing must be done carefully so that the fibre comes out in good lengths and not in broken bits. The best method of pealing is shown in Ryan Foundation Handout 156 and 118.

Uses for this fibre are very many. Ruggets, Organic manure packing bags, ropes etc, can be made. Thick ropes can be used to make the roof frame-work for building low-cost houses with village materials as 'Explained in the book shelter with village materials for self-help settlements published by the Ryan Foundation For various other uses fibre can be put to see Handout 233 released by the Ryan Foundation,

HOLY BASIL (TULSI)

Botanical- Ocimum basilicum Linn. family- *Labiatae.* Hindi and Bengali *Baburi Tulsi* Tamil- *Karpura. Tulsi* or *Tirnirupachai.* Talugu-*Bhutulasi,* Kannada-*Kama Kasthuri.*

There are ever so many species in Tulsi and the common variety Kept in homes for purposes of worship by the Hindus is called Ocimum Sanctum.

Basically there are four distint types:

1. European type in which the principal costituent *is linalool* but no camphor.

2. The "Reunion type which contains more of methyl chavicol and camphor and considered inferior to the European variety.
3. Methyl Cinnamate type which does not contain camphor.
4. Eugenol Species which contains eugenol. as the main constituent.

While the right species is to be chosen for preparing different medicines all types are equally good for preparing herbal tea and more or less the flavour is the same in all types.

Considered" as a sacred plant in India, it is grown in homes, temples and religlos centres. The fruits are small and the seeds yellowish or reddish, all parts of the plant are medicinal.

The oil of Tulsi has the property of destroying insects and bacteria. The juice of the leaves is useful in treating bronchitis, catarrah, digestive disorders and minor skin troubles; A decoction of leaves is used to cure common cold and cough, to increase urination and to bring about sweating in malarial fever. Juice of the leaves is also applied as a nasal douch. Seeds are roasted and eaten or ground fresh and taken with honey to relieve piles and constipation, According to herbal scientist Pruthi the plant is considered stomachic, anthelmintic, alexlphar-mic, antipyretic, stimulant and pectoral. An infusion of the plant is given for cephalalgia and gouty joints and used as a gargle, for foul breath". Leaves are used in poultices pores and sinuses and in treatment of cough, for which waerm juice with honey is given.

"Roots, bark and leaves are cyanogenetic. Alcohol extract, of leaves and alcoholic -yid aqueous extracts of flowers possess anti-bacterial activity against Micrococcus pyogenes Varaureus. Seeds possess demulcent, stimulant, diaretic, diaphoretic and cooling properties."

Analysis report of the American Spice Trade Association (ASTA USA, records that Basil or Sweet Basil oil contains protein 11.9 percent, carbohydrates 41.2 per cent, fibre 20.5 per cent, total ash 16.7 per cent and calaroies value (food energy) 325 calaroies per 100 gm of dried herb. Methyl chavicol is the main in constituent of Sweet Basil Oil.

PRESERVE FRESH FLOWERS FOR YEARS

Beautiful fresh flowers can be preserved in their original colour, tint and shape, framed like pictures, displayed in wall plaques, vases, or made into briquettes and wrapped in cellophine paper. They look very natural and beautiful.

Step One: Take ordinary sand of fine grains. It may be river or sea sand or dug out earth. Pound the sand to powder in a pistle or grind in a grinding stone and sieve in a kitchen sieve, muslin cloth or gauze. Wash the sand in clean water and dry and repeat the washing and drying process ten times. Finally soak the powdered sand overnight in preserved rain water (or demineralised water) and dry it again. Repeated washing is necessary to remove salt, soap, acids, chemical and dirt. Thereafter boil the sand in rainwater to kill all bacteria that might eat the petals. Finally dry and seave the sand once more and then only it is ready for use.

Step Two: Take a suitable container like a chocolate or biscuit tin or a wooden box. Size of box and quantity of sand depend on the size and number of flowers you want to preserve. Bread box or glass jars may also be used.

Fill one third of the container with the prepared sand, pick the flowers by the stem without touching the petals and place them gently on the sand bed petals upward. Then gently fill the remaining two third of the container with the prepared sand. Take care to cushion the petals without forcing them even a bit out of their natural shape. Tap or jiggle the container gently so that sand powder penetrates all the curves and cresies. With this the process is over. You may lable the name and number of flowers and the date of selling and leave it to dry in sun or shade for three to four weeks with the lid on. Then open and remove gently.

Three Step: While setting the flowers set also leaves of the same plant in the same way in another container. Cut also six twigs of the same plant of the size 15 cms, 20 cms, 25 cms and dry them in the open sun, paint and bring back to look green and fresh. Paste, tie or drill holes and Insert the flowers and leaves in the prepared stem. Wax or nail polish may be used for sticking.

NOTE: The same sand may be recycled for drying a second set of flowers provided they are sieved again and dried well. Washing again is not necessary.

Buds and semi bloomed flowers give excellent result. Garden flowers best suited are Zinnias, tulips, daisies, dahlias, roses, hollyhocks, lotus and billies and almost all forest flowers come out well.

THE HUMBLE PLANT

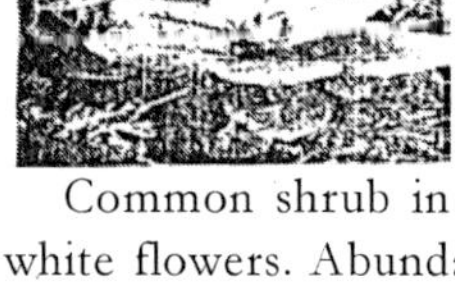

Botanical - *Calotropis Gigantea.*
Sanskrit - *Armand or Arka.*
Tamil - *Erukkam.*
Hindi- *Muddar or Ak.*
Family- *Euphorbiacsae.*

Common shrub in many tropical countries with bunches of pale white flowers. Abundant and uncared for in the Indian subcontinent Found all along road sides in urban and rural areas and waste lands. When the broad pale-green leaves are plucked or branches broken a milky juice drips. This milk is called *Muddar* in North India and Yerukku in South India and it is applied on boils, bruises and cuts for quick healing. Left in the wild it grows as high as two mts. with branches about an inch in thickness. The shrub is extremely drought resistant and cattle do not eat the leaves.

Uses:

1. According to Himal Botany (page 275) the plant is reported to yield sugar. (so far not commercially exploited).
2. The leaves are excellent plant manure cum insecticide and they are commonly used by farmers as 'trash mulch.
3. The stem yields fibre which is spun into thick thread (count one or two) and woven into coarse cloth by the tribals and used as rugs and carpets.
4. Ropes made out of this fibre are used in tieying thatched roofs as insects don't attack them.
5. Roots, when dried and powdered are excellent as insecticide.
6. The poisionous oil in the leaves is steam distilled by the village process and the oil is rubbed to cure skin diseases. The oil is applied on fibre ropes and wooden poles to save them from white ants.
7. Tribals mix the oil with much other non-edible oil from nuts and seeds found in the forests and use the mixed oil to make flame torches and carry the burning fire when they cross jungles for light and warmth and also to scare away wild animals and snakes.
8. They also pour the oil in termite hills to kill dangerous ants.
9. Branches of the fully grown shrubs can be used to make frames' to make oven-sack tiles (RF Handout 192).
10. Dried branches are made into briquettes for domestic cooking. (See RF handout No 319).
11. The roots of Calotropis, Vasaka, datura and Vinca Rosea, dried, powdered and mixed in equal proportion has the effect of high quality insecticide.

The manufacturing of this root insecticide is an excellent rural industry and can provide employment for thousands of families in hundreds of villages in Third countries.

The leaves of Calotropis, dried and ground to granules also have properties of insecticides but powdered roots are much more effective and ideally suited for orchids and home gardens. As they are purely organic they can be used inside the house in boxes and storing places to control moths and mosquitoes, pests and parasites.

BEER FROM SORGHUM

Botanical-Holcus sorghum. Sorghum in English Jowar in Hindi. Solam in Tamil (this is different from Makka Cholam called corn in English. *Sorghum* is the smaller variety of corn otherwise called maize.

Sorghum is used as raw material in malting industry and as a source of starch in fermentation industry for manufacturing industrial alcohol and acetone. The grain grows commonly in many Third world Countries with little care under drought conditions.

To make good beer out of sorghum it is pound first into fine flour. Then double its quantity of water is added to the flour by volume and boiled. After cooling the water is filtered and left for a day. The next day the filtered Sorghum water is boiled again. After cooling Yeast is added (one tablet or half tea-spoon of Yeast powder for every glass) the beer is ready on the following day and it should be consumed fresh in a day or two. Thereafter it becomes stale and intoxicating. Left for four or five dayrs it can turn sour and poisonous.

Oxfam News of Summer 1989 explains this recepie as followed by the Titao Womens Group of Yatenga Province where Oxfam works. The reporter Toby Milner writes about the beer thus: "It was good - not so far away after all, in taste atleast from some of the real ales of Britain."

NOTE:

1. Brewing beer is an offence in some countries and needs a permit from the Government
2. Soft water gives better beer than hard water.
3. The Sorghum must be cleaned and dried well before powdering.
4. It is better to use ready-made Yeast tablets or powder than to make your own yeast.
5. If properly done this beer is like a health tonic.
6. The price can be kept low so that many people, women included, may take fresh beer with mild fermentation for good health and cheer:

7. Care must be taken to consume the beer within a day or two to avoid over fermentation.
8. Cottage-scale brewing of sorghum beer can give a good income for several families in the same village provided people of the village have earning capacity to buy beer and are adequately disciplined to limit their Intake to 3 or 4 pints a day.
9. Corn, millet, barley, wheat, rice can all be used in a similar process and in Nepal many families brew beer out of rice which is good for healthy and tasty (the author took a full glass in Oct. 1989 and felt fine) The process in Nepal is slightly different. Theysteera cook the rice in a specially made pot with perforations and the beer they make preserves for several months.

Too Much Alcohol is Bad For Health and Family But Mild Beer is Good

Curry leaf

Poor villagers in warm countries can make about Rs 6000 per month if they cultivate the highly drought resitant curry leaf (Murraya Koenigil Sprengel) which requires little care and water (For culinary and medicinal properties of curry leaves sea Ryan Foundation Handout 359)

Healthy seeds from luxuriously growing plants or trees should be taken for raising a nursery. When the saplings are about three to four months old and about 15 to 20 cms high they are carefully removed with roots and transplanted into tiny pits of about 20 cm X 20 cm X 20 cm and one metre by per imetre apart. The pits may be given some 3 wood-ash and cow dung for a start.

For raising a nursery the variety with red stalk (red-petioled typo) may be selected as this species has a very strong and pleasant smell. Each of the for corners of the plot may be allowed to grow a tree to give shoots for propagation, i.e., they should not be pruned like the rest.

In home gardens we sea curry leaf allowed to grow into big trees but for commercialising they have to be pruned as soon as they reach a metre and a half high. Chemical fertilisers need not be used as they thrive well with or. gain manure and mulch Cobs of corn, millet or ragi are excellent fertilisers for the plant and some cow dung when available may be thrown. Each plant may be given a kilo of manure and a bucket of water once a month. Too mouch water is bad and bright sunlight is good.

In about 13 to 14 months, the plant grows high enough and can be harvested. The first two or three harvests will give a low yield but after two or three prunings the yield will be large and the plant will look bushy. If pruning is done leaving a stub as short as 30 to 40 cms from ground level the plant can be harvested once in three months.

Weeding must be done once in two weeks and this is very necessary. If delayed, pests set in and weeds take away soil nutrients.

Harvest is usually left to contractors.durge.

If the poor do not have land they may cultivate the plant in waste lands and enjoy the benefits. Care must be taken to fence the cultivation with thorny plants or fibre nets.

Recently curry leaf "Tea". is attracting western markets, in some combination of leaves or roots for herbal *TEA*. curry leaf forms an important ingredient. The leaves can be dried, powdered, packaged, marketed and even exported. The Ayurvedic system of medicine recommends curry leaf powder with honey as a general tonic.

Packing is usually done in polythene bags. The leaf has high potentialities to enter international markets from developing countries. The Western world does not have curry leaf and they are waiting for suppliers from the tropics.

HEALING FENUGREEK

Botanical - *Triconella Focnum-graecum L.*

Family- *Leguminosae* Tamil- *Vondhiam.*

Hindi-Bengali and Gujarati - *Methi.* Telugu- *Mentulu.*

Native of South Europe, seeds yield dicsgenin, precursor of steroids. Fenugreek is the dried fruit of an annual herb. Seeds are small, light brown and slightly bitter.

Seeds contain many substances such as starch, protein, mucilage, sugar, volatile oil, mineral matter, enzymes, vitamins and much of essential amino acids, (Chemical analysis was done by the Central Food Technology Research Institute of the Government. of India, Mysore and the composition, food value and medicinal properties were established. The Gujarat Ayurvedic University, Jamnagar and the Drug Research Institute (*CSMDRI*) Madras have also done investigations and reported.

The leaves are rich in calcium, carotene (Vitamin A), iron and ascorbic acid. The Vitamin C content of raw leaves averages between 43.10 mg/100 g.

The Ancient Greeks believed that fenugreek stimulated the digestive process and toned up the general metabolism and they ate the seeds raw, boiled, or with honey.

Seeds are used to relieve colic flatulence diarroehea, dysentery, chronic cough, dyspepsia, loss of appetite, enlargement of liver and spleen, rickets, diabetese and gout. Recent findings of the Indian Council of Medical and Scientific Research throws much light on the medicinal property of Fenugreek to reduce sugar level in the body and diabetic patients in India are increasing the intake of fenugreek in various forms. Some take powdered fenugreek put into gelatine capsules, others soak it in water and eat or mix the powder with honey and swallow.

Recent studies in UK have indicated that the seeds contain diosgenin which is used as a starting material in the synthesis of sex hormones and oral contraceptives. Thus, a regular intake of Fenugreek is expected to reduce the fertility of people and control the growth of population.

Medical papyri from ancient Egyptian tombs reveal that it was used to reduce fevers and as a cure for baldness in men, Pruthi reports-that in Java today fenugreek is used in hair tonic preparations and in cosmetics. The seeds contain a fixed oil which has a very strong and pleasant smell and in recent years it has attracted perfume manufacturers

In Egypt and Ethiopia fenugreek is popularly used in bread making known to the Arabs as Hulba and in Ethiopia as Abish. In the United States of America fenugreek is commonly used for making chutneys. Thus, in many parts of the world and even the ancients, knew the food and medicinal and preventive health maintenance value of fenugreek.

CURRY LEAF

Botanical – *Harraya Koenigii (Linn) Sprengel.*

Family – *Rutaceas.*

Hindi – *Mitha neea* or *Kadhi-neem.*

Gujarati – *Goranimb.*

Teluga – *Kapapaka.*

Kannada – *Karibeve.*

Bengali – Barsanga.

The Central Pood Research Institute of the Govt of India has researched and established the chemical composition and medicinal properties of curry leaves. The leaves contain free amino acids such as serine. aaparagine, glutmic acid, aspartic ecidv alanine, threnine. proline, tryptophane tyrosine, phenylalanine, lsoleucine, leucine. histidine end arginine. The leaves also contain crystalline glycoside; remain, exit Koenigil and some potash.

An infusion of the roasted leaves is used to stop vomiting and the tender green are eaten raw to cure dysentery. several ayurvedic preparations include curry leaves and the ayurvedic system recommends dried curry leaf powder with honey as a general tonic.

The leaves contain a volatile oil the major chealea constituents of which are sabinene, dipoantone, pinene. terpenal cadinene end caryopaylene. The CFTRI reports that beta-pinene is present in curry leaves.

Curry leaves are grown in many homes and farms and used commonly in Indian cookery for flavour and taste the Indian housewife is always happy to have a curry leaf tree in her backyard.

References:-

1. Research papers of the Cptri Hyoore.
2. *Ayurvedic Cure for Common Diseases* by H.L. Sharma, Head of the Shalya - Shalakya Dept, Moolechand Hospital, New Delhi.
3. *Spices and Condiments* by J.S. Pruthi. Orient Paperback Scientist, Winner of World Prize and Gold Medal and National Awards on his Research Findings in the Field of Spice. and condiments published by the National Book Trust.
4. *Home Remedies* by Hakeem Abdul Hameed Saheb. Head of the hamadard Dawakhana and laboratories Published by Orient Paperbacks, New Delhi 1988.
5. *Medicinal Plants* by S.K. Jain, Director, Botanical Survey of India, Calcutta and his Other books Herbarium Methoda, Olimpeea of Indian Ethnobotany etc.
6. *Dictionary of Economic Plants in India* by Twrao singh Wadhwani and Johri Published by the Indian Council of Agricultural Research of India. New Delhi.1988
7. *Everyday Indian Processed Food* by K.T. Acharya, also Published by the National Book Trust of India.

USEFUL DESERT/AXYLANCL SHRUB

Botanical - *Capparis decidua.*
English- *Kair.*
Hindi- *Kair.*
Family- *Capparidoeceal*

Description A shrub tree that looks like, grows quick and wild like acacia. Thrives well in regions with temperature as high as 50 degrees C and rainfall as low as 150 mm and in very saline soils. Small green leaves are found only on the twigs and not on the big branches but red flowers are found on the branches in clusters away from the leaves. The tree blooms twice a year and the red petals are oblong and narrow. The fruits look similar to Cherry

Distribution: Native of many tropical countries including the desert and dry lands of India. Grow. wild also in African countries, Egypt, Arabia, Madagascar and several Indian ocean Islands.

Uses: Excellent for consolidating and holding sandy soils and sand dunes. The berries, while still green contain a high percentage of vitamin C and its protein content is as high as 8.6 percent (more than what a Guava fruit has) Seeds contain 20.3 percent oil, 68.6 percent unsaturated fatty acids and 31.4 percent saturated acids.

The tree yields very hard and strong wood which is used as pillars and rafters in building construction and as railway sleepers. They are also used as building foundation base-planks as they stay like stone-slabs and insects don't eat the wood.

About two Kgs of green berries and about eight kgs of ripe ones may be picked from each tree every day at regular intervals. In India dried and processed fruits fetch Rs 70 to 80 per eight Kgs.

Poor people living in areas where this tree grows use the bark, the fruit, the leaves and the nuts for preparing several medicines but so far these have no scientific sanction in the alopathy system. However, they are recognised and liberally used in Ayurvedic system.

Animals eat the leaves, and the berries are used for making pickles and 'chutoys'. In Africa liquor is brewed from this fruit.

This desert plant which lives by the water provided by Nature for its survival has tremendous potentialities and with minimum care can be promoted and multiplied in many hot regions and exploited for human progress. They can give means of livelihood both to the poor who care for them and give the urban society fuel, fruits, building wood and medicines.

The twigs of the shrub-tree are excellent for making briquettes as explained in BP Handout No 319.

MEDICINAL MINT

Botanical - *Mentha Arrensis L.*
English - *Corn Mint* or *Field mint*,
In many Indian languages it is called *PODINA*.
Family- *LABIATE*.

There are several varieties of mint but the most important species is MENTH PIPERITAL, This species is cultivated in several parts of India and some other countries and Japan has plenty of different species of mint.

The dried loaves and flowering top of mint Pipertta are medicinal and are used to relieve rheumatic pain, headache, stomach disorders, indigestion and cough. They are also used as an anticeptic, carminative, refrigerant, stimulant and diuretic. The dried leaves do not have a pleasant taste but they act as a good expectorant, kidney tonic and help the liver, spleen and asthma. The leaves contain antispasmodic properties and help cure jaundice. Patients of elephantiasis and varicose veins get relief when they consume mint. Ground leaves (Pudina chutney) is popular for flavouring fish, meat, stews, soups, ice cream, jellies and salads.

In medicinal and tonic preparations only *MENTHA PIPERITA* should be used and the other species which have low medicinal properties should not be mixed.

The roots, flowering tops and leaves of Mentha Piperinta are dried, stored and taken as 'tea' in Japan and China for toning up general health. The Japanese claim that mint tea is good for preventive maintenance of health and Japan is the homeland of mint.

References

(1) *Spices and Condiments* by J.S. Pruthi (p. 159-163). Authority on Spice Technology. Director GMA.RK Laborotaries of the Govt of India. Scientist in charge Council of Scientific & Industrial Research, Govt of India (Trivandrum Complex).Published by the National Book Trust of India, 1976 followed by several editions.

(2) *Medicinal Plants* by S.K. Jain, (p. 102 & 103). Director, Botanical Survey of India, Calcutta, and Fellow of the National Botanical Research Institute, Lucknow, Published by the National Book Trust of India. First edition 1968 and thereafter several editions.

(3) *Home Remedies* by Hakeem Abdul Saheb, Scientist and Chief Trustee of the Hamdard Dawakhana Laboratories, Delhi, Very distinguished and successful Practitioner of Home Health Care based on home remedies. Published by Orient Paper Back, Delhi in 1982 and subsequently revised and Published. (2nd edition 1988)

(4) *Directory of Economic Plants in India* (page 139) by Umrao Singh, Wadhwani and Johri (of the IARI, TCUP, and University of Delhi respectively.) Published by the Indian Council of Agricultural Research, Govt, of India, 1955 and 1983.

5) Some issues of Ancient Science of Life, *Journal of International Institute of Ayurvedic*, Coimbatore, South India.

HERBAL CAPSULES FOR DIABETES

The wellknown book "*Where there is no Doctor*" written by Dr David Verner and translated from Spanish into English and published by the Hesperian Foundation of USA was revised and adopted for India by The Voluntary Health Association of India and translated into Hindi. Like many other books on herbal medicines, including the 1988 revised publication by the Indian authority Hakeem Abdul Saheb, Dr Verner's book recommends decoction of Catharanthus Reseus (English-*Periwinkle* or *Vince Rosea*, Tamil-*Nithiya Kalyani* or *Sudu-kattu Malli*) and seeds of Jambol (botanical Eugenia Jambolana Lam) called *Nagam palham* in Tamil. Bitter Gourd (*Pavakkai*), neem leaf and Touch-me-not (Momosa Pudua) are also recommended. There are reputed native doctors and many wellknown books which also recommend in-take of Fenugreek (Botanical-*Trigonella Foenam Nees*) called *Methi* in Hindi and *Vendhiam* in Tamil. The Indian Council of Medical Research (ICWR) of the Government of India also recommends Fenugreek.

Many laboratories in India and the West have established the active ingredients in these herbs, leaves and seeds and the percentage of insulin-equivalent that they contain. (The insulin injection that is now commonly given to diabetic patients is extracted from pancreas glands of pigs).

While the injection does (or supplements) the work of the panves gland in the human body the green medicine strengthens the gland without disturbing the natural metabolism. Hill tribes and villagers have been taking these herbal medicines from time immemorial and observe no side effects and therefore more and more alopathy doctors are prescribing these native medicines with the full backing and research support of the World Health Organisation of the United Nations which has released several books and reports on herbal medicines. The UNCTAD, ILO, FAO, UNICEF, etc are all now very much in the field of research and development. "Avoid injections and chemicals" is the call of the day.

RYAN Foundation has been generating employment in the rural parts of Third world Countries directly and through various organisations by organising the collection and processing of medicinal herbs and leaves. They are dried and ground without adulteration and under hygienic conditions and packed in geletine capsules, ready-made and easy to swallow. Capsule cases are supplied and recently a programme was launched by the Foundation in the Kanyakumari district in Peninsular India with aid from the MISEREOR of Germany.

Very soon capsuling medicinal herbs, leaves, seeds, nuts and barks in powder form should give a living for millions of people in India and other Third world

Countries as the demand for these non-chemical herbal remedies are increasing. The time is not far when India will be the leading exporter of capsules of herbal powders to the West. Already, some pharmaceutical companies like the Himalaya Drug Co. in Bombay have entered the field in a big way but the raw materials for this industry is in the hands of rural people. It is for agencies working in rural areas to organise and promote this industry and ensure that there is no adulteration.

RYFO PULP AND MORTAR BOARD

Several uses for water Hyacinth have been experimented and demonstrated. There is detailed explanation of many uses for Water Hyacinth in the book, "*Plants and Trees that Generate Employment*" by Dr Felix Ryan, environmentalist. This handout explains how the pulp of Water Hyacinth and RYFO Mortar mixture can be blended to produce hard boards like asbestos sheets, both plain and corrugated to be used for roofing low-cost houses.

Process: The entire acquatic weed (roots, stem and leaves) are dried well in sun and ground to small particles and kept aside.

Tamarind seeds powdered or chopped dried cassava or yam powdered or granuled is boiled in water to get glud (gum) and kept aside.

RYFO Mortar mixture prepared as explained in RYFO Handout 270 and kept aside.

All these three are then mixed in equal parts by volume with an equal part of water to make a semi-liquid pulp and spread out on a large sieve framed like a picture. The size of the frame is 180 cm x 90 cm and its thickness 4 cm above the mesh and 4 cm below the mesh (to get sheets of three cm thickness).

The semi liquid mixture prepared as explained above is poured on the sieve and spread out uniformly to form a 3 cm layer or sheet and left in the sun to dry. The sieve is oiled before the pulp is spread on it to avoid sticking. The water in the mixture not only evaporates, but also drips through the sieve. When completely dry, the board is ready. It is hard but breaks if hammered or dropped from a height. For a stronger board the sheet is made thicker, may be 6 cm or 9 cm thick. To get corrugated sheets a thick metal mesh is put on a asbestos or galvanised corrugated sheet and a mould is made out of the mesh. The prepared pulp is spread out on this corrugated mesh mould.

For strength and durability it is better to standardise the size to 180 cm x 90 cm.

These sheets can be used just like asbestos sheets but they are lighter, cheaper and can be hand moulded by villagers in their village with local raw materials.

GRASSES AND GUMS FOR DIFFERENT USES

Following are some common grasses available in many tropical countries of the Asia-Pacific Region:

For Paper Making (Botanical names)

1. *Eulaliopsis binata*

For Fodder (Botanical Names)

1. *Andropogon*
2. *Bothriochloa intermedia*
3. *Bothriochloa Sp*
4. *Bothriochloa pertusa*
5. *Bromus Spp*
6. *Cenchrus Ciliaris*

For matting (Botanical names)

1. *Arundo Spp*
2. *Cyperus Corymbosus*
3. *Phragmites Spp*
4. *Saccharum munja*
5. *Typha elephantina*

For Rope making (Botanical names)

1. *Desmostachya bipinnata*
2. *Eulaliopsis binata*
3. *Saccharum munja*
4. *Saccharum spontaneum*
5. *Themeda arun dinacea*

For Thatching (Botanical names)

1. *Heter opogon Controtus*
2. *Imperata Cylindrica*
3. *Saccharum munja*
4. *Saccharum spontaneum*

For Miscellaneous Uses (Botanical names)

1. *Thysanolaena maxima*
2. *Vetiveria Zizaniodes*

Gum Giving Trees

1. *Acacia Catechu*
2. *Acacia Modesta*
3. *Acacia nilotica Spp Indica*
4. *Acacia Senegal*
5. *Anogeisus latifolia*
6. *Bauhina retusa*
7. *Cochlospermum religiosum*
8. *Lannea Coromandelica*
9. *Pterocarpus marsupium*
10. *Sterculia urens*
11. *Sterculia Villosa*

Hairwash for Luster

Ingredients

1. Botanical - *Sapindus trifoliatus linn.*
   English - *Soap nut.*
   or — 200 grams
   Acacia Concinna.
   Tamil – *Shikakai.*
2. Botanial- *Vigna radiate.*
   Family - *Papilionaceae.*
   English - *Green gram.* — 200 grams
   Hindi – *Mung.*
   Tamil - *Pacha payre.*
3. Botanical - *Trigionella foenum-graecum.*
   Family – *Papilionaceae,*
   English – *Vendiam.* — 100 grams
   Hindi – *Methi.*
   Tamil – *Vendhiam.*

4. Botanical - Citrus aurantifolia.
   English - *Lime* (skin to be dried and powdered). — 200 grams
   Hindi – *Nimbu*
   Tamil – *Elumicham*

5. Any rose petal dried in shade 100 grams
6. 20 neam leaves

Dry the six ingredients powder, sieve and keep them separately.

Then mix them in the proportion indicated and bottle them.

Instead of applying soap on the head apply this powder. Only if you mix the ingredient No. 1 you will get a little lather and no soap is required at all. If your preparation does not contain ingredient No.1 take some foam of a soap in your palm and then apply the powder.

After the bath your hair will have a good luster. It is enough to use it once or twice a week. The wash prevents dandruff and helps hair to grow healthy and long.

The powder may be used also for body wash.

MESTA FOR Paper

Some pulp giving grass are explained in RF Handout 153. Other common wood pulp for making paper are crop wastes such as grasses like esparta, (stipa tanacissima). cotton stalks, cereal straws, mesta (hibiscus Spp), mediteranean grass, marshmallow (Althea officinates), marsh plant (sesbania sp) and crotolaria (Crotolaria juncea). Of these, mesta is of greatest use In India average area under cultivation of this plant (Hibiscus cannabinus and Hibiscus Sabdariffa) is about 360,000 ha yielding about 820,000 bales of dry fibre.

Mesta is more profitable as raw material for paper making than cotton and jute and it can be cultivated under different soil and climatic conditions with less care and without irrigation. In the Western Ghats, many paper factories have been using mesta, pulp. Cultivation of mesta in wastelands can promote employment for thousands of families and bring down the cost of paper.

Mesta is called in English Bimlipatam Jute, or Kenaf. In Hindi it is called Patsan or Ambari and it belongs to the Malvaceae family.

A prickly shrub native of Africa is now grown in W. Bengal, Assam, UP, M.A. Andhra, Tamil Nadu, Bihar and Punjab (it is grown but perhaps unidentified in many tropical countries.

Fibre from stem is also used for making ropes, and rough sack cloth. Edible seed oil is also used for burning lights and as a lubricant. It is good for making soaps, lineleum and paints. Seed-cake is used as cattle feed. Tender leaves are edible.

FRAGRANT TUBEROSE

Botanical name - *Polianthes tuberosa.* Family - *Amaryllis* (native of Mexico). Tuberose is a beautiful white flower with a pleasing smell and it is commonly used in flower boquettes and garlands. The plant grows well in warm climatic conditions especially in coastal areas. In winter the bulbs remain dormant and in summer they bloom. It is soil tolerant and grows in almost any type of soil but needs good drainage.

Tuberose can be planted any time during the year and a spacing of 20 cm by 30 cms between plants is recommended. Walking path in between the cultivation must be laid to facilitate the collection of flowers.

Within three months from planting Tuberose bloom. They may either be sold as cut flowers or used for extracting oil. Some stalks have two flowers but others have a single flower. The single flowers are rich in oil and the oil and the stalk oil is usually extracted by steam distillation. The flower provides honey for bees. The steam distillation method see RYFO Handout 344.

During the first year of cultivation nearly 200 quintals of flowers can be harvested from a hectare. In the second year the yield is slightly higher and drops considerably during the third year. Not much watering is needed and the plants are quite sturdy and tolerant to varying weather.

The price of flowers naturally dependos on the region and the demand.

Propagation is by bulb planting fresh bulbs are stored in shade and watered. Their storing place must be changed every day to prevent formation of fungal infection. Low temperature and high humidity helps healthy storing.

Ryan Foundation recommends the cultivation of this flower plant between wetland crops and to pool the flowers grown by different growers for extracting Tuberose oil which is much in demand.

Vegetable Dyes

Following are some important Vegetable Dyes commonly available in some selected countries of the Asia-Pacific Region.

Wood Based Dyes (Botanical names)

1. *Acacia Catechu*
2. *Artocarpus heterophyllus*
3. *Artocarpus lakoocha*

4. *Caesalpinia Sappan*
5. *Pterocarpus Santalinus*

Bark Based Dyes (Botanical names)

1. *Acacia Concinna*
2. *Acacia farnesiana*
3. *Acacia Leucophloea*
4. *Alnus Spp.*
5. *Casuarina equisetifolia*
6. *Manilkara littoralis*
7. *Myrica esculenta*
8. *Terminalia tomentosa*
9. *Ventilago medraspatana*

Flower and Fruit Based Dyes (Botanical names)

1. *Bixa Orellana*
2. *Butea monosperma*
3. *Mallotus philippensis*
4. *Mammea longifolla*
5. *Nyctanthes arbortistic*
6. *Toona ciliata*
7. *Woodfordia florebunda*
8. *Wrightia tinctoria*

Root based dyes (Botanical names)

1. *Berberis aristata*
2. *Datisca Cannabina*
3. *Morinda tinctoria*
4. *Punica granatum*
5. *Rubia cordifolia*

Leaf Based Dyes (Botanical names)

1. *Indigofera tinctoria*
2. *Lawsonia inermis*

Herbal Wines

Fruit wines are produced from the juice of fruits and a proportionate quantity of sugar which on completion of the time of fermentation give wine.

If fruits of herbs do not contain natural juice or plenty of it, they must be crushed and extracted in a careful manner to retain maximum essence, and properties of the product.

Method

There are several methods of preparing home made wines. The fermentation process takes place in a closed atmosphere, to prevent contamination from wild yeast. After the fermentation the wine is not boiled to sterlise as this will cause the natural essence to evaporate, and make the wine "Cooked".

Natural Proess

The natural process which is explained, produces wines of excellent flavour and colour which get better by an aging process.

Basic Wine Type

The natural process of wine production must be controlled from the beginning to end to obtain. DRY table wine medium Dry, Medium sweet or sweet Wine. These groups are further defined by the tannic clinging taste in the mouth to the citrous flavour, considered most appropriate to the type of wine being produced.

Technology

The basic technology is now available in India to make good wine extracted from local herbs for their properties. These medicinal wines as called in the Eastern Countries are much priced and patronised by the locals for their curative effects. Herbal wine is tasty, healthy and convenient to be taken as a tonic.

Samples

Dry Wine Zanblon: Best consumed at 9-12 months (three month old). Medium Dry Golden Apple (two month old) Best consumed at 9-12 months.

This wine lends itself well to sparkling. At two months, the clarification is still incomplete.

Medium Dry Pine Apple	(5 years)
Medium Sweet Banana	(5 years)
Sweet Plum	(5 years)

ASTHMA POWDER

The plants listed below are commonly found in India and many tropical countries and elders and villagers know to identify them and their uses.

1. (*Adhatoda Zeylamica Milk*-Botanical). (*Adhotota Vasaaka*-English). (*Adhathoda*-Tamil). For more information and picture see Handout 230. Leaves are to be dried and powdered. Most of the cough syrup in the market have Vasaka as an important ingredient.
2. (*Salanum Surattense Bum* Botanical). (*Kankakari*-Common name). (*Kantan Kathari*-Tamil). Roots are to be dried and powdered. The IMPCOS tablets made out of this leaves are effective and popular. See Handout 224.
3. (*Tylophora Indica*-Botanical). (*Tylophora Asthmatica*-English). (*Antamul*-Hindi). (*Kagitam*-Tamil). See Handout 224, Roots are to be dried and powdered. The All India Institute of Medical Science has tested this on several patients and announced its effectiveness.
4. (*Ocimum Sanctum*-Botanical). (*Holy Basil*-English). (*Tulasi*-Tamil). See Handout 358. Leaves are to be dried and powdered.
5. (*Acalypha Indica*). (*Indian Acalypha*-English). (*Kupoamani*-Tamil). See Handout 237. The whole plant including the roots is to be dried and powdered. Ref S.K. Jain, Director, Botanical Survey of India in his book *Medicinal Plants*. National Book Trust. Govt. of India.
6. (*Emblica Myrobalan*-Botanical). (*Gooeseberry*-English). (*Nellikai*-Tamil). See Handout 149. Seeds are to be dried and powdered. S.K. Jain and H.K. Bakhru in Foods that Heal. Orient paper back.
7. (a) Dried ginger (*Sukku*-Tamil) (b) *Black pepper* (*Melegu*-Tamil) (c) *Long Pepper* (*pippili*-Tamil), (*Piper Longum*-Botanical), Dried fruits (pods) are powdered. *Pippili* is readily available in the culinary market. The plant is an ever-green bush/shrub. (d) *Termeric* (Manigal-Tamil).

Powder of atleast any three of the first five and any two of the last 4 are taken separately and then mixed in equal parts and bottled air tight. Half teaspoon of the mix is taken after every meal with honey, milk or plain water. The powder is not a quick cure but a slow tonic to fortify the lungs. There are cases of complete cure. Results can be noticed only after 6 to 12 months. There is no side effects. The powder can be taken as a general lung tonic by anybody, young and old, in these days of pollution and pesticides that induce asthma. The powder may be put in capsules boiling into decoction and taken. It can also be mixed with equal part of honey and kept like jam for ready use. When there is breathing difficulty half spoon may be put in boiling water and Inhaled.

GARLIC IN HONEY OR CAPSULES

Botanical - *Allium Sativum.*

Hindi - *Lahsau.*

Tamil - *Vella Poondu.*

As with many other folk remedies, a scientific base for the use of garlic has been established. For a long time it has been known that garlic contains sulphur and sulphur had antibiotic effect. Research has now established that it lowers blood lipids or fats and cholesterol and so helps protect the blood vessels from developing atherosclerosis. It also has an anticoagulant effect, ie. it reduces blood clotting and helps heart patients. It is useful to builduup resistance of the lungs and protect and strengthen respiratory. tract and therefore widely used in lung medicines. It also finds a use in the treatment of lencoderma, ringworms and skin diseases.

According to the *Directory of Economic Plants in India* published by the Indian Council of Agricultural Research, Govt of India, since garlic has antibacterial properties, it is widely used in infectious diseases. Antibacterial activity is due to allicin which is found to inhibit growth of several micro-organisms. Plant has germicidal properties. Garlic is strongly antiseptic; taken internally it destroys worms and applied externally rids the skin of parasites.

The best way to take garlic is to remove the skin of the pods, soak the pods in honey for about a month and swallow two pods every night before bed to avoid unpleasant smell in breath during the day. Alternatively, garlic pods may be dried well after removing the skin powdered and capsuled. A capsule or two a day will keep the doctor away.

Now-a-days garlic preparations are available in the form of powder, pearls, capsules and liquids. But the best is pods soaked in honey hygienically prepared at home. It is good home industry and can be put in small bottles and sold. Better to avoid plastic containers.

BAOBAB OF AFRICA

Botanical - *A dansonia Digitata Linn.*

Family - *Bombacaceae.*

English - *Monkey-Bread Tree* or *Cream of Tartan Tree.*

Indian - *Choyarichichy, Gorakhaamti* or *Gorakh Chinch.*

Eventhough native of Afrieca this tree has been in existance in many parts of India for the past several centuries. It is seen in Madras, Bombay, Calcutta etc. but most common along the Western Coast of India.

Description: Strange looking. rather short for the very broad trunk; soft wood, thick branches. In Africa there are trees the diametre of which is over 10 mts (or 30 m growth). So broad, that people make a hollow in it and live inside the hollow. It is said that the life of the tree is 5000 years. The tree is erect seldom going over 20 m high. The leaves look like those of the silk cotton tree but almost double in size. White flowers (with a touch of purple) or attractive. The fruit 20-30 cm long hangs from thickened stalk. They are oval in shape and grayish or light brown in colour. The fruit has a rough outer woody coat and contains a meaty pulp with numerous seeds. Some people eat the pulp but it is not palatable. It has an acid taste and in summer it is refreshing.

Uses: Useless for carpentry but good for making match sticks and soft toys. The fibre of the bark is very strong when the bark is incised it yields a gum. The ash of the bark is caustic. The tribals boil the ash in oil and use it like soap. The dried fruits are used as floats by fishermen. The fibre is excellent for making high quality paper.

Medicinal: The pulp of the fruit is given for dysentery. In Africa and in India people prepare a soft drink (Sherbet) which is said to remove the heat in the body. A decoction of the bark is given for malaria in the place of quinine. Tea made of the dried leaf, the Africans claim, is good for kidney troubles. The gum from the bark is applied on wounds and boils, especially on domestic animals.

TARO FOR TROPICS

Botanical - *Colocasia esculanta.*

English - *Taro or Arum.*

Hindi - *Arvi or Kachalu.*

Native of South East Asia. Belongs to the Yam family, Tubers are starchy and tasty. They are made into cors and corals, roasted, baked or boiled and eaten. leaves and petiolas are eaten as vegetable. *TARO* is rich in Calcium, iron, carbohydrates, Vitamin A and C and phosphorus. In drought ridden villages in many countries it is the staple food. It is a drought resistant crop, grows in any soil and it is tolerant to bad weather. April-May is the best time to plant the tubers and with irrigation facilities it can be cultivated throughout the year. The soil must be mulched before planting and farmyard manure used liberally.

Cormels are planted in 15 cm deep prepared pits. They may also be raised in beds and ridges with a spacing of about 50 cms between cornels. About 700 kgs of cormels must be planted in a nectare to get about 30,000 plants. Organic manure may be given periodically, The manure may be soaked in a pool of water for a couple of days and that water used for the plants. Regular weeding has to be done. In about 20 days, the cormels sprout and in about 30 days thereafter the leaves spread out.

Taro can be grown as an intercrop in banana field, rice fields and coconut groves. Nitrogen fixing legumes such as cowpea or cluster beans blend very well with Taro.

In about 175, days when the leaves turn yellow the crop can be harvested without damaging the skin of the tubers as damaged tubers rot quickly and spoil other tubers in storage. About 20 tonnes of side tubers (cormels) and two tonnes of mother corms can be got from an irrigated field.

Taro tubers are eaten by cows, goats and pigs and the dried skins given to pigs. By boiling the tubers with little water a sticky paste (gum of starch) is obtained which can be used as a binder in several uses. The tubers can be completely dehydrated, powdered and preserved and different types of eats can be made out of them. Sap of Taro leaves a permanent black stainton clothes and can be used as a black dye.

WONDERFUL MUSHROOMS

Mushrooms are considered to be plants even though they are not like plants. Unlike all other plants, they lack chlorophyll in their leaves (they don't have leaves) and therefore cannot build food such as fats, proteins and carbohydrates from organic matter. In fact, mushrooms can only alter or destroy existing compounds and form fungi. They can be described as "fungi" or "destroyers" of compounds found in nature.

Fungi are plants that lack leaves having the green pigment called Chlorophyll, which helps leaves to manufacture food, aided by water and sunlight. The leafless fungi do not produce their own food but derive nourishment from bodies of plants, birds, animals or fish. They subsist on the waste of their hosts or thrive as parasites. In effect, fungi break complex organic matter and add to soil fertility. Fungi are very useful to mankind; penicillin, cortisone, yeast, citric acid, gluconic acid, (alcohol out of yeast) etc. are products made from fungi as base material.

The umbrella or Oyster like "thing" that usually springs up after some rains is actually the fruit. The plant which produces the fruit is called "spawn" and it is a mass of very fine threads that grow away from the spot, where a spore landed carried by wind or watar and germinated The threads discharge enzymes which break up food out of the threads to be absorbed later on by the threads in the form of solution. Some of this absorbed material is utilised to produce mushrooms.

In other words, under the umbrella like mushroom lies the vital hidden part, underground as a tangled web of strands called "hyphae". The entire hyphal mass is called "mycelium" and it abounds in luxuriant litter, in heaps of foliage, paddy straw, or rotting logs. Mycelium is whitish hair-like matter and it is the root of the fungi, the leaf and the stem, all three in one.

The mycelium survive very long periods, drought and dry conditions and when moisture sets in the fruiting bodies develop. They sprout as roundish buttons and shoot up like umbrellas overnight.

But the mushroom plants die after making use of all that they can find in the plant. But before they die they produce the fruits (mushrooms) and this fruit gives rise to a myriad tiny spores which are released and carried by air currents or water. When they land they germinate if their growth is supportable. Thus their life cycle is continued.

RAUVOLFIA SERPENTINE FOR EXPORTS

Botanical - *Rauvolifia Serpentine.*

Family - *Apocynaceae*

Origin India: Above 2,000 feet and with good rain fall.

Description: Plant grows over a metre high.

Flowers twice a year and flowers are pinkish white with a deep orange Corolla tube.

Medicinal: Very rich in alkaloids and about 80 alkaloids have been identified and isolated from the roots. The more important alkaabids are ajamaline, ajmalicine, rescinnamine, and serpentine. These are use to cure neuro-physical disorders, cardiae arrythemia, hypertension and psychiatric disorders.

Inern Wester Alopathy synthetic substitutes such as phenothiazine, chlopramaize, methyldope etc. are available but today natural organic medicines are preferred and are in demand.

The alkaloids are extracted from the roots and over 350 tonnes of the roots are being exported every year from India and India is not able to meet the ever rising export demands. About 100 tonnes of the roots are consumed within India mostly by ayurvedic doctors and pharmacies.

The plant can be introduced by cuttings or transplanting and they propagate by themselves in the wild. Rural people living near hills and hill tribes grow this plant and supply the roots to exporters. The plant seems to be a speciality of India and the other country where it is seen commonly in Malagaski. Cutting or sapling can be had from Botanical Research Centres.

TURMERIC FOR DYE

Botanical - *Curcuma Longa Linn.*

Family - *Zingiberaceae.*

English - *Turmeric.*

Tamil - *Manjil.*

Hindi - *Haldi* or *Haridra.*

Description: Perennial root-stock with bright yellow tubers (inside), Pale yellow flowers, Petiolo as long as leaf blade, about 40 cms long, deeply channelled.

Distribution: Throughout India, Pakistan, Bangladesh and Sri Lanka. Grows in a limited way in other countries with similar climate.

Uses: The rhizome is a very valuable commodity in trade and commerce after it is boiled and dried. A deep yellow dye is extracted from the rhizome. The colouring matter is called Curcumine (Kachcha Haldi) and it varies from yellow to orange and turns red with alkali. Curcumine is a pigment. Cloth or fibre dyed with Curcumine does not bleed or fade but gets dull when constantly exposed to light. But if alum is used as a mordant this does not happen. Turmeric dye is usually used as an additional colouring matter or by mixing with other dyes to get different shades. Turmeric dye is usually used to colour leather, fibre, carpets, paper, cotton, silk, wool, country made furniture etc (for RYFO wood paint with turmeric as an ingredient see Handout 567). Well dried and powdered turmeric is used in Indian cooking, cosmetics, medicines and also as an ant repealleant. When a dried rhizome is burnt it repells mosquitoes.

Medicinally turmeric is used as stomachic, blood purifier, anticeptic and applied externally on boils, wounds and certain skin ailments.

Hindus consider turmeric as something auspicious and keep it on a plate during wedding ceremonies, social and temple functions. -

SWEETER MELONS FROM SALTY FIELDS

The National Research Council of the US National Academy of Sciences Published in 1990, the 140 pages report of a four year study by some 100 experts in over 30 countries on salt tolerant plants and trees (halopytes) suitable for developing countries.

About 100 plants and tree species are reviewed and some of them appear rather exotic like Disticils, Salicornia and Sporbolus. There are also some surprisingly familiar crops listed such as wheat, barley, rice, cotton and asparagus that can be selected for salt tolerance and cultivated. The book also lists several valuable crop, fuel and fodder plants that can be irrigated with sea water but warns that sea water should not be used to substitute good water but exploited only for dry and drought areas and mixed with good water in suitable proportions if necessary as they do in Israel.

Salt-tolerant species are not always cultivated for production or edible purposes. Fixing sand dunes, growing shadow trees or wind breakers, lowering of salt content of the soil or the water table could be the primary objective. Some plants remove salt from the soil at the root level by concentrating it in the leaves, while others help to drain the soil where a high or brackish groundwater is the problem, thereby helping to rehabilitate marginal land.

Moderate levels of salt, the report explains, are not always a disadvantage. Many halophytes grow better with than without salt. Salt stress can make some crops tastier. Near East Farmers, for instance, have often found that the sweetest melons are growing on salt fields or on sea shores.

Clarification on Eucalyptus

(1) Eucalyptus for Pulp: Eucalyptus Hybrid (mainly, E. Tereticornis) and E.grandis are the two common species of Eucalyptus used in India for pulp and paper manufacturing. Cut of the two E. Grandis is better than E. hybrid.

(2) For oil: Essential oils obtained from several species of Eucalyptus leaves by steam distillation are of commercial importance. The two species popularly used in India for oil are:

1. Eucalyptus globulus (medicinal oil).
2. Eucalyptus Citriodora (Oil for perfumery).

(3) For Gum: Most of the Eucalyptus species are popularly known as gum trees in Australia, although exudation from them is not a gum but an astringent, tanniferous substance called Kino. The two species given below give a good yield of Kino.

1. Eucalyptus Camaldulensis
2. Eucalyptus Citriodora

(4) Kino or *Kino gum*: The dried resinous juice of several tropical trees of the genera Pterocarpus, Butea and Eucalyptus are used in medicines used for curing throat infection and in tanning.

Kino or Kino gum or Ki-no is the name commonly used by people of West Africa in their local languages. As said already, it is the dried resinous juice of several tropical trees. The Kino gum cannot really be used as a gum for sticking or pasting. It is more lime starch with properties of stickiness. However, the resigness juice in consentrated form can be used as a binder for certain purposes.

When the juice is mixed with gummy starch such as tamarind seed starch, casava starch, starch of yam or cluster, beans it enhances the sticky property of the liquid, increases the volume and makes the gum cheaper for commercial use.

Addition of a small quantity of powdered mineral lime and sugar or jaggeary enhances the sticky property of the solution.

Gum, thus made, has to be commercialised for large scale use and the industry can provide employment for thousands of people.

Some Prosopis Species

The genus prosopis includes more than 40 species out of which five are prominent in tree planting projects and social forestry. They are:

1. The most popular Prosopis Juliflora (also known as mesquite in America and "Mad Tree" in several countries because it grows in deserts, inbetween rocks, on the sea-shore, with water, without water and stands severe changes in climatic conditions.
2. P. Chilensis.
3. P. Tamarugo
4. P. Cineraria
5. P. Pallida

All these five trees (species) thrive well in light and sandy soils; adapt well to arid conditions; root well in hard and rocky soils; most important of all, tolerate alkaline or saline soils and grow well along seashore. They withstand drought for nearly eleven months in a year in desert temperature. Most of these trees have thorns and fruits, appear as pods containing several seeds. (about 10 an average). The pods contain 13 per cent crude protein and four per cent Carbohydrate. Ripe pods ground into flour can even be backed as food for humans.

Most of the prosopis listed above yield good honey. A coffee like drink is made out of the dried seeds. The bark of the tree is crushed and used in leather tanning. Some of them have medicinal properties.

The species mentioned above reproduce easily from seeds or cuttings. The pods gathered from the tree or collected from the ground must be dried in the sun for atleast ten days and then used in a nursery. Before sowing the seeds must be doused in boiling water and allowed to soak a day or two until the natural swelling that bursts the endocarp from within.

GLYRICIDIA MECULETA

This is a fast growing dryland tree and needs no watering after the roots catch the soil. It is tolerant to all sorts of soils and weather conditions.

Usually it is propagated through seedlings. When the sapling is about 50 cms it is transplanted during rainy season into a 30 cm hole made in the soil. The tree takes a year to grow 3 mts high and should be protected from cattle. If propagated by cuttings watering for about three months is necessary if the soil is not wet.

Meculeta sheds its leaves during winter and flowers during Feb-March. Whitish pink flowers are in clusters and contain honey. During April pods with seeds appear. During summer the tree developes several branches and plenty of leaves which are rich in nitrogen and used as green manure.

Dry branches of this tree burn well and give high calorie of heat. The weak branches must be cut and the tree pruned every year, before monsoon. Pollarding, ie, cutting the tree to a height of a man should not be done even though the tree survives if cut that way. It does not flower if pollarded.

In rural areas the tree can be planted in rcws with a gap of three mts inbetween and the leaves of this tree make excellent fodder and increase the yield of milk. Goats love the leaves.

The great advantage with *Meculeta* is that the week and irregular branches can be cut regularly every year throughout one's life time and the tree keeps on growing and flowering and providing fuel and fodder. Moreover, the roots of this tree go deep and do not spread out and so can be kept near homes in small open grounds.

Meculeta leaves make better foliage than Subabul or Eucalyptus. Unlike Suba and Euca, Meculeta develops horizontal branches and provides good shade and flowers.

This is a tree to be propagated in rural areas in urban homes that have open space and also as avenue trees to line city roads.

Saline Agriculture

The following information has been culled out from the 143 pages book entitled Saline Agriculture: Salt-Tolerant plants for Developing Countries published by the National Academy of Sciences-1990.

Salt tolerant plants (halophytes) usually have poor agronomic qualities (e.g., there may be wide variations in germination and maturation times). They may be cultivated in land and water that are unsuitable for salt sensitive plants.

1. Leucaena Leucocephala is growing in coastal sandy soil in Pakistan irrigated by saline water. Trees even survived when 20 per cent seawater was used although yield came down by 50 per cent.
2. *Jojoba* grows near the Dead Sea in Isreal with brackish water irrigation.
3. *Quinoa* germinates in a mixture of 1/3 sea water and 2/3 fresh water, and it did not continue to grow for a long time. In the salt flats of Southern Bolivia, Quina is grown.
4. Azadirachta indica-(Neem) grows successfully in Pakistan on sandy soil using irrigation water with about 10,000 ppm salt(pure sea water is 35,000 ppm). A neem plantation has been established near Mecca in Saudi Arabia to provide shade for Muslim pilgrims. Water with about 2500 ppm salt was used for irrigation.
5. Beets and date palms grow very well in brackish water.
6. *Asparagus* is remarkably tolerant of salt. In Tunisia, where irrigation water contains 6,500 ppm salt, asparagus yields are about the same as in areas irrigated with fresh water.
7. *Barley* is the most salt-tolerant cereal grain. At the University of Arizona good results have been demonstrated. California experiment produced 458 kg of barley from one ha of land when cultivated entirely by sea water.

The book or further information may be obtained from the Board of Science and Technology for International Development, Publications and Information Services, Office of the International Affairs. National Research Council, 2101 Constitution Avenue, Washington D.C 204 18, USA.

Seaweeds on Fibre Ropes

Thousands of Fishermen in the coast of Philippines have been shifting from fishing to seaweed cultivation during the past decade and claim that seaweed farming is more profitable than fish farming. The farming is based on appropriate technology. They do not go into the sea neck deep in search of weeds but have them grow on coconut fibre ropes tied to Casuarina poles planted five mts away from the shore and drawn to the shore and tied to a line of poles on the shore.

Small lengths of fresh sea weeds are tied to the ropes and in about six weeks under water the weeds are harvested. Some weeds are left on the ropes to grow again and the cycle continues.

In 1990, these weeds were taken from the Philippines and introduced in the coastal areas off Tanzania in Zanzibar island. Reports say that the harvest is much better in the African region and two business companies are promoting the weed and selling them to a factory which extracts from the weeds Carageenan, which is a popular binding agent in food products. Appropriate Technologists not see possibilities of promoting this weed in several regions and also promoting other quick growing weeds and China grass on fibre ropes. Much research and investigation has to be done, but seaweed farming has already thrown open several alternative employment possibilities for poor fishing communities. What we need now is collecting, processing and exporting Centres.

Halophyte Potentialities

1. Marine algae has great potentials as livestock feed, fertilizer and raw materials for several industries. They are a rich source of numerous minerals and live saving medicines. The liquid seawater fertilizer recently researched and developed is becoming popular in several countries. Some fresh algae, including *Spriluna*, *Chlorella* and Scenedesmus, rich in edible protein, are widely sold as health food in Western Countries and Japan.

2. In Benin people cultivate a bean called *Ablat* which requires very little water to grow. They first put some compost around the foot of the plant and it produces bean all round the year. If the atmosphere is water borne the plant grows quicker and healthier. With sea water vapours in the atmosphere *Ablat* can be grown in dry and drought lands.

3. The Central Salt and Marine Chemical Research Institute of Bhavanagar, India, has been experimenting on the cultivation of Jojobe - an oil bearing plant in coastal sand dunes under semi-arid conditions in the West Coast of Gujarat and in Sub-humid regions of Ganjam district of Orissa. Experiments have established that Jojobe can be grown successfully in Coastal sand dunes and the oil obtained from the plant could be used as a lubricant for making soaps and for other purposes.

4. A halophyte grows excellently well in arid zones and saline soils and improves habitat of wild life and birds and serves as fodder for livestock and reclaiming sandy soil. It grows wild in the salt Steppes of Eastern Asia, low lying salt plains of Australia, the Red Sea basin and the South American Pampas. It is an easy to propagate annual and perennial herb.

5. In 1990, The Philippines ranked fourth among the worlds producers of Red Sea-weed, exporting about US $ 48 million of dried sea weed and *CAAGRENAN* – a derivative from it which is used as a binding agent in food products.

Tapping Sea Water by Bamboo Pipes

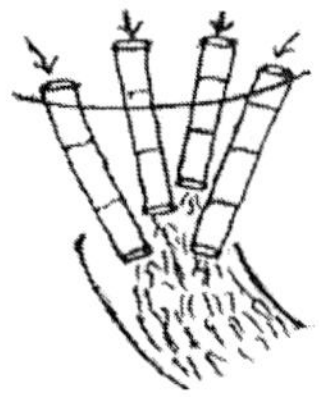

There are several ways of drawing water from the sea into land to fill dry ponds and lakes. The appropriate technology shown in Ryan Foundation booklet "*Pumps Without Water*" are quite inexpensive and feasible. Yet, all rural communities may not be able to instal them with their own initiative and financial resources.

In RYFO handout 579, a method is shown to draw sea water in bamboo pipes through a brick and mortar chamber. The purpose of the chamber are - 1) land mark, 2) level fixing, 3) double 'flow block' 4) a steady out flow and 5) a sense of community ownership and participation in getting water into their village.

However, sea water can also be drawn straight away without building a brick chamber as shown in this handout. In fact, this method is cheaper, quicker, easier and absolutely safe but can serve only one or two villages because of limited flow.

All that is required are bamboo poles of uniform size in thickness and the number of poles required depends on the extent of sand to be covered on the shore by length. The bamboos may be cleared and cleaned inside, for free flow of water (handout 323) and laid as shown in this handout. Joining of the bamboo pipes may be done as a carpenter joins two pieces of wood and glued (joinery). If necessary joints may be wrapped with plastic or rubber sheets (cut car tube) or thick cloth or jute cloth and tied well to reduce leakage as much as possible.

Where the sea water enters the bamboo a strong cloth should be tied to act as filter. The bamboo must be buried about 15 cm below mean sea level and it may have to go about a metre or two into the ground as it comes out of the water to be laid on the shore. It may be buried in a slightly slanting position as shown and at the 'out flow' end the community may dig a channel to lead the water to the nearest dry lake or pond or catchment area and from there take the water by channels to other places.

To stop the flow one has merely to go into the sea knee deep and insert a bottle into the inlet end. Alternatively, a bottle or stopper may be inserted at the 'out flow' end. Thus, all the materials required are some bamboos, discarded car tubes or plastic sheets, old cloth, fibre ropes, country-made glue and an empty bottle.

It is better to lay four or five pipes all leading to the same channel to get a good flow into the village. Instead of bamboo, cement or earthen ware pipes used in sewerages may be used if available. Metal pipes will corrode in sea water.

JERUSALEM THORN

Parkinsonia aculeata (Botanical).

Native of tropical and subtropical America, has been introduced in Africa, Asia the middle and the Far East. The tree can:

1. Withstand light frosts and high temperature,
2. Tolerate saline soil where there is no waterlogging,
3. Tolerate drought for about nine months,
4. Grow in sandy soil, in desert grasslands and pebbly soils.

In English this tree is called *Jerusalem thorn* or *Horse-bean* tree. The tree is fast growing and reaches a height of about 10 mts. The trunk is crooked but the branches are long, thin and straight, covered with sharp shines. Hence the name Jerusalem thorn.

The foliage makes good fodder for goats, rabbits and sheep. The round pods contain many seeds which can be easily removed out of the nods.

The endocarp must be removed before sowing by sprting in boiling water for about three minutes. Seeds may be planted in poly bags at the rate of three to four seeds per bag. germination takes place in four to six days. When the seedlings are about 10 weeks old they may be transplanted and protected from animals.

Wood of this tree is heavy but brittle. Therefore it makes good charcoael and fuel wood. The flowers contain plenty of honey and the sweet fruits are edible.

The tree produces plenty of seeds and carried by wind sprout lavishly during rainy season but grows only in tropical countries and cannot tolerate much cold.

URENA LOBATA, A NEW FIBRE CROP FOR THE TROPICS

Introduction

Urena Lobata an excellent Jute substitute fibre crop grows annualy in the temperate regions, and as a perennial in the tropics. Urena grows wild in many parts of the tropics, including East Africa. The plant is branched and shrubby in the wild state, but when closely cultivated for its fibre it acquires a tall (8 ft-13ft.), straight and unbranched form. The fibre of Urena is obtained from the bark of its long stem. It has been commercially grown for fibre in Ghana, Belgian - Congo, Madagascar, Cuba, Brazil, and Nigeria.

The variety (Ex-Mokaw) which is grown for fibre production has a growing season of about one to four months during which period the plant needs moderately moist conditions. Rainfall of 25 to 30 inches during the growing season is considered sufficient. Climatic conditions are suitable wherever the wet season averages more than four months in length and six inches of rain falls in each month. These conditions are widely found in West, East and Central Africa. The plant cannot withstand flooding.

Soil Requirements

For good growth, urena requires a medium textured, well drained soil. The soil must be moderately fertile. The tap root of the plant reaches 18 inches, so that this is the minimum soil depth required. Although the nutrient demands of the crop may not be very high, there are nevertheless large differences in yield which can be attributed to soil factors. This was noticed in the Congo and Ghana where heavy, compact soils were found to be inferior to medium textured soils. Soil aeration, solid moisture relationships and rooting depth are often more important for this plant than chemical factors.

Cultivation and Preparation of Soil

Proper and deep ploughing of soil is essential. Fields are then harrowed to produce the fine tilth neceasary for seed planting. Soil preparation should begin soon after a good rainfall.

Time of Planting

Seed should be planted at the beginning of the wet season when about one to 1/2 inches of rain has fallen. In warm countries seeds should be planted between late April and mid May.

Seed Treatment Before Sowing

There is a tendency for the seeds to germinate unevenly. Therefore, seeds should be soaked in mater overnight before sowing. This treatment increases the percentage of germination

Seed Rate and Spacing

40 lbs to 60 lbs of seeds may be planted per acre. The seeds should be sown about 1/2 to one inch below the soil surfaces. and the soil should be

lightly rolled after the seeds have been sown. The seeds may be cast or sown in rows (in case a drilling machine is available). A Ferguson seed drill may be used to sow the seeds in rows. The following spacings can be used: 7 in x 2 in, 9 in x 4 in, or 10 in x 4 in. Row Planking helps to reduce cost of cultivation and facilitates inter-cultural operations and increases fibre yield. For seed production, wider spacing of 2 ft x 2 ft or 4 ft x 4 ft can be used or seeds may be broadcast at the rate of 10 to 20 lbs per acre.

Fertiliser Application

Application of ammonium sulphate, single superphosphare and potassium sulphate at the rate of 214 lbs (54 lbs N_2/acre 150 lbs (27 lbs $P_2$05/ acre) and 54 lbs (27 lbs K_2O/acre) per acre, respectively. is said to result in yields of 1,500 lbs to 2,500 lbs of dry fibre per acre. The fertiliser should be applied at the time of sowing of seeds.

It has been reported that, in Ghana, amnxontum. sulphate and triple superphosphate each at the rate of 3/4 Kilogram per acre gave yield increases of 11 to 12 per cent.

Pests

The first weeding should be done 3 weeks after sowing of seeds and the second should be 5 weeks after sowing. There-after the crop can suppress the weed growth.

During August, September it is often necessary to scare birds away to prevent nesting and damage to the plants.

Harvest

The best time to harvest the corop is between flowering and early pod formation. If the seeds were sown in May, the crop is ready to be harvested in September, i.e., 120 days after sowing. During harvest the crop should be cut at the ground level. After harvest, the plants are left in the field in small bundles for two or three days to shed leaves before retting.

Retting and Processing

The fibre may be retted in a slow moving stream. To ensure uniform retting, bundles of stem should be placed upright in water for two to three days. After that the bundles should be placed horizontly and well below the surface of water (at least six inches below the water surface). Concrete blocks, stone slabs, logs of wood, etc (other than mango and banana, which contain tannion) are quite suitable for weighing down the bundles under water. After two to four weeks in water, the soft part of the outer bark will have rotted sufficiently for the bark to be slipped off the stem easily. It is better to examine the bottom part of the stem and if the fibres are separating from the bark, the fibres are ready for stripping and washing. Too long retting makes the fibre weak; similarly, it is difficult to extract the fibre from the stem if stripping is done early. Green stems are best retted soon after harvest. Soft water produces best quality of fibre, whereas hard water delays retting. The same also happens if the volume of water is small. Treatment of wet fibre with dilute extract of tamarind fruits (Tamartndus indtca) fruit or sour fruit removes black colour of the fibre.

Drying of Fibre

Washing over the long strips are hung on poles and quickly dried. After drying, the fibres are separated, usually by rubbing over a pole and beating the fibre with a wooden hammer.

Field

The fibre yield usually varies between 1700 lbs and 2500 lbs per acre, depending upon the soil, growing conditions and season.

Quality of Fibre

Urena fibre resembles Jute. It is fine and can be spun to the fine counts to which Jute can be spun. The best quality fibre is equal to the best Jute and can be prepared and spun in ordinary Jute machinery without any change of machine. Urena is superior in strength to Jute and kenaf when well prepared, but it is not as durable as kenaf fibre.

The fibre is graded according to the quality, colour (silky white is prefered than greyish colour), length and strength. Its cleanliness is determined by the presence of such foreign matter as stem and bark fragments.

Uses

Urena fibre is used for making sacks, ropes, carpets, etc.

WATER HYACINTH FOR A MILLION JOBS

Initiated by the Commonwealth Science Council (CSC) and with a grant from the United Nations Environment Programme (UNEP), the Regional Research Laboratory at Jorhat of the Government of India conducted several investigations and established that high quality paper can be made out of water hyacinth Eichornia Crassipes which is the most prolific aquatic plant, the volume of which doubles every fifteen days. This floating weed grows in any water almost under any climate and is considered an environmental hazard because it clogs drainage ditches, shades out other aquatic vegetation and obstructs boating, shipping and fishing and also breeds mosquitoes and water snakes. A pond of about one hectare of water hyacinth can produce nearly 1.8 tonnes of dry mass of weed every day.

Jorhat Report

The Jorhat Laboratory has produced high quality paper from the pulp of the stalk of the weed and not so high quality paper from the leaves, and has commissioned model cum demonstration plant at Hyderabad to manufacture various types of paper out of the weed and the samples produced are very impressive.

In a booklet, the laboratory has published the research results and recorded that the pulp of the weed produces excellent cover paper, document paper, file boards, blotting paper, greeting cards, invitation cards, degree/diploma certiricates etc but yields itself best for making grease proof paper. Details of the process and a scheme with lull particulars to manufacture the items mentioned above is also given. A typical whole green plant, the report reveals, contains 24.8 per cent root, 41.9 per cent stalk and 33.3 per cent leaf and the stalk gives the finest quality paper. The average length of the fibre is 1.604 mm and the average diameter is 5.5 micron.

Organising Collection

The findngs must encourage thousands of developmnet workers and NGOs in the poor Countries to organise the village people to collect the weed, remove and separate the roots, the stalk from the leaves and have them packed in jute bags or HDPE Woven sacks. The collections may be sold by weight to nearby paper and card-board factories and stalk should fetch more than the leaves. The dried roots and leaves mixed with other "burnables" like rice-straw, corn-cobs, wood-shavings foliage etc makes excellent alternative wood fuel for the rural kitchen when used in the Fuel Pump invented by the author of this article. For particulars see RF booklet on the subject.

Collecting Method

Four hooks welded together and tied to a strong rope (diagram above) may be given to the people to collect the Weeds. They have only to hold fast to the end of the long rope and fling the bunch of hooks into the pond or river as far as it would go and then draw it back and the hooks will drag the Weeds out of the pond or river on to the bank. The distance between one hook and another in the bunch should be about 30 Cms so that the "drag" is plentiful and the thickness of the hooks should be atleast one Cm.

The cleaning, sorting and packing operations may be done on the bank of the ponds then and there and a heavy knife and a block of wood used to chop off the roots from the stalk. The organisers of the industry may provide a yard to store the collected weeds and the packed bags and arrange to transport the bags either directly to paper factories, collection and baling centres or to wholesale dealers.

If National and International Governments encourage the private sector in starting more paper, card-board and grey-board factories, this aquatic weed Collecting Industry can provide employment and a family living wage for a million people in the Third World. Most LDCs and many D.Cs which are now importing paper and board can export them and earn foreign exchange.

If more of quality paper is made, India's paper exports will pick up. Fine hand-made paper can also be made out of the stalk pulp and perhaps the Khadi and Village Industries Commission of the Government of India which is specializing in the making of hand-made paper and runs well-established demonstration, training and production units in several places can exploit the water hyacinth.

Solution to Jute Crisis

In Bangladesh and India there is now a crisis in the Jute Industry and India has restricted the use of HDPE Woven sacks by fertiliser, sugar, cement and other factories in order to protect the jute industry. As a result the Woven Sack Industry is terribly hit for want of market, but if the Weed Collecting Industry picks up, there will be more demand both for jute bags and HDPE woven sacks. Owing to shortage of paper in India, exports of certain varieties of paper are totally banned. The water hyacinth Industry can also solve the paper shortage and save many soft wood trees from being cut for making paper and save ecology.

Training

The Regional Research Laboratory of the Council of Scientific and Industrial Research, Government of India in Hyderabad and the Khadi and Village Industries Commission of the Government of India should be happy to train paper and board factory engineers in the use of water hyacinth in their mills. The UNIDO, ILO or the UNEP may arrange for such training at Hyderabad with financial support and promote similar training institutes in other countries as well, and work in this field should start without further delay.

Fuel Briquetting

There is yet another good use for water hyacinth. According to an article published in Research and Industry, Vol 28, Dec 1983 (PP 251-253), it can be effectively used as a new material to produce fuel bricks and this fuel will not pollute the atmosphere.

Briquette making machine are common now and many countries are making them. The National Small Industries Corporation of the Government of India manufactures and sells on hire-purchase an excellent briquette fuel manufacturing plan which can be fed with different types of "burnables" including dried water hyacinth. Some reputed private factories such as the Pauls Engineering Enterprise in Calcutta are making small electrical/hand-operated machines. The College of Agricultural Engineering, Jabalpur in Madhya Pradesh, has developed a simple and cheap hand operated machine to grind agricultural waste or water hyacinth and also a simple pelleting machine. See RYAN Foundation booklet.

The UNITAR/UNDP Centre on small energy resources, Italy, has very valuable informaton in its Newsletter No.4 of September 1986 on bio-mass briquetting and gasification and the Swedish Academy of Sciences too has a store of information.

Silage for Cattle

Under the Kerala Agricultural University experiments conducted by the Department of Nutrition, College of Veterinary and Animal Sciences, have revealed that water hyacinth can be profitably converted into silage for cattle. Their chemical analysis showed that the weed contains about 6.3 per cent crude protein and 21.9 per cent crude fibre.

One important finding was that wilting the water hyacinth to 30 per cent dry matter was optimum for the maximum recovery of good silage, and at 15 per cent dry matter, the wilted material will have to be mixed with other dry fodder like paddy straw in the ratio ten to one to produce quality silage.

Weevil to be Withdrawn

It is a pity that a few years back the Indian Institute of Horticultural Research, Hessaraghatta, Bangalore, brought from USA, *Weevil*, the tiny darkish brown beetle, technically known as Neochetina - Eichhomiae to slowly and steadily destroy water hyacinth. The multiplication of this beetle should be arrested immediately and the weed must be introduced and promoted in more rural areas to employ people.

Efforts of ATIC

The RYAN Foundation International founded by the author of this article is already organising the collection of stalks, leaves and roots of water hyacinth from raral parts through some Church Agencies and negotiations are under way with nearby paper and board factories for their sale. Factories may be slow to change over to, or add on, this new raw material but R F believes that the idea will catch on, the weed supply trade will be established and thousands of people, especially, women and children will be gainfully employed. A very important factor to be noted is that the investment for promoting the collection in the rural sector will be almost nil as only the collecting hooks and some sacks will be required initially. It should also be noted that the Weed trade besides keeping the environment clean will promote mass communication by the paper (press) media. Indeed water hyacinth has employment potential and an expanding market and therefore should be fully exploited to give work for the youth and a living for the poor, on a large scale in many countries.

O Welcome, Beneficent Weed

The Water Hyacinth has moved fast from despised and feared pest of pests clogging waterways and eutrophying waters to bearer of good tidings and a cornucopia of blessings, according to a publication of the UN Environment Programme. Water hyacinth has the potential to. act as the focal point for an integrated rural development scheme for high production of food and energy The high growth rates of water hyacinth allow rapid production of a food supplement for non-ruminants such as pigs and rabbits. After drying, it is also a valuable food supplement for cattle and goats. The animal wastes are readily processed in simple digesters to yield high grade energy in the form of methane gas for cooking and Highting. The digester effluent fertilises water hyacinth ponds to enable rapid growth. A section of the pond is kept free of water hyacinth cover to allow the growth of algae which promote aerobic conditions in the pond. The aerobic conditions lead to the destruction of most parasites and pathogens. Algae act as food for fish such as Surotherodon ('Tilagia") species. Nutrients in the oxidised water are directly available to agricultural crops by hand or mechanical irrigation The crops con-tribute to animal and human food requirements. Roots from the water hyacinth are exposed to the sun to kill absorbed pathogens and bacteria and then used as a mulching agent to improve the soil condition and fertility.

Rabbits are considered to be especially valuable as a component of integrated rural development Their hind gut digestion allows benefit to be gained from consumption of large amounts of water hyacinth. The meat is a high grade protein readily digested by humans. The fat content is lower than most other animals. Most species have fur which can form the basis of ornament, toy and clothing industries the reproductive capability is high and 40 to 60 young per year may be readily reared from one doc Their small size allows number to be easily kept on a family basis in a small area They offer much potennal to yield high grade protein from water hyacinth and other readily available high roughage foods. The droppings are dry and if kept in this state non-offensive.

WATER HYACINTH, UNEP, Nairobi, 1984

Ryan Foundation booklet on Rabbit raising Published by the Rotary club, Madras (South).

CRISIS IN ECOLOGY

Many planners, politicians and even agronomists do not understand top soil or that layer of soil that covers the earth on which humanity depends for its existence ever since Adam came out of paradise. A well cared for and regulated ecology gives us the food we eat, the clothes we wear, the houses we live in, most chemicals we need and even our industrial life. Indeed it is the thin layer of top soil that sustains all living creatures and when the plants and the animals, the birds and the bees perish humanity would perish as well.

In the ages past the kings and the empires and the governments cut their trees and sold their resources. And when the land became barren, the dried out and dead surface of the earth got washed by the rivers and vanished. The trees fell, the birds and the bees died, the land eroded, people perished and countries fell like house of cards and passed into history books. Alexander the great cut trees to build warships and king Solomon to build the famous temples. The whole of north Africa, once the granary of the Roman Empire, is now only a desert stretching to the horizon.

Plato lamented the loss of top soil in ancient Greece: "Our land is now like the skeleton of a body wasted by disease, the soft parts are gone and all that remains is the bare carcass." Herodotus wrote: "You could walk across the North of Africa and always in the shade of trees." It is not so today. There is only sand now, and you could see lost empires, lost fertility, famine and frustration on the face of the people.

All but a few trees have been felled in Ethiopia and the uprooted soil has literally gone down the river to the Aswan Dam. The globe is facing the crisis of top soil; crops are failing and millions are starving to death. And yet, saws are now very busy cutting those few trees that still remain.

"Over the last quarter century, an average of more than 6 million acres a year has been taken out of cultivation. Often it's the best farmland gobbled up for other uses" (USN & WR Chart. Basic data. US Dept. of Agriculture). The UN estimates that 80 million Asians, pressed by overcrowding and inequities in land ownership, cut roughly 48 million acres a year, only some of which regrows when the farmers move on.

In Indian newspapers we read nightmarish stories of entire per capita income of only about $ 180 a year, the 135 million people of Indonesia rank among the worlds poorest.

About one-third of the world is already a desert and about ten million acrests of deserts are added every year. Says John Larmuth, Director of desert research, Cambridge, "In 1872, desert occupied 14 per cent of the world's potentially usable land area (i.e., excluding tundra, polar and high mountain regions permanantly inaccessible to agriculture), and in the 80 years upto 1952 a further 21 per cent lost bringing the total to 35 per cent. During the last 25 years., there has been a dramatic 300 per cent increase in the rate of loss so that by 1977 over half (55 per cent) of all potentially usable land became deserted. This is an average loss of 175 million acres every year for the last 25 years which represents £ 9000 million in lost agricultural output each year. Every five years land equal to the whole surface area of the UK becomes useless."

Meanwhile the world population is doubling. From where will our children find food? Have they to live on camel milk and dates in Oasts? Jacques Ellul in 1935 was one of the first modern philosophers to sound the warning that society was becoming enslaved by a science and technology that proceeded with its own rules of logic with no thought of welfare of families committing suicide to end the agony of slow death by starvation. The ancient country is losing thousands of once cultivated land now to the deserts every year. Roads costing millions in foreign aid are thrown by landslides into rivers already running chocolate brown with mud. Down-stream in India, six million tons of top soil - ten tons for every person in the country - slip away each year. Says Ledec, "It is ironic but countries that would go to war if someone tried to move their border back a yard, are losing millions of tons of soil a year to erosion." Man-made deserts -are swallowing the top soil in the Philippines, Nepal, Java, Indonesia and parts of Malaysia. Vast stretches of Mexico which were once covered with trees have little trees now to provide food for the people and wood for the carpenters. Two thirds, of Latin America's original forest is gone or seriously depleted. Thailand has lost one quarter of its forest in the last ten years; once a leading producer of teak the country actually spent $ 100 million in 1980 to purchase wood products from abroad. At Balikpapan in east Kalimantan a $ 36 million logging operation run by the P.T. International Timber Corp produces about 3.5 million cubic feet of timber every month in Indonesia. The worlds poorest people are literally destroying their future. When the Europeans arrived there after Christopher Columbus they found the land rich and fertile. There was a green carpet of marvellous trees with apples and oranges and plenty of forests with teak and timber. Where are they now? Gone are the trees and one can visibly see wind and water erosion. The Americans are losing about 4 million tons of their precious, irreplacable top soil annually. When they arrived there, they enjoyed about 20 inches of nutitious top soil but they are down to six inches now. Below that six inches the soil is as lifeless as the moon. No amount of artificial manuring can ever bring back the original life and fertility of the soil.

The Amazon forests stretching from Andes to the Atlantic across several south American countries have the worlds largest growth of tropical forests. They are rich with millions of plants, trees, birds, animal species and a share of old timber to supply the world with hundreds of important industrial oils, resins and dyes. But these forests are also coming under axe, bulldozers, chain saws and fire and the trees are falling much faster than Nature or man can replace them. Peru plans to settle some two million peasants in the jungle over the next five years. Colombia and Ecuador are planning to lay oil pipe lines. But nobody paid attention.

Yet demands for wood are growing rapidly. In his address to the 8th World Forestry Congress in Jakarta, the Director General of the FAO predicted, on the best available statistics of trends that consumption of wood and wood products would rise by 75 per cent in the next 16 years to 4,000 million in 1944. In the same address the Director General estimated that the forest area of the Developing Countries is being destroyed at the rate of up to 16 million hectares a year.

Half of all the wood cut in the world is used as fire-wood, for essential cooking and heating. In developing countries this constitutes, about 90 per cent of the wood used and represents one third of their total energy consumption.

According to a Crown Agency Quarterly review published in 1980 by the overseas government and Administrations of England it is estimated 400 million tons of dung is burnt as fuel in Africa because of the shortage of other fuel. And yet dung is desperately needed as fertiliser for the land instead of being a form of energy.

The destruction of top soil in the United States against the wish of god who wanted to keep the garden with good care (Genesis 2:9, 15) God meant that the trees in the garden must be looked after and cared for. This is exactly what is required now of our forests and woodlands. God's command holds good unto the day for the progress of mankind.

The fact of the trouble is we have been on a wrong track for many years; we have had a blind and a wrong belief about modern technology dreaming of ourselves as masters of Nature, not fully realising that man can only convert and not create. We are not the masters, we are only part of nature. If we destroy nature we destroy ourselves.

Dr Toynbee, that great historian who had studied the rise and fall of empires and civilisations predicted the end of our civilisation in about a century and Mike Benge of the Agency for International Development says, "The real crisis today is not oil but wood".

We ripped off the earth. All she ever asked of us, that we put back what we take out. Replant forests after we cut and put back all the nutrients that we took out. But our greed got in our way.

Railway lines across these forests and Brazil has already built the Trans-Amazon Highway.

The farmers of Japan always say, "What is good for the fathers is not good for the sons", thereby meaning that if the fathers had used machine made fertilisers the sons must get back to natural manuring. And it is a well known fact that China's soil fertility is due to natural manuring where chemical fertilisers are supplemented. After a close study of soil, substance and fertility many sensible people say that there is only one rule of good farming and that is leave the soil better than when you found it.

The balance of nature depends partly on certain portions of the surface of the earth being covered with trees. To some extent this can be compared to the skin of a human being in the body system. A certain percentage of the skin can be burnt or ruined by disease and the man can still survive. But if the critical point is surpassed the whole life system will fall and the man will die.

When God created *Adam and Eve* he put them in a garden with plenty of trees, fruits and flowers. Adam was told to dress Gautama Buddha included in his teaching that every man who calls himself a good Buddhist should plant and grow one tree atleast once in five years. When this teaching was followed India, Burma, Ceylon and Japan were full of trees, plenty of water and shade and food and the trees provided several raw materials for trade and industry and gave fuel. Even today, if only people go back to follow the teaching, countries like India would have during the next five years some 500 million more trees. It is easy to imagine the economic value of this. If only the more useful trees are planted and promoted the results would be greater even than what all the five year Plans have achieved and it could be done without a penny of foreign aid. There will be no big problems of savings, investment or taxes. The effort would produce more food, more clothes, more water and industrial raw materials. It can in fact produce most of the things that man needs for a contented life. As Gandhiji said:, "Earth provides enough to satisfy every man's need, but not every man's greed".

TECHNICAL INFORMATION ON DEHYDRATION OF FRUITS AND VEGETABLES

Introduction

An old method of preserving certain fruits and vegetables is by drying them in the sun. These days drying is done in closed chambers by mechanical means under controlled conditions and this process is known as dehydration.

The keeping quality of fruits and vegetables depends on their water content. In the dehydration process, the water content is reduced to a level where micro-organisms cannot grow. Dehydration reduces the weight of the material dehydrated and, therefore, the packing and transportation costs are less than those of fresh fruits or vegetables. Dehydrated stuff can also be compressed for further savings in cost of packing and transport. Moreover, they can be packed in inexpensive packings and do not necessarily require cans.

Process of Manufacture

Most fruits and vegetables can be dehydrated, but those that are commonly done are mangoes, bananas, jack fruits, apples, apricots, grapes, peaches, pears and pineapples. Vegetables which are usually dehydrated are spinnach, potatoes, peas, cauliflower, cabbage, beans, ladies fingers, onions, tomatoes, carrot, beat, celery, sprouts etc. Peas rank first among the dehydrated vegetables in India. Dehydrated onions are being exported from India.

The first operation is sorting, grading and washing. The fruits and vegetables are peeled if necessary. Peeling is done by hand with knives or by abrasion peelers. Some fruits are peeled by dipping for about three minutes in a: boiling solution of 1.5 to 2.5 per cent caustic soda or lye. In some cases, the fruits or vegetables are scaled for 0.5-1 minute in boiling water to loosen the peal. Fruits are cut into pieces and their inner unwanted materials such as stores, seed and core are removed.

In some cases, fruits and vegetables are blanched for few minutes (2-10) in boiling water or steam before drying. Bleaching destroys undesirable enzymes which are responsible for deterioration in food products. The advantages of blanching are: good keeping quality of the dried products, expulsion of air from tissues, reduction in drying time and retention of vitamins.

Fruits are often treated with sulphur dioxide fumes before drying. Sulphur dioxide fumes are obtained by burning sulphur (about two-four kgs per ton of fruit). Fruits are placed in trays and the trays so stacked that the fumes react with the fruits readily. The sulphur must be fresh and free of oil. Vegetables are often given a sulphitation treatment i.e treated with sodium or potassium sulphite or bisulphite solutions. A 50:50 mixture of 0.6 per cent sulphite and 0.6 per cent bisulphite solutions give good results. Sulphur dioxide treatment and sulphitation increase the storage life of the dried products and also help in the drying process. These processes also improve the colour and protect the vitamin content of the vegetable or fruit. Sulphitation may be done by adding sodium sulphite in the bleaching water.

Fruits and vegetables are then loaded into trays. Trays are available in various sizes (2' x 3', 3' x 3', 3' x 6', 3' x 8') and may have slotted or solid bottoms. They may be made of wood, galvanized iron but aluminium trays are better because of the non-corrosive nature. The trays may be lubricated with mineral oil to prevent sticking. drying may be done in various types of driers such as tray or chamber drier, kiln drier, tower or stack drier, cabinet drier, tunnel drier etc. Drying may be done by natural circulation or by forced draft. Drying under vacuum is preferred when the material to be dried is sensitive to high temperature and oxidation. Products such as tomatoes which are dried in liquid form are dried in drums or spray driers. Parallel-current and counter-current systems of drying are used and sometimes the product is first dried at high temperatures in a parallel-current system and then at lower temperature in a counter-current system. Each fruit or vegetable has a critical temperature beyond which it should not be heated. During the early stages of heating when there is a large amount of water in the product, drying may be done at high temperature. However, in the last stages of drying, the temperature should be less. For most of the fruits and vegetables, the critical temperature

After dehydration, the weight of the fruits and vegetables is reduced due to the removal of moisture. Also, there is loss in preparing (washing, peeling, cutting, blanching, etc.). The reduction in weight is expressed as dehydration ratio. Dehydration ratio after preparation is the ratio of prepared raw product on the tray to the finished dried product; and before preparation it is the ratio of raw product as purchased to the finished dry product. Similarly on soaking in cold or boiling water the dried product absorbs water and its weight is increased. The increase is expressed as rehydration or inconstitution ratio to the weight of the dried product.

DEHYDRATION OF FRUITS

Bananas

Green bananas are blanched before peeling to loosen the skin. They are sliced, sulphured for 15 to 30 minutes and dried at about 60°C. Drying takes 18-20 hours. Ripe bananas are peeled and dried whole and when dried, they are known as 'banana figs'. If the ripe fruit is sliced lengthwise and sulphured for 20 minutes before drying a fine product is obtained. The dried banana product may be ground to obtain banana powder. The yield is 14–20 per cent.

Mangoes:

Mangoes are not dried as such but their juice is dried to obtain "Am Ka Papad" in a crisp state with good keeping quality. The fresh juice of ripe mangoes is spread out in trays to a depth of 1/8' and dried first at a temperature not exceeding 60°C for four-six hours in a shelf drier and then at 60°C for one hour in a vacuum drier. Addition of cane sugar (10 per cent) improves the taste, and treatment of juice with sulphur dioxide improves the colour but affects the flavour.

Pineapples:

Ripe pineapples/are peeled and cored by hand, the loss in weight being 45%. They are then sliced into 3/8" thick pieces. The slices are brought to boiling in a syrup of 40 Brix. made of sucrose and corn syrup in equal proportions plus water to give 40° Brix. and allowed to stand for 3 hours, before drying. Drying is done at 65°C in an airblast dehydrator at 600 ft min air velocity.

DEHYDRATION OF VEGETABLES

Washing over, potatoes, carrots, turnips and beets are peeled by abrasion or by treatment with hot lye, hot brine or steam at high pressure. Peeling may be done by heating over gas flames. Flame peeling is good for onions and pressure steam peeling for beets, these processes are employed on commercial scale in USA. Tomatoes may be peeled on flame peelers or by scalding in water. The vegetables are then cut into slice about ¼" x 3/8" or smaller. Spinach, chord, string beans and turnips are benefited by sulphitation. Peas should not be sulphited because it destroys the thaminc in it.

The tray load varies from 0-75 to 1.5 lb./sq.ft. with carrots about 1 lb./ sq.ft. for cabbages. Other vegetables may be loaded like carrots and leafy vegetables like cabbages. Too heavy loading results in slow and uneven drying.

Even spreading is extremely important because with uneven spreading large lumps may remain wet long after the rest of the product in the tray is well dried. The material in trays is now dried in a suitable drier. If a parallel counter current two-stage method is used, most of the vegetables may be dried in the parallel section of the dehydrator at 90 to 95°C (Near the end of drying period much lower temperature (60°–70°C) are usually necessary.

Peas

The pods of peas are shelled and graded for quality and maturity. They should not be too mature for dehydration otherwise, drying is difficult. Peas are blanched in hot water containing 0.5 per cent potassium bisulphite for five minutes. They are spread on trays in layers about ¾" deep. The centres (core part) of the peas, dry slowly, hence they should be dried until entirely crisp, which is usually to below 5% moisture content. At 35°C peas are dried in 12 hours but higher temperature upto 60°C may be used to increase the drying rate. The drying ratios on unprepared and prepared basis are 20.1 and 7.3:1 respectively. The rehydration ratio is 1:3.

BHINDI (LADY'S FINGER)

The stalks are cut and the small pods are dried whole. Large pods are cut lengthwise in halves or quarters or crosswise in circular pieces 1/4" thick. Blanching is done in hot water for two minutes and rinsed in cold water to remove the geletinous coating. Drying at 40°C takes about 10 hours but they also be dried at higher finishing temperature below 60°C to reduce drying time. Drying ratios on prepared and unprepared basis are 9.8:1 and 7.7:1 respectively.

Tomatoes

Unpeeled sliced tomatoes may be dried but the quality will be better if peeled. Peeling is done after scalding in boiling water for 1 minute. Tomatoes are cut into 1/4-3/8" thick slices. They are usually not blanched. Slices are dried below 65°C/ until they become crisp and break on bending. Drying takes 9-10 hours. Dehydration ratios on unprepared and prepared basis are 5.85:1 and 5.58 respectively and rehydration ratio is about 4:1. The colour of dried slices may be improved by sulphuring the slices for 20-30 minutes before drying. In the manufacture of tomato powder, the tomatoes are first pulped and the juice concentrated to 18-25% solid content. The puree is then dried on drum driers.

Dried vegetables are compressed into blocks and packed. They are heated to 60–70°C in a current of warm air and pressed while warm in steel moulds at 130-200 kgs./sq.cm. for 10-45 seconds. This treatment is suitable for vegetables containing high percentage of soluble solids, e.g, carrots, etc. The compressed material is packed in containers previously treated in phoshbate or chrome bath, lacquered to prevent corrosion. Cans are sometimes filled with nitrogen or carbon dioxide. Packed vegetables and fruits should be stored below 28°C. Dehydrated vegetables like peas may also be packed in polythene bags for retail markets.

EQUIPMENT AND MACHINERY

Machinery and equipment required for a small scale vegetable dehydration plant with an estimated capacity of 100 kgs per day are as under:-

(1) Preparation tables with aluminium tops 5' x 3' x 2.5' (2 Nos.).

(2) Vegetable washing tanks with spray arrangements 5' x 3' x 1.5' (2 Nos).

(3) Peeling machines (1 No).

(4) Aluminium blanching tank with steam pipe connections and false bottom 4' x 3.5' **x** 2.5' (2 Nos).

(5) Cross flow drier steam heated with provisions for recirculation of air and controlled thermostatically (1 No).

(6) Boiler with 300 kg./hr. steam capacity at 100 psi (1 No).

(7) Cooling tank of masonry construction '4 x 3' x 2.5' (1 No).

(8) Can reforming unit with flanger and seamer (1 unit).

(9) Platform type weighing machine capacity 300 kg (1 No).

(10) Empty can washer and sterilizer (1 No).

(11) Miscellaneous equipments like knives, gloves, hand slicers, instruments, bickets, trolleys, hoists, laboratory equipments.

COST ANALYSIS

For a small unit producing 100 kgs. day of dehydrated vegetables (the quantity of fresh vegetables will depend on the type of vegetables dried) the cost of equipment and machinery is estimated at Rs 200,000. The covered area required is 300 sq. m. The return on total capital investment will be about 30 per cent.

CODE OF CONDUCT FOR RURAL DEVELOPMENT WORKERS

1. Do not attempt any economic activity for your people if you do not find either the raw materials, techniques or the markets locally.
2. Locate or create raw materials locally by promoting vegetation, trees, poultry, fish ponds, live-stock, etc.
3. Take your people from agriculture to agro-industries, from agro-industries to cottage industries and from cottage industries to small industries, and not straightaway jump from agriculture to small industries.
4. Always restrict the initial investment during the first three months to a few hundreds and not to a few thousands (As for as possible produce samples on trial basis). Even Honry Ford made, only one car first!
5. Pass on the responsibility of production and distribution and management to the producing family gradually and cautiously and not right from the start

6. Do not form partnership or cooperative forms of organisations unless under extraordinary conditions; first teach people to operate and then only to co-operate.
7. Always start from the marketing end and always assist in the marketing, even after the entire responsibility is taken over by the producing unit.
8. Check accounts every week in a friendly way and make your findings known to everybody concerned.
9. Build up for the producers infrastructure such as water, transport and safety.
10. Exploit all available local ran materials and investigate every plant, tree livestock institutional waste materials available.
11. Always talk to the entropreneurs about quality and cost which are the heart and soul of business.
12. Guarantee a fixed off-take during the first year of production and find a way to dispose of that off-take.
13. Insist on cash transactions and discourage consignment sale.
14. Make people and institutions within the area or elsewhere patronise the products made in the area.
15. Introduce only those lines first which can give a living or a family wage to the people without having to wait long for returns.
16. Insist on the successful units setting apart a small reserve fund for expansion and invest it profitably.
17. Put a celling on production and earnings for every activity and not allow expansion beyond a limit more the producers, harder the disposal.
18. Repeat successful lines to other families in the area for their livelihood without giving room to cut-throat competition.
19. Provide a common centre for collecting and selling the unsold goods that have the proper quality and price.
20. Have a full time multipurpose specialist to be in full charge of all economic activities.
21. Start projects as independent of the Government as possible. That community which is least dependent on the Government will always prosper.

22. Tap all donations, grant-in-aid and whatever help that is forthcoming from the local people and institutions.
23. Train people on the job instead of sending them here and there for institutional training.
24. Always talk to the people optimistically and encouragingly.
25. Promote Appropriate Technology and only Appropriate Technology.

N.B. The two most important out of these 25 codes are:

(1) "Thou shalt always start from the marketing end".

(2) "Thou shalt promote appropriate technology and only appropriate technology".

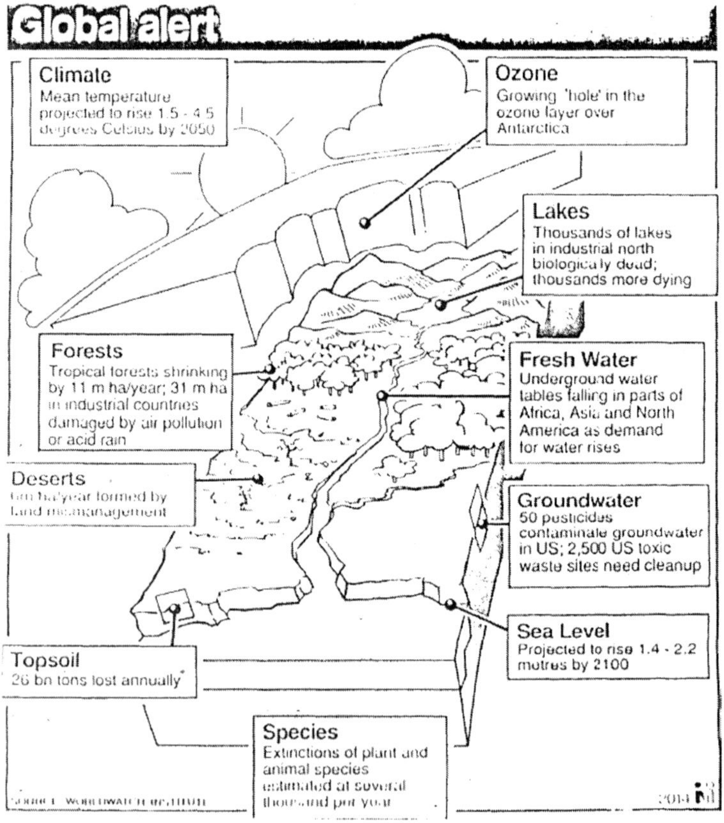

In your own country you may obtain seeds and saplings for the plants and trees explained in this book from:

1. Argentina CARD Forage Seed Project, P.O. Box 766, Friars Hill, St. John, Antigue, Buenas Aires, Argentina.
2. Australia Australian Seed Co, Albert Pk.119 Ashworth St. Melbourene. Vic.3206 Australia.
3. Australian Tropical Plant Supplies, P.O. Box 5 Mount Molloy, Queensland 4880 or Pinnacle Rd, Julaten 4880, Old Australia.
4. Conservation Commission of the Northern Territory, Forestry Unit, P.O. Box 1046, Alice Springs N.T.5750, Australia.
5. Conservation Commission of the Northern Territory, Forestry Unit, P.O. Box 38496, Winnellie, Darwin NT 5789, Australia.
6. Conservation and Land Management Department, 50 Hayman Road, Como, W.A. 6152, Australia.
7. Dendros Seed Supplies, P.O. Box 144, Weston Creek, ACT 2611, Australia.
8. Department of Conservation, Forests & Lands, G.P.C. 4018, Melbourn, Victoria 3001, Australia.
9. Division of Tropical Corps & Pastures, Cunningham Laboratory, 306 Carmody Road, Sta Lucia, Queensland 4067, Australia.
10. D. Orriell-Seed Exporter, 47 Frape Avenue, Mt. Yokim Perth, Western Australia 6060, Australia.
11. Ellison Horticultural PTY Ltd., P.O Box 365, Nowra N.S.W. 2541, Australia.
12. Flamingo Seeds Pty. Ltd., P.O. Box 1046, East Nowra 2541, N.S.W., Australia.
13. Forest Department, Australia, GPC 104 Como, S.A. 6152, Australia.
14. Forestry Commission of New South Wales, P.O. 119 Coffs Harbour Jetty, NSW 2451 Australia.
15. Forestry Commission, Tasmania, G.P.C. 207B Hobert Tas.7001, Australia.
16. Forestry Co. vission, Victoria, G.P.C 4018, Melbourne 3001, Australia.
17. Fruit Spirit Research Nursery ana Gardens, Dorroughby 2480, N.S.W. Austraila.
18. H. Grant-Austrailan Seeds, 2 Sandra Place, Dubbo, *NSW* 2830, Australia.

19. H.G. Kershaw PTY Ltd., P.O. Pox 84 Terry Hills, N.S.W. 2084, Australia.
20. J.H. Williams & Sons Pty. Ltd., P.O. Box 102, Murwillumbah 2484, Australia.
21. Kimberly Seeds, 51 King Edward Road, Osborne Park, W.A. 6017, Australia.
22. Kingston Rural Management Pty, P.O. Box 47, Maryborough 46500 old, Australia.
23. Kylisa Native Seed Supplier, 1 Gould Court, Taralgon, Via 3844, Australia.
24. M.L. Farrar Pty Ltd, P.O. Box 1046, Bomaderry, N.S.W.2541, Australia.
25. Nindethana Seed Service, Narrikup Wa 6326, Australia.
26. Phoenis Seed Association, P.O. Box 9, Stanley 7331, Tasmania, Australia.
27. Queensland Dept. of Forestry, P.O. Box 944, Brisbane, old 4001, Australia.
28. Royston Petrie Seeds, P/L P.O. Box 77 Dural, N.S.W. 2158, Australia.
29. Seeds Australia Pty Ltd., P.O. Box 30, Cloverdala, WA 6105, Australia.
30. Seeds for Preservation, Lot 6, Badgerup Road, Wanneroo, WA 6065, Australia.
31. Silvan Improvements Pvt Ltd, P.O. Box 42, Watson, A.C.T. 2602, Australia.
32. Southern Seed Sales, 35 Wilhelmina Ave, Lauceston, Tas 7250, Australia.
33. Tasmanian Forest Seeds, Summerieas Farm Kingston, Tas 7150, Australia.
34. Vaughans Wildflower Seeds, P.O. Box 66 Canberra 2600, A.C.T. Australia.
35. Western Wildlife Supply, Terrara, P.O. Box 90, Gtlgandra, N.S.W. 2827, Australia.
36. Yates Agricultural Seeds, P.O. Box 616, Toowoombe, Queensland, 4350. Australia. Bangladesh.
37. The Director, Forest Research Institute, P.O. Box 273, Chittagong, Bangladesh.

Belizil

38. Chief Forest Officer, Ministry of Agriculture, E. Block, Belmopan, Belize, Brazil.

39. The Director, Centro de Desarollo Forestal, Ministerio de AA. CC.Y. Agropecuories, Casiila 3548, La Paz Bolivia. C.P.
40. Embrapa/IAPBS. Km 47. 23460, Seropedica RJ Brazil.
41. EPAMIG Caiza Postal 295. CEP 35.700 Sete Lagaos, Minas Gerais, Brazil.
42. Reserve Florestal de CVRD Calxa Postal 91 CEP-29900 Linhares. ES Brazil.

Canada

43. Canadian Forestry Service. Petawawa National Forestry Institute, Chalk River, Ontario, Canada.
44. Ontario Ministry of Natural Resources Biomass Institute, Maple, CNT. *LCTI*EC Canada.
45. Chile Institute Forestal (INFCR) Huerfanos 554, Casilla 3085, Santiago, CHILE.
46. Centro de Semillar Forestales, Corporacion Nacional Forestal, Castilla 5, Chilian, Chile.

Colombia

47. Banco de Semillas Forestales, INDERENA Estaction Forestales La Florida, Apartado Aerao 57596, Bogota D.E., Colombia.
48. Centro Internacional Agriculture Tropical, Apartado Aereo. 6713 Call, Colombia.
49. INDERENA - Banco de Semillas. A.A. 13458, Bagota DE. Colombia.
50. Investigacion Forestal, Apdo, Aereo 219 Call, Colombia.
51. **Costa Rica** Banco de Semillas Forestales, Direccion General Forestal, Apartado 10094 San Jose 1000 CASTA RICA, Central America.
52. Banco Latinoamericano de Semillas Forestales (BLSF), Turrialba, Costa Rica.
53. Centro Agroseconomico Tronical de Investigaciones Y. Ensenanzas (CATIE), Turrialba, Costa Rica.
54. Latin American Forest Tree Seed Bank, CATIE Turrialba, Costa Rica.

Cuba

55. The Director, Centro de Investigaciones Forestales. Calle 174 No.1723. E/17. By 17C, Siboney, Playa, Cuidad, Hawana.

Cyprus

56. Department of Forestry, Ministry of Agriculture and Natural Resources., Nicosia Cyprus.

Denmark

57. DANIDA Forest Seed Centre. K rogeruprej 3A. DK-3050 Humla back, Denmark.

Ecuador

58. The Director, Dept de capacitacion Y Experimentacion. Ministrio de Agricultura Y. Ganaderia, Quito Ecuador.
59. EL SALVADOR Banco de Semilas Forestale. Dept. Conser de Res. Nat. Ministerio de Agr. Y. Ganaderia Sazopango. San EL SALVADOR.
60. Centre de Recursos Naturales (CENREN) Apartado Postal 2265 Canton el Matasano Soyapango, San Salvador EL.

England

61. Commonwealth Forestry Institute, South Parks Road, Oxford OX41EP. England.
62. Dept. of Plant Sciences, University of Oxford, South Parks Road, Oxford
63. Henry Doubleday Research Assn. (HDRA), RYTON-on-Dunsmore, Coventry. England.
64. Heath, West Sussex. England.

Ethiopia

65. Forestry Research Centre. P.O. Box 1034, Addis Ababa., Ethiopia.
66. International Livestock Centre for Africa (ILCA) P.O. Box 5689, Addis Ababa, Ethiopia.

France

67. Centre Technique Forestier Tropical 45 bis Avenue de la Belle, Gabrielle 94130, Nogent sur Marne. France.
68. Versepuy. 43000 Le puy France.

Guatemala

69. Banco de Semillas Forestales, 7 Avenida 7-00 Zona 13, Cludad, Guatamala.
70. Banco de Semillas Forestales Bansefor Institute Nacional Forestal Inafor Edificio Galeries de Espana 7a Ave 11 63 Zona 9, Cuided de Guatemala.
71. Exportacion de Semillas–Seed Export Anartads Postal/543. Guatemala City.

Honduras

72. Banco de Semiliias – ESNACIFOR. Apartado Postal 2. Siguatepeque Depto-de Comayagua. Honduras.
73. Banco de Semillas. Escuela Nacional de Ciencias Forestales, Apartado Postal 2 Signatepeque, Honduras.

India

74. Aggarwal Nursery & Seed Stores. Panditwadi. P.O. Prem Nagar, Dehra Dun 248007. (U.P.), India.
75. Agronomist & Principal Investigator, AICRP on Agroforestry. Agricultural College, Dharwad 5. India.
76. Bhoratiya Agro-Indust. Found. Kamedhenu, Sena pathi. Bapat Marg, Pune 411016, Maharashtra.
77. Central Arid Zone Research Institute, Jadhpur. Rajasthan 342003, India.
78. The Director, Forest Research Institute & Colleges. P.O. New Forest, Dehra Dun 248006, U.P., India.
79. India Nursery & Seeds Sales Corpn., P.B. 4341, 36/962 DDA Flats Kalkaji, N. Delhi-19.
80. Indian Grassland & Fodder Res. Jhansi, U.P. 284003, India.
81. Kumar International, Ajitmal 206121, Etawah, UP, India.
82. Nand Prakash & Company, P.O. New Forest, Dehra Dun 248006, UP.
83. National Botanical Research Institute, Rana, Pratap Marg, Lucknow 226 001, UP.
84. Nimbkar Seeds Pvt Ltd., Phaltan, Maharashtra 415523, India.
85. PAL Seed Traders, Kaulagarh, P.O. Kaulagarth, Dehra Dun, UP.
86. Regional Research Lab, Canal Road, Jammu Tawi, India.
87. Shivalik Seeds Corpn, Panditwadi, P.O. Prem Nagar, Dehra Dun - 248 007, UP, India.
88. Tamil Nadu Forest Dept., Forest Genetic Div., Bharathi Park Road, Coimbatore - 43, T.N., Madras, India.
89. The Bharatiya Agro Industries Foundation, Kamadhenu, Senapati Bapat Marg, Pune 411 016, India.
90. Titaghur Paper Mills Co Ltd, 95 Park St, Calcutta 700 016, India.

91. Tosha Trading Co., 161 Indira Nagar Colony, P.O. Indira Nagar, Dehra Dun - 248 001, UP, India.
92. Vijay Seed Stores, P.O. Ranjhawala (Rajpur), Dehra Dun -248 008, UP, India.
93. UAS/KDDC Fodder Project, University of Agri Science, Hebbai, Bangalore - 560 024, India.

Indonesia

94. Agricultural Polytechnic, Uni. of Nusa Cendans Jl. Adisucipto, Penfui P.O. Box 153, Kupang, Indonesia.
95. Biotron, Seameo Reg. Centre for Trop Biol, P.O. Box 17, Bogor, Indonesia.
96. Firma Pangkalredjo, Jl.MH Thamrin No.57, Semarang, Indonesia
97. FForest Research Inst, Gunung Batu, P.O. Box 66, Bogor, Indonesia.
98. Hortimary Utama P.T, Jl., Taman Tanah Abang 111, 31 Tanan, Abang, Jakanta, Indonesia.
99. INTI AGRCPURA. Jl, Kebon Jeruk III, 154 Sawah Besar, Jakarta, Indonesia.
100. Parta Tani, Jl, Senopati 43A Jakarta 12190, Indonesia.
101. Proyek Kalikonto. Jl, Guntur No.27 Malang 65112, Indonesia
102. PT Bibit Baru, P.O. Box 632, Medan 20001, North Sumatera, Indonesia.
103. State Forest Corpn., Direksi Perum Perhutani, Jalan Jenderal Galot, Subroto 17-18, Jakarta, Indonesia.
104. Toko Pertama. Jl, Baluwerti, No.32 Surabaya, Indonesia.
105. Yayasan Tananua, Tromolpos 3, Waingapu Sumla Timur, N.T.T., Indonesia

Israel

106. Forestry Div, Agri Research Org., Illanot Doar Na Ler Hasharon 42S05, Israel.
107. Arava Seeds Suppliers, P.B. 45109, Haifa, Israel.
108. Institute for Applied Research, Ben Gurion University of the Negev, P.B. 1025, Beer Sheva 84110, Israel.
109. Israflora, Forest Seeds of Arid Zones, Kiryat Blalik 2700, P. Box 502, Israel.

Italy

110. Florasilva Ansaloni, Casella Postale 2100, 40100, Bolongna, Italy.

Jamaica

111. Dept. of Forestry and Soil Conservation, 173 Constant Spring Road, Kingston 8, Jamaica.

Kenya

112. Baobob Farm Ltd, P. Box 90202, Mombasa, Kenya.
113. East Pokot Agricultural Project, Kositec, P.O. Marigat Via Nakuru, Kenya.
114. Head of Environ & Silviculture Div., Kenya Agri Research Inst., Box 74, Kikuyu, Kenya.
115. Kenya *Forest* Seed Culture, Box 74, Nairobi.
116. Tree Seed Programme, Ministry of Energy & Regional Development, PB 21552, Nairobi.
117. UNESCO IPAL, P. Box 30592, Nairobi.

Korea

118. Forest Research Inst., Chunguangni-Dong, Dongdaemun-Ku, Seoui, Korea.

Malawi

119. Forest Research Inst. of Malawi, PB 270, Zomba, Malawi.
120. National Seed Co. of Malawi Ltd, P.B No. 30050, Lilongwe 3, Malawi.

Malaysia

121. Forest Research Centre, (Seed Officer), P.B. 1407, Sandakan, Sabah, Malaysia.
122. Forest Research Inst., Selangar, Malaysia.
123. Senior Research Officer, Pusat Penyelidi, Kan Hutan, P.P. 1407, Sandakan, Sabah, Malaysia.
124. Sabah Softwood Adn. Bhd., P.B. No. 137, Tawan, Sabah, Malaysia.

Mexico

125. 62000 Apdo Postal 1082, Cuernavaca Morelos, Mexico.
126. Banco de Germoplasmo, Inst. Nacional de Investigacion, Sobre Reurses Bicticos (INIREB) Apartado, Postal 63.
127. Banco de Mexico, Calle 58, No.389, Merida, Yucatan, Mexico.
128. Ciapas/INIA/SARH, Apdo 98, Tapachula, Chiapas, Mexico.

129. Institute Nacional de Investigacion Forestal, Ave Insurgentes, Sur No.694, 10 Piso, Col del Valle. 03100, Mexico, DF.

130. Instituto Nal-de Investigaciones Forestales, Depto-de Plantaciones, Av. progreso No.5. Viveros de Coyaocan 64110 DF. Mexico.

131. The Director, Centro de Investigacion, Esenanza Extension en Ganderia Tropical, C/o. Martinez la Tovee Vera Cruz, Mexico.

132. **Nepal** Tree Seed Unit, Hattisar, Naxal, Kathmandu, Nepal.

Netherlands

133. Medigran, P.B. 731, 1180AS Amstelveen, Netherlands.

134. Setropa Ltd., P.B. 203, 1400 AE. Bussum, Netherlands.

135. Timmers & Leyar, PB 17, Heemstede 2100 AA, Netherlands.

New Zealand

136. Peter B Dow & Co, Dowseeds, PB 695, Gisborne, New Zealand Nicaragua.

137. Banco de Semillas Forestales, IRENA Aptdo Postal 5123, Manegua, Nicaragua.

Pakistan

138. Elite Nurseries Inc., 3 Street 67 Sector F 7/3, Islambad, Pakistan.

139. Pakistan Forest Inst., Gatwala Faisalabad, Pakistan.

Panama

140. Banco de Semillas Forestales, RENARE, Paraiso, Corregimiento Ancon Apartado Postal 2016, Panama, Central America.

Papua New Guinea

141. Office of Forests, P.O. Box 5055, Boroko Papua New Guinea.

Philippines

142. Agtalon-Agro. Technical Assistance & Livelihood Opportunities in the North, 2nd St. Gracia Village Urdanets 2428 Pangasinan, Philippines.

143. Abet Ramos, Barangay Quirino Bacnotan La Union, Philippines.

144. Dave Deppnex, C/o. Rey Capares, New Forest Project, 241 Caballero St., Pozorrubio, Pangasinan, Philippines.

145. Dept of Horticulture, UPLB College, Leguna 4031, Philippines.

146. Development Alternatives Inc. C/o. DENR Visayas Ave, Quezon City, Phillppines.

147. Ecosystem Research & Development Bureau (ERDB) Seed Bank, College of Forestry UPLB College, Laguna 4031, Philippines
148. Ernesto Cadaweng, DENR, Visayas Ave., Quezon City, Philippines.
149. Evergreen Gardens Inc. Ismena Village Maguikey, Mandaue City, Philippines.
150. Inst. of Plant Breeding, UPLB College, Leguna 4031, Philippines.
151. IIRR, Silang Cavite, Philippines.
152. Keystone Seedhouse Corpn, 807 San Andres St, Malate, Manila, Philippines.
153. Magbabaul Foundation Bismartz, Masipag Don Carlos, Bukidnon, Philippines.
154. Magseysay Foundation, 1640 Roxas lvd, Manila, Philippines.
155. Makinabang Enterprises, 470 Makibang Baliwang, Bulacan, Philippines.
156. Manila Seedling Bank Foundation, Quezen Ave Ext Cor E. de los Santos, Quezon City, Philippines.
157. Mindanao Baptist Rural Life Centre (MBRL) PB 94, Bansalan, Davao del Sur Philippines.
158. Nasipit Lumber Co, Agusan, Philippines.
159. Nestle Phil Inc, Butcidnon, Philippines.
160. Paper Industries, Corpn of the Philippines (PICOP), Forest Research Dept, Tabon Bldg, Surigao del Sur 8311, Philippines.
161. Rayos marketing, 78 Molave St, Proj - 3, Quezen City, Philippines.
162. Visayan Seedling Centre, PB 879 Rcom 219, LK Bldg, Subangdaku, Mandaue City, Cebu, Philippines.
163. Wood Development Corpn, Kitting Bldg, Busa Cagayan de oro City, Philippines.
164. World Neighbours MAG-UUG mad Foundation, 524-C del Rosario Ext., Cebu City, 6000 Philippines.

Puerto Rico

165. Southern Forest Experiment Station Inst. of Tropical Forestry, P.O. Box AQ, Rio Piedras, PR00928, Puerto Rico.

Senegal

166. Centre National de Recherches Forestieres, B.P. 2312, Dakar, Senegal.

167. Inst. Senegalais de Recherches Agricoles, Centre National de Recherches, Laboratoire de Graines, Parc Forestier de Hann B.P. 2312, Dakar, Senegal.

Sierra Leone

168. Forestry Division MANR Youyi Bldg, Brookfields, Freetown, Sierra Leone.

Singapore

169. The Inland & Foreign Trading Co P.B. 2098, Maxwell Road, P.O. Singapore, 9040.

Solomon Islands

170. Forestry Div. PB 79, Munda Solomon, Islands.

South Africa

171. Directorate of Forestry Seed Section, P.B. 727 Pretoria 0001, S. Africa.

Sudan

172. Forestry Research Centre, PB 658, Soba Khartoum, Sudan.

Tiwan

173. Yilin Co. 24 Fu-Jen 2nd St, Huallan, Tiwan.

Tanzania

174. Dept. of Forest Biology, Faculty of Forestry, Sokoine Univ. of Agri, PB 3009, Morogoro, Tanzania.

175. Tanzania Forestry Research Inst., Silvicultural Research Centre, P.B. 95, Lushoto, Tanzania.

Thailand

176. ASEAN—CANADA Forest Tree Seec Centre (ACFTSC) Muak-Lek, Saraburi, 18180 Thailand.

177. Benjavan Rerkasem, Multiple Cropping Project, Chiang Mai University, Chiang Mai, Thailand.

178. Rupert Nelson, PB 29, Chiang Mai 50000, Thailand.

United Kingdom

179. Kins Plants Ltd, Woodcote Grove, Ashley Road, Epson, Surrey, KT 18 5 BM, UK.

180. Royal Botanical Gardens, Kew Richmond, Surreys, U.K.

181. Unit of Tropical Silviculture. Dept of forestry, Commonwealth Forestry Inst., South Parks Road, Oxford, UK.

United States of America

182. Carter Seed Co., 475 Mar Vista Drive Vista California, 92083, USA.

183. Hudson Seedsman, Redwood City, California, USA.

184. Hurovs Tropical Seeds, PB 1596, Chula Vista, California, 92012, USA.

185. ECHC, 17430 Durrance Road, North Fort Mayers, Florida 33917, USA.

186. USDA-ATS Regional Plant Introduction Station, Experiment Georgia 30212, USA.

187. Regional Plant Introduction Station, Georgia Experiment Station, Experiment, Georgia 30212, USA.

188. National Tree Seed Laboratory Seed Bank, Rt. 1, Box 182B, Dry Branch, Georgia 31020, USA.

189. Amorient Inc., PB 131, Kahuku Hawai 96731, USA.

190. Dept of Agronomy & Soil Science, University of Hawai at Manoa 3190, Maile Way Honolulu, Hawaii 96822, USA.

191. NIFTAL Project, Univ of Hawaii, PB 'O' Pala Hawaii 96779, USA.

192. Nitrogen Fixing Association (NFTA), PB 680, Waimanalo Hawaii 96795, USA.

193. Tree Seeds International, 2402 Esther Court, Silver Springs, Madison 20910, USA.

194. Plant Introduction Officer, USDA-ARS BLG 001, RM 322, BARC—West, Beltsville, Maryland 20705, USA.

195. Dept. of Forestry, Michigan State Univ., East Landing, Michigan 48824, USA.

196. Univ of Minnesota, Alderman Hall 1970 Forwell Ave St, Paul Minnesota 55108, USA.

197. Caesar Kieburg Wildlife Research Centre Campus, PB 218, Texas Ad I Univ of Kingville, Texas 78363, USA.

198. Duglass W. King Co, PB 203320, 4627 Emile Road, San Antonio, Texas, USA.

199. Native Plants, 360 Wakara Way, Salt Lake City, UTAH 84108.USA.

200. WINRCCK International, 1611 N. Kent, Arlinton, Virginia 22209, USA

201. Tree Seed International, 10 15 18th Street, N.W. Suite 802, Washington DC, 20036, USA.

Uruoguay

202. Coordinator Depto Forestal Facultad de Agromia, Avdą Garzon 780, Montevideo URUGUAY.

Venezuela

203. Estacion Experimental de Semillas Forestates, MARNR. EL Limon, Maracay Estado de Aragua, Venezulla.

Vietnam

204. Faculty of Forestry, Univ of Agri & Forestry Thu Duic, Ho Chi Minh, City, Vietnam.

Zambia

205. Forest Geneticist, Div. of Forest Research, P.B. 22099, Kitwe, Zimbabia.

Zimbabwe

206. Divisional Manager, Sustainable Agriculture, P.O. Box HG 595, Highlands, Harare, Zimbabwe.

207. National Herbarium & Botanic Garden, P.O. Box 8100, Causeway, H*araxe* Zimbabwe.

TREE PLANTING IN DIFFICULT SITES

Reproduced with courtesy from CARITAS INDIA Bulletin-Feb-June 1989 for mass communaction by RYAN FOUNDATION registered Public Charity 8. West Meda Sr. Srinagar Colony, Madras-6000015.India.

Water logged areas

Tree species with high transpiration rates are preferred for this area. Some species yielding good results on road, canal, rail side depressions and other Waterlogged areas are:

Eucalyptus robusta
E. tereticornis
Syzigium cumini
Terrainalia arjuna
Barringtonia acutanguta
Dalbergia sissoo
Acacia catechu
A. nilotioa
A. auriculiformis
Lagerstroemia specicsa
Bombax ceiba
Trewia nudiflora

Pongamia pinnata	Millingtonia hortensis
Anthocephalus chineusis Salix sp	Bischofia javonica

Planting of all plants is done on mounds of suitable dimensions so that they do not get submerged during the rainy season. In some areas after water dries up the seedlings are attacked by termites which would necessitate use of aldrex or other pesticide. Planting with the pre-monsoon shower is advisable.

Ravine Lands

The problem in such lands is low soil fertility, pan sandy layers and soil moisture deficiency. Acacia catechu, Dalbergia sissoo are preferred on gully slopes and humps to overcome moisture deficiency. For saline and alkaline patche in gully beds Acacia nilotica, Azadirachta indica Albizia sp should be preferred. Gmelina arbore and Dendroculamus strictus have also been planted successfully in the gully beds. In sloping areas contour trenches are made.

Saline Soil

A proper method of soil working is of utmost importance. Pits are filled with imported soil or amendments are added to provide a favourable medium for initial growth. Trench-ridge method has been fairly suitable. In this method ridges provide a relatively salt free condition and a favourable medium for root proliferation.

Among various species tried Albizia spp. Eucalyptus tereticornis, Dalbergia sissoo, Acacia auriculiformis were more promising. Among the fast growing species Lcucaena leucocephala has shown good results.

The experiments in Haryana showed:

— Soils with clay pan were not suitable for afforestation.

— Soils with calcareous pan at a depth more than one metre could be used for raising trees with short rotation (6 to 10 years).

— Eucalyptus tereticornis, Prosopis chilensis and Acacia nilotica were successful where the percentage of salt was not more than 0.5 to 0.8.

— Shads trees were useful in preventing the upward movement of salts.

Prosopis juliflora, Acacia nilotica and Eucalyptus tereticornis were successfully planted in sodic soil. yptus hybrid, Eucalyptus citriodora, Artocarpus *integrifolia* and Grevillea robusts.

For coastal areas

Anarcardium occidentale, Ailanthus malabarica, Acacia Auriculiformis, Casuariana equisitifolia, Pongamia glabra, Thespesia populnea, Calophyllum inophyllum, Mangifera Indica, Grevilea robusta, Cassia siamea.are recommanded, for coastal areas.

Shrubs and grasses

Agave species, Sesbania aegyptica, Sesbania aculeata, Glyricidia maculata, Cassia auriculata, Vitex negundo Dodonea, Vissosa Euphorbia tericulli, Jatropba spp., Thevetia neirifolia, Grasses, Sacchanim, spp., Cynodon dectylon, Elusive coracana, Cenchrus ciliaris, Euleolopsis binata and other fodder grasses.are recommanded.for castal areas.

Pattern of Planting

Shelter belts should be in one or more rows of trees.

As the sheltered area is 15 to 20 times the height growth the protection afforded will many a time cross the fields of the farmer. Hence raising of these belts should be on a cooperative basis, as land holdings are small in India.

The belts should be triangular in cross section. Tall trees are planted in the centre and shorter ones at sides. A mixture of species is advisable.

As far as possible species should be selected on the basis of their coppicing power. Spacing should be one metre for shrubs, 1.5 metres for trees in the row, each row being 1.5 to 4 metres apart and there should be five rows for proper protection.

Hot and Arid Areas

The local tree species of the region are not only meagre in number but they are also slow growing and it therefore becomes essential to introduce tree species of higher rates of growth and resistance to drought and cold, from iso-climatic regions of the world. It is mentioned that between 1958 and 1969, 103 species of Eucalyptus., 58 species of Acacia, 8 species of cassia and 63 species of other genera were trought. from Australia, Israel, the U.S.A., the USSR, to Rajasthan. Few species of Eucalyptus including E. Camaldulensis, E. Tereticornis, E. Tessellaris and E. Melanophoia were among the promising species. Among Acacia spp., A. tortilis proved most promising. Its performance on sand dunes and skeletal soils was extremely good. The most exotic species showed susceptibility to frost.

Dune Fixation

Sowing of seeds directly on dunes has failed almost universally. The basic principle in dune fixation is to immobilise the sand long enough to enable either natural or planted vegetation to establish itself. Natural vegetation will invade the dune if their movement is completely checked and there is sufficient vegetation in the vicinity to supply seed.

Crust forming chemicals such as bitumen emulsion can be sprayed to immobilise sand dunes. This method in India has not been found either economical or feasible. The techniques of sand dunes reclamation have been standardised in India. Three processes are involved:

- Protection against biotic influence;
- Treatment of shifting sand dunes by fixing barriers in parallel strips or chess board design from the crest down to the heel of the dune, using local shrub material, to protect the seedlings from burial or exposure by the blowing sand; and
- Afforestation of such temporarily fixed dunes by direct sowing and planting.

Mined Lands

Neither expertise nor experience is available in India in the field of rehabilitation of mined (derelict) land. Some have given an account of an experiment on derelict land where open cast mining for bauxite had been done previously. After levelling the area was full of laterite boulders and bauxite rejects and was devoid of any soil. Soil PH was 5.5 to 6.75. In 1979, 2.5 hectares were planted by digging 45 x 45 x 45 cm. and filling them with soil brought from a nearby sal forest. Cowdung manure at the rate of a half kg per pit was added and spacing was kept at 2 x 2 *m*, Poly-potted plants were used.

Among the indigenous species Shorea robusta and Pongamia pinnata and among exotics Eucalyptus camaldulеusis pinus caribaea, Grevillea robusta and G. Pteridifolia showed good results. The results are from three years old plantations.

Derelict lands present many problems which may vary from site to site. Generally in these areas normal soil texture or structure does not exist, the water holding capacity of the waste material may be poor and the soil may have acidity, toxicity or salinity. All derelict lands have nutrient deficiency. Therefore, a systematic and well planned method is required suited to specific area. Top soil conservation in new mining areas could be done. The application of top soil obtained from other areas may be costly or impossible.

Natural pioneers and colonisers generally constitute more suitable species. Some leguminous trees such as Acacia spp. and shrubs are useful for their nitrogen fixing capacity.

Table: Techniques of Sowing Planting, and Utilities of Tress Grown Under Social Forestry Schemes

Sl. No.	*Botanical and Common names*	*Family*	*Time of flowering*	*Time of seed collection*	*Time of sowing*	*Technique and time planting*
1.	*Acacia Catechu* (Khair)	Mimosaceae	June-Sept.	Jan.-Feb.	May-June	June-July, Direct sowing & Entire planting
2.	*Acacia arabica* (Babul)	Mimosaceae	June-December	May	May-June	July, Direct sowing and Entire planting
3.	*Adina cordifolia*	Rubiaceae	June-August	April-June	May-June	July, Entire planting
4.	*Ailanthus excelsa* (Maharukh, Mahaneem)	Simarubaceae	Feb-March	April-May	July	Entire, planting, Direct sowing, stump cutting
5.	*Azadirachta indica* (Neem)	Meliaceae	March-May	June-July	July	August. Entire seed
6.	*Bombax ceiba* (Simal)	Malvaceae	Jan.-March	April-May	June	July-August
7.	*Boswellia serrata* (Salai)	Burseraceae	Feb.-April	May-June	April	July, Entire root suckers planting,
8.	*Chloroxylon swietienia*	Meliaceae	March-April	May-July	June	July-August
9.	*Dalbergia sissoo* (Shisham)	Papilionaceae	April-May	December-January	March-April suckers	July, Direct sowing, Entire planting. Branchcutting, root
10.	*Dalbergia Latifolia sissoo*	" "	August-Sept.	Jan.-Feb.	Feb.-March	July-August, Direct sowing, Entire planting
11.	*Melia azadirachta* (Bakain)	Meliaceae	May-June	Nov.-Dec.	Feb.-April	July, Direct sowing, S. Planting

(contd.)

N.B.—D.S.–Direct Sowing, E.P.
Planting, S.C.—Stump Cutting, B.C.–Branch Cutting, R.S.–Root Suckers.

Shape and size of trees	Types of trees	Time for exploitation	Utilities	Climatic zone
Middle sized	Deciduous	30-50 years	Fodder Fuel, Poles, soil conservation & Katha etc.	Dry & Moist Tropical
" "	Evergreen	" "	Fodder, Soil conservation agricultural implements, Bark as medicine Tannin and fuel.	Dry & Most Tropical
Big sized tree	Deciduous	30-35 years	Planks Doors, Furnitures Mathematical instruments.	Dry & Moist Tropical
Big sized tree	"	8-15 years	Avenue trees	All through out India except costal regions.
Big to medi-um size	"	8-20 years	Planks, Tooth Brush & medicine (Bark, Leaves, Gum)	Hot Zone
Direct sowing Entire Planting	"		Match sticks, packing case plywood, soil conservation Roots used as medicine.	Moist Tropical to Sub-Tropical
Big sized tree	"	20-25 years	Match sticks gams, packing case.	Moist Tropical to Sub-tropical
Middle sized tree	"	20-30 years	For ornamental purpose	Dry to Moist Tropical
Big	"	25-50 years	Timber, fodder, fuel, soil conservation	Dry to Moist Tropical
Big	" years	20-30	Fodder, Timber, Fuel Tropical	Moist
Big	Deciduous years	15-20	Avenue tree Tropical to	Moist

(contd.)

Sl. No.	Botanical and Common names	Family	Time of flowering	Time of seed collection	Time of sowing	Technique and time planting
12.	*Petrocarpus marsubium* (Bija sal, Piu sal)	Papilionaceae	Sept.-Oct.	Dec-Jan.	March-April	July-August, Entire planing S. planting D. sowing
13.	*Shorea robusla* (Sal, Shakhua)	Dipterocar-paceae	March-April	June-July	May-June	July-August D. sowing E. Planting, S. Planting
14.	*Tectona grandis* (Sagaun)	Verbenaceae	July-August	Nov. Jan.	April-May	July, S. Planting E. Planting
15.	*Terminalia toman tosa or alata* (Ason Sain)	Combretaceae	March-April	June-July	Feb.-May	June-July, E. Planting
16.	*Terminalia arjuna* (Arjun)	"	"	" "	Feb.-May	June-July, E. Planting
17.	*Gmelina* *arborea* (Gamhar)	Verbeuaceae	Nov.-Dec.	April-May	May-June	July, E. Planting
18.	*Acacia auriculiformis* (Babul)	Mimosaceae	October-November	March-April	April-May	July, E. Planting
19.	*Acacia* *Chundra* (Lal Khair)	"	June-Sept.	Decem-ber	April-June	July-August January
20.	*Aegle marmelos* (Bel)	Rutaceae	Nov.-Dec.	April-May	May-June	July, E. Planting
21.	*Albizia* *chinemis* (Kala Siris)	Mimosaceae	Sept.-Nov.	Feb.-April	July-August	July-August E. Planting
22.	*Albizia Procera* (Safed Siris)	"	" "	" "	" "	" "
23.	*Artocarpus hetrophyllus* (Kathal)	Moraceae	Dec-January	May-June	July-August	Direct sowing
24.	*Artocarpus lakhncha* (Barhar)	"	May-June	June-July	July	July, D. Planting E. sowing
25.	*Anthoceph-alus chinemis* (Kadam)	Rubiaceae	July-August	Sept.-Oct.	March-May	July, E. Planting

(contd.)

Shape and size of trees	Types of tree	Time for exploitation	Utilities	Climatic zone
				Sub-tropical B. cutting R. suckers
Big	"	30-40 years	Fodder, Timber, fuel and medicinal	Moist Tropical
Big sized tree	Deciduous	20-40 years	Structure and Industrial Timber, pole, Fuel, Tannin.	
Big	"	20-40 years	Structure and Industrial Timber, pole, fuel, Tannin ornamental & medicinal use.	Dry and Moist Tropical
"	"	20-30 years	Industrial Timber, Tannin, gum, medicinal, pole, fuel.	Tropical
"	"	20-30 years	Industrial timber, small poles fuel, fodder, Timber ornamental medicinal use (Bark)	Tropical
"	"	20-30 years	Furniture wood	Tropical
Middle sized tree	"	10-15 years	Denuded Place Tannin, fuel, Ash used as washing soda for clothes	Big to Moist Tropical
Middle sized tree	"	20-30 years	Timber, Pole, Fuel, Tannin. soil conservation	Dry Tropical
"	"	10-20 years	Fuel, Tooth brush, fruits (Bark & Gum used as medicine)	Dry to Moist Tropical
Big	"	10 years	Timber, poles, fuel, medicinal	Tropical Moist Sub-tropical
"	"	10 years	Fuel, medicinal	" "
Middle sized tree	Evergreen	8 years	Fruit, ornamental, Timber fuel (Leaves, roots and flowers used as medicine)	Moist Tropical
Big	"	10 years	Fruit, Timber, fuel	" "

(contd.)

Sl. No.	Botanical and Common names	Family	Time of flowering	Time of seed collection	Time of sowing	Technique and time planting
26.	*Emblica officinaiis* (Amla)	Euphorbia-ceae	July-Aug.	Oct.-Nov.	May-June	E. Planting
27.	*Madhuka latifolia* (Mahua)	Sapotaceae	Feb.-May	June	July-Aug.	July, E. Planting
28.	*Mangifera indica* (Am)	Anacardiaceae	Feb.-March	April-May	June-July	July, E. Planting
29.	*Psidium guayava* (Amrud)	Myrtaceae	June-July	Dec-Jan.	March-April	June-July
30.	*Tamarindus indica* (Imli)	Caesalpini-aceae	Oct.-Nov.	March	April	July-Aug. D. Planting E. Planting
31.	*Terminalia chelula*	Comberet-aceae	July-Aug.	Dec-Jan.	Feb.-May	June-July, E. Planting D. Sowing
32.	*Ziziphus jujuba* (Ber)	Rhamnaceae	July-Aug.	Dec.-Jan.	Feb.-April	July-Aug. E. Planting D. Sowing
33.	*Anacardium accidentale* (Kaju)	Anacardiaceae	Nov.-Dec.	March-April	June	July, D. Sowing E. Planting
34.	*Prunus armeniaca* (Apricot)	Rosaceae	Nov.	—	Sept.-Oct.	July, E. Planting
35.	*Prunus persica* (Baddam)	Rosaceae	Nov.-Dec.	Feb.	April-July	July
36.	*Syzyglum cumini* (Jamun)	Myrtaceae	March-April	June-July	June-July	July-Aug.
37.	*Moringa oleifera* (Sahajan)	Meringacea	Sept.-Oct.	March-April	April-June	July, stem cutting, E. Planting
38.	*Sesbania grandiflora* (Basna, August)	Papilionaceae	Oct.-Nov.	Dec-Jan.	June-July	July-Aug. E. Planting
39.	*Schletchera oleosa* (Kusum)	Sapindaceae	Feb.-March	July	June-July	July-Aug. E. Planting
40.	*Saraca asoka* (Ashok)	Caesal Piniaceae	March-April	Dec.	Match-Apr	June-July, E. Planting
41.	*Santalum album* (Sandal wood, Chandan)	Santlaceae	Sept.-Dec.	March-April	May-Aug. Oct.-Dec.	June, D. Sowing E. Planting,
"		Deciduous	10 years	Fodder, fuel,	Pulp wood,	Moist to

(contd.)

Shape and size of trees	Types of tree	Time for exploitation	Utilities	Climatic zone
			ornamental	Tropical
Middle	Deciduous	8 years	Fruit, Fuel, ornamental,	Dry to wet
			medicinal	Tropical
Big to middle	"	15 years	Flower, fruit, Timber fodder, oil (Bark seeds, Flowers as medicine)	Dry to
Moist Tropical				
Big to Middle	Semi	10 years evergreen	Fruit, Timber, fodder medicinal (Seeds, Leaves, Bark)	Moist Tropical
to Sub-	tropical			
Middle &	Evergreen	10 years	Fruit, fodder, Fuel	Tropical
Subtropical				
Big	" "	15 years	Fruit, fuel, Medicinal, Timber Leaves, Flowers	Dry to
Moist				as medicine
	Tropical			
Big	" "	15 years	Fruit, fuel, medicinal plants	Tropical
Moist				
Middle	semi	10 years Evergreen	Fruit, fodder, poles	Sub-
tropical				
Middle	Deciduous	8 years	Fruit, fuel	Temperate
Middle	"	8 years	Fruit, small Timber, poles ornamental, soil conservation	"
Middle	"	8 years	Soil Conservation, Tannin Medicinal use	"
Big	Evergreen	10 years	Fruit, Timber, Fuel Medicinal (Flowers, Fruits)	Moist Tropical
Middle	Deciduous	10 years	Fruit, fodder Medicinal (Leaves and Fruits)	" "
Big	"	15 years	Flowers, Fence post, Tannin, fodder, fuel Pulp medicinal use Fodder for milch cattle.	Moist to Subtropical
Big	Deciduous	15 years	Industrial Timber, small timber, fuel, edible fruits, oil, ornamental, soil conservation, Tannin, medicinal use, Lac host trees.	Tropical
Big to Middle	Evergreen	10 years	Ornamental, medicinal use	Tropical,

(contd.)

Sl. No.	*Botanical and Common names*	*Family*	*Time of flowering*	*Time of seed collection*	*Time of sowing*	*Technique and time planting*
"	Tropical	"	15 years	Industrial timber, oil, ornamental oil, medicinal		Sub-Tropical, Dry Tropical Dry
42.	*(A) Morus alba*	Moraceae (Mulberry, Tont)	Oct.-Feb.	April	April-May	July, Stem cutting
	(B) Morus serrata (Mulberry)			May		D. Sowing E. Planting
43.	*Pongamia pinnata* (Kuranj)	Papilionaceae	Aug.-Sept.	March-May	April-May	July, E. Planting
44.	*Bauhinla variegata* (Kachnar)	Caesalpini-aceae	Feb.-March	April-May	May	July, E. Planting
45.	*Bauhinia retusa* (Kural)	Caesalpini-aceae	Sept.-Dec.	Feb.-March	May	July, E. Planting
46.	*Bauhinia racemose* (Jhangora)	"	April-June	Nov.-Feb.	April	July, E. Planting
47.	*Bahunia chinemis* (Kanehan)	" "	" "	" " "	" "	
48.	*Cassia fistula* (Amaltas, Sonari)	" "	May-Aug.	March-April	March-April	July-Aug., E. Planting S. Planting D. Sowing
49.	*Cassia siamea* (Chakundl, Beati Kasond)	" "	March-April	April-May	April-May	July, E. Planting S. Planting D. Sowing
50.	*Juglans regia* (Walnut)				Jan.-Feb.	Dec.Jan., D. Sowing
51.	*Michelia champaca* (Champa, Champ)	Magnoliacea	April-May	July	Nov.-Dec.	March-April E. Planting
52.	*Populus spp.* (Poplar)	Salicaceae	—	—	Feb.-March	Jan.-Feb. Branch cutting, E. Transplanting
53.	*Pitheclolbiu-*	Mimosaceae	Jan:-Feb.	April-	April-May	July-Aug.

(contd.)

Shape and size of trees	Types of tree	Time for exploitation	Utilities	Climatic zone
	mdulce		June	D. sowing
(Vilayati, Imli)				E. Planting. B. cutting
54. *Prosopis chil-ensis* (Kabuli Kikar)	"	Sept.-Nov.	March-April May-June	Aug. D. sowing E. Planting

Shape and size of trees	Types of tree	Time for exploitation	Utilities	Climatic zone
			use, soil conservation	
"	"		Fodder, fruit, sports goods Timber, fuel, silk worm trees	Moist Tropical to Sub-tropical
Middle sized tree	Deciduous	10 years	Flowers used as fertiliser, Branch used as tooth brush, seeds for oil, fuel, soil-cons-ervation (Roots, Leaves Flowers oil used as medicine)	Dry to Moist Tropical
"	Evergreen	8 years	Fodder, food & Timber, leaves and flowers are used as vegetables, Medicines	Moist Tropical to Sub-tropical
Middle sized tree	"	8 years	Medicinal sweet meat, Gum & fodder	Tropical to Sub-tropical
"	"	8 years	Fodder & fuel	" "
"	"	8 years	Medicinal Plant	Sub-tropical
"	Deciduous	10 years	Medicinal & fuel, ornamental	Tropical Moist
"	Evergreen	10 years	Soil conservation, fodder fuel, ornamental	Dry to Moist Tropical
Middle	Deciduour	15 years	Fruit, carving and Ornamental (Timber, Gum, Butter).	Temperate
"	Evergreen	20 years	Poles, Industrial Timber, fuel, Ornamental, Soil conservation, Medicinal flowers, are more valuable for ladies	Sub-tropical to Temperate
"	Deciduous	10 years	Soil conservation, fodder, Packing cases, pulpwood fuel, matchbox and Splints.	Sub-tropical to Temperate
Middle	Deciduous	15 years	Tannin, Fuel, medicinal use.	Tropical
"	"	8 years	Fodder, fuel, soil	Dry to

(contd.)

Sl. No.	Botanical and Common names	Family	Time of flowering	Time of seed collection	Time of sowing	Technique and time planting
				conservation in sand dunes zones.		Moist
Tropical						
"		"	10 years	Fuel, Timber good in coastal area for plantation		Tropical
"		"	10 years	Industrial Timber, poles,		Temperate
55.	*Casuarina equisetifolia* (Chok, Jhau)	"	May	June	Feb.-Nov.	June-July, E. Planting
56.	*Cupressus cashmiriana* (Cypress)	Coniferal	—	—	April-May	June-July
57.	*Eucalyptus camaldulensis* (Eucalyptus)	Myrtaceae	June-July	Dec.-Jan.	Sept.-Oct.	July-Aug., E. Planting
58.	*Eucalyptus globulus*	"	June-July	Dec.-Jan.	Sept.-Oct.	July-August., E. Planting
		(Blue Gum)				March-
April						
59.	*Eucalyptus teriticornis* (Mysore gum)	"	"	"	March-May	July-Aug., E. Planting Sept.-Oct.
60.	*Ficus religiosa* (Pipal)	Moraceae	Feb.-March	March-April	March-May	June-March, E. Planting
61.	*Ficus bengalensis* (Bar)	"	" "	" "	" "	"
62.	*Ficus tinctoria* (Pakar)	"	" "	" "	" "	"
63.	*Ficus glomerata* (Gular)	"	" "	" "	" "	"
64.	*Delonix regia* (Gulmohar)	Caesalpini-aceae	April-June	Dec-Jan.	April	May-July, E. Planting
65.	*Leucaena leucocephala* (Su-babul)	Mimosaceae	July-Nov.	Dec-Jan.	June	July, E. Planting
66.	*Pterocarpus santalinus* (Raktachardan)	Santalaceae	—	—	April-May	July-August, D. sowing B. cutting
67.	*Quercus incana* (Banj)	Fagaceae	April-June	Aug.-Sept.	Dec.-Feb.	July, D. sowing E. Planting
68.	*Querlus spp* (Indian oak)	Fagaceae	April-June	Aug.-Sept.	Dec.-Feb.	July, D. sowing

(contd.)

Shape and size of trees	Types of tree	Time for exploitation	Utilities	Climatic zone
			soil conservation, ornamental oil	Subtropical
"	"	8 years	Pulpwood, fuel, Timber	Moist Tropical & Subtropical
"	"	8 years	Fuel and Pulpwood. Tropical	Dry to Moist
"	Deciduous	10 years	Avenue, trees, fodder, fuel fruit, medicinal	Moist Trypical
"	"	10 years	Avenue, trees, fodder, fuel fruit, medicinal	" "
"	"	10 years	" " "	" "
"	"	10 years	" " "	" "
"	Semi Ever-green and Deciduous	10 years	Ornamental, Avenue, trees	" "
Middle duous	Semi Deci-	5 years	Poles, fodder, fuel, soil conservation Evergreen	Dry to Moist Tropical
"	Deciduous	10 years	Timber, fodder, Gum	Dry tropical
Middle sized tree	Evergreen	15 years	Poles, fuel, fodder, Tannin, ornamental, soil conservation, Industrial Timber.	Temperate
Middle sized tree	Evergreen	15 years	Fodder, fuel, silk cocoon host trees.	Temperate
" "	"			
Big sized	"	10 years	Fuel soap, nut for washing clothes	Temperate
"	Semi Ever-green	15 years	Poles, Gum, Tannin, Industrial Timber, ornam-ental and soil conservation	Sub-tropical Tropical Moist
"	Deciduous	8 years	Fodder, Gum, Poles, Indus-trial use, Soil conservation,	Dry Tropical Moist Tropical

(contd.)

Sl. No.	*Botanical and Common names*	*Family*	*Time of flowering*	*Time of seed collection*	*Time of sowing*	*Technique and time planting*
						E. Planting
69.	*Salix spp* (Willow)	Salieaceae	Oct.-Nov.	May-June	Feb.-March	Feb.-March, B. cutting
					pollards	
70.	*Sapindus mukorossi* (Ritha)	Sapindaceae	May-June	Dec.-Jan.	March-April	June-July, D. sowing E. Planting
71.	*Sweetenia-mahagoni* (Mahogany)	Meliaceae	April-May	July-Aug.	Dec.-March	June-July, D. sowing E. Planting, Stump planting
72.	*Dendrocalamus strictus* (Bamboo)	Gramineae	March-April	April-May	May-June	July, E. Planting
73.	*Legerstromia perviflora* (Sidha benteak)	Lythraceae	July-Aug.	Dec.-Jan.	Jan.-March	June-July, E. Planting
74.	*Holoptelea integrifolia* (Chilbil,	Ulmaceae	March-April	May	June	July-Aug., D. sowing E. Planting
		kanju)				S. Planting
75.	*Hardwickia binata* (Anjan)	Caesalpiniaceae	July-Aug.	Feb-March	May-June	July-Aug., D. sowing E. Planting
76.	*Lannea coromandelica* (Jhingan)	"	—	—	May-July	July, after one year D. sowing E. Planting
77.	*Mesua ferrea* (Nagesar)	Guttiferaceae	Feb.-June	Aug.-Oct.	April-May	July-Sept., D. sowing E. Planting
78.	*Erythrina subersoa* (Pangra, Burumarar)	Papilionaceae	March-April	April-July	June July	June-July, S. Planting B. cutting, Root stuckers Root cutting
79.	*Grewia spp* (Dhanian)	Tiliaceae	July-Oct.	Dec.-Jan.	April	July, E. Planting (contd.)
					B. cutting	
80.	*Pinus roxburghii* (Chir Pine)	Coniferal	Feb.-April	September	Feb.-April	June-July, E. Planting
81.	*Pinus wallichiana*	Coniferal	April-May	Septe-	Feb.-April	June-July, E. Planting

Shape and size of trees	Types of tree	Time for exploitation	Utilities	Climatic zone
			Medicinal Fodder, fuel, Gum, Tannin	
Big sized	"	15 years	Pole, Timber, ornamental, soil conservation.	Tropical Moist
Big sized tree	Evergreen	10 years	Gum, oil, Tannin ornamental soil conservation, Industrial Timber	Dry to Moist Tropical
"	"	10 years	Fodder, fuel, Timber	Tropical Moist
Big sized	Evergreen	15 years	Fodder, fuel, agricultural implements.	Dry Tropical
" "	Deciduous	15 years	Fencing posts, soil conservation	Moist Tropical
" "	Evergreen	20 years	Poles, fuel, Edible fruit, Gum, oil seeds, Industrial Timber, Tannin, soil conservation, Medicine.	Tropical to Moist
Mindle	"	10 years	Fuel and soil conservation	Moist Tropical
"	"	10 years	Fuel and fodder. to Temperate	Sub-Tropical
Big sized	"	15 years	Gum. Tannin, oil, resin, rosin, Poles, Industrial timber, ornamental and soil conservation.	Sub-tropical
Big sized	Evergreen	15 years	Gum, Tannin, oil, resin, rosin, Poles, Industrial timber, ornamental and soil conservation.	Sub-tropical

SOURCES

1. Prakash M. Shingi, Patel M.S., & Sanjay Wadwalkar; '*Development of Social Forestry in India*'; Oxford & IBH Publishing Co., 66, Janpath, New Delhi-110 001; 1986.
2. Sholto Douglas, J., Robert A. de J. Hart & G. Shankar Ranganathan; '*Forest Farming—Prosperity for India*'; Natraj Publishers. 17 Rajpur Road, Dehra Dun, India; 1982.
3. Prasad, V.N.; '*Principal and Practices of Social cum Community Forestry*'; International Book Distributors, Dehra Dun-248001; 1985.
4. Irshad Khan; *Wastelands Afforestation; Techniques and Systems*'; Oxford & IBH Publishing Co. Pvt. Ltd., Delhi-1; 1987.
5. '*Our Common Future*'; The World Commission on Environment and Development; Oxford University Press, Delhi; 1987.
6. '*For Every child a Tree*'; The SOS, Children's Villages of India, 507 Vishal Bhawan, 95, Nehru Place, New Delhi.
7. Sitaram Rao M; '*Introduction to Social Forestry*'; Oxford & IBH Publishing Co., 66, Janpath, New Delhi-110 001; 1979.
8. Desmond D'Abrco; *People and Forests; The Forest Bill and a New Forest Policy*'; Indian Social Institute, New Delhi; 1985.
9. Walter Fernandes; '*Forests, Environment and People*'; Indian Social Institute, New Delhi; 1983.
10. Shishupal Singh Kunwar; '*Hugging the Himalayas; The Chipko Experience*'; Dasholi Gram Swarajya Mandal, Gopeshwar (Chamoli) U.P., India; 1988.
11. Peter F. Folliott & John L. Thomas; 'Environmentally Sound Small Scale Forestry Projects (Guidelines for Planning)'; Codel—Vita Publication, 1815 N. Lynn Street, Suite 200, Arlington, VA 22209, U.S.A.
12. 'The State of Indian Environment'; The Second Citizens' Report; Centre for Science and Environment, New Delhi; 1985.
13. 'The Disappearing Forests;' An Article published in *Encology*, Volume 3, No. 5; October 1988.
14. Prof. JAmes Brewbaker; 'An Article on Nitrogen, Fixation and the Nitrogen; 'Fixing Trees'.

15. 'Green files'—A Selection of Clippings on the Environment; Issues: January to December 1988 and January, February, March, April 1989.

16. Plant trees';—A Selection of Clippings on Forestry Development; ISO/ Swedforest Consultants in Forestry, A-3/2 Vasant Vihar, New Delhi-110 057; June 1988.

Sea Water Kitchen Gardens

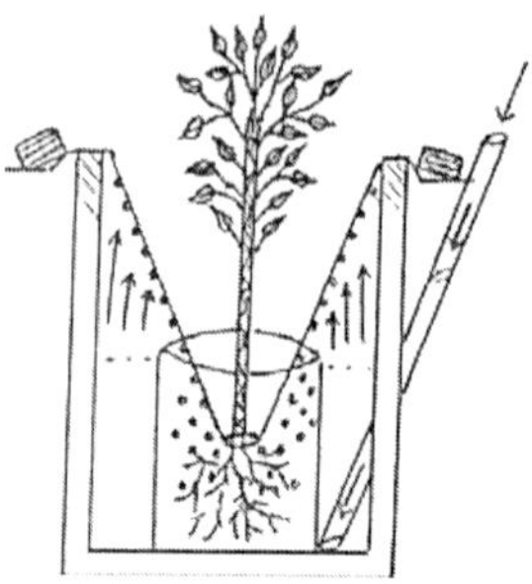

Plants and trees that cannot stand saline soil or brackish water can be raised by this method innovated by the Ryan Foundation. Experiments conducted in some African countries have proved very successful.

Materials required are three sq. metre of thin transparent plastic sheet, 200 hand-compressed and sun-dried bricks, a 20 liter garden or kitchen mud pot, RYFO mortar (no cement) and a 6 cm. dia hallow bamboo about 120 cm. long.

First, a one metre × one metre pit is dug and the floor and sides are lined with bricks and plastered with mortar. While building a side wall the bamboo is placed slanting as shown in the diagram. The mud pot is placed in the middle of the pit as shown and filled with good earth mixed with organic manure. (RYFO manure is recommanded).

In the middle of the plastic sheet a circular hole of 10 cm. diameter is cut. The pit is covered with the sheet and the central portion of the sheet taken down into the mud in the middle pot as shown. Weights are placed on the color of the sheet around the pit as shown and sand heaped around the pit on the plastic to prevent air entering the pit.

The required vegetable, say the quick growing Okra (lady's finger) is sowed or planted in the middle of the central pot as shown.

Sea water is poured through the top end of the bamboo and the mouth of the bamboo is plugged.

During day the sea water evaporates, hits the sides of the plastic sheet, gets condensed and rolls down the sheet to the roots of the plant. Thus, the plant gets something like pure rain water and flourishes. The method can be adapted also to growing trees in the middle of deserts provided man-made sea water canals are taken into the deserts. The sea and the tree hold the key for human progress.

Jused out tubes of tube lights, metal ends removed, ay be used in the place of bamboos. Table and Kitchen waste may be mashed and put around the plant as mixture

Vegetables for Family Nutrition

Household garden should include vegetables that are rich in protein, carbohydrates, minerals and vitamins.

Carbohydrate/Energy Sources

- *Cajanus cajan* (pigeon pea), pods
- *Colocasia esculenta* (taro), tuber

- *Dolichos lablad (hyacinth* bean), dried beans
- *Ipomoea batatas* (sweet potato), tuber
- *Manihot esculenta* (cassava), tuber
- *Pachyrrhizus erosus* (yam bean), tuber
- *Phaseolus aureus* (mungbean), pods
- *Phaseolus calcaratus* (rice bean), pods
- *Phaseolus lunatus* (lima bean), pods

Vitamin A Sources

- *Amarathus gracilis* (amaranth), leaves
- *Baselia alba* (alugbati, leaves
- *Capsicum anuum* (green pepper), leaves
- *Capsicum frutescen* (hot pepper), leaves
- *Colocasia esculenta* (taro), leaves
- *Corchorus oliturios* (Jute), leàves
- *Cucurbita maxima* (squash), tops
- *Daucus carota* (carrot), tuber
- *Hibiscus sabdariffa* (roselle), leaves
- *Ipomoea batatas* (sweet potato), leaves
- *Momordica charantia* (bittergourd), leaves
- *Moringa olelfera* (horseradish), leaves
- *Portulaca oleracea* (purslane), leaves
- *Psophocarpus tetragonolobus* (winged bean), leaves and flowers
- *Talinum triangulare* (Philippine spinach), leaves

High Vitamin C Sources

- *Amaranthus gracilis* (amaranth), leaves
- *Baselia alba* (alugbati), leaves
- *Brassica chinensis* (petchay), leaves
- *Brassica juncea* (mustard), leaves
- *Colocasia esculena* (taro), leaves
- *Ipomoea aquatica* (swamp cabbage), leaves
- *Momordica charantia* (bittergourd), fruits and leaves
- *Moringa oleifera* (horseradish), leaves
- *Psophocarpus tetmgonolobus* (winged bean), leaves and flowers
- *Talinum triagulare* (Philippine spinach), leaves

High Protein Sources

- *Cajanus cajan* (pigeon pea), pods
- *Canavalia ensiformis* (jack bean), pods

- *Dolichos lablab* (hyacinth bean), pods
- *Moringa olelfera* (horseradish), leaves, pods
- *Pachyrrhizus erosus* (yam bean), pods
- *Phaseolus calcaratus* (rice bean), pods
- *Phaseolus lunatus* (lima bean), pods
- *Psophocarpus tetragonolobus* (winged bean), pods
- *Vigna sesqulpedalls* (string beans), pods

Iron-rich Crops

- *Amaranthus gracilis* (amaranth), leaves
- *Baselia alba* (alugbati), leaves
- *Brassica chinensis* (petchay), leaves
- *Brassica juncea* (mustard), leaves
- *Cajanus cajan* (pigeon pea), pods
- *Capsicum anuum* (pepper), leaves
- *Colocasla esculenta* (taro), leaves
- *Corchorus oiltorius* (Jute), leaves
- *Dolichos lablab* (hyacinth bean), pods
- *Ipomoea aquatica* (swamp cabbage), leaves
- *Ipomoea batatas* (sweet potato), leaves
- *Momordica charantia* (bittergourd), leaves and fruits
- *Moringa oleifera* (horseradish), leaves
- *Pachyrrhizus erosus* (yam bean), pods
- *Phaseolus aureus* (mung bean), pods
- *Paaseolus lunatus* (lima bean), pods
- *Psophocarpus tetragonolobus* (winged bean), pods
- *Phaseolus calcaratus* (rice bean), pods
- *Talinum triangulare* (Philippine spinach), leaves

Calcium-rich Vegetables

- *Amaranthus gracilis* (amaranth), leaves
- *Basella alba* (alugbati), leaves
- *Colocasla esculenta* (taro), leaves
- *Corchorus olitorius* (Jute), leaves
- *Dolichos lablab* (hyacinth bean), pods
- *Hibiscus sabdariffa* (roselle), leaves
- *Ipomoea batatas* (sweet potato), leaves
- *Momordica charantia* (bitter gourd), fruit
- *Moringa oleifera* (horseradish), leaves
- *Pachyrrhizus erosus* (yam bean), pods

- *Phaseolus calcaratus* (rice bean), pods
- *Phaseolus lunatus* (lima bean), pods
- *Talinum triangulare* (Philippine spinach), leaves
- *Vigna sesqulpedalls* (string bean) pods

Vegetables With Multiple Edible Parts

Scientific Name	Common Name	Edible Parts
Cucurbita maxima	Squash	fruit, seeds, flower, shoots
Psophocarpus tetragonolobus	winged bean	pods, shoots, flowers
Moringa oleifera	horseradish	pods, flowers, leaves
Colocasia esculenta	laro	corn, leaves, petiole
Hibiscus sabdariffa	red serrel	fruits, leaves, petiole
Sesbania grandiflora	sesbania	fruits, flowers, leaves
Ipomoea batatas	sweet potato	tubers, leaves, petiole
Vigna sesquipedalis	string bean	pod, shoots
Sechium edule	chayote	fruits, shoots
Raphanus sativus	radish	roots, leaves
Momordica charantia	bitter gourd	fruits, shoots
Capsicum anum	green pepper	fruits, leaves
Allium cepa	onion	bulbs, leaves
Allium sativum	garlic	cloves, leaves
Vigna sinensis	cowpea	pods, shoots
Dolichos lablab	lablab bean	pods, shoots
Pachyrrhizus erosus	yam bean	tubers, young pods
Apium graveolens	celery	leaves, stems
Brassica oleracea var. *acephala*	kale	leaves, stems
Petroselinum crispum	parsley	leaves, stems
Ipomoea aquatica	swamp cabbage	leaves, petiole
Citrullus vulgaris	water melon	fruits, seeds
Abelmoschus esculentus	ladyfinger	fruits, seeds
Brassica chinensis	pechay	leaves, flowers
Brassica juncea	mustard	leaves, flowers
Amaranthus gracilis	amaranth	leaves, seeds

Produced by the International Institute of Rural Reconstrution Silang, Cavite, Philippines

COCONUT SUGAR

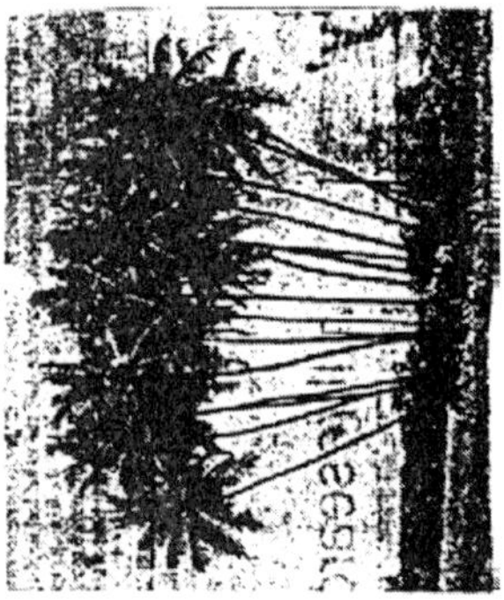

There are now 83 countries in the world where coconuts grow naturally. Other countries, like the Gulf countries, are introducing coconuts as they grow well on the sea shore and saline soil. Production of sugar from the sap of the tree is a profitable business but most of the countries do not make sugar. However, in Indonesia, Thailand and certain parts of Tamil Nadu and Kerala, sugar is produced in the villages using open pans.

The experience in countries like Thailand, Indonesia or Srilanka is that earmarking trees for tapping sap for sugar is more profitable than leaving them for producing nuts and copra. In Indonesia farmers leave about *30* per cent of the trees for sugar production

Trees may be used both for production of nuts and production of sugar. This is done by tapping only alternative spathes or by restriciting tapping to about six months of the year.

In the Philippines, experiments demonstrated that the same spathe could be used for production of sap and nuts by tapping only half length of the sheath and leaving the other half for production of nuts.

A general research results in many countries showed, that it is more profitable to leave about 25 per cent of the trees only for the production of sugar.

In the provinces of Samut Songkharm, Samut Parkhan and Samut Sakhan of Thailand, coconut gardens are maintained only for the production of sugar and when they are five years old, the sap is tapped for sugar in these gardens. For about ten months the tapping is done and then the trees are left to recoup their health, for the next cycle of production. Thus they are tapped every year for ten months only.

In about 30 Provinces of Indonesia the Government encourages production of sugar and sugar making is a popular cottage or rural industry in these provinces.

Local organisations help these sugar units and organise the sale of the sugar for the domestic and export markets.

It is reported that the annual production of coconut palm sugar in Indonesia is more than a million tonnes. In 1985, the Industrial sector of the country absorbed 36 per cent of coconut sugar, produced locally. The major consumer was the soya - sauce industry.

In 1991, the average monthly demand of coconut sugar from West Asia, New Zealand, USA, Australia and Europe was over 1,000 tonnes. More and more people in the advanced countries prefer to consume no-chemical natural sugar in preference to chemically defined cane sugar.

As more people demand coconut sugar, the production will increase and the cost of sugar will come down. Cultivation of coconut palm on coastal areas will pick up and provide livelihood for people directly and indirectly.

NEEM INSECT SPRAY

Neem smell add spray drive away several insects including mosquitoes and cockroaches to some extent. Some new generation mosquitoes and cockroaches, like the new generation youth are very stuborn and defeat neem. How to prepare the spray: Neem fruit is collected from the ground or from the tree. If the branches are shaken vigourously when the trees are fruiting many fruits will fall. Fruits are crushed by hand or in a pistle and mortar, the pulp and the seeds are dried in sun for a week. Dried seeds are stored in a basket or cloth bag.

When spray is required for the kitchen-garden, the lumber room, or cupboards, a handfull of seeds are taken, ground to a coarse powder and stired well in a liter of water and left overnight.

The mixture is cloth-filtered the next morning and sprayed or sprinkled with a fibre brush or a bunch of neem leaves (twigs with leaves held together). Use the prepared spray the same day as it loses much effect the following day. They spray is very effective in controlling pests in stored food grains and keeps toilets disinfected.

In wardrobes plain green neem leaves may be spread on each tray (shelf), paper or plastic sheets spread on it and clothes arranged on top.

In grain pots or containers neem leaf is put at the bottom below a sheet of paper and then the grains put in. In villages the leaves are dried in shade, powdered, mixed with cloth and used to plaster the inside of grain pots or granaries (20 gms of leaf powder for one kg on clay). This lining keeps away insects for over a year. Some villagers mix one kg powdered leaves but leaves are good enough.

Neem is salt tolerant and can be grown in soils with low fertility. It's main active ingredient, Azadirachtin was isolated by British Scientists end of 1970 and found to be effective against over 100 insect species in very small quantities. They discovered that neem upsets the harmone balance of insects permanently. Neem has about 20 other active ingredients and it is difficult for any insect to develop resistance to all of them.

Facts about Soyamilk

1. Soya. The richest source of natural protein in the-world.
   That's right.
   Soya is the world's richest source of natural protein. Not meat. Not fish. Not eggs. Not dal.
   Every 100 gms o f soya gives you 40 gms of protein. That's a lot more than any other natural food or drink can give you.
2. The complete protein.
   Soya is not just packed with proteins, it's packed with proteins of the quality that your body needs for growth and muscle development. In fact, of the 22 amino acids (components of protein) found in nature, soya is one of the few foods that has 20 of these.
   Further, it has all the essential amino acids in good proportion. The presence of Lysine in soya helps the assimilation of proteins into the body and stimulates growth and development.
3. Vitamins minus pills or frills.
   Some diets are deficient in vitamins. Soya is rich in the B Complex vitamins including Thiamin, Niacin, Riboflavin and Nicotinic Acid. These are necessary for the utilisation of nutrients by the body and for the steady release of energy from food.
   Moreover, soya contains Vitamin A which is good for the eyes; and Vitamin E which retards the ageing process in body cells.
   Soya is also rich in minerals such as calcium, phosphorus and magnesium. One of the most common mineral deficiencies is that of iron, leading to anemia. Soya can help correct this deficiency because it is specially rich in iron.
4. Goodbye allergies!
   Research shows that many allergies are caused by the most ordinary of foods: dairy milk, eggs and wheat.
   That's why doctors recommend soyamilk for both infants and adults who are allergic to dairy milk.
   Soyamilk is also an important lifeline for those infants whose systems cannot tolerate Lactose, a sugar present in all animal milk.

5. The healthy alternative.
   Although most of us grew up on dairy milk, recent medical research has shown that soyamilk could be a healthier alternative.
   To start with, dairy milk contains cholesterol. And cholesterol, we all know, has been linked to hypertension and hardening of the arteries.
   On the other hand, soyamilk has absolutely no cholesterol and even the low fat content in soyamilk is almost entirely made up of polyunsaturated. The beneficial effects of polyunsaturated fatty acids in protecting against heart disease is medically recognised.
6. Front-line Food Technology. processing Modern food processing technology has released the true potential of the versatile soyabean. Today, soya can be converted into just about any texture, taste, shape or colour: Confectionery, ice cream, breakfast food, cakes, breads. And of course, soyamilk. Another marvel of modern technology is the aseptic processing of soyamilk where by soyamilk is sterilised by momentary heating to a high temperature, followed by rapid cooling. This ensures the retention of all the nutritional, taste and flavour characteristics of the product while ensuring total hygiene. It gives a long shelf life without the need for expensive refrigeration.
7. The taste that grows on you.
   Soya has been the major source of food protein in the diets of Chinese and Japanese for over 3000 years. Today, people all over the world are discovering the goodness of soya.
   In Hong-Kong, soya drinks out sell Coca-Cola.
   In the U.S., they put soya into burgers.
   In Britain, they spend millions of pounds on soya foods every year.
   In Sri Lanka, soya flour is added to bakery flour.
   All over Europe, soya yogurt is already a rage. And very soon, you will come face to face with this amazing food drink

Preserving Pulp of Fruits

A simple traditional method of keepings mangoes, for example, is to spread the mango pulp on a bamboo mat or aluminum tray with or without addition of sugar and let it dry in the sun for four to six days until it has a leathery consistency. The dried product is then rolled or cut into pieces for sale. Although the freshly prepared product is of good quality, standards are virtually non-existent and the storage life is relatively short-only two to three months.

Main Raw Material Required to Prepare Approximate 100 kg of Fruit Bars.

Type of Fruit	*Fruit required in kg.*	*Pulp obtained in Kg.*	*Sugar required in Kg.*	*Yield (per cent of fresh fruit)*	*Yield (per cent of pulp)*
Mango	720	360	33	13.8	27
Banana	600	360	30	16.6	21
Guava	406	325	60	24.6	30
Mango +	540				
Banana	150	360	35	14.5	27
Papaya +	500				
Banana	140	336	54	23.4-	29

After mixing the fruit pulp and sugar in the proportion given above add for every kg. of it juice of one small lime fruit, one table spoon full of fresh ginger juice, one table spoon of honey, half tea spoon of salt and half tea spoon of mineral lime (chunam) Mix well and spread out on a mat or plate like biscuits to a thickness of one or two cm. Thinner the biscuits, quicker the drying and longer the preserving quality.

Jojoba for Shore Cultivation

Jojoba, a native shrub of Arizona, USA, pronounced as Ho-Ho-ba, is botanically known as simmondsia Chinoris, R&D done for about 4 years by the Central Arid zone Research Instituted (CAZARI) India, confirmed that Jojoba is highly drought tolerant and salt resistant and can convert desert and sea-shore sands into an oasis of prosperity. Several years of research done by the Central Salt and Marine Chemicals Research Institute, Bhavnagar, in the waste and coastal lands of Northern Gujarat also confirms that Jojoba is highly draught and salt tolerant.

Agricultural economists consider this shrub a gold mine and the FAO of the United Nations and the World Bank recommend the introduction and propogation of this shrub in waste lands and saline soils.

In the international market a tone of Jojoba seeds fetches about 8000 The money is paid for the oil which the seeds contain. The oil is very much like the whale oil in physical and chemical properties and better than almost all commercial substitutes for whale oil, which is getting scarce by the restrictions laid on whaling.

Israel is cultivating the shrub already on a large scale. Australia, Costa Rica, Brazil, S. Africa, Mexico, are among the fore runners in the promotion of jojoba. India, China, Philippines and some East African countries are also promoting the shrub now.

Jojoba oil, golden in colour, is totally free from alkaloids and resins. Cosmetic industry in the West consumes a large quantity of it. The oil is also used in the preparation of high quality candles, polish, varnish, lubricants, antifoam agents, fire-retardants and in the making of soaps. The oil is edible and has a low-calorie. But the most important and indispensible need for the oil is by the engineering industry to replace sperm whale oil which is scarce and costly to be used as a high pressure lubricant. The Ben Gurion University of Israel reports that the oil relieves pain and cures skin diseases.

Jojoba shrub thrives in temperatures ranging from 5 to 50 degrees Celsius and live 50 to 200 years. The shrubs are propagated by direct sowing, stem planting, or tissue culture. A plant yields about 125 gms of seeds in the first 5 years and thereafter about 2 Kg. The plant tolerates salinity level of 10,000 parts per million making it absolutely suitable for desert and coastal areas. CAZRI estimates a return of 1.8 lakh rupees per year from one ha of Jojoba.

Some Common Plant Dyes

Name of Plant or plant matter	*Mordant (agent which helps to fix the colour)*	*The colour obtained*
• Red groundnut skins	Gum tree bark and copper Sulphate	Brownish red
• Onion (Outer skins)	Alum or cream of tartar	Yellow
• Maize skins(red husk variety)	None needed	purple
• Eucalyptus (blue gum) leaves	Alum	Yellow
• Mango skin and seeds	Gum tree bark and copper Sulphate	Brownish orange
• Red Sorghum (finely crushed leaves)	Vegetable ash and lemon juice	Red
• Indigo (Legume)	None needed	Deep Blue
• Grenadilla skins (Passion fruit)	Alum and Chrome	Brown
• Black Soya Beans	Iron Rustwater	Silver grey
• Eucalyptus (Blue green) leaves	Gum tree bark and copper Sulphate	Green
• Black Soya Bean Skins	None needed	Deep Blue
• Mango skins and seeds or leaves	Gum tree bark and alum	Yellow

• Walnut Shells	None needed	Dark Brown
• Lichens (Different spices)	None needed	Different shades (depends on species)

Commonly used Moderants: Copper Sulphate, alum, ferrous sulphate, potassium dichromate, tannin, salt, wood ash, vinegar etc. By mix 2 or more moderants you can get different colours.

Quantity: Boil half kg of plant matter in 20 litres of water. Boil the material to be dyed. (Cotton, would, fibre or hair) and keep turining to spread the colour uniformly. By mixing different colours you can get different shades. After repeated experiments you can standardise the colour, concentrate the liquid and bottle it for the consumer market. Permutation and combination can give a wide range of colours and shares.

Cheese making made easy

Take one kg of leaves and stalks together of Calotropis gigantea or Calotropis procera (different species but about the same and both are medicinal) Calotropis Procera is also called Apple of Sodom or Dead Sea Apple-shurb. Crush the leaves and tender stem and take the juice. Use this juice as the rennet to Coagulate and add about two ounces of the juice to about one liter of milk under low fire. The Calotropis juice contains an enzyme that makes the milk Coagulate. It is orally consumed mixed in medicines and not poisonous or harmful.

Before the mixture solidifies sieve the liquid in a muslin cloth. A clean bandage cloth or mosquito curtain close may be used. Sieve the mixture directly into very hot milk and within a short time the milk Coagulates. The curd thus obtained is boiled for about fifteen minutes or for a longer time if the quantity is large. Then pass the contents through a strainer and allow solidify. Now the cheese is ready. Before it solidifies it may be put into a mould of desired shape. About 5 liters of milk will yield one kilo of soft cheese. Thereafter, it is allowed to dry on sterelised straw bed. Dried Cheese is hard and keeps for several months. People in Benin, West Africa, usually fry this Cheese and then eat it but some people eat it raw.

Sometimes they boil millet stems or millet chaff, obtain a red coloured water from it and then boil the cheese in it to give it a red colour. It is also boiled with beetroot for red colour.

It was reported by PPEA (NGO) of Benin that in 1993 about 2,500 tonnes of this cheese was produced and marketed and it is a very good source of income for the poor of that country. This way of Cheese making is ideal to preserve excess milk.

This author has eaten this cheese in West Africa and thinks that it is safe to fry, boil or otherwise cook it and eat it. In India they squeeze a lime when the milk boils, make it curdle and prepare a sort of cheese which they call "Paneer". Paneer lumps are cut into size and cooked; can be kept only for about a day or two. From the preservation point of view the Benin cheese is fine and healthy.

Plant Treatment for Animal Diseases

As reported by M. A. Mohamed Salith of the Scandinavian Institute of African studies in the IIED paper No. 32, March, 1992.

The plant species cited are common in Nigeria, Africa, perhaps they are also found in other countries of Africa and may be introduced into other warm Countries.

Some Medicinal Plant Species for Treatment of Animal Diseases

Fulfulde	*Latin*	*Parts used and application*
Bakkurehi	***	Bark. dried, pounded, mixed with salt and used to speed up delivery.
Bodi	Terimalia avicennioides t.glancescens and t.laxiflora	Bark- pounded and powder mixed with salt and used to treat habitual abortion (Brucellosis)
Bokki	Cucumis pustulantus	Bark-dried, pounded and powder mixed with salt and given to cows to speed up labour and relieve delivery pains.
Burle	Dichrostachys cinerea	Seeds-soaked in water and given to calves to treat worms, goli (haemonchosis).
Hanohi	***	Barks-soaked in water and given to calves to treat worms.
Kahi-Katki	Aristolochia	Barks-soaked in water and given to calves to treat worms, goli
Konkehi	***	Same as above
Hanohi	***	Same as above
Narchi	Parkia clappertoniana	Same as above
Naudi	Bridelia ferruginea	Barks-pounded, soaked in water and salt and used to treat poisoning.

(*** Latin name not identified).

Physic Shrub keeps away Crabs

In Peninsular India, one can notice farmers here and there cultivating the shrub called safed or Arand in some Indian languages. In English, the shrub is called *physic nut shrub* and in Nepal where it is common it is called *Hatlikane* or *Sajwon*. The shrub or small tree is native to tropical America and it is now cultivated along the west coast of India. The oil from the seed is used for manufacturing candles, soaps and also used as a lubricant and for burning lamps. Tribals use the oil as a purgative, use the tender twigs for brushing their teeth and-cook the tender leaves. The botanical name of this useful shrub is Jatropha Curces L. (family Euphorbiacese) The dried and burnt leaves are used as fertilizer and insecticide. When the dried fruits are set fire to, they burn long like a candle. In some villages in Nepal, the plant is grown as hedge row to control enemies that attack crops.

One important and interesting use of this shrub must be highlighted as it has not caught the attention of many. When these shrubs are planted as hedge rows or boundary plants to fence a field, the shrub keeps away rats and crabs, crabs in particular keep far away from this shrub. Farmers who know that this shrub chases away rats and crabs plant stem cutting of this shrub and reports say they get a better yield as the grains are saved from pests. Ryan Foundation recommends the planting of this shrub as hedge rows and appeals to botonists to research on this shrub. Perhaps it has several other uses. It may be possible to dry and powder the roots of this shrub to be used as rat poison and cockroach poison. The Foundation will be grateful to get any feed-back on this subject.

Latex Extraction from Papaye

Latex for Papain production is extracted from more than half mature (nearly ripe but fully green) fruits when they are still on the tree. A clean stainless steel knife or sharp bamboo splinter is used to make incisions. The incision is usually made early morning before the sun comes up and they are done lengthwise from the stalk end to the tip of each fruit. Aluminium or glass vessels are used to collect the latex (milk) that drips from the incisions. The vessel is tied on held below the fruit. The incisions can be made every 4th day on the same fruit for collecting the latex.

The latex is usually sun dried but sometimes simple artificial driers are used. The ideal temperature for drying is about 50° C. The atmosphere should not have humidity while drying. For every kilo of latex one tea spoon full of chunam (mineral lime) may be added to henance the keeping quality of the papine.

Latex yield is high during winter and low during summer Papain can be stored in tight containers for about 6 months. A yield of 200 kg of papain per ha during the first year and 100 kg in the second year can be expected.

Fruits from which latex has been extracted do not lose their flesh quality in anyway but only their outer appearance. Such fruits are mostly used for canning or for making mixed fruit jams or for dehydrating.

During the productive life of 18 months, the latex yields of Papaya is about 1,750 kg. from one ha. and the fruit yield is about 125 kg.

The Enzo/chem Laboratories Pvt. Ltd., P.B. No. 28, Yeola, Dist Nasik, Maharashtra pays Rs 50 per kg. of latex which works out to about Rs 87,500. The fruits yield about Rs 62,500. Thus the total income is Rs 1,50,000 per ha in 18 months.

For supply of seeds end buy-back of latex contact Enzo/chem Lab.

THE BARNA

Botanical - *Crateva Magna.*

Sanscrit - *Varuna.*

Family - *Capparaceae.*

Hindi - *Barna.*

Tamil - *Marilingam.*

Malayalam - *Nirmathalam.*

Description: Medium size ornamental tree good for home gardens. Grows wild in nature; also cultivated; propogated through seeds. The saplings have sharp roots and grow in light or rocky soils. Seeds should be planted deep and while transplanting the sharp roots should not be damaged.

During warm months the leaves fall and during April-May green flowers appear with 4 clawed petals. As they mature and open the flowers turn white, creamy and yellow and they are just beautiful to look at. The leaves are ovate-lance shaped, 6 to 12 cm long and pointed. The tree flowers for nearly a month and as they fade and fall new leaves appear.

Uses: From ancient times the pulp of this tree is used in the building industry. By mixing the pulp of the fruit with mortar a strong and quick setting cement is obtained.

The bark of the tree is medicinal and it is used by villagers and tribals of India as a laxative, demulcent, diuretic and a cure for kidney stone. The twigs make good fuel, wood and leaves are eaten by cattle.

Clarification on Eucalyptus

1. *Eucalyptus for pulp*: Eucalyptus Hybrid (mainly, E. Tereticornis) and E.grandis are the two common species of Eucalyptus used in India for

pulp and paper manufacturing. Out of the two E. Grandis is better than E.hybrid.

2. *For oil*: Essential oils obtained from several species of Eucalyptus leaves by steam distillation are of commercial importance. The two species popularly used in India for oil are:
   1. Eucalyptus globulus (medicinal oil)
   2. Eucalyptus Citriodora (Oil for perfumery)
3. *For Gum*: Most of the Eucalyptus species are popularly known as gum trees in Australia, although exudation from them is not a gum but an astringent, tanniferous substance called KINO. The two species given below give a good yield of KINO.
   1. Eucalyptus Camaldulensis
   2. Eucalyptus Citriodora
4. *Kino or Kino gum*: The dried resinous juice of several tropical trees of the genera Pterocarpus, Butea and Eucalyptus are used in medicines used for curing throat infection and in tanning.

Kino or Kino gum or Ki-no is the name commonly used by people of West Africa in their local languages. As said already, it is the dried resinous juice of several tropical trees. The Kino gum cannot really be used as a gum for sticking or pasting. It is more like starch with properties of stickiness. However, the resigness juice in concentrated form can be used as a binder for certain purposes.

When the juice is mixed with gummy starch such as tamarind seed starch, casava starch, starch of yam or cluster-beans it enhances of the sticky property of the liquid, increases the Volume and makes the gum cheaper for commercial use.

Addition of a small quantity of powdered mineral lime and sugar or jaggary henances sticky property of the solution.

Gum, thus made, has to be commercialised for large scale use and the industry can provide employment for thousands of people.

Fibre Food good for Constipation and Cholesterol

Studies reveal that fibre in the diet increases the tolerance of Glucose in diabetics. Dietary fibre such as pectin decreases the concentration of blood glucose by reducing the dijestion of Carbohydrate and the rate of absorption in the intestine. Carbohydrates present in certain food stuffs are absorbed more slowly than those in others. For instance, those in ragi are absorbed more slowly than those present in rice.

Generally speaking, fibre in the diet brings about a reduction in the serum Cholesterol by preventing the absorption of Cholesterol. Several types of fibre have been shown to lower the serum Cholesterol and lipid levels in people suffering from atherosclerosis. Pectin has a definite hypercholesterolemia effect.

Some common foodstuffs which contain a high percentage of fibre are:—

1. Safflower seeds 34.9 per cent in 100 gms of edible portion.
2. Sundakkai (Tamil, also in English) 17.6 per cent.
3. Dried Colacasia leaves - 116 per cent.
4. Dried tamarind leaves 10 per cent.
5. Amla - 3-4 per cent
6. Gooseberry 3-2 per cent
7. Guava fruit 3.2 per cent
8. Cardamom 20 per cent
9. Dry chillis 30.2 per cent
10. Cloves 9 per cent
11. Corriander — 32.6 per cent
12. Cummin seeds 12 per cent
13. Fenugreek seeds 7.2 per cent
14. Black pepper — 14.9 per cent
15. Tamarind pulp - 6.6 per cent

To relieve constipation, Cholesterol and to reduce body weight, Ryan Foundation recommeend Surdakkai, Tamarind leaves, cardamom, corriander, fenugreek and black pepper. These may be dried, powdered, made into tablets or pellets and taken everyday. Two tabs after every meal.

Some Prosopis Species

The genus prosopis includes more than 40 species out of which five are prominent in tree planting projects and social forestry. They are:

1. The most popular Prosopis Juliflora (also known as mesquite in America and "Mad Tree" in several countries because it grows in desserts, in between rocks, on the sea-shore, with water, without water and stands severe changes in climatic conditions.
2. P. Chilensis.
3. P. Tamarugo
4. P.Cineraria
5. P. Pallida

All these five trees (species) thrive well in light and sandy soils; adapt well to arid conditions; root well in hard and rocky soils; most important of all, tolerate alkaline or saline soils and grow well along seashore. They withstand drought for nearly eleven months in a year in desert temperature. Most of these trees have thorns and fruits appear as pods containing several seeds. (about 10 on an average). The pods contain 13 per cent crude protein and 4 per cent Carbohydrate. Ripe pods ground into flour can even be backed as food for humans.

Most of the prosopis listed above yield good honey. A coffee like drink is made out of the dried seeds. The bark of the tree is crushed and used in leather tanning. Some of then have medicinal properties.

The species mentioned above reproduce easily from seeds or cuttings. The pods gathered from the tree or collected from the ground must be dried in the sun for atleast ten days and then used in a nursery. Before sowing the seeds must be doused in boiling water and allowed to soak a day or two until the natural swelling that results bursts the endocarp from within.

Principle 23 of Rio Decleration says, "The environment and natural resources of people under oppression, domination and occupation shall be protected." Let the affluent usher an austerity revolution to save our planet. Poverty degrades not only those who suffer it but also those who tolerate it

People need work and water, not weapons and wars:

NEEM, THE WONDER TREE

Botanical - *Azadirachta Indica A. Juss.*
Family - *Meliaceae.*
English - *Neem Tree or Margosa Tree.*
Tamil - *Vepa Maram.*
Malayalam - *Vepam.*
Hindi - *Nim.*

"I think I shall never see a poem lovely as a tree, poems are made by fools like me, But only God can make a tree", poet Joyce Kilmer.

A deep rooted common radside and household tree in most tropical countries producing bunches of small, white and sweet scented flowers. Native of India and Burma. Hardy neem grows luxuriously even in marginal and leached soils upto an elevation of 1,000 m. The seeds yield. useful oil called Margosa oil and the oil is excellent for soap making oil cake is used as manure and fertiliser. Leaves act as insect repellant and green leaves are used as insecticide and manure. Leaves are dried, burnt and the ash is used as tooth powder. Oil is effective in treatment of skin diseases and leprosy and the Kernel gives 45 per cent oil and the oil when used in wick lamps repells mosquitoes. Leaves in poultice are used for healing of wounds. Ripes fruits are edible. Seed oil is also used as antiseptic and for burning lamps, especially in temples. Bark yields tannin and the amber-hued gum that exudate from the bark is used in medicines as a stimulant and for dyeing silk.

The bitter principles of neem oil are obtained by alcohol extraction and the main component of the oil is Nimbidin which is very bitter. Nimbidin is used in the making or several pharmaceutical and auyervedic perparations such as ointments, liquors, emulsions, lotions, hair tonics, etc. Timber is strong and of medium quality. As they are not attacked by white ants they are used for making agricultural and farm implements and furniture.

Neem grows under different climatic and soil conditions and tolerates salinity. Nature propogates them. If planted during the rainy season nature cares for them. Animals do browse but don't relish them since the leaves are bitter.

RYFO Germicide Spray

Chemical Germicide and insecticide sprays are now common all over the world and their harmful effects on soil, plant and human health is well known. Several organic matter is now being used as a substitate for chemical substance and most of them are leaf based.

RYFO Germicide spray (liquid) can be prepared by villagers out of the leaves of trees and shrubs available in and around their village.

There are several leaves containing insecticidal and Germicidal properties listed in RYFO Handout. on Mosquito Smoke. Three or four of these leaves which are common may be collected. They may be Eucalyptus, Neem, Vasaka, Papaya, Adhathoda, Vinca Rosia, Datura etc. Neem and Eucalyptus leaves are most effective.

One bucket full of the mixed leaves is boiled in 4 buckets of water and kept aside.

Separately, Caustic soda is extracted in two earthern pots out of banana skins, barks, Vasaka Stems, mulberry stemps etc. by the method explained in RYFO Handout 45.

Also, separately half kg of mineral lime, quarter kg of turmeric powder and quarter kg of Chilli powder is mixed in two kg of country-brewed alcohol like toddy, or two kg of kerosine or 2 parts of any low density non-edible oil such as the oil extracted from the leaf of humble plant (Handouts 332).

The three mixtures may then be combined together and mixed thoroughly in equal quantity of water by Volume, stored and sprayed.

Spraying is done either with a fibre brush or the liquid mixture is filled into an old automobile lorry tube and air blown into it to make it bulge double its size. A small hole made with a pin in the tube sprays the liquid. The tube may be hung on the shoulder and the spray allowed to fall on plants.

Grape Cure

Delicious grapes which is grown world over has about 15 per cent glucose and fructose and the fruit is easily disgested. The fruits contain tartaric acid resinic acid and mellic acid which is like tonic for kidneys and intestines. They also contain over ten per cent of carbohydrates and plenty of Vitamin A, B and C. Ayurvedic science claims that grapes improve eye sight and clear phlegm (flem in the respiratory tract).

In villages near Madurai, the poor people administer grape juice, ginger juice, (in equal parts mixed with milk and honey with equal parts) to relieve conjestion of the lungs with flem. Large size dried grapes, (seeds removed) is soaked in honey and taken as a desert in some European countries and it is said to help blood circulation and constipation.

Commercial table grapes belong to the species Vitis Vinifera and there are over 125 other species. Grapes tolerate saline soil and different weather conditions.

All varieties of grapes can be dried. on a cottage scale the fruits are punctured and pressed gently to extract as much juice as possible. Grape juice thus pressed makes a good drink. After removing nearly half the juice the fruits can be sun dried and while drying a spoonful of mineral lime (Chunam) powder may be sprinkled on the fruits along with same fresh lime juice and honey. For one kg of fruits one spoonful of lime, one spoonful of lime juice and spoonful of honey may be mixed. Fruits thus dried may be stored in sterilised bottles and preserved. A pinch of salt may be added to taste. Drying should be done when the temperature is over of or in Ryan Foundation Biscuit tindrier.

To preserve grapes with seeds the fruits must be slit first and the seed removed. The skin of black grapes can be dried well powdered and used as a food colouring.

DEEP PURPLE

Jammu (Syzyqium Cumini Skeels)

Botanical - *Syzygium Cumini Skeels*, Family - *Myrtaceae*, Hindi - *Jammun*. Tamil - *Nagam Palham*.

Hardy Horticultural tree wide spread in the forests of peninsular India is not usually attacked by pests. Grows in diverse soil and climatic conditions and can be introduced in several third world countries having more or less the climate of South India. Requires dry weather at the time of flowering and fruiting and grows well in waste and marshy land provided the soil is hard. Generally propagated by seed during May-June though inarching, and air layering methods are possible. Saplings can be raised in seed beds and when one year old trans planted into one cubic meter pits filled with a mixture of top soil and farm yard manure (50-50) and watered for about a month. No fertilisers are required other than some cow dung during the first month of planting.

The fruits which look like large black grapes (but longish) is used for making wine, vinegar, pickles, jelly, jam and *"chutneys"* can also be dehydrated (sun dried) and preserved. Children love to eat the fruit raw as it is juicy with good flavour.

From time immemorial tribals and villagers have been taking Jamun, particularly the powder of seeds as an antidote for diabetes and to reduce sugar in urine. The seed is rich in Calcium, Carbohydrates and Protein and small quantities of the powder can be mixed for making biscuit or "Chappatis". The fruit has scientific sanction as an antidote against diabetes.

In many villages in Kerala, people prepare "tea" out of the tender leaves and drink it to cure stomach disorders and take "tea" made out of the seed powder to get tid of worms in the stomach. Like pomogranate leaves, Jamun leaves are also given to cattle and chicken for deworming. When grown out of seeds the tree bears fruits in ten years and if grafted in seven years.Trees grown from seeds give more and larger and more juicy fruits and have a longer life span. February and March end is the season for flowering and the tree is in full bloom by the middle of March. Most flowers drop off and only about 15 per cent ripen as fruits in April-May. In the tenth year, each tree gives about 100 kgs of fruits. This tree must be promoted in tropical countries for its commercial, medicinal and food value and to generate rural employment and for deworming cattle.

Flowering Tress Courtesy B.A. Rama Rao

Botanical Name	*Common English and Tamil Name*	*Erect or Spreading*	*Colour of flower*	*Rate of growth*	*Height in feet*	*Spread in feet*
Bauhinia varieties	Ebony or camel foot tree (Mandari)	Spreading	Pink, white, purple and yellow	Quick	20—25	20—25
Brownea coccinea		Spreading	Scarlet	Slow	15—20	20—25
Calophyllum inophyllum	Alexandrian laurel (Pinnal)	Spreading	White	Medium	20—25	20—25
Callestamen speciosa	Bottle brush	Stragly drooping	Scarlet	Medium	15—20	20—25
Cassia fistula	Indian laburnum	Spreading	Yellow	Slow	20—30	20—25
Cassia varieties	(vakai, kirudam)	Spreading	White pinkish, pink, yellow	Slow	20—30	20—25
Citheroxylon subserratum	Fiddle wood tree	Erect	White scented	Quick	20—25	10—15
Cordia sebastina	Aloewood tree	Spreading	Orange	Medium	10—15	15—40
Couropita guianensis	Cannon ball tree (Nagalingam)	Erect	Orange red, scented	Slow	35—40	15—20
Erythrina indica	Coral tree (Kalyana murungu)	Erect	Scarlet	Quick	30—35	10—15
Gliricidia maculata	Madre tree (Kona maram)	Spreading	Whitish pink	Quick	15—20	15—20
Guaicum officinale	Lignum vitae	Spreading	Blue	Slow	25—30	25—35
Lagerstroemia flosregina varieties	Pride of India Queen's flower (Kadali)	Spreading	Mauve, pink, whitish mauve.	Medium	20—25	20—25
Mimusops alengi	(Maghudam).	Spreading	Cream scented	Slow	30—40	30—40
Millingtonia Hortensis	Indian cork (Marsmalli)	Erect	White scented	Quick	30—40	15—20
Peltophorum ferrogineum	Rusty Shield bearer (Iyalvagai)	Spreading	Yellow	Quick	40—50	40—50
Poinciana regia	Gul Mohar (Panchala maram)	Spreading	Orange red	Quick	35—40	40—50
Plumeria varieties	Pagoda or Temple tree	Spreading	White with yellow throat, white scented. red and pink	Quick	15—25	15—20
Saracca Indica	Ashoka (Asogam)	Spreading	Bed	Slow	15—20	15—20
Spathodia Companulata	Tulip or Fountain tree (Patadi)	Erect	Orange red	Medium	40—50	20—25

Reproduced by Ryan Foundation with courtesy to B.A. Rama Rao.

RAUOLFIA SERPENTINE FOR EXPORTS

Botanical - *Rauvolifia Serpentine*; Family - *Apocynaceae*.

Origin India: Above 2000 feet and with good rain fall.

Description: Plant grows over a metre high.

Flowers twice a year and flowers are pinkish white with a deep orange Corolla tube

Medicinal: Very rich in alkaloids and about 80 alkaloids have been identified and isolated from the roots. The more important alkaloids are ajamaline, ajmalicine, rescinnamine, and serpentine. These are used to cure neuro-physical disorders, cardiac arrythemia hypertension and psychiatric disorders.

In Wester Alopathy synthetic substitutes such as phenothiazine, chlopramaise. methyldope etc. are available but today natural organic medicines are preferred and are in demand.

The alkaloids are extracted from the roots and over 350 tonnes of the roots are being exported every year from India and India is not able to meet the ever rising export demands. About 100 tonnes of the roots are consumed within India mostly by ayurvedic doctors and pharmacies.

The plant can be introduced by cuttings or transplanting and they propogate by themselves in the wild. Rural people living near hills and hill tribes grow this plant and supply the roots to exporters. The plant seems to be a speciality of India and the other country where it is seen commonly in Madagascar. Cutting or sapling can be had from Botanical Research Centres.

SUPERFINE SOYABEAN

Soyabean and various products and by-products made out of it are having a rising demand the world over. The average yield per ha in India is 990 kg. 80 per cent of Indian's Soyabean comes from the State of Madhya Pradesh. In 1989-90 Soy exports from India earned 361.23 crores. Soy is rich in minerals proteins (40 per cent) oils (20 per cent, Carbohydrates (26 per cent), minerals (4 per cent) and Phoslolipids (2 per cent). It is a good source of lacithin and phosphorus and therefore used for nervous disorder. Because of its low carbohydrate content it is very good for diabetic patients and those suffering from high blood pressure.

Soyflour can be mixed with wheat flour, maida or Atta to make "Chapatis and puris". It can even be mixed with rice flour to make "Dhosa" or "Idlies" or Vermecelli.

The antibiotic manufactures of India consume over 10,000 tonnes of Soyflour every year.

In Japan and China and now in USA. Soyamilk is very popular and infants are fed with it. Curds and cheese are prepared out of Soyamilk and Soy oil and milk have a rising demand in India. Sakthi Soya of Coimbatore and Arbindo Ashram in Pondy are promoting Soya in a large way.

In Columbia and Israel, compulsorily by law five per cent of Soyaflour must be added to bread. It is high time that more and more developing countries increase and improve their Soya cultivation to better health and nutrition of people. The small soya plant is highly drought resistant, bad soil and climate tolerant. Soya, mushroom, rabbits and fish can salvage people out of hunger and poverty.

GRAFTING MANGOES

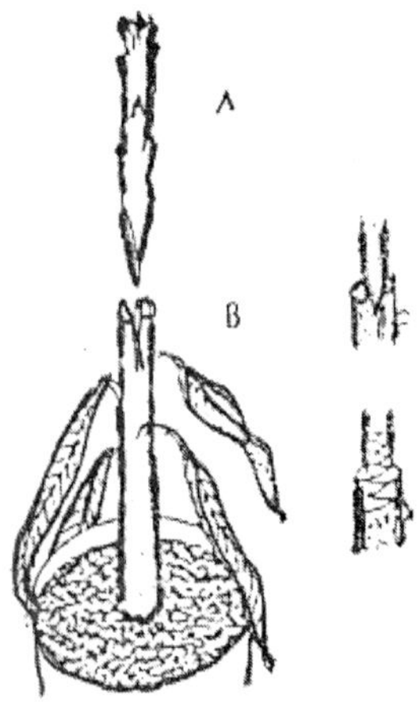

The art of grafting is now practiced all over the world by people from backward tribals to advanced botanists. It is a quick and easy way of increasing quantity and quality of fruits. If a small branch six cm thick and 15 cm long is cut from a healthy mango tree which produces excellent fruits is cut and grafted (attached skin to skin) on the stem of another good variety of mango tree sapling which grows healthy in the ground, as shown in the diagram, the two grafted species blend as one tree and produces very superior quality of fruits and the yield is high. While grafting, care is taken to ensure that the soft tissues are in contact so that they blend and grow together as one tree.

If grafting is to be successful, the scion stick (stick or branch of the parent tree) and the seedling stick (or stem) must be about the same size and age.

A tasty ripe mango is plucked directly from the tree (not a fallen one) and after eating the fruit the nut is put into a bucket of water. If the nut floats it is not good for grafting. A good seed which settles in the bottom is removed from the bucket, dried well and then buried in a pot or plastic bag filled with common earth without lumps. Some cow dung and a handful of neem leaves may be added. When the seed grows into a sapling with a stem as thick as a human finger it is ready to take the graft. Only the main stem of the sapling is allowed to grow and the side shoots are removed.

The most suited method for grafting mangoes is the claft method in which the bud stick that is to be grafted on a growing sapling is selected from **a** tree which the buds are about to sprout. The bottom of bud stick is cut tapering or either side as shown. The sloping cut may be 31/2 cm. long to form the wedge. The seedling stock on the ground is cut about 30 cm above the soil and one straight verticle cut is made in it, 30 cm. deep. The wedge of the bud stock is pushed firmly into the claft of the root stock leaving 1/3 of the cut on it outside the root stock. Then cow dung and sand is plastered on the joint and bandaged with a thin cloth like bandaging a broken limb. Shoots growing below the graft are removed.

If the grafted portion dies out allow one or two shoots to come up in the root stock and six months thereafter remove the top dead portion and try a fresh grafting.

PINEAPPLE FIBER

Pineapple grows abundantly in several parts of India, Sri Lanka, Hawaii, Madagascar, many countries in the African continent, the Far East, Republic of Seychelles, Marutius, Fiji and almost in all countries with tropical climate. The fruit is eaten raw, preserved in wet or dry form (dehydrated). However, the fibre from the leaves have not been commercialised so far. Only now in 1991. the Southern India Textile Research Association (SITRA) has fabricated a machine after much R & D to extract the fibre to be woven into cloth. The machine which is not expensive and simple to operate can be introduced in all pineapple growing countries to extract the fibre and weaving blended cloth in handlooms.

Pineapple Fibre

The R and D which was funded by the United Nations Development Organisation (UNIDO) has generated a wide variety of spin off products, including non-woven felt, cords, for conveyor belts, tapes, wicks, reinforced corrugated roofing sheets, shoe laces, floor mops etc. The waste and dust dropping during the extraction can he used to make compressed fuel pallets and briquettes in Cinva Ram or hand moulds (RYFO methods).

Further, the waste can be used as organic fertiliser or to compose humus along with the prickly peals of the fruit.

In the Republic of Seychelles, some families used to soak the prickly peels and rotten pineapples in Jerry cans with yeast for over a month, steam distill the rotten contents and get good quality colourless alcohol like white rum.

With the R and D already done on pine apple fibre by SITRA the fruit and its bye-products are bound to earn pride of place in trade and commerce from Tropical countries.

MALTA LEMON

Malta Lemon which is vegetatively propagated is very juicy with fine lemon fragrance. The plant grows into a bush and bears fruit within a year of planting and the fruits are seedless. The bush grows to an average height of two metres with several branches. From the second year each bush yields about 400 lemons and from the fourth year the yield is about 1,000 lemons per year.

Botanically lemons are called Citrus lemons and limes are called acid limes. Lemons are sturdier than limes and pests don't usually attack lemons and a lemon bush yields fruits well upto twenty years or quarter century. They require sunshine, watering drainage and organic manure and no chemicals. The bushes must be pruned drastically three years after they begin to yield the first batch of fruits and they yield fruits all through the year.

Cuttings should be planted in pits of 60 cubic cms. and filled with good farm yard manure. The distance between two pits must be atleast two metres.

There are two types of Malta Lemon and both are seedless. The more common variety is globular with prominent beaks, each fruit weighing on an average 200 gms. The globular type has a thin skin and each fruit yields about 70 ml of juice. The other variety is conical with comparatively a thick skin. This type contains less juice - about 50 ml per fruit.

These lemons are easily propagated by cuttings. They flower profusely and there is practically no shedding of flowers. Fruit dropping is very rare if watering, manuring and pruning is done regularly.

The conical variety is excellent for making pickles and the globular type, for making squashes. The skin of both varieties may be dried in a "RYFO biscuit tin dryer" and stored for making lemon "tea" (they are used in the place of tea leaves and taken without milk. If one likes one may add some tea leaves in the extraction and have a mix. Lemon tea is rich in Vitamin C and it is good for people suffering from cold and urinary infection.

There is a friend in Royapuram, Madras, who grows plenty of these Malta Lemons in his third floor terrace inside small cement tanks filled with earth. There are several uses for limes and lemons, their skin and seeds, which are explained in other handouts of Ryan Foundation.

DANDELION

Botanical - *Taraxacum officinate.*
English - *Common Dandelion.*
Hindi - *Dulal or Barau.*

A common herb in the temperate Himalayas to Peninsular India. Common all over Africa, throughout Europe, North America and Central Asia. The shrub grows about a metre high with yellow flowers and triangular leaves looking like a sword with sharp side blades. The shrub is highly drought resistant and tolerates high salinity. Investigation reveals that the shrub is a store house of Vitamins and every part of it - leaf, stem, flower, sap etc. are all useful. The leaves contain Vitamin A and C and the European settlers in Africa and the natives use them as salad leaves. The roots are also cooked. Leaves and flowers are used to prepare alcoholic drinks. Rhizomes and roots constitute drug known as Taraxacum which is used as diuretic, hepatic, stomachic and tonic. The shrub propogates itself and animals don't browse the leaves or the flowers. It is ideal for cultivation in marshy lands, sea-shore and open sewerages. Dried leaves and stalk burn well and keep out mosquitoes. The flowers produce honey and attract honey bees. For commercial propogation a main root of a plant may be cut into several parts and buried at a distance of one metre between plants. It is a perenial shrub but look lively with bright yellow flowers only during winter. Dandelion wine is made out of the flower. The roots are dried and roasted until they are brittle and then used as a coffee substitute. The sap or milk of the plant is a source of latex. As the shrub tolerates different types of soil and climate and very high salinity it is suitable to be grown on the sea shore or on the banks of sea water canals. That the shrub does not attract cattle or children at play is an added advantage for shore cultivation. In Africa people boil the whole plant with sugar, lime and ginger and take out the syrup and preserve it. It not only tastes good but also gives energy and builds up stamina. Honey from the flowers of this shrub is said to be pure and rich and the flowers yield plenty of honey. Intercroping this shrub with Soya or Jujibe (pronounced as Ho ba) has produced very encouraging results. Ryan Foundation advocates the propogation of this shrub in drought ridden and coastal areas.

THE IDEAL SOIL BINDER

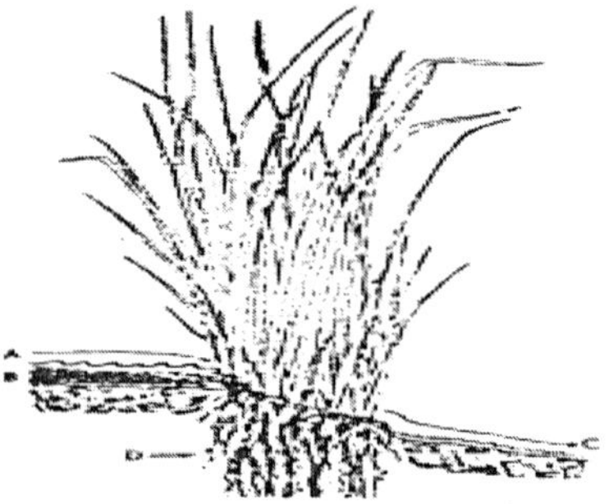

Figure 1. Cross Section of a Vetiver Hedge

Vetiver (*vetiveria Ziganioides*) is an ideal soil binder. It is also good for moisture conservation. Over the years, many trees, plants, shrubs, herbs and grass have been tried as soil binders but vetiver has proved to be the best for the following reasons:

1. It is perennial and requires very little care and maintenance.
2. The sharp aromatic leaves and roots of it repel rodents, pests and snakes.
3. It forms a permanent and dense hedge soon after planting.
4. As it's grown below the ground it is protected against overgrazing and fire.
5. The strong fibrous roots of it penetrates the soil to a depth of about three metres.
6. It is practically sterile and does not produce rhizomes and stolons and therefore will not become a weed.
7. The roots and leaves of vetiver are reistant to most diseases.
8. It is said to have associated nitrogen fixing mycorrhiza which explains the green growth of it round the year.
9. It is easy to remove when not wanted.
10. It can withstand long periods of drought or waterlogging as it is both a xerophyte and a hydrophyte.
11. It has no negative effect on the yield of neighbouring food crops.
12. It grows in areas with average annual rainfall between 200 and 600 milimetres.

13. It grows in all types of soils, regardless of pH, fertility or salinity and grows well on sea shore.
14. It grows also in soils which include shales, gravels and aluminium toxicity.

IPOMOEA CARNEA JACO

Botanical name is Ipomoea Carnea Jaco

Other names are not given because different people call it by different names in different parts of the country and sometimes in the same village people call it by different names. In Tamil Nadu many villagers call it Velli Kathan since it is grown as a fence but they also call v*asaka* as *Velli Kathan*. Confusing.

Villagers in peninsular India make baskets out of the finger thick stem of this shrub when it is green (before it dries up). Picture shown baskets being made out of the stem. The baskets are usually made in the shape of a big basin as the sticks will not bend much like cane or bamboo. Fruit and vegetable vendors carry this basket on their head with vegetables or fruits. Fibre of the same shrub is used to tie and hold the corners and ends of the basket.

Road workers also commonly use these baskets like a metal bond to carry cement, sand or stone. As the basket has holes and crevices they spread a plastic sheet or used cement bag or old newspaper on it and then fill it with sand or cement.

Another use: The stem is hammered, dried, pounded, sieved and the pulp is used for making cardboard as 'sal'. Mulburry stems are used in China, Japan and Indonesia to make paper umbrellas with painted designs on them. See RYFO Handout 450 and 451.

A third use is to burn the dry stem and use the ash to extract caustic soda to make soaps as explained in RYFO Handout 115.

Before soap came to India, washermen used to burn the stem of Vasaka to wash and whiten clothes.

PROLIFIC YIELDING MORINGA

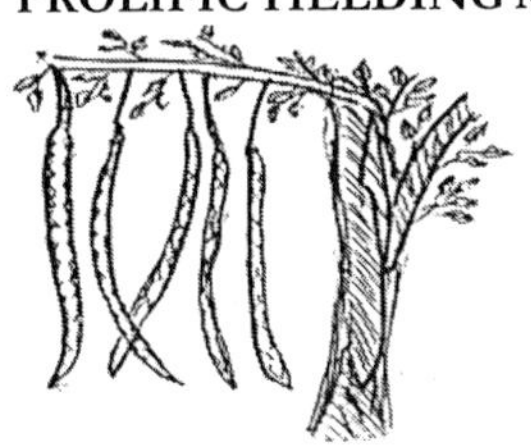

An improved moringa variety named PKM-1 and released by the University of Agriculture, Coimbatore, India, is getting more and more popular in Peninsular India. The pods are long and they yield fleshy and tasty drum sticks six months after sowing the seeds.

There are two types of Moringa - the perenial ones which are propagated by limb or stem cuttings such as the Jaffna variety and the annual variety propagated by seeds. PKM-1 is the annual type.

Sowing is done in pits of 45 cubic cms. at a distance of 2.5 metres between pits. With liberal farm yard manure. two or three seeds are put in each pit. Sowing is done in July - August at the rate of 500 gms. of seeds per/ha when the plants reach a height of about a metre the top is pinched at 75 cms height to encourage profuse branching. From the third month of sowing plenty of farm yard manure is given. Watering may be done by drip irrigation and the pots filled once in two weeks.

Peak harvesting is from February to April and the pods are harvested when they attain a length of more than 60 cms. In the month of May, the trees are thoroughly pruned followed by a light pruning in July. For rationing the trees must be cut at 90 cms from ground level. Long side-branches must be cut and removed in November to get more pods.

Some common pests attack Murunga after they germinate but they can be easily controlled by spraying organic fertilisers (RYFO Fertilisers).

The trees live for three years and during that period inter cropping of several plants have approved successful. Such as vegetables and pulses, soyabean grows very well between all types of Moringa.

The seeds yield oil and like all other Muringa the seeds of this variety also may be used to purify drinking water. The leaves and pods of Murunga have plenty of vitamin A and are good for the eyes. Moringa pods and leaves are very frequently eaten by the rural poor and what they want now is better and quick growing varieties.

SAMPHIRE FOR SEA WATER

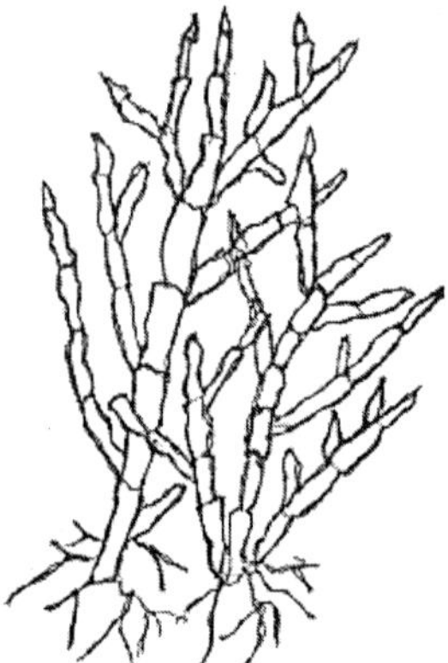

In torrid regions, trapped between sea and sun, growing crops with sea water is a long time dream of farmers. After several years of research on this plant, Samphire, the Environmental Research Laboratory (ERL) of the (University of Arizona has succeded in releasing a species of Samphire called Salicornia bigelovil Torr, rich in oil and protein which thrives in sea water. Samphire which is an halophyte is classified as a mangrove and has a stout leafless stem and one may mistake it for a Cactus. The stem contains a large quantity and good quality of Caustic Soda and can be extracted by the RYFO method (Handout 45).

After crossing several species of Samphire the researchers of the University produced a giant variety which they named SOS-7 which grows to a height of 50 cms. in hot and very hot climates and in sandy soi1.

SOS-7 produces 25 per cent oil, rich in edible linoleic acid, which compares well with Soybean oil. The residue after extracting the oil makes good cattle and chicken feed.

SOS-7 yields about two tons of seeds per hectare, but more research is on to improve yield and quality. Experiments are currently on also in Egypt, Kuwait and Saudi Arabia.

This is an useful addition to the halophytes listed by the Ryan Foundation for its Survival By Sea Water Movement.

SWORDBEAN

Botanical - *Canavalia ensiformis.*

Other names - *Jack bean* or *one eyed bean.*

Descriptiont: Eerect legume growing to a height of about 80 cm. Bears sword like green pods each upto 30 cm long -may be smaller when young. Each pod contains about a dozen big seeds with a black hilum. A single plant yields about two dozen sheeths (pods) weighing nearly two kgs.

In about 45 days from the date of sowing, the pods appear and they should be harvested when they are green. If left on the plant without picking they slowly turn brownish and fall from the plant in about 3 months. Dried seeds are hard and cannot be cooked but can be powdered.

The plant can tolerate severe drought and can be grown on field bunds and dry lands. It is resistant to a good extent to pests and plant moths. After one cycle of yield the plant is usually removed and used as fodder or green manure and the seeds are sown again for the second harvest. Propagation is easy.

Contents: The Sword bean seeds contain 91 per cent dry matter including 30 per cent crude protein. 2 per cent fat, 12 per cent crude fibre and 3 per cent ash and no oil.

Sowing sword bean is quick and easy. The rate of germination is high and almost every seed germinates. Hence, just one seed in every hole is sufficient. The finger holes to plant may be 6 cm. deep and the spacing between the holes may be 40 to 45 cm. Farmyard manure helps growth.

It is a legume which can be easily introduced, cultivated and promoted in many Third Countries and Ryan Foundation recommends Sword bean to relieve poverty and hunger and to feed cattle and fowls.

BUSSA BEER

The purpose of releasing this handout is not to initiate people into alcoholic drinks but to wean those addicted to alcohol by giving them a mild, harmless, inexpensive home-made substitute.

Bussa is popular in Kenya. This recipe was obtained from the Food Science Club, University of Nairobi. It is an alcoholic beverage prepared out of maize and millet. The major substrate used is maize and the fermenting power is provided by yeast. Ready made yeast tablets may be purchased from the market if available. But market yeast may be avoided and instead raw potato may be chopped and soaked for 2 clays in a cup or bowl of coconut water; on the third day it becomes concentrated yeast. Instead of a potatoes, a slice of bread may be soaked in coconut water to get yeast.

Ingredients and Equipment

1. Milled maize - 20 kgs
2. Germinated millet malt- 2 kgs
3. Yeast -200 gms
4. Metal pan for frying (Large)
5. Drums to ferment the beer
6. Cloth to sieve

Botanical (Maize or Corn-zea mays L) (Millet-Pennisetum typhoides)

Method

(A) Preparing the Maize (the Substrate)

Maize (ground to powder) meal is mixed in water to get a paste- equal part of water to equal part of maize by weight. The paste is placed in a container and allowed to ferment at about 25°C (or room temperature in the tropics) for about 10 days. The fermented product is fried on open charcoal fire for about 30 minutes. While frying the alcoholic flavour and brown colour develops.

(B) Preparation of Malt out of Millet

Millet grains are soaked in water and then placed in open pans which are well ventilated and allowed to germinate, for eight days. The germinated millet malt is then dried in the sun and is now called kimera in Africa (Kenya). Kimera is ground to a coarse form either manually between two stones or in a machine. It is usually ground manually in African rural homes.

(C) Fermentation

The dried kimera is mixed with the fermented and roasted maize from A above, at the rate of two kg kimera to 20 kg of maize. This is then thoroughly mixed. The mixture is placed in large open drums and water is added one part of water to three parts of solids. The slurry is allowed to ferment for three days at about 20° C (or room temperature in the tropics). Thereafter, the product is sieved through a thin cloth (mosquito curtain cloth or bandage cloth). The filtrate obtained is Bussa which may be served hot or cold. Cold Bussa (iced) is very refreshing in summer.

(D) In hot weather the fermentation takes place fast and so in warm countries or under direct sun the duration of fermentation must be reduced. Bussa beer should have 5 to 6 per cent alcohol. At any rate it should not be allowed to exceed 10 per cent. It should be consumed within 24 to 30 hrs. If kept longer it can ferment further, turn sour and even poisonous. More than 10 per cent alcohol is bad for health and working efficiency. Keep it under control. For heaven sake keep alcohol under control. Excessive alcohol damages health, career, family and future.

(E) Honey, sugar syrup or glucose may be added to Bussa if sweet taste is desired. Bussa should not be marketed as it has to be consumed within 24 hours. Follow the law of your country regarding alcohol.

(observed in Africa and recorded by Dr F.A. Ryan).

FIBRE/STRAW ROOF

Paddy straw 'Korai' grass and all types of fibre are the cheapest and most easily available materials for low-cost rural housing and they are traditionally used in several countries. Some fibre yielding plants and trees are listed in ATIC Handout 167 and some simple ways of extracting fibre are explained in handout 156. Paddy straw or fibre (or both together) may be combed with one's own fingers and got into uniform bunches and tied on to the roof frame-work as shown in the diagram. It is not necessary to make the entire roof frame-work with bamboo or Casurina poles. Well twisted six cm fibre ropes can be tied to make checks on four strong pillars and a square pole frame (only the four sides) and the fibre bunches laid on the network.

If a big plastic sheet or agrifilm is available it may be spreadout first on the top square frame and then the network tied on top of it. Alternatively, used and thrown away cement or fertilizer bags may be stitched together and used. The plastic lining will prevent rain water penetrating the roof. Two cm thick fibre ropes may be used to tie the bunches to the framework and the ropes can be easily twisted in villages with available fibre. The spun ropes may be rolled in wooden shuttles as shown in the dia to make work easy.

When the entire roof is laid and tied to stay extra ropes may be taken over the roof and tied frame to frame in a criss-cross fashion to prevent breeze lifting.

Straw and fibre ropes do not last long as they are eaten by moths. To prevent this and to preserve them for five to six years they may be soaked in big oil drums or a cemented garden tub in a semi-liquid solution of neem-leaf/chillie and turmeric or in any other paste-solution of leaves listed in ATIC Handout 112 and 130 having insecticide properties.

If a hard roof is wanted a semi-liquid mortar solution may be sprinkled on top of the fibre roof and allowed to set and harden.

SOYA COFFEE

Soya coffee is excellent for appearance, taste, smell and preserving quality of powder. A standard recipe to process and prepare soya powder for coffee is explained below. More and more people are switching over to Soya Coffee in the place of usual coffee. Soya can be grown in gardens by families to meet their domestic needs. Preparing the powder is easy and inexpensive. The coffee is good for health. The prepared powder can be packeted and marketed for an income.

After washing, the seeds are boiled well in clean water for about 40 mins. and all the time the water must keep boiling.

The water in which the seeds were boiled is thrown to plants (kitchen gardens) as it is nitrogenous with fertilising effect.

The boiled seeds are dried well under the open sun. The dried seeds are then roasted in a dry pan - no water, no oil. They are then pounded in a pistle and mortar, a stone, or any domestic grinder and sieved to a fine powder.

The large particles which stand in the sieve is pounded again and sieved again and thus all the seeds are got out in fine powder form.

The powder is stored in airtight containers and used like the usual coffee powder.

If one wants the usual coffee flavour they may mix some usual coffee powder to the Soya powder for coffee flavour.

Soya coffee powder may enter the market in small sealed packets and priced at half the price of coffee of same quantity or weight. Soya is very good for health, heart and cholesterol.

Tapping Palms for Cheap Sugar

A report produced in 1981 said that out of about 60 million palmyrah trees in India the State of Tamil Nadu in peninsular India alone had 40 millions. Out of these only 6 million trees were tapped for neera (juice) and 5 million were utilised for making products from the fibre and leaves. Nine million were reported to be unfit for use due to negligence and the remaining 20 millions still remained unutilised.

A recent study reveals that a man can climb atleast 50 trees everyday and get about 3 litres of juice (Neera) per tree.

Women heat the juice for several hours before pouring them into moulds for getting them into blocks (Palmgur). The maximum that a family can get out of 100 trees is about 15 kg. of gur or sugar. on an average only 100 litres of neera is tapped during season. But a male tree yields only about 50 litres. The difficulty faced by the tappers is that most of them do not own the trees that they tap but share the profits with the owners and the sharing is usually on 50-50 basis. Merchants purchase palm gur for Rs 10 (1994 price) per kg and sell it for double the price. Thus the middlemen take a big profit and also put up the market price. Another difficulty of the trade is that it is seasonal - January to April. A third difficulty is the tax which the government levies on palm sugar instead of treating palm sugar as on agrieultural commodity.

Ryan Foundation study reveals that making products like baskets, brushes and beams is not as profitable as making sugar. Marketing sugar is easier than marketing other products made from the tree as sugar is always in demand and gets or can get a good profit. If more and more palm tree tappers are encouraged to make palm sugar the price of crystal white open market cane sugar will also fall. People know that palm sugar is (or can be) cheap and healthy. Their demand has to be met to the advantage of both the producer and the consumer. Where there is no demand it has to be created. More palmyrah trees must also be promoted as they are highly drought resistant, tolerate high salinity and can be grown on sea-shores.

WEST INDIAN CHERRY

Botanical name: *Malphigia Punicifolia.*

Native of the Barbadoes Islands in the Carebbian (West Indies).

Evergreen bushes reaching an average height of two m. Spreads easily by layering. Blooms about six to seven times every year if watered and cared for. A month after flowering fruits appear. They come up very well in black cotton soil as a rain fed crop. A single tree yields about 30 kgs of fruit under rainfed conditions.

The sweet smelling fruits are red in colour, contain three triangular seeds, and very high content of Vitamin C. As the fruits get spoiled very fast soon after harvest they must be made into jams or squashes.

Cherry Jam: Pulp of fruit is extracted. For 4 cups of pulp add 4 cups of sugar, juice of 4 lime fruits, and Juice of ginger which are 3 cm thick and 10 cms long. Mix well, boil and store in glass bottles.

Cherry Sauash: Juice of fruit is extracted and strained (one cup). one cup of sugar is dissolved in two cups of water and put on slow fire. Sugar solution is filtered and cooled. Then the fruit syrup is mixed with the sugar solution. One spoonful of lime juice and one spoonful of ginger juice is added to the sugar solution while boiling. Add also a pinch of salt for taste. Mix well and preserve. If not kept in a refregirator, consume within a month.

Pickles may also be made out of the half ripe fruits in the usual way of making pickles with lime or mangoes.

ZACHUN-OIL TREE

Botanical - *Balanites aegyptiaca.*

Grows in very arid conditions deserts and on sea shores. More drought resistant than Acacia. Has thick and shiny leaves with a thick coat of ware which protects against hot dry air. The plant has a twin root system and goes into the ground vertically deep and horizontically broad, spread to several metres. When the leaves fall photosynthesis continues through the branches and spines. The leaves make fodder. The wood which is not attached by white ants is used for making low quality furniture and agricultural implements. The spines are used as pins.

The fruits which are hard and not very sweet or fleshy is inferior than dates in quality. They yield a sugary syrup when boiled in water. The syrup is used in making sweet meat and for washing silk.

The leaves and barks of Zachun tree are said to be medicinal for treating jaundice and rheumatism.

The kernel contains 50 per cent oil by weight and more protein than groundnut, sunflower or cotton.

The tree must be introduced on an intensive scale in drought ridden and semi-desert areas and on the coastal belt and along the sea shore of warm and dry countries.

Cheese making made easy

Take one kg of leaves and stalks together of Calotropis gigantea or Calotropis procera (different species but about the same and both are medicinal). Calotropis Procera is also called Apple of Sodom or Dead Sea Apple-shurb. Crush the leaves and tender stem and take the juicie. Use this juice as the rennet to coagulate and add about two ounces of the juice to about one liter of milk under low fire. The Calotropis juice contains an enzyme that makes the milk coagulate. It is orally consumed mixed in medicines and not poisonous or harmful.

Before the mixture solidifies sieve the liquid in a muslin cloth. A clean bandage cloth or mosquito curtain cloth may be used. Sieve the mixture directly into very hot milk and within a short time the milk coagulates. The curd thus obtained is boiled for about fifteen minutes or for a longer time if the quantity is large. Then pass the contents through a strainer and allow to solidify. Now the cheese is ready. Before it solidifies it may be put into a mould of desired shape. About five liters of milk will yield one kilo of soft cheese. Thereafter, it is allowed to dry on sterilised straw bed. Dried Cheese is hard and keeps for several months. People in Benin, West Africa, usually fry this Cheese and then eat it but some people eat it raw.

Sometimes they boil millet stems or millet chaff, obtain a red coloured water from it and then boil the cheese in it to give it a red colour. It is also boiled with beetroot for red colour.

It was reported by PPEA (NGO) of Benin that in 1993 about 2500 tonnes of this cheese was produced and marketed and it is a very good source of income for the poor of that country. This way of Cheese making is ideal to preserve excess milk.

This author has eaten this cheese in West Africa and thinks that it is safe to fry. boil or otherwise cook it and eat it. In India they squeeze a lime when the milk boils. make it curdle and prepare a sort of cheese which they call "Paneer". Paneer lumps are cut into size and cooked; can be kept only for about a day or two. From the preservation point of view the Benin cheese is fine and healthy.

Sane Common Plant Dyes

Name of Plant or Plant Matter	*Mordant (agent which helps to fix the colour)*	*The colour obtained*
1. Red groundnut skins	Gum tree bark and copper sulphate	Brownish red
2. Onion (Outer skins)	Alum or cream of tartar	Yellow
3. Maize skins (red husk variety)	None needed	Purple
4. Eucalyptus (blue gum) leaves	Alum	Yellow

Name of Plant or Plant Matter	*Mordant (agent which helps to fix the colour)*	*The colour obtained*
5. Mango skin and seeds	Gum tree bark and copper sulphate	Brownish orange
6. Red Sorghum (finely crushed leaves)	Vegetable ash and lemon juice	Red
7. Indigo (Legume)	None needed	Deep Blue
8. Gerenadilla skins (Passion fruit)	Alum and Chrome	Brown
9. Black Soya Beans	Iron Rustwater	Silver grey
10. Eucalyptus (Blue green) leaves	Gum tree bark and copper sulphate	Green
11. Black Soya Bean Skins	None needed	Deep Blue
12. Mango skins and seeds or leaves	Gum tree bark and alum	Yellow
13. Walnut Shells	None needed	Dark Brown
14. Lichens (Different spices)	None needed	Different shades (depends on species)

Commonly used Moderants: Copper sulphate, alum, ferrous sulphate, potassium dichromate, tannin, salt, wood ash, vinegar etc. By mix 2 or more moderants can get different colours.

Quantity: Boil half kg of plant matter in 20 litres of water. Boil the mater to be dyed. (Cotton, wood, fibre or hair) and keep stirring to spread the colour uniformly. By mixing different colours you can get different shades. After repeated experiments you can standardise the colour, concentrate the liquid and bottle it for the consumer market. Permutation and combination can give a wide range of colours and shades.

JOJOBA FOR SHORE CULTIVATION

Jojoba, a native shrub of Arizona, U.S.A. pronounced as Ho-Ho-ba, is Botanically known as simmondsia Chinoris, R&D done for about 4 years by the Central Arid Zone Research Instituted (CAZARI) India, confirmed that Jojoba is highly drought tolerant and salt resistant and can convert desert and sea-shore sands into an oasis of prosperity. Several years of research done by the Central Salt and Marine Chemicals Research Institute, Bhavnagar, in the waste and coastal lands of Northern Gujarat also confirms that Jojoba is highly drought and salt tolerant.

Agricultural economists consider this shrub a gold mine and the FAO of the United Nations and the World Bank recommend the introduction and propagation of this shrub in waste lands and saline soils.

In the international market a tone of Jojoba seeds fetches about **$ 8000.** The money is paid for the oil which the seeds contain. The oil is very much like the whale oil in physical and chemical properties and better than almost all commercial substitutes for whale oil, which is getting scarce by the restrictions laid on whaling.

Israel is cultivating the shrub already on a large scale. Australia, Costa Rica, Brazil, S. Africa, Mexico, are among the fore runners in the promotion of jojoba. India, China, Philippines and some East African countries are also promoting the shrub now.

Jojoba oil, golden in colour, is totally free from alkaloids and resins. Cosmetic industry in the West consumes a large quantity of it. The oil is also used in the preparation of high quality candles, polish, varnish, lubricants, antifoam agents, fire-retardants and in the making of soaps. The oil is edible and has a low-calorie. But the most important and indispensible need for the oil is by the engineering industry to replace sperm whale oil which is scarce and costly to be used as a high pressure lubricant. The Ben Gurion University of Israel reports that the oil relieves pain and cures skin diseases.

Jojoba shrub thrives in temperatures ranging from five to 50 degrees Celsius and live 50 to 200 years. The shrubs are propagated by direct sowing, stem planting, or tissue culture. A plant yields about 125 gms of seeds in the first 5 years and thereafter about two Kg. The plant tolerates salinity level of 10,000 parts per million making it absolutely suitable for desert and coastal areas. CAZRI estimates a return of 1.8 lakh rupees per year from one ha of Jojoba.

INCOME FROM FOLIAGE BRIQUETTES

Selling RYFO foliage briquettes, home made, hand pressed, using Cassava starch as binder, in the Jalalaqsi refugee settlement in Somalia where the author lived and worked for the Ethiopian refugees. The briquettes are made out of dried leaves of the thorny shrub, Prosopis Juliflora, which is found in abundance throughout Somalia and in all tropical countries. Most deserts have plenty of Prosopis Juliflora of different species, including trees like the Babool.

Eucalyptus and Water hyacinth are also found in large quantities in dry countries which are excellent for making RYFO briquettes.

Many development projects are frustrated because local resources are not exploited.

RYFO Briquettes

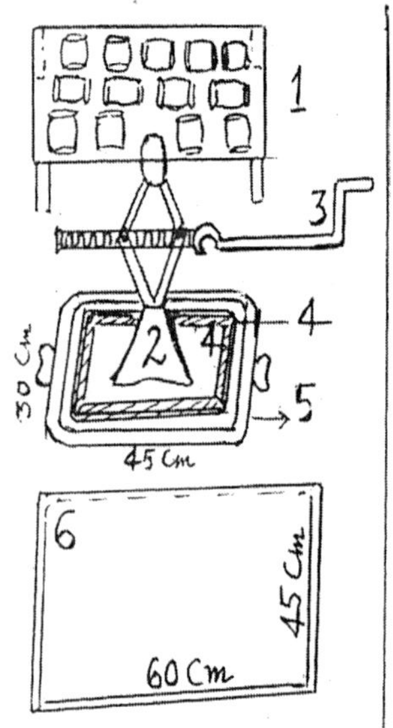

RYFO Briquettes are made out of foliage (all sorts of fallen leaves) dried well and pound or ground to small granules (like tea leaves in packets, or even smaller). Ryan Foundation has innovated several contraptions for grinding. The sea-saw grinder cum crusher appended to this is a RYFO innovation. The traditional Indian and Nepalese grinder cum crusher are also appended.

The leaves may be broken to bits by hand pounding in a pistle and mortar, if easier methods are not available. A village woman may adopt the method most suited for her. Grinding of foliage may be done whenever she finds time and the granules may be kept in store in a dry place. To bind the leaf-granules into blocks or briquettes a binder and a press are required.

The best binder to bind foliage briquettes is tamarind seed glue, the simple preparation of which, is explained and attached. Fish glue is also very good and the preparation process of it is also attached. But both these glues require fuel to cook. To avoid fuel RYFO recommends starch of casava, sweet potatoes or yam. The best is casava and almost every village in every poor country has it or can have it.

How to extract casava starch in a Village?

1. Take a strong wooden plant, atleast one inch thick, 60 cm long and 45 cm broad. This serves as the base plate or foundation board (Diagram 6).
2. Find an old wooden cot or table and cut the legs to make the height just one foot. Alternatively, turn it upside down and rest it on 4 corner stones. (Diagram 1).
3. Push the base board under the cot or table and load the cot or table with as many sand, bags as possible without breaking the cot (or table).
4. Take a metal tray commonly used to serve tea to visitors of the size atleast 45 cm x 30 cm and atleast 3 cms deep (diagram 5).

5. Place the tray right in the middle of the base board.
6. Make a strong wooden box of the size 40 cm x 30 cm and depth of 10 cms. Without the lid and the bottom (just a deep frame) (diagram).
7. Secure a strong plank to sit into this frame i.e., slightly smaller than the box frame, in length and breadth. (not shown).
8. Take a car or lorry jack. It may be any type of jack of any four wheel vehicle (The scissor jack is shown in the diagram 2)
9. Fill the box without the bottom with chopped casava. The skin need not be removed.
10. Place the loose plank on the casava inside the box.
11. Place the car jack on this plank under the cot and lift the cot and lift the cot (or table) by the jack which has all the weight of the sand bags.
12. Lift it about ten cm high and leave it like that overnight (in lifted position).
13. The next morning you will find the milk of casava (the starch) filling the tea tray.
14. Take this milk, mix it well with the already prepared foliage granules. If you don't use the milk within 24 hours it will solidify and become hard (out of which tapioca pearls are made).
15. Remove the crushed casava under the jack and cook it or give it to cattle.
16. Now fill the frame box with the foliage granules mixed with wet casava starch and press this by the "Cot-Jack" press as you pressed the casava to take out the starch and leave it over night in the lifted position.
17. The next day you get a solid briquettes in the shape of a flooring tile. It will be as long and broad as the frame but only four to six inches in thickness. If you make it thicker than that, the middle portion, will take several days to dry. Six cm will be ideal thickness. Each slab, or may be two slabs, can boil a pot of rice or prepare a full dish.
18. Every family must prepare these foliage briquette out of the foliage sweeping collected from their frontage and backyard and keep piling the slabs in a dry place - may be in a separate shed built out of RYFO walls for protection and for use during rainy days. About a dozen slabs may always be kept around the cooking stove.
19. What the village family requires to prepare these briquettes, from outside the village, are just a tea tray and a car jack.
20. Where even these are not available casava may be chopped and pound by the traditional village methods and the starch may be pressed out. By this way the yield of starch will be less.
21. In the absence of a jack and a tea tray the foliage-starch mix may be hand pressed into the wooden frame and compressed to the extent possible.

22. Alternatively, they may rolled and pressed between the palms of the hands and shaped like tennis balls. But when made like this the burning time will be short. Harder the compression, longer the burning time.
23. The leaves available in large quantities are those of acacia, Eucalyptus, Pongamia, Neem etc. Any leaf may be used. But research has proved that water hyacinth and seaweeds and leaves, give a very high calory of heat almost as good as coal. All leaves can be mixed.

In many Third Countries the famous Cinva Ram (mud block press) is available. Several improved versions on the cinva ram are also available. Where one is available, it may be used both for pressing out the starch from casava and for binding the briquettes. Diagram of the Original Cinva Ram and the V.S. Cinva Ram (a German improvement of it) are attached.

Ryan Foundation appeals to NGOs world over to provide one V.S. Cinva Ram to every village to make abode blocks for low cost houses, for extracting starch, oil from certain oil seeds. (ground nuts, castor etc.) and for compressing briquettes.

The author demonstrated the extraction of starch from casava and making foliage briquettes using a cot and a jack to the Ethiopean refugees in Somalia and the successful demonstration drew crowds. But as internal trouble started in the country about that time the technology did not click there.

Medicinal Plants

IV. Charak Gan: Based on their uses, plants have been classified into 50 group (Gan) of 10 plants each, in the ancient Ayurvedic Text Charaka Samhita.

(A) Shothahar: Plants in these gan are useful in the treatment of inflammation.

Sr. No.	*Botanical Name*	*Sanskrit Name*	*Local Name*
1.	Stereospermum suaveolens	Patla	Padal
2.	Oroxylum indicum	Shyonak	Tetu
3.	Premna serratifolia	Agnimanth	Agnimanth
4.	Aegle marmelos	Bilva	Bael
5.	Gmelina arborea	Gambhari	Shivan
6.	Solanum indicum	Brihati	Chichurdi
7.	Splanum xanthocarpum		
8.	Desmodium gangatioum	Kantkari	Ringani
		Shalparni	Salvan
9.	Uraria picta	Prushnipart	Pithvan
10.	Tribules terrestris	Bokshuru	Gokhru

(B) Kushtaghna: Plants useful in skin diseases.

1.	Acacia catechu	Khadir	Khair
2.	Terminalia chebuls	Haritaki	Hirda
3.	Emblica officinalia	Haritaki	Hirda
4.	Curcuma longa	Haridra	Haldi
5.	Semcarous anacardium	Bhallatak	Bibba
6.	Alstonia scholaris,	Saptaparna	Satvin
7.	Cassia fistula	Aragvadh	Bahava
8.	Nerium indicum	Karvir	Kanher
9.	Embelia ribes	Vidang	Vavding
10.	Jasminum grandiflorum	Jati	Jai

Reproduced by Ryan Foundation. Courtesy- Academy of Development Science, Kashola, Kharjat Raigad Dist. Maharashtra-410201. For saplings contact the academy.

Fruits, Oil-seeds and Medicinal Plants

Following are some common fruits, nuts, and medicinal plants available in many tropical countries of South Pacific Regions.

Fruits (Botanical)

1. Aegle Marmelos (bel)
2. Amorphophallus Campanulatus
3. Anacardium Occidentale (Kaju)
4. Annona Squamosa (custard apple)
5. Artocarpus lakoocha (barhal)
6. Buchanania lanzan (chironji)
7. Carissa Sp (Karaunda)
8. Dioscorea Sp.
9. Emblica Officinalis (aonla)
10. Feronia elephantum (Kaitha)
11. Ipomoea aquatica
12. Juglans regia (akhrot)
13. Madhuca indica (Mahua)
14. Madhuca longifolia (also Mahua)
15. Moringa Oleifera (drum stick)
16. Pinus gerardiana (chilgoze)
17. Syzygium Cumini (jamun)
18. Tamarindus indica (tamarind)
19. Zizyphus jujuba (ber)

Oil Seeds (Botanical)

1. Actinodaphne Sp.
2. Azadirachta indica
3. Garcinia indica
4. Madhuca indica
5. Mangifera indica
6. Pongamia Glabora
7. Salvadora Oleoides
8. Schleichera trijugr
9. Shorea Sp.

Medicinal Plants (Botanical)

1. Atropa acuminata (Belladona)
2. Cassia angustifolia (Senna)
3. Costus Speciosus
4. Datura innoxia
5. Datura metal
6. Datura Stramonium
7. Dioscorea Sp.
8. Rauwolfia Serpentina
9. Solanum Sp.

Multipurpose Moringa

For treating drinking water on a large scale chemical coagulants are added to the water. The coagulants cause the suspended particles stick together (Coagulate) and sink to the bottom of the tank. Then the clean water is separated and distributed to the public but the correct chemicals are not available in small quantities for the small user and when available the price is high. Homes and villages should therefore turn to coagulants available in nature such as the Moringa oleifera also known as drumstick or Horseradish

This is a quick growing drought tree of the tropics which reach a height of four metres and bears harvestable pods within a year. Pods can be harvested all round the year if the trees are cared for but usually harvesting is done twice a year.

The Environmental Engineering Division of the Leicester University, UK, has been studying the potential uses of Moringa as a natural coagulant for some years and has established that:

1. Seed pods should be left to mature on the tree and harvested when dry.
2. The thin wings and shells of the seeds are removed easily separating the white seed kernels.
3. The white kernals are to be ground or crushed to tiny particles.
4. To treat about 20 litres of water about 2 grams of crushed seed is required. Alternatively, 2 level 5 ml teaspoons.
5. A small amount of clean water is added to the crushed seeds to make a paste.
6. The paste is put in a clean bottle (full soft drink bottle is the right size) and shaken well for about 5 minutes).
7. The action activates the chemicals in the crussed seed.
8. The solution is then filtered through a clean cotton cloth into a 20 liter bucket of potable water (Well or river water).
9. For 2 minutes the content is stirred vigorously and then for 15 minutes slowly.
10. During the slow "shaking" period the moringa seeds bind together (covariate) the fine particles and the bacteria present there into large particles and settle to the bottom of the vessel. Some 2 hours later the clear water from the top can be separated.
11. The University has announced that this process removes 99.5 per cent of the bacteria and cleans the water.
12. However, to remove the small percentage of micro-organisms that are still present treated water may be filtered through clean sand, gauze, or boiled.
13. Only healthy seeds are taken, and the dried seeds may be powdered and stored for about a year but the paste must be prepared fresh every time. About 100 mg of ground seed is reguired for one liter of water.
14. The seeds of Moringa contain 40 per cent oil by weight.
15. Laboratory tests at Leicester have confirmed that the residue (cake) after extracting the oil still contains the active coagulants and can be used to purify water as explained.
16. The pressed cake can also be dried and stored for an year or longer.
17. The advantage with the pressed cake is that it is a by-product of the Moringa oil extraction industry and can be collected free or for a small price.
18. Moringa oil, which is rich, can be used as a cooking medium, for making soaps, as a lubricant and for lighting lamps.
19. The oil is a mosquito repallent.

20. Moringa leaves have a high protein context of 27 per cent and have plenty of Vitamin A and C, besides calcium, phosphorus and iron. They can be dried and stored and used in cooking as dried leaves.

Gum from Tamarind Kernel

Step by step instructions:

1. Collect and soak Tamarind seeds in water for one week.
2. On the 8th day rule them between the two palms of your hand and the brown seed coat (skin) will drop out.
3. Then dry the kernel in hot sun for three days and thereafter roast it in a kitchen frying pan at 1100° C for 20 minutes (The skin may be shelled even after roasting).
4. Powder the Kernel and sieve it in 180 mesh (on a domestic scale a domestic grinder or mixi may be used and on a commercial scale a common mini pulvariser may be used.
5. Separately grind mineral lime (chunam) and equal quantity of cheap jaggery or cheap sugar, dry, sieve and store. If mineral lime is not readily available roast sea or river shells, bird or animal bones, egg or crab shells, powder, sieve and store.
6. For about one kg of Tamarind Kernel powder add 2 table spoonful of lime or sea or river shell powder, (roasted and ground) and 2 spoonful of jaggery.
7. After mixing them with the Kernel powder sieve and store in dry condition.
8. Pack powder in one kg. plastic pouches (sachets) for domestic use, and like cement in sacks for commercial supply.
9. The user has only to mix 200 per cent water to the powder by volume (2 times the quantity of powder) and boil to get good adhesive.
10. The cost of this gum is very low. The powder stores long and transported easily to markets.
11. For a chemical process, after boiling the Kernel powder in twice its quantity of waters add by weight 5 per cent glucose, 4 per cent formalin and 12 per cent Sodium Carbonate. (but chemical process is not recommended by Ryan Foundation).

Common Uses

1. The product is a good as sizing material in the textile, tanning, paper, board, and jute industries. It contains Polysaccharides. It is also used to clarify and concentrate latex in the rubber industry.

2. The hard and brown skin (testa) is source of good tannin and can be sold to tanning industry. Tannin can also be extracted on a rural scale under the open sky.
3. The roasted kernel powder when ground and used in the confectionery industry can reduce cost as the kernel contains 70 per cent carbohydrates, 20 per cent protein, 3 per cent erude fibre and three per cent ash.
4. Raw tamarind seeds are crushed (or roasted and crushed) and mixed with cattle feed and chicken and duck feed.
5. The gum is also mixed with clay, surki and chunam to add to the binding property of sun dried bricks.
6. The kernel powder contains seven to eight per cent fatty oil which can be extracted and used for soap (50.2 per cent) and olilce acid (19.6 per cent). It also contains linolenic acid (2.8 per cent) and behenic acid (9 per cent).
7. About five lakh tonnes of tamarind fruit is produced in India every year which leaves 1.5 lakh tonnes of seed which can yield 10,000 of oil per annum.

PRESERVING PULP OF FRUITS

A simple, traditional method of keeping mangoes, for example, is to spread the mango pulp on a bamboo mat or aluminium tray, with or without addition of sugar, and let it dry in the sun for four to six days until it has a leathery consistency. The dried product is then rolled or cut into pieces for sale. Although the freshly prepared product is of good quality, standards are virtually non-existent and the storage life is relatively short-only two to three months.

Main raw material required to prepare approximate 100 Kg. of fruits bars

Type of Fruit	*Fruit required in kg.*	*Pulp obtained in Kg.*	*Sugar required in Kg.*	*Yield (per cent of fresh fruit)*	*Yield (per cent of pulp)*
Mango	720	360	33	13.8	27
Banana	600	360	30	16.6	27
Guava	406	325	60	24.6	30
Mango +	540				
Banana	150	360	35	14.5	27
Papaya +	500				
Banana	140	336	54	23.4-	29

Tomato Paste

1. Take the desired quantity of tomatoes, say 10 kgs.
2. Blanch it in nearly boiling water for three minutes.
3. Pulp it by hand, or in a mixer.

4. Remove the skin and seeds (sieve).
5. Tie the pulp in a thin cloth and hang for one full hour.
6. Clear, tasteless waste will drip out.
7. Remove the hanging bag and add table salt and hang the pulp for yet another hour.
8. The weight of the pulp (after draining) will be only one third of the weight of the fruits taken.
9. Use no-energy or pressure.
10. The final product in the hand is pure and fresh tomato paste.
11. Add a teaspoon of sugar and a teaspoon of turmeric powder to every kilo of paste.
12. Expose the paste to bright sun in a RYFO tin dryer.
13. (Sugar, salt, turmeric and sunlight are all natural preservation)
14. Out of a refrigerator the paste stays fresh for a month.
15. If kept in a refrigerator it can be stored and used for six months.
16. Paste of many edible fruits can be made and preserved in the same way.
17. If equal quantity of sugar is added to the paste, mixed and boiled with pure juice of the same fruits used, a good quality jam can be obtained.

HOW TO MAKE VINEGAR

It is not necessary **to** use fresh fruit juice to make Vinegar. It is technically possible to make good Vinegar from solid or liquid fruit waste. Any edible fruit waste may be used. Even the skins may be washed well and added. The waste should be shredded (a domestic mixi may be used) and boiled for about half hour to sterilise the liquid and separate the sugars. In the liquid that is collected several lots of waste may be boiled to get sugar concentration. What is in the pot is then filtered through a thin sterilised cloth to separate the solid pulp and then the liquid is cooled and inoculated with yeast. For a liter of liquid one spoon of raw rice and one spoon of raw wheat may be powdered and mixed in the place of yeast, and left for a month to ferment.

The steps involved are:

1. Selection, cleaning and weighing the fruit waste.
2. Boiling and liquidizing
3. Adding 2 litres of water per kg of fruit pulp and 120 gms of sugar to one liter of water.
4. Adding one small mashed banana to control acidity.
5. Adding the yeast (Rice and wheat powder)
6. Adding diluted good Vinegar from previous batch or from the market.

7. Leaving the Vinegar to ferment for 2 months.
8. Filtering, boiling to a temperature of 80° to 90° cooling and bottling in glass bottles (not plastic).

Halophyte Potentialities

1. Marine algae has great potentials as livestock feed, fertiliser and raw materials for several industries. They are a rich source of numerous minerals and live saving medicines. The liquid seawater fertiliser recently researched and developed is becoming popular in several countries. Some fresh algae, including Spriluna, Chlorella and Scenedesmus, rich in edible protein, are widely sold as health food in Western Countries and Japan.
2. In Benin, people cultivate a bean called ABLAT which requires very little water to grow. They first put some compost around the foot of the plant and it produces bean all round the year. If the atmosphere is water borne the plant grows quicker and healthier. With sea water vapours in the atmosphere ABLAT can be grown in dry and drought lands.
3. The Central Salt and Marine Chemical Research Institute of Bhavanagar, India, has been experimenting on the cultivation of Jojobe - an oil bearing plant in coastal sand dunes under semi-arid conditions in the West Coast of Gujarat and in Sub-humid regions of Ganjam district of Orissa. Experiments have established that Jojobe can be grown successfully in coastal sand dunes and the oil obtained from the plant could be used as a lubricant for making soaps and for other purposes.
4. A halophyte grows excellently well in ariel zones and saline soils and improves habitat of wild life and birds and serves as fodder for livestock and reclaiming sandy soil. It grows wild in the salt steppes of Eastern Asia, low lying salt plains of Australia, the Red Sea basin and the South American Pampas. It is an easy to propagate annual and perennial herb.
5. In 1990, the Philippines ranked fourth among the worlds Producers of Red Sea-weed, exporting about $ 48 million of dried sea weed and CAAGRENAN - a derivative from it which is used as a binding agent in food products.

JOJOBA FOR SHORE CULTIVATION

Jojoba, a native shrub of Arizona, USA, pronounced as Ho-Ho-ba, is Botanically known as Simmondsia Chinoris, R&D done for about 4 years by the Central Arid Zone Research Instituted (CAZARI) India, confirmed that Jojoba is highly drought tolerant and salt resistant and can convert desert and sea-shore sands into an oasis of prosperity. Several years of research done by the Central salt and Marine Chemicals Research Institute, Bhavnagar, in the waste and coastal lands of Northern Gujarat also confirms that Jojoba is highly drought and salt tolerant.

Agricultural economists consider this shrub a gold mine and the FAO of the United Nations and the World Bank recommend the introduction and propogation of this shrub in waste lands and saline soils.

In the international market a tonne of Jojoba seeds fetches about 8,000. The money is paid for the oil which the seeds contain. The oil is very much like the whale oil in physical and chemical properties and better than almost all commercial substitutes for whale oil, which is getting scarce by the restrictions laid on whaling.

Israel is cultivating the shrub already on a large scale. Australia, Costa Rica, Brazil, S. Africa, Mexico, are among the forerunners in the promotion of jojoba. India, China, Philippines and some East African countries are also promoting the shrub now.

Jojoba oil, golden in colour, is totally free from alkaloids and resins. Cosmetic industry in the West consumes a large quantity of it. The oil is also used in the preparation of high quality candles, polish, varnish, lubricants, antifoam agents, fire-retardants and in the making of soaps. The oil is edible and has a low-calorie. But the most important and indispensible need for the oil is by the engineering industry to replace sperm whale oil which is scarce and costly to be used as a high pressure lubricant. The Ben Gurion University of Israel reports that the oil relieves pain and cures skin diseases.

Jojoba shrub thrives in temperatures ranging from 5 to 50 degrees Celsius and live 50 to 200 years. The shrubs are propagated by direct sowing, stem planting, or tissue culture. A plant yields about 125 gms. of seeds in the first 5 years and thereafter about two kg. The plant tolerates salinity level of 10,000 parts per million making it absolutely suitable for desert and coastal areas. CAZRI estimates a return of 1.8 lakh rupees per year from one ha of Jojoba .

MARKING NUT TREE (ENGLISH)

Botanical - *Samecarpus anacardium.*

Hindi - *Bhilawa.*

Family - *Anacardiaceae.*

Medium size drought tree can be seen in countries which have very warm 00weather. Common in South Indian forests.

Black resin obtained from pericarp of fruit, is used as marking ink to write on cloth or canvas. Washerman and artists use the ink.

Vesicant juice known in trade as Bhilawan Shell Liquid (BSL) is obtained from Bhilawan nuts and is rich source of phenols. The resin from the pericart of the fruit is used in paints and plastic industries and in varnish making, hacquers, water proofing, enamels and insulation materials.

Chlorinated derivatives of phenolic constituents of BSL are used as anticeptic, ant repellent, insecticide and moth proofing agents. Constituents of BSL are also used in herbicides, detergents and fireproof plastics.

The kernel of the fruit yields a semi-drying oil which is used as wood preservation. The oil kills white ants. The oil can also be used in soap making but not usually done as there are cheaper alternatives for making soaps. Buts of this tree are used as tan and the tree itself serves as a host for lac insects out of which sealing wax, shoe polish etc. are made.

This being a wild tree with wide uses it must be introduced and promoted in hot countries with poor soil. If commercial quantities are made available several livelihood and income generation activities can be started based on various parts of this tree.

The raw leaves of this tree are crushed and used as insecticides inside boxes and storing places and the wood is used as firewood. The tree has a long life.

Acknowledgement

1. Mr.S.John Joseph, I.F.S., the Principal Chief Coservator of Forests, Government official esteemed as an authority on trees, forests, environment, ecology and social forestry for writing the foreword.
2. My niece Miss. Rosalind Alphonse for typing several pages of the book.
3. First cousin Bernard, for proof-reading the typed script.
4. Good friend Miss Gloria Miranda for applying her artistic hand to my drawings and sketches.
5. Mr. S. Santiago, Consultant on Human Development to several International German agencies for encouraging my R&D whenever he read through pages and parts of the book.
6. Wife Jaya and son Sajee for all the help they gave me in investigating neglected plants and trees and their uses.
7. Mr. N. V. Masilanani for helping me to identify some drought tolerant trees .
8. Mr. Kumar Raj for Drwing my attintion to server useful inddor plants.

Index